GENDER

MW01199702

Series editors:
Lynn Abrams, Cordelia Beattie, Pam Sharpe and Penny Summerfield

The expansion of research into the history of women and gender since the 1970s has changed the face of history. Using the insights of feminist theory and of historians of women, gender historians have explored the configuration in the past of gender identities and relations between the sexes. They have also investigated the history of sexuality and family relations, and analysed ideas and ideals of masculinity and femininity. Yet gender history has not abandoned the original, inspirational project of women's history: to recover and reveal the lived experience of women in the past and the present.

The series Gender in History provides a forum for these developments. Its historical coverage extends from the medieval to the modern periods, and its geographical scope encompasses not only Europe and North America but all corners of the globe. The series aims to investigate the social and cultural constructions of gender in historical sources, as well as the gendering of historical discourse itself. It embraces both detailed case studies of specific regions or periods, and broader treatments of major themes. Gender in History titles are designed to meet the needs of both scholars and students working in this dynamic area of historical research.

Women against cruelty

Manchester University Press

WOMEN AGAINST CRUELTY

PROTECTION OF ANIMALS IN NINETEENTH-CENTURY BRITAIN

Diana Donald

Manchester University Press

Published by Manchester University Press
Altrincham Street, Manchester M1 7JA
www.manchesteruniversitypress.co.uk

British Library Cataloguing-in-Publication Data
A catalogue record for this book is available from the British Library

ISBN 978 1 5261 1542 3 hardback
ISBN 978 1 5261 5046 2 paperback

First published in hardback by Manchester University Press 2020
This edition first published 2021

The publisher has no responsibility for the persistence or accuracy of URLs for any external or third-party internet websites referred to in this book, and does not guarantee that any content on such websites is, or will remain, accurate or appropriate.

Cover: George Frederic Watts, *A Dedication (to all those who love the beautiful and mourn over the senseless and cruel destruction of bird life and beauty)*; also known as *The shuddering angel*, oil on canvas, 1898–9. © Watts Gallery Trust, Compton, Surrey. The painting shows an angel sorrowing over a pile of tropical birds' wings and plumage, sacrificed on the altar of fashion.

Typeset by Servis Filmsetting Ltd, Stockport, Cheshire

Contents

Figures

Cover: George Frederic Watts, *A Dedication (to all those who love the beautiful and mourn over the senseless and cruel destruction of bird life and beauty)*; also known as *The shuddering angel*, oil on canvas, 1898-9. © Watts Gallery Trust, Compton, Surrey. The painting shows an angel sorrowing over a pile of tropical birds' wings and plumage, sacrificed on the altar of fashion.

Preface

Many studies of animal advocacy groups in the modern western world have revealed the striking prominence of women among the activists.[1] Gender also seemingly affects attitudes towards animals among the population at large. For example, one researcher in the 1990s found that, statistically, gender had 'the greatest total effect on opposition to animal research' (vivisection), while 'feminist attitudes had the second greatest total effect'.[2] Also in the 1990s Carol Adams, Josephine Donovan and others proposed a theoretical basis for these proclivities. They argued that patriarchal attitudes still prevalent in society bear down on both women and animals, establishing a sense of common cause between them. For these feminist writers, an 'ethic of care' – fellow-feeling with animals and a sense of moral responsibility for their wellbeing – is preferable to abstract theories of animal rights. The latter place a premium on rationality, a quality which is often associated with ancient but discredited theories about the 'masculine' mind and women's supposed irrationality or animality.[3]

The reasons for the apparent difference between the sexes in their readiness or their capacity for sympathy with other species nevertheless remain open to further investigation.[4] Does women's attachment to animal causes partly stem from some innate 'mothering' instinct? Or does it arise solely from their life experiences, especially their consciousness of male domination? Perhaps 'sentiment' or tenderness is socially induced, when treated as a desirable aspect of femininity or of female pursuits? Is women's special feeling for animals in fact constant through the centuries, or is it a fluctuating and historically contingent phenomenon? It is only this historical dimension of the subject that my study of women's work for animals in nineteenth-century Britain can have any hope of addressing. I set out to show how these women responded to the problem of cruelty in British society at many levels – with strong emotion impelling them to direct action, but also with analytic thoughtfulness and imagination. By the 1890s, some were led to formulate ideas about the special bond between women and animals that anticipate feminist views of the present day, while their rejection of controlling anthropocentrism resonates with the recent emphasis on animals' own subjectivity and agency in history.[5]

Several authors, notably Mary Ann Elston, Moira Ferguson, Barbara Gates, Susan Hamilton, Hilda Kean and Coral Lansbury, have made key contributions to our knowledge of women's roles in the Victorian animal protection movement. However, a connected history of this subject – its leading figures, literature and institutions – has been lacking. There is certainly a need for such a history, to counter the trivialisation, disdain and neglect evinced by many authors of standard works. The biographers of Charles Darwin write dismissively of how his daughter Henrietta, 'a confirmed hypochondriac, had jumped on the bandwagon' of opposition to vivisection.[6] One is glad to know that Darwin himself took Henrietta's principled objections to the practice more seriously.[7] The author of a classic history of *The Naturalist in Britain* suggests that the women who founded the future Royal Society for the Protection of Birds (RSPB) typified 'people on the search for something to protest about', prone to 'hysteria, often absurdly impractical' … 'Obsessed with propaganda', and resistant to the (male) scientific advice that would have guided the Society in its early days towards sound conservationist measures.[8] What is distressing in these and similar judgements is less their misogyny than the travesty of historical facts that is often involved. If my own version of events is open to criticism as *parti pris* in its celebration of Victorian women's achievements in animal protection, it at least brings to attention the wealth of archival and other primary source material available to scholars who may wish to research the aspect of gender in the history of animal advocacy more widely, and from different disciplinary or ethical perspectives – embracing women's writings as well as their practical initiatives. At a time when animal history is expanding in many new directions, there is unlimited scope and promise in this field.

It only remains to apologise to the reader for the solecism of referring to 'animals' and 'humans' throughout the book, as though they were discrete categories. At present there seems to be no concise alternative.

I am very grateful to those who have helped me to bring the book to completion, and firstly to the Culture & Animals Foundation, whose generous grant, in itself a great honour, funded the early stages of my archival research. I should also like to thank David Allen, Philip Browning and their colleagues at the Royal Society for the Prevention of Cruelty to Animals (RSPCA) headquarters for giving me unstinted access to the Society's archive over several years; the distant sound of dogs' woofing in the offices was a pleasant accompaniment to work there. At the RSPB, Lisa Hutchins and Elizabeth George were exceptionally knowledgeable and helpful in retrieving items from the archive. At a time when charities' resources are under great strain, and many debar researchers from access to their archives, such hospitality is especially appreciated. I have greatly benefited from conversations with Hilda Kean and with Chien-hui Li, both of whom have given me many valuable thoughts and references. Many other individuals have kindly offered information or responded to my enquiries; here I should especially like to thank Conrad Cherry, Christopher Christie, Felicity James, Miles Lambert, Louise Logan, Judith Bailey Slagle and Julie-Marie Strange. I have also greatly profited from the wise advice of Emma Brennan and her colleagues at Manchester University Press during the process of preparing the work for publication. Finally, my family – Trevor, Paul and Alice Donald and Fiona Roberts – have given me the benefit of their knowledge and their reassurances throughout the book's rather problem-strewn process of gestation. I could not have completed it without their kind encouragement.

Notes

1 Carol J. Adams and Josephine Donovan (eds), *Animals & Women: Feminist Theoretical Explorations* (Durham, NC and London: Duke University Press, 1995), p. 5. Emily Gaarder, *Women and the Animal Rights Movement* (Piscataway: Rutgers University Press, 2011).
2 Linda K. Pifer, 'Exploring the gender gap in young adults' attitudes about animal research', *Society and Animals*, 4:1 (1996), 37–52.
3 Carol J. Adams, *Neither Man Nor Beast: Feminism and the Defense of Animals* (New York: Continuum, 1994). Carol J. Adams and Josephine Donovan (eds), *The Feminist Care Tradition in Animal Ethics: A Reader* (New York: Columbia University Press, 2007).
4 Lyle Munro, 'Caring about blood, flesh, and pain: women's standing in the animal protection movement', *Society and Animals*, 9:1 (2001), 43–61.
5 For example, Philip Howell, 'Animals, agency and history', in Hilda Kean and Philip Howell (eds), *The Routledge Companion to Animal-Human History* (London and New York: Routledge, 2019).
6 Adrian Desmond and James Moore, *Darwin* (London: Michael Joseph, 1991), p. 615.
7 See 'Unpublished journal offers new take on Darwin's daughter', at www.cam.ac.uk/research/news, accessed July 2018.
8 David Elliston Allen, *The Naturalist in Britain: A Social History* (Harmondsworth: Penguin Books, 1978), pp. 198–9.

Prefatory note: the archive of the Royal Society for the Prevention of Cruelty to Animals

The main categories of documents relevant to study of the Society's nineteenth-century history are indicated below, headed by the abbreviations used in my notes.

RSPCA executive committee minutes

Manuscript minute books survive from the beginning of the Society in 1824. Minutes were kept more fully and systematically from March 1832 onwards.

RSPCA ladies' committee minutes

CM/89: A manuscript minute book covers the period from the creation of the ladies' committee in 1870 down to 1904. However, there is an unexplained break between January 1871 and November 1891, although the ladies' committee continued to exist during that time.

RSPCA *Records*

CM/1–17: An anonymous typescript in seventeen volumes collates and transcribes (with minor inaccuracies) material relating to 'the general progress of public opinion, with reference to the prevention of cruelty to animals'. It covers the years 1800–1876. Sources include parliamentary reports and records, press articles and letters to editors.

RSPCA *Report(s)*

Annual reports were published from 1832 onwards; or, at least, that for 1832 (titled the 6th) is the first to be preserved. They contain detailed records of speeches and debates at the annual meetings, data on the Society's prosecutions and finances, membership and subscription lists etc.

RSPCA 'Sermons and Reports'

CM/171: A bound collection of printed pamphlets, collated in 1900 by Mrs Florence Suckling, provides information about lesser-known late-nineteenth-century groups involved in various aspects of animal advocacy.

Introduction

In 1893 the Chicago World's Fair became the first international exhibition to include a section on women's work, showing the part it had played in the 'moral and social progress of the world'. Baroness Burdett-Coutts, the most famous female philanthropist of the day, assembled a British exhibit and composed a report which contained descriptions of the many benevolent projects that women had undertaken to meet 'human need'. They included nursing, teaching in 'ragged schools' and reform of conditions in workhouses: all aspects of women's growing commitment to organised public work that characterised the Victorian era. However, the report also included, more surprisingly, a chapter on 'Woman's work for animals' in Britain. This, too, was written by Burdett-Coutts, herself a pioneer in the field, but out of modesty she requested the Hon. Mrs Muir Mackenzie, her colleague on the ladies' committee of the RSPCA, to sign it in her place.[1]

It was a proud record of achievement that was sent to Chicago. Burdett-Coutts explained that the movement for animal protection had begun in London in the early nineteenth century, a time when 'either from ignorance … heedlessness, or wanton brutality, animals were generally subjected to extreme ill-treatment, and even torture'. The lower classes of the British people 'naturally … ignored the rights of dumb animals' altogether, but even among the higher classes, those who protested against cruelty were at first a derided minority. Nevertheless, laws were gradually passed that protected working animals and livestock from extreme abuse, and these had been enforced by the Society for the Prevention of Cruelty to Animals, founded in 1824, which prospered as the *Royal* Society or RSPCA, and gradually won over public opinion. The RSPCA's ladies' committee was formed in 1870 to further its educational mission, and the women's influence proved to be 'both wide and deep', especially through the organisation of 'Bands of Mercy' to teach children to be kind to animals.[2]

At the same time, women had initiated and led many 'kindred associations', which carried the work of animal protection into more specialised fields. They included Mary Tealby's Home for Lost and Starving Dogs (now the Battersea Dogs' Home), Ann Lindo's Home of Rest for Horses (now the Horse Trust), and 'societies ... whose object is the better protection of birds' – foremost among which was the body that became the RSPB, started by Emily Williamson and others in 1889.[3] Burdett-Coutts was naturally keen to emphasise the role of women in establishing the institutional framework of animal protection in Britain, but at grassroots level, too, their work had been indispensable, in running branch societies, alerting the authorities to local occurrences of cruelty, fundraising and making their own generous donations to the cause. By 1900, 65 per cent of legators and 69 per cent of listed subscribers to the RSPCA were women, and this percentage does not, of course, include women whose contributions were made under their husbands' names.[4] Moreover, while mentioning inducements to women to 'write stories and poems in promotion of the general cause', Burdett-Coutts says nothing about the outstanding quality of much of the polemical and imaginative literature that female authors produced in the course of the nineteenth century, from Frances Power Cobbe's anti-vivisection tracts to Anna Sewell's *Black Beauty*.[5] As in other fields of endeavour, Victorian women could exert an influence through their writing that compensated for their continuing exclusion from many areas of public life. Indeed, they were prepared to ponder the deeper philosophical aspects of the human–animal relationship, and the social and psychological causes of cruelty to animals: matters which – despite Burdett-Coutts's upbeat assessment of progress – often seemed more problematic at the end of the nineteenth century than at its beginning.

The historiography of the animal protection movement

The organisations mentioned by Burdett-Coutts have become venerable and highly regarded national institutions, of unquestioned status in British society. Yet despite the volume of recent works on Victorian women's philanthropy in many fields, a comprehensive study of 'woman's work for animals' has still to be written. In fact the historiography of the animal protection movement as a whole is, even leaving aside its failure to appraise the importance of gender, still very much open to debate and revision. On one side are the authorised, celebratory histories of the RSPCA, the Battersea Dogs' Home, the RSPB and other nineteenth-century foundations, which, like Lady Burdett-Coutts's report, present a tale of virtuous endeavour and progress in improving conditions for animals – the very longevity and present-day prestige of these organisations seeming to confirm their 'onwards and upwards' trajectory.[6] On the other side are accounts of the animal protection movement which treat it as a case study in the field of Victorian philanthropy and social formations. Writers of this latter school of thought sometimes have little apparent interest in the peculiar features and problems of animal protection and little sympathy with its advocates; in the preoccupation with institutional politics, the actual nature and extent of the cruelties experienced by animals also tend to disappear from view. Brian Harrison's scholarly work on the RSPCA has been particularly influential. He is principally concerned with the Society's policy of 'Prudence complemented by professionalism'; in other words, cautious moderation and conciliatory approaches to government and powerful interest groups. From this perspective, failures to end particular forms of cruelty (for example vivisection or field sports) merely exemplify the limits of the possible, and represent a shrewd rejection of self-defeating zealotry. In the same vein, Harrison tends to treat specialised offshoots of the RSPCA as groups with potentially 'radical' tendencies that were prudently ejected by the parent body in order to dissociate it from their likely 'tactical errors' or their fanaticism. Leaving aside the special case of anti-vivisection, this view of the situation is, I believe, at odds with much of the primary evidence.[7]

Many authors have emphasised the idea of the RSPCA as an arm of the state or of the establishment, as allegedly an instrument of social control, the main purpose of which was to discredit and reform the mores of the lower classes. Proponents of this view find plenty of ammunition in the many nineteenth-century complaints about discrimination in the pattern of RSPCA prosecutions: the inevitably harsh treatment of working animals by poor labouring men was punished, while the cruel practices of the rich were seemingly inviolate.[8] In an understandable reaction against the Whiggish tendencies of histories of animal protection, some recent writers have also questioned the notion of gradual enlightenment and progress in humane attitudes, and stressed instead the cultural relativism involved in perceptions of cruelty. Here there has been a particular attention to the abolition of popular blood sports such as bull-baiting and staged animal fights in the late Georgian era.[9] E.P. Thompson's brilliant exposition of the 'field of force' operating in social relations between the ruling classes and 'the crowd' – traditional paternalism gradually being displaced by hard-nosed modern capitalism and work-discipline – still colours the thinking of historians of plebeian pastimes.[10] However, the suppression of baiting was actually never more than a side-issue for the RSPCA, albeit an important symbolic triumph in the early years of the Society's existence; and historians' focus on victimisation of the lower classes has limited attention to the much more serious struggles between animal protectionists and the vested interests of the business and scientific worlds that occurred later in the nineteenth century. Moreover, such attributions of veiled socio-political or other ulterior, even unconscious, motives to the reformers tend to preclude any searching examination of their own stated views, which, as Chien-hui Li remarks, are simply ignored or discounted.[11] At the extreme of this tendency, one writer hypothesised that 'the concept of animal rights is only marginally concerned with animals'; another has concluded that the 'principal focus' of the RSPCA's 'moral mission ... could *not* have been animals'.[12] Yet any analysis of the actual debates among protectionists suggests the painful fellow-feeling with animals and agonies of conscience that were often involved. So far from sitting back in a mood of self-congratulation over the taming of the lower orders, reformers became more and more conscious of the intractability of cruel behaviour at every level of society.

In the present context, it is important to note that historians' tendency to homogenise or typecast animal protectionists has obscured *gendered* distinctions in their attitudes and motives for action; distinctions that operated despite the fact that activists of both sexes tended to be drawn from the same privileged social classes. There was, for much of the century, a preoccupation with offences committed in public places, in effect those committed by men. These included the barbaric treatment of working animals in the city streets, especially drivers' abuse of horses and donkeys; drovers' and slaughterers' inflictions of pain on cattle and sheep; and – higher up the social scale – the cruelties of trap pigeon shooting matches, driven shoots, steeplechasing and road races between horses for wagers. Women played little part in any of these occupations other than as spectators, and they were credited with a natural gentleness that offset male brutality. Nevertheless, such brutality was often seen as a natural response to the exigencies of the working world; as an exercise of customary practices; or even as an expression of manliness. In those circumstances, the tendency of women to sympathise with animals lacked operative power. Such pity could be idealised as a feminine trait, but at the same time dismissed as unrealistic and 'sentimental'; and so women intent on ameliorating conditions for animals needed to find routes that avoided conflict with male values and prerogatives. Even from Burdett-Coutts's brief account, it is clear that they were especially active in moral education of the young, and in what would now be called 'welfare'. The *care* of animals and the relief of suffering were more attainable and (according to Victorian notions) more appropriate objectives for women than the punishment of cruelty through criminal prosecutions, which was undertaken by the RSPCA's male leaders. Yet on what principles could legislation against cruelty be based, if not on instinctive sympathy with the pain and misfortune of sentient creatures?

Traditions of thought on the treatment of animals

Expressions of sympathy with animals and arguments for their entitlement to human kindness occur sporadically throughout European history, making it difficult and sometimes misleading to periodise changes in attitudes. However, in eighteenth-century Britain, sermon-writers, essayists and poets were inspired by the cult of universal benevolence stemming from Lord Shaftesbury's *Characteristicks* (1699) and by the tenor of religious thought to write on this subject with increasing frequency.[13] For Anglican evangelicals, Quakers and Methodists in particular, the fate of animals in this world and the next became an important issue.[14] The cult of sensibility that stemmed from the writings of Rousseau, Sterne and Mackenzie also inflected the tone of humane literature, and, as we shall see, it had, by the end of the eighteenth century, acquired a particular association with feminine responses to the sight of suffering.

There was, nevertheless, a wide difference between the public's appreciation of the sentiments expressed in moral treatises or in romantic poetry and a readiness to impose standards of conduct on the populace through legal coercion. The authority of traditional religious teaching seemed to be the likeliest means of changing men's behaviour, short of punitive laws. Thus the whole understanding of human–animal relations was to be grounded in biblical texts. According to the Book of Genesis, God made man in His own image and gave him dominion over the animals, as His regent on earth: a lordship signalled by the delegation to Adam of the task of naming every species. After the great flood, human supremacy was confirmed in harsher terms: God assured Noah that all beasts and birds would henceforth fear man – 'into your hand are they delivered'.[15] If animals were not actually created for man's use, many kinds were nevertheless destined to be his slaves or his food. However, Christian humility and lovingkindness – Christ's blessing on the merciful – palliated the exercise of this human right of dominion, for man and the animals were alike the children of God, all fitted for their respective situations and intended to enjoy their lives on earth. As Francis Hutcheson remarked in his *System of Moral Philosophy*, 'Here is plainly a well ordered complex system, with a proper connexion and subordination of parts for the common good of all'.[16] Natural hierarchy arising from man's superior mental powers and spiritual destiny was unquestioned (it was habitually expressed in the designation of non-human species as the 'lower' animals, a term that was used throughout the nineteenth century); but the whole chain of authority and responsibility was to reflect the benignity of the Creator's purposes. Kindness to animals became a mark of spiritual grace, and, conversely, 'wanton' or gratuitous cruelty was a symptom of unregeneracy: 'by their fruits ye shall know them'.[17] Furthermore, as habitual cruelty was thought to be not only indicative of character but also formative of it, the acculturation of the young became, as we shall see, a matter of critical importance.

In all this body of teaching on man's relationship to other species, it was always assumed that the prioritisation of human interests was legitimate and absolute. Animals were not viewed as independent agents, but as useful tools for the realisation of human objectives. Theories of animals' *rights* to happiness and equity did flourish briefly in the era of the French revolution, and were famously expressed by Jeremy Bentham in his note on 'Interests of the inferior animals improperly neglected in legislation'.[18] However, such ideas gained little traction until the 1890s, and were indeed looked on with suspicion in loyalist circles as a sign of warped values and a challenge to the status quo. Thus when Edward Augustus Kendall, in his touching story of a dog, *Keeper's Travels in Search of His Master* (1798), looked forward to a time 'when men shall acknowledge the RIGHTS; instead of bestowing their COMPASSION upon the creatures, whom, with themselves, GOD made, and made to be happy!', the conservative Anglican writer Sarah Trimmer was shocked by his unorthodoxy.[19] Animals should not be viewed as man's near-equals: there were, she protested, 'distinguishing marks of *sovereignty* on one side, and of *subjection* on the other'. Certainly these subject creatures should be kindly treated – Trimmer's own *Fabulous Histories: Designed for the Instruction of Children, Respecting Their Treatment of Animals* (1786) was a much-reprinted classic; but talk of rights was 'subversive of that dominion which the Almighty himself established', and a recipe for 'great confusion'. 'We have long been used to hear of the RIGHTS OF MAN, and the RIGHTS OF WOMEN; but the levelling system, which includes the RIGHTS OF ANIMALS, is here carried to the most ridiculous extreme.'[20] At just this time, too, the conservative politician George Canning, in his *Anti-Jacobin* poem 'New morality', sarcastically accused the representatives of 'Sweet SENSIBILITY' and '*French* PHILANTHROPY' of caring more for 'the crush'd Beetle ... the widow'd Dove' than for their parents, friends, king and country endangered by revolutionary upheaval.[21]

A belief in hierarchy was essential to the ordering of society and to the proper degree of paternalistic care for lesser creatures – a belief that was sustained through most of the Victorian era, and lingered on even after Darwinism had established a very different view of the natural order. As the pronouncements of Trimmer and Canning make clear (particularly in the reference to Mary Wollstonecraft's *Vindication of the Rights of Woman*), this system of subordination was all-embracing. Wives were to submit to husbands, servants to their employers; and working or domestic animals were themselves valued as servants or slaves of a kind – 'dumb, uncomplaining beings, which move in a *lower* Sphere of existence', according to one clergyman writing in the 1790s.[22] Their patient labours for mankind entitled them to gratitude and reciprocal benefits: it was always *their* treatment, not that of wild animals, that preoccupied the moralists, at least until the last two decades of the nineteenth century. Nevertheless, 'mercy' to these passive beings from motives of pity or gratitude or from consciousness of the will of God could only ever be voluntary – a question of individual conscience, not of obvious legal obligation. Thus when animal advocates began to propose laws that would arraign and punish those deemed guilty of cruelty, they were entering quite new territory; for, as one writer has pointed out, it was necessary for the first time to formulate 'a strong argument for the more or less intuitive certainty that … abuse of animals was reprehensible'.[23]

Parliamentary debates in the early 1800s: the problem of justifying the criminalisation of cruelty

We have seen that sympathy with animals and anxiety over their abuse had a long history in European philosophy and literature; but a legal historian has shown that 'The prevention of cruelty to animals is, as a conception of the State, a pure product of the nineteenth century'.[24] At a time when abolition of the slave trade was being debated in parliament and the country as a moral issue, the propriety of affording legal protection to another helpless, subject group of beings became conceivable. For the first time, it was proposed that mistreatment of the creatures that served man – hitherto regarded simply as private property – should be liable to public interference and judicial punishment. A succession of bills was presented to the British parliament in the first decade of the century that in various ways aimed to protect animals from ill treatment. None succeeded – a law that punished those found guilty of cruelty to horses and livestock was passed only in 1822, and became the foundation for more comprehensive legislation in later years. Nevertheless, the early initiatives were highly significant. For the first time, the issue of cruelty to animals was scrutinised in a public forum, and discussed by the leaders of a nation, and their debates, widely reported in the press, brought to the surface problems that would be endemic to animal protection throughout the nineteenth century.

The gendered nature of attitudes to the animal kingdom immediately became evident, and there were the first indications of disproportionate female support for reform. Initially, the most flagrant kinds of cruelty under attack were the baiting of bulls and badgers, cockfighting and other animal fights, and the abuse of horses and livestock on the roads; and all, as we have noticed, were offences for which men and boys alone were held responsible. Indeed, a focus on bull-baiting in parliamentary bills of 1800 and 1802 articulated a conflict of ideas on the very nature of masculinity or 'manliness'.[25] William Windham, the government's Secretary at War, was alarmed that a law to prohibit the blood sports of the common people would – at a time of political unrest – foment popular discontents. It would aggravate resentment of the game laws and the harsh punishment of poachers, and might open the door to a wider debate on the moral legitimacy of aristocratic field sports. Indeed, defence of the latter was to impede anti-cruelty legislation over a broad front throughout the century. Windham thus argued at great length that bull-baiting was no crueller than hunting and shooting wild animals in the field. This was an early deployment of the *tu quoque* line of argument, which seeks to invalidate efforts for reform of one kind of abuse by pointing out another kind, equally heinous, which has allegedly been passed over – thereby demonstrating the supposed inconsistency or bias of the would-be reformer. This tactic was, as we shall see, widely deployed throughout the Victorian era, implying the hopelessness of *any* attempt to change entrenched attitudes and practices. However, Windham was justified when he claimed that a focus on the prosecution of working men for street cruelties would be discriminatory, and his accusation that an anti-cruelty law would simply reflect the way in which the ruling classes set themselves up as a moral authority over their social inferiors was often reiterated by other critics. Windham also went so far as to assert that the tradition of baiting bulls with fighting bulldogs, or running bulls through the streets, was beneficial to the nation, as it inspired bravery and patriotism in the spectators: 'the amusements of our people were always composed of athletic, manly, and hardy exercises, affording trials of their courage, conducive to … ambition and … glory', and preparing men for the battlefield.[26] In response, an anonymous member of parliament, writing in 1800, accused Windham of confusing courage with cruelty, 'manliness with *ferocity*', and of sneering at anything that 'wears the aspect of religious seriousness' or that aimed to 'stop the violent torrent of corruption of manners'. The writer added that 'an accomplished lady, well known in the literary world' (probably Hannah More) was equally disgusted by Windham's speech, which indeed contradicted all the reforming intentions of the evangelical Anglicans in the Clapham sect.[27]

Supporters of the abolition bills were sure that true gallantry and manliness had nothing to do with brutality. Moreover, such cruelty to animals was alien to the sensibilities of mothers and children. According to Wilberforce, Windham had forgotten that the alleged 'happiness derived from bull-baiting ... was confined to an individual, while his wretched family, excluded from any participation of the spectacle', was left to rue the waste of money in gambling that it often entailed.[28] Indeed, during the Commons debate of 1802, Sir Richard Hill remarked that many letters and petitions showed that 'The amiable sex, in general, were advocates for the bill'; but this female support, he jocularly assumed, did not encompass the whole social scale:

> There might, indeed, be some exceptions ... staggering out of a gin-shop in St Giles's; perhaps sitting over an oyster-tub, or riding in a cinder-cart, but it could not strictly be said of any one of these ladies, 'Grace is in all her steps, Heaven in her eye; in all her gestures dignity and love' ... [a free quotation of the description of Eve in Milton's *Paradise Lost*].[29]

However, even the highly respectable middle- and upper-class ladies who were sneeringly indicated as the supporters of reform could easily be accused of hypocrisy or double standards. Windham insinuated that the members of parliament intent on abolishing labouring-class blood sports were 'influenced by a species of philosophy dictated by their wives', who affectedly recoiled in horror at the sight of bull-baiting, but were unconcerned by their husbands' shooting expeditions.[30] At a deeper level, men on both sides of the argument – engaged as they were with competing models of masculinity – betrayed a sexual preoccupation, and in particular a sense of *affinity* between women and animals, that was all the more potent for being at the same time humorous, misogynistic and rooted in history. 'The higher orders had their Billington' remarked Colonel Grosvenor, referring to the stout operatic diva Elizabeth Billington; 'and why not allow the lower orders their bull?'[31] Even Milton's Eve, invoked by Hill, was, as his listeners would have recalled, created by God as a direct substitute for Adam's animal companions; and Windham himself, when complaining about his opponents' undue attention to little isolated incidents of cruelty to baited animals, made a Swiftian analogy with a woman's face. 'Nothing could be more pleasing to the eye than the sight of female beauty; but even if the fairest complexion were contemplated through a microscope, deformities would appear, and hairs unobservable to the naked eye would present themselves as the bristles on the back of a boar.'[32]

Such denigration of women, used as a means of ridiculing the animal cause, did not pass unnoticed, and was bitterly resented by many writers. John Lamb, brother of the essayist Charles Lamb, published *A Letter to the Right Hon. William Windham* in 1810, and in it he raged against a facetious speech made by George Canning in 1800 to discredit the first anti-baiting bill – at just the time when the latter was also satirising female sensibility in the *Anti-Jacobin*. Canning had suggested that the bill was trivial in its object – as trivial as seeking to legislate on the basis of seeing a bull, on its way to slaughter, run amok and gore so insignificant a person as a poor old woman in a red cloak on Ludgate Hill; 'by what turn of mind', Lamb asked, 'can misery only excite mirth?' Flippancy not only insulted the old woman, in a way that was 'as shocking to reason as the laugh … of a demon': it also demonstrated 'most forcibly the little consideration the generality of people are likely to bestow upon the brute creation'; for cruelty to animals and to human subalterns had the same cause – incapacity for sympathy.[33] As late as 1814, in Margaret Cullen's novel *Mornton*, the identification of pity for animals with female weakness or inconsequence still rankled. A boorish devotee of field sports, callous in his treatment of animals and of the local villagers alike, tells his sister that if men were to treat domestic animals 'as women often do … we should become quite effeminate. *Womanish humanity* would render men good for nothing. Mr Windham even thought bull-baiting necessary to keep up the courage of Englishmen'.[34]

In 1809, parliamentary debate on the question of cruelty to animals took a new turn. Thomas Erskine, formerly Lord Chancellor and famed as the barrister who had secured the acquittal of the accused radicals in the great treason trials of 1794, introduced an anti-cruelty bill in the House of Lords. In the nature of the offences it was intended to cover, it differed significantly from the earlier bills to ban bull-baiting. Sidestepping the culture wars which the latter had provoked, Erskine, a noted animal lover, focused on the evils of cruelty to horses and livestock. More significant than the detailed provisions of the bill, however, was its preamble, articulating a 'grand efficacious principle' that was intended to guide all future protective legislation. Avoiding the politically dangerous ground of animal 'rights', Erskine gave fresh expression to the traditional doctrine of human dominion over animals ordained by God, and the sacred 'trust' this entailed. He was, however, acutely aware of the difficulties of framing and enforcing a law which rested only on a moral principle – particularly as the four-legged clients he represented were themselves of a questionable moral status. He admitted that there 'can be no law for man' with respect to his treatment of animals, 'but such as he makes for himself': animals themselves could not be party to it, nor be deemed to have legal responsibilities. Kind and merciful treatment of them was, in legal terms, only an 'imperfect obligation': it was a course of action that was not enforced by any existing law, but was motivated by moral compunction, which might, he admitted, be felt or interpreted in variable, subjective ways by different people. Only the sure 'standard in the human heart' could distinguish between inadvertent and deliberate cruelty, and reach judicial verdicts accordingly.[35] Thus early in the century an important truth had to be faced. There was no objective, ascertainable and universally accepted reason (biblical injunctions aside) why mankind should treat animals well. One could appeal only to the 'human heart'; and, as quickly became apparent, the 'human heart' could easily morph into '*"Womanish humanity"*'.

Two years after parliament's abolition of the slave trade, Erskine set up a principle of 'disinterested virtue' against not only the rights and powers conferred by individual ownership of animals, but also private, commercial interests of all kinds. Although he stressed the moral imperative of 'softening' the labouring classes, wealthier people would also be affected by the proposed law, while being far more difficult to bring to court. The gross overworking of horses by competing stagecoach firms, and beating of cows and sheep by the employees of cattle dealers and butchers, were certainly targeted; and, although Erskine was equivocal in the matter of field sports, his 'grand efficacious principle' might eventually encompass these too, bringing 'the whole living world' – wild as well as tame – within the scope of the law. He spoke of the 'letters upon letters' he had received in support of this project. Although his speech was apparently received with open derision in parliament and the bill ultimately failed, the degree to which his views tallied with those of a sector of the educated public is manifest in the many favourable responses in the press.[36] Windham, putting himself forward once again as the main opponent of punitive legislation, noted that 'fashionable female circles', in particular, appeared to have been 'very diligently canvassed' in favour of the bill.[37] He knew, however, that the game had changed: while the earlier bills against plebeian blood sports might be countered through appeals to traditional notions of British-bulldog masculinity, Erskine's bill, with its reference to widely recognised forms of abuse of domestic and working animals, had to be countered by the presentation of more fundamental objections to the very notion of cruelty to animals as a definable offence.

Windham therefore reiterated his earlier objection to a law of this kind, that it would be socially biased: a 'parade of virtue' and an 'exercise of power' that harassed the poor as badly as they harassed their animals. Working men – drivers, carters and drovers – could easily be convicted of cruelty on the evidence of over-zealous, busybody witnesses, drawn from the higher classes and oblivious to the stresses of labouring life. The cruelties of the rich themselves, meanwhile, would remain untouched – not just their field sports, but their role as demanding passengers in hired vehicles – it was to meet *their* selfish demands that cab and coach horses were so wretchedly exploited. Once again, women in particular were accused of rank hypocrisy: 'the same ladies who express horror at whipping of horses may excuse and praise their own guilty coachmen for being "so clever in a crowd" and getting them to "Mrs. Such-a-one's half an hour before anyone else" '.[38] But Windham was at his most effective when he undermined the tenets of Erskine's philosophy – the set of beliefs which, as we have seen, was foundational to eighteenth-century thinking about cruelty to animals. If God had made *all* His creatures to be happy in their lives, why should one make a distinction between man's duty to the domestic working animals that served and depended on him, and to the wild ones that remained free? In the case of the latter: why, because they had not sought man's protection, 'were they to be liable in consequence to be persecuted and tormented by him?' To ward off the hostility of the field sports enthusiasts, Erskine had deployed their own argument: sports were beneficial in preventing over-population of the hunted species, and in allowing wild animals to avoid the pains of physical decline. Windham in riposte pointed out that the hunted species were in fact artificially bred and protected; and, 'when humanity was the question', why should men be so ready to act as their executioners?[39] Here again, Windham's arguments were prophetic. A sense of Christian duty to underlings and a principle of reciprocity meant that domestic animals and livestock were the focus of protectionists' concern for most of the Victorian period. Only in the last two decades of the nineteenth century did the treatment of 'wild' animals begin to occupy the minds of reformers, as an effect of a much wider shift in attitudes associated with evolutionary theory and the dawning of environmental concerns.

Many of Windham's debating points were banter based on devil's advocacy, but he made a serious and lethal attack on Erskine's interpretation of the central principle of human dominion, the very cornerstone of Christian belief on the subject of man's relationship with animals. It had always been assumed that man's interests were to take precedence over those of the 'lower' creatures. But where was one to draw the line between human desires or necessities and animals' entitlements? Meat eating and the use of animal products, together with the extermination of dangerous or pest species, had traditionally been treated as human prerogatives; but humans, as Erskine had acknowledged, made up the rules, which seemed to Windham to admit of some 'striking exceptions', even 'wretched evasions and subterfuges'.[40] It was claimed that both nature and revealed religion instructed man to treat animals with a benevolence modelled on that of God himself; but, if so, should this not entail avoidance of *any* action that caused them suffering or death? The uncertainty of such ethical demands made kindness to animals an imperfect obligation, as Erskine had conceded, on a par with the wealthy classes' voluntary charitable provision for the poor: but it also made cruelty an unfit subject for legislation. It would be another thirteen years before Windham's view was gainsaid, in the very limited anti-cruelty Act of 1822; and each subsequent campaign to expand the terms of that Act had to overcome similar objections.

Thus Windham's arguments, though dismissed angrily as sophistry or twisted logic by supporters of protective legislation, had struck home. The philosophical weaknesses or contradictions he had identified in the pleas of the reformers would haunt their Victorian successors; all the more when views of nature were transformed by Darwinism, and a belief that man's unique spiritual status legitimated his subjugation of other species could no longer be unquestioningly maintained. Responsibility for cruelty – whether it was systemic or individual, upper class or labouring class, a relic of the past or a symptom of moral decline – would continue to be debated; and, despite the positivity of Baroness Burdett-Coutts's account of 'woman's work for animals', reforming groups such as the RSPCA would likewise be accused throughout the nineteenth century of high-handed assaults on personal liberties and oppressive social discrimination. In particular, the *gendering* of attitudes which had surfaced in the Commons debates emerged as a crucial issue. We must now turn to the history and nature of those sexual constructs which shaped women's contribution to animal protection.

Notes

1 'Woman's work for animals', in Baroness Angela Burdett-Coutts (ed.), *Woman's Mission: A Series of Congress Papers on the Philanthropic Work of Women by Eminent*

Writers, produced for the Royal British Commission, Chicago Exhibition, 1893 (facsimile edn, Warrington: Portrayer Publishers, 2002). Minutes of the RSPCA ladies' committee for 13 March 1893 reveal that Burdett-Coutts drafted the report, but asked Mrs Muir Mackenzie to sign it.

2 Ibid., pp. 329–32.

3 Ibid., pp. 332–3.

4 Frank K. Prochaska, *Women and Philanthropy in Nineteenth-Century England* (Oxford: Clarendon Press, 1980), pp. 29, 233, 251. My own calculations, based on the list of subscribers in the RSPCA report for 1897, exactly coincide with Prochaska's figure for 1900 – 69 per cent women.

5 Angela Burdett-Coutts, 'Woman's work', p. 333.

6 For example, Arthur W. Moss, *Valiant Crusade: The History of the R.S.P.C.A.* (London: Cassell, 1961); Garry Jenkins, *A Home of Their Own: The Heart-Warming 150-Year History of Battersea Dogs and Cats Home* (London: Bantam Books, 2011); Tony Samstag, *For Love of Birds: The Story of the Royal Society for the Protection of Birds, 1889–1988* (Sandy: The RSPB, 1988).

7 Brian Harrison, *Peaceable Kingdom: Stability and Change in Modern Britain* (Oxford: Clarendon Press, 1982), especially pp. 4, 25, 83–4, 103–8, and Harrison's article on Colam in the *Oxford Dictionary of National Biography*. (British Academy and Oxford: Oxford University Press, 2004).

8 Harrison, *Peaceable Kingdom*, pp. 116, 127, 137f. Keith Thomas, *Man and the Natural World: Changing Attitudes in England 1500–1800* (London: Penguin, 1984), pp. 185–7. Harriet Ritvo, *The Animal Estate: The English and Other Creatures in the Victorian Age* (Cambridge, MA: Harvard University Press, 1987), pp. 129–55.

9 Emma Griffin, *England's Revelry: A History of Popular Sports and Pastimes, 1660–1830* (Oxford and New York: Oxford University Press, 2005), pp. 223f.

10 E.P. Thompson specifically mentioned popular sports in *The Making of the English Working Class* (Harmondsworth: Penguin, 1968), pp. 443f., and in chapters 2 and 6 of his *Customs in Common* (London: Merlin Press, 1991). Cf. Robert W. Malcolmson, *Popular Recreations in English Society, 1700–1850* (Cambridge: Cambridge University Press, 1973); James Turner, *Reckoning with the Beast: Animals, Pain, and Humanity in the Victorian Mind* (Baltimore and London: Johns Hopkins University Press, 1980), p. 25.

11 Chien-hui Li, *Mobilizing Traditions in the First Wave of the British Animal Defence Movement* (London: Palgrave Macmillan, 2019), p. 5. Cf. Diane L. Beers, *For the Prevention of Cruelty: The History and Legacy of Animal Rights Activism in the United States* (Athens, OH: Swallow Press/Ohio University Press, 2006), pp. 8–9.

12 Keith Tester, *Animals and Society: The Humanity of Animal Rights* (London and New York: Routledge, 1991), p. 48. Rob Boddice, *A History of Attitudes and Behaviours Towards Animals in Eighteenth- and Nineteenth-Century Britain* (Lewiston: Edwin Mellen Press, 2008), p. 165.

13 Dix Harwood, *Love for Animals and How It Developed in Great Britain* (1928), ed. Rod Preece and David Fraser (Lewiston: Edwin Mellen Press, 2002). E.S. Turner, *All Heaven in a Rage* (London: Michael Joseph, 1964). Thomas, *Man and the Natural World*, pp. 143f. Kathryn Shevelow, *For the Love of Animals: The Rise of the Animal Protection Movement* (New York: Henry Holt, 2008).

14 For the Methodist belief in animal immortality: John Wesley's sermon 'The

general deliverance', and Samuel Thompson, *Essays Tending to Prove Animal Restoration* (Newcastle: Edward Walker, 1830). Many Christians of other denominations shared this belief.

15 Genesis 1:26–8; 2:19–20; 9:2–3.

16 Francis Hutcheson, *A System of Moral Philosophy, in Three Books* (Glasgow: R. and A. Foulis, and London: A. Millar and T. Longman, 1755), vol. 1, p. 313.

17 Matthew's gospel, 7:20.

18 Jeremy Bentham, *An Introduction to the Principles of Morals and Legislation* (1789), ed. J.H. Burns and H.L.A. Hart (Oxford: Clarendon Press, 1996), pp. 282–3.

19 Anon. [Edward Augustus Kendall], *Keeper's Travels in Search of His Master* (London: E. Newbery, 1798), pp. iv–vi.

20 Sarah Trimmer, *The Guardian of Education*, 5 vols (1802–1806), ed. Matthew Grenby (Bristol and Tokyo: Thoemmes, 2002), vol. 1, pp. 393–400.

21 Anon. [George Canning], poem later titled 'New morality', *The Anti-Jacobin; Or, Weekly Examiner*, 36 (9 July 1798), pp. 282–7.

22 Revd Luke Booker, *Sermons on Various Subjects* (1793), 2nd edn (London: Rivingtons, 1794), pp. 289, 292–3.

23 Andreas-Holger Maehle, 'Cruelty and kindness to the "brute creation": stability and change in the ethics of the man-animal relationship, 1600–1850', in Aubrey Manning and James Serpell (eds), *Animals and Human Society: Changing Perspectives* (London and New York: Routledge, 1994), p. 91.

24 J.E.G. de Montmorency, 'State protection of animals at home and abroad', *Law Quarterly Review*, 18:69 (January 1902), 31–48 (31).

25 Bills introduced in the House of Commons by Sir William Pulteney, 2 April 1800, and by John Dent, 4 May 1802, to suppress bull-baiting.

26 Windham's speeches of 18 April 1800 and 24 May 1802 in William Cobbett and John Wright (eds), *The Parliamentary History of England* (London: Longman, 1812–20), vol. 35, cols 203–8, and vol. 36, cols 831–41.

27 Anon., *A Letter to the Right Hon. William Windham, on His Late Opposition to the Bill to Prevent Bull-baiting: By an Old Member of Parliament* (London: W. Stratford, and Cadell and Davies, 2nd edn, 1800), pp. 10, 11–12. Turner, *Reckoning with the Beast*, p. 21.

28 Wilberforce's speech supporting Dent's bill of 1802, in *Parliamentary History*, vol. 36, col. 847.

29 Hill's speech in ibid., cols 830–1.

30 Windham's speech in ibid., col. 840.

31 Grosvenor's speech in ibid., col. 844.

32 Windham's speech in ibid., col. 833.

33 Anon. [John Lamb], *A Letter to the Right Hon. William Windham, On His Opposition to Lord Erskine's Bill, for the Prevention of Cruelty to Animals* (London: Maxwell and Wilson, 1810), pp. 31–4.

34 Margaret Cullen, *Mornton: A Novel in Three Volumes* (London: J. Mawman, and York: Wilson and Sons, 1814), vol. 2, p. 40.

35 Erskine's speech in the Lords, 15 May 1809, in *The Parliamentary Debates from the Year 1803* (London: T.C. Hansard, 1812), vol. 14, cols 553–8, 569. Turner, *All Heaven in a Rage*, chapter 10.

36 Erskine's speeches of 31 May and 2 June 1809, in *Parliamentary Debates*, vol. 14, cols 805, 852, referring to correspondents who had offered to give evidence in support of the bill.

See the sympathetic reports in the *Times* (30 May 1809), p. 3, and *Gentleman's Magazine*, 79, new series 2 (July 1809), 645–8.
37 Windham's speech in *Parliamentary Debates*, vol. 14, col. 1037.
38 Ibid., cols 1036–7.
39 Ibid., cols 1039–40.
40 Ibid., col. 1040.

1

Sexual distinctions in attitudes to animals in the late Georgian era

As we have seen, the very first debate on the nature of cruelty to animals to take place in the British parliament had already involved notions of proper masculinity and femininity, reflecting age-old assumptions about the characteristics of the sexes.[1] Ruthless domination of working, hunted and baited animals was assumed to be a function of masculinity; but where did 'manliness' (control, robustness, bravery) end, and reprehensible brutality begin? Conversely, femininity was expressed by pity for all helpless creatures, and by attempts to dissuade men and boys from cruelty towards them. Priscilla Wakefield, in *Instinct Displayed* (1811), gave this commonplace view both a biological and a cultural basis. One of her imagined female letter-writers tells another that boys, 'from false notions of courage and spirit, are suffered to take birds' nests, to tyrannize over horses and dogs, &c. till their feelings are blunted' for ever after. 'Women are more tender-hearted than men; which may partly be attributed to a wise provision of nature, to qualify them for the maternal office. But they are also indebted to education: cruelty is discouraged in girls, as unamiable, and discordant with their natural character; so that an affectation of great sensibility has, of late years, been very fashionable.' Only people endowed with genuine sensibility would perceive, sympathise with and seek to relieve the suffering of animals; but this impulse might be feigned for effect, misdirected, transient or foolishly excessive. It was also liable to be inconsistent, as an effect of prejudice and partial judgement to which women were believed to be especially prone. They might wring their hands over particular cruelties, real or imagined, while perpetrating greater ones themselves. William Howitt, in *The Rural Life of England* (1838), defended hunting from its detractors in 'A word to the too sensitive': a 'delicate lady' of his acquaintance wept pleasingly over a sentimental novel, while condemning the live turkeys in her kitchen to the agony of suspension and slow bleeding to improve the flavour of the flesh.[2]

Many women came to resist the imputations of shallow emotionalism or illogic which were raised against them; they began to undertake a systemic analysis of the deep-seated causes of cruelty in society, and sometimes risked practical interventions of their own to resist it. Yet in making these efforts they encountered a negative construct of femininity more established and ingrained than was displayed merely in the depreciation of sensibility. It was widely believed that women were not just likelier than men were to identify with animals: they were actually more *akin* to animals, as the supposed preponderance of intuition and instinctive feelings in their behaviour suggested. In this chapter, I shall explore the gendering of attitudes to animals, and its effects in shaping the work of female reformers themselves.

The notion of affinity between women and animals

The idea that only males were capable of rational, abstract thought had an ancient history. In the writings of Aristotle, femaleness was a kind of natural 'deformity', while nevertheless complementing maleness as matter complemented spirit. Women's supposed kinship with 'nature' and animals and their incapacity for intellectual or ethical pursuits placed them in a proper subjection to men, just as animals were subjected to human beings.[3] This was a view that, as we shall see, persisted and even grew stronger in the later nineteenth century under the influence of evolutionary theory, taking on a scientific or psycho-sexual guise. Milton's Eve, though created out of Adam's body, was inferior to him, 'in the mind/ And inward faculties'. Her lack of spirituality and wisdom, and even her physical form, meant that she reflected less clearly than Adam did the image of a masculine deity. Nor could she lay claim so indubitably to that right of 'dominion' over the irrational creatures which the deity had conferred on man. Indeed, she was soon to fall victim to the blandishments of the evil tempter in the form of an erected snake.[4] Women's proximity to animals in the scale of being was also signalled by their alleged sensuality. Fear of women's sexuality and the disgust excited by female bodily processes haunted the male consciousness throughout European history, from Juvenal's description of Messalina to Swift's evocation of 'The lady's dressing room'. In the latter, the 'lady' takes on beast-like characteristics, needing tweezers to remove 'Hairs that sink the Forehead low,/ Or on her Chin like Bristles grow', and manufacturing her night gloves out of her deceased lapdog's skin.[5] Indeed, the link between repulsive carnality and animality was especially symbolised by the imagined libidinous relationship between such women and their pet dogs, a theme which occurs also in Pope's *Rape of the Lock* and many other eighteenth-century poems and essays. Moreover, the physical vanity that was imputed to women could also take on animalistic features; even in the later Victorian period, cartoons depicting women wearing furs and feathers virtually transform them into hybrid creatures with crests and claws (see figures 27 and 28).[6]

If women shared with animals an essentially non-reasoning persona, they also felt a bond with them created by common victimhood. In Fielding's *Joseph Andrews* (1742), the beautiful and tender-hearted Fanny tries to save a hunted hare, exclaiming 'with tears in her eyes against the barbarity of worrying a poor innocent defenceless animal out of its life' – only to become herself the intended prey of the hunting squire.[7] In fact, the language of hunting was and is suffused with sexual metaphors and analogies, stressing the varied sensuous attractions of the quarry, the mounting excitement of pursuit, the pleasure in admiring but also in defeating the animal's evasive stratagems, and the ecstatic gratification of capture and conquest. The imagined aptitude of the hunted hare (always referred to as 'she', whatever its actual sex) to *being hunted*, and the supposed 'Coquetries' of its wiles in trying to thwart the hunters, offer a particularly strong parallel with the language of sexual predation.[8] Even the hunted fox could take on sexual allure: a Victorian writer thought that its scent trail was 'as incomprehensible as woman ... when you trust it, it may suddenly jilt you; when cold, may turn as suddenly hot', keeping the hunter's 'passion evergreen'.[9]

The engagement of women themselves in field sports, which had been accepted by the aristocracy in earlier centuries, was increasingly anathematised, with direct effects in a gendering of attitudes towards these pursuits. Sports*women* now represented a perversion of the natural order, as the assertion of mastery involved in hunting and shooting was assumed to be essentially and exclusively masculine. In the view of Joseph Addison in the *Spectator* and later of Hannah More in *Coelebs in Search of a Wife*, such sporting viragos or 'Amazons' were likely to evince a taste also for politics or 'party rage' and for intellectual dispute that represented a further intrusion into the male sphere, and a betrayal of their own proper female roles.[10] Moreover, as William Alexander noted in his *History of Women* (1779), men who were habitual hunters and 'trained up in the exercise of every cruelty against the brute creation' became so unfeeling that 'even the tender and inoffending fair sex are subjects upon which they exercise that ferocious temper'.[11] For all these reasons, a lust for the chase was wholly inconsistent with the timidity, 'softness', gentleness and empathy with suffering fellow-creatures that were considered ideal qualities in women. In the words of Humphry Primatt: 'What a contrast to the tenderness of Rebecca' – the Old Testament heroine who voluntarily drew water for Abraham's camels – 'is the hardheartedness of our *sporting* females, who can testify their delight in the piercing groans of the dying and more delicate STAG. In minds so abominably callous, Religion can have no place'.[12]

Such vehement condemnation reflected a genuine fear that, through women's acquired 'hardheartedness', animals were likely to lose their domestic defenders; but the reflexive effect of hunting and other field sports on the characters of women who engaged in them was of equal concern. Thus sensitive ladies' aversion to the killing of hares, deer and wild birds could be celebrated, even as those sports continued to be ratified and enjoyed by male participants. Francis Noel Mundy's poem, 'On reading verses by the Hon. Julia Curzon, *On Hare Hunting* – December 1792', is full of suave gallantry, in its evocation of her touching distress over the animals' suffering:

> Indignant now she points her pen,
> To urge their plea with savage men;
> And pours a strain so sweet, so strong,
> (For Innocence inspires her song,
> Humanity and warmth of heart,
> And Pity do the Muse's part),
> That thoughts so elegantly drest,
> Win on the most obdurate breast.

Nevertheless, a footnote admits that Mundy himself indulged in hare coursing (setting greyhounds on a hare released from a trap), and being made 'conscious' of the cruelty of the sport was not imagined as really 'winning' on him to desist. Indeed, he wrote another poem about the pleasures of hunting a hare with beagles.[13]

In Mundy's poem, the aristocratic Julia Curzon's 'innocence' and sweet 'pity' typify the more idealising images of women's affinity with nature that developed in the romantic period, countering the negative stereotype of female animality. Other examples can be found in the early poems of Wordsworth recalling his childhood, such as 'To a butterfly', written in 1802. When he and his sister ran after a butterfly

> A very hunter did I rush
> Upon the prey: – with leaps and springs
> I follow'd on from brake to bush;
> But She, God love her! feared to brush
> The dust from off its wings.[14]

Masculine boldness and activity, feminine sweetness and compassion, were now supposedly complementary qualities of the sexes, allotting to women a civilising or 'softening' function in society. However, complementarity did not imply equality of force – female distress over cruelty was a pleasing foil, not a corrective to masculine behaviour. In practice, the value placed on female passivity and the exclusion of women from the public sphere severely restricted any practical effects which their advocacy of kindness to animals might bring about; and, as we shall see, this was a fundamental problem that had to be confronted by the many women who sought to effect a change in attitudes to other species in nineteenth-century Britain.

Field sports, in particular, were perceived as belonging so entirely to a prestigious, upper-class masculine realm that the pleasure they gave was beyond the comprehension of women, and arguably exempted from their criticism. Sarah Trimmer, in her *Easy Introduction to the Knowledge of Nature* (1787), was intent on teaching children to recognise animals as God's creatures, and to treat them, therefore, with respect and loving kindness. However, 'Gentlemen often take great diversion in hunting Stags' – captive, semi-tame animals that were 'carted' to the meet, and then let loose to be chased. 'I suppose there is pleasure in hunting, but I think the poor creature should be allowed to return to his Park again' after the hunt, rather than being killed. So too with hare hunting: 'I don't know how it is with Gentlemen, Henry, but I should feel so much for the poor little frightened creature, as would destroy all enjoyment of the sport.' Yet it emerges that Henry's Papa 'goes a shooting' and coursing hares.[15] The appeal of hunting to men simply bemused the majority of women writers, rather than making it their prime target for suppression; and indeed one finds in the Victorian era what seem to be glaring inconsistencies between women's efforts to reform the treatment of domestic animals, and their toleration of grand-scale hunting among their own male kinsfolk. Feeling for the sufferings of animals, such as that evinced by Julia Curzon or Sarah Trimmer, was pleasing in women. It seemed to do honour to human nature, reflecting in particular the civilised Christian values that were supposed to characterise British society at the end of the eighteenth century; but its pertinence and moral authority in the field of practical action was much more questionable.

The vexed role of female sensibility in attitudes to animals

Expressions of 'sensibility' – a tender, emotional response to the sight of suffering, including that of animals – were associated particularly with the writings of Rousseau, Sterne and Henry Mackenzie; but in the later decades of the eighteenth century, sensibility was increasingly looked on as a female trait.[16] For some writers, it represented all that was distinctive and admirable in the character of women. In 1808 John Bowdler questioned the wisdom of a 'Proposed Improvement of Female Education'. 'Women are not profound scholars and philosophers: it is admitted'; but they possess a peculiar 'delicacy and justness of feeling', together with an 'enchanting' but wayward or even irrational faculty of imagination. All these qualities would be disturbed by 'mental discipline' or by an exposure to the world's insoluble woes. 'Sensibility is the first of charms; but woe to the wretch, who, regardless of the coarseness and apathy of mankind, cherishes feelings exquisitely alive to every sentiment of pain and pleasure … imagination is the rack of exalted spirits.'[17] However, it was precisely this kind of gratuitous, over-susceptible display of high-flown feeling, often artificially heightened by affectation, which brought female sensibility into disrepute. It had no necessary connection with useful action to relieve suffering: indeed, it was often prompted by merely trivial objects or spectacles – and here distress for suffering or dying animals furnished the prime examples. The fictional literature of the period is full of women who agonise over pets but neglect their duty to humankind. The conservative writer Hannah More, in her early poem on *Sensibility*, deplored the often 'counterfeit' nature of its 'external marks' or poetic expressions, referring here to writers of both sexes:

> There are, who fill with brilliant plaints the page,
> If a poor linnet meet the gunner's rage:
> There are, who for a dying fawn display
> The tend'rest anguish in the sweetest lay;
> Who for a wounded animal deplore,
> As if friend, parent, country were no more.[18]

In her *Strictures on the Modern System of Female Education* (1799), More again alluded to 'all the images of grief, and love, and fancy' in poetic 'elegies' for animals, and blamed them for the growth of *false* feeling in girls; they were a distraction from 'rational' studies and from progress in religion and morality.[19] As if to illustrate such shortcomings, in More's didactic novel of 1809, *Coelebs in Search of a Wife*, Lady Melbury is genuinely attached to her maid Toinette and feels 'real compassion' when she is ill. Yet her ladyship spends so long 'setting to music an elegy on the death of her Java Sparrow' and choosing items of millinery that the maid dies before she is ready to visit the bedside.[20]

Excessive fondness for other species even smacked of misanthropy or frustrated sexual passions: it was allegedly indulged at the expense of humans

In Old Maid treating a favorite Cat to a Duck and Green Peas.

1 Richard Newton, *An Old Maid treating a favorite Cat to a Duck and Green Peas*, 1792, hand-coloured etching. The grotesque spinster gives her cat delicacies, while her servant boy goes hungry. Framed portraits of other cherished cats adorn the wall.

(relatives, friends or servants) to whom such ladies had a real moral obligation. In Jonas Hanway's words, 'an immoderate love of a brute animal, tho' it may not destroy a charitable disposition, yet it often weakens the force of it', and may even co-exist with indifference to animals in general.[21] In numerous Georgian caricatures, witch-like old 'tabbies', whose characterisation reflects a hostility to ageing single women typical of the time, are seen doting obsessively on their cats, whose catty nature they are presumed to share (figure 1).[22] The tradition continued into the nineteenth century in works like Landseer's drawing of 'The ladies' pets' (1823) (figure 2), where an overweight pug and beribboned spaniel pant along in the wake of their fashionably dressed owners. As late as 1879, William Lauder Lindsay, describing *Mind in the Lower Animals*, suggested that the companionship of women was generally an 'evil' influence

2 Edwin Landseer, drawing of 'The ladies' pets', dated 1823; in a set of engravings after
Landseer's designs published by Ernest Gambart, London, in 1848.

on dogs; life in the boudoir, with 'injudicious petting and pampering', made the
animals disdainful and selfish.[23] Such negative tropes had a damaging effect on
public perceptions of anti-cruelty campaigns: the allegation that 'old women'
were the principal backers of any parliamentary bill to improve the lot of animals was a favourite weapon of opponents throughout the Victorian era. In
1898, even a champion of animals' rights, Edward Evans, in his *Evolutionary
Ethics*, noted that 'charitable foundations for animals' were viewed as 'manifes-
tations of a mild and harmless monomania peculiar to old maids and withered
beldames, who … pour the flood of their pent-up affections into this channel';
the 'channel' could even become 'the waste pipe of suppressed and soured emotions'. As Brian Luke has noted, women's 'rage' over the treatment of animals
was, and often still is, dismissed in this way as 'sentiment' or 'hysteria'; it is 'thus
divested of political significance by interpreting any female reaction against the
established order not as a moral challenge to that order, but as a biosexual phenomenon to be ignored or subdued'. In these circumstances, strong and overt
female support for animal protection measures in the nineteenth century could
be more of a liability than an asset, and 'sentiment' needed to be emphatically
disclaimed by activists of both sexes.[24]

When, however, one turns from the diatribes and condescension of critics to the imaginative writings of women themselves, it becomes clear that in many cases their thoughts about human relationships with animals go much beyond mere sentimental effusion. In their identification with despoiled nature and with suffering creatures, they suggest poignant analogies with the fate of women themselves, and in their direct expressions of feeling they are quite different from the witty ironies of Laurence Sterne in his famous encounters with downtrodden donkeys or imprisoned starlings.[25] As early as 1762, Sarah Scott, in her remarkable novel *A Description of Millenium* [*sic*] *Hall*, imagined an all-female community in whose idyllic grounds all field sports and the capture and caging of wild animals were forbidden. 'Man never appears there as a merciless destroyer, but the preserver, instead of the tyrant, of the inferior part of the creation', and animals were granted 'a perfect equality in nature's bounty'.[26] Similarly, in Anna Letitia Barbauld's influential writings about animals, the psychology of human relationships with other species is explored in new ways, moving subtly between personal feeling and universal concerns. 'Epitaph on a goldfinch' describes a caged bird, 'scarcely permitted to view those fields, to the possession of which he had a natural and undoubted charter. Deeply sensible of this infringement of his native and inalienable rights, he was often heard to petition for redress' in song. 'At length, wearied with fruitless efforts to escape, his indignant spirit burst the prison which his body could not, and left behind a lifeless heap of beauteous feathers.'[27] The tone of this 'Epitaph' may affect one's reading of Barbauld's much better known and apparently more humorous poem 'The mouse's petition' (1773), in which a mouse, caught and caged with a view to being used in one of her friend Joseph Priestley's experiments on the properties of gases, pleads with him for release. In imagining its thoughts and feelings, the poem expresses the difference between our attitude to animals en masse, often slaughtered without compunction, and to those *individual* animals which, encountered at close quarters, take on identity and inhibit the killing instinct – a theme which Barbauld was to explore more fully in another poem, 'The caterpillar' (c.1816). Yet the mouse also stands for all animals: referring to Priestley's thoughts on the problematic nature of the connection between body and spirit, Barbauld speculates on the likelihood that animals possess 'a kindred mind', a 'brother's soul', linking them closely to humanity. All living creatures may then be imagined as sharing man's longing for, and right to freedom, and 'The chearful light, the vital air', are blessings to which all are entitled.

The well taught philosophic mind
To all compassion gives;
Casts round the world an equal eye,
And feels for all that lives.[28]

Coleridge, writing in *The Watchman* in 1796, remarked that 'thanks to Mrs. Barbauld, and to Berguin [Arnaud Berquin, author of *L'ami des enfans*], it has become universally *fashionable* to teach lessons of compassion towards animals'; and, given the continuing popularity of Barbauld's writings in the Victorian era, that lesson was sustained.[29] Her works demonstrated that women, deprived of opportunities to act in the public sphere, might yet influence public attitudes to cruelty through literature: a lesson that was not lost on her successors. She and some other female writers of the period had, moreover, shown that women's response to animal suffering could be different in kind from that of men: more empathetic, more urgent, and at the same time more inclined to view cruelty to animals as an aspect of wider cruelties endemic to society: cruelties which only moral education of the young could correct.

The subject of cruelty to animals in educational works

Many sources suggest that cruelties committed by young boys (mainly involving domestic animals, birds, frogs and toads, insects, mice and other 'pest' species) were rife at this period and indeed throughout the nineteenth century, involving behaviour that would be thought intolerable, even psychopathic, in present-day western societies. Yet parents' acceptance or actual encouragement of such conduct had been roundly condemned by Lord Shaftesbury, John Locke and many influential Georgian writers: habits of cruelty contracted in childhood would, they believed, lead on to greater crimes in adulthood.[30] Thomas Young, writing in 1798, explained that 'Cruelty, like all other vices, is progressive and ingenious; it calls continually for stronger gratifications, and is driven upon refined methods of satisfying its cravings': what began with birds-nesting might end with the murder of fellow-humans.[31] Revd Thomas Crowe, in *Zoophilos* (1820), deplored the fact that boys were introduced to 'sanguinary sports' almost as soon as they left the nursery, as 'pursuits of manhood'. He believed that even the horrors of the Napoleonic wars might be traced to the source of children's license to inflict 'death or torments on other animals'.[32]

Exhortations to reject cruelty accordingly became a standard, almost an obsessive feature of improving books for young children, a spate of which appeared in the later Georgian period.[33] The first was the anonymous story of *Goody Two-Shoes*, a woman who teaches kindness to animals, and adopts those in distress.[34] Later, the great majority of such books were written by women, and a fictional mother, aunt or other female mentor takes on the task of instructing children in the proper, humane treatment of animals. Their popularity was such that many were reprinted in new, updated editions well into the Victorian era. Maria Edgeworth's stories of 'Lazy Lawrence' and 'Simple Susan', for example, from her book *The Parent's Assistant*, first published in 1796, can be found combined in a freshly illustrated edition of 1868; and Mrs Barbauld's *Lessons for Children*, published from 1778 onwards, was reissued as late as 1869.[35] These nursery classics cemented the association in readers' minds between women and animal protection, preparing the way for the homilies and children's story-books of Victorian writers such as Caroline Bray and Anna Maria Hall, and for a leading female role in the educational activities and publications of bodies such as the RSPCA.[36] Indeed, female authors' admonitions to be kind to animals were so vehement and, in some ways, so much at odds with normal male-dominated practices of the day, that G.J. Barker-Benfield has called them 'a kind of surrogate feminism'.[37]

Some of these books were intended for the improvement of the lower classes, who – closely connected as they were with the everyday management of working animals, including the driving of horses – were thought to be especially in need of attitudinal reform. Sarah Trimmer's *The Two Farmers* of 1787, for example, was a 'short tract for the poor', sold for use in Sunday schools; and indeed her guidelines for such schools in *The Oeconomy of Charity* (1787) included a regular 'Evening Admonition' to the children not to 'torment dumb creatures'.[38] The playwright and poet Joanna Baillie wrote *A Lesson Intended for the Use of the Hampstead School* in 1826, to guide its pupils – destined for a life in domestic service or manual labour – in humane treatment of animals. Her wish that 'the Ladies, who have the goodness to examine the School' should read out the lesson to the children periodically, interpolating their own thoughts and observations, marks an early stage in the enlistment of middle- and upper-class women in the educational mission that would later develop into the 'Band of Mercy' movement.[39] However, the best-known works concerned with the moral instruction of children, such as John Aikin and Anna Letitia Barbauld's series *Evenings at Home* (1792 onwards), were expressions of the values held by the *bien pensant* middling orders, in many cases Unitarian writers, to be imparted to their own offspring and social class. Thus the stories centre on parental exhortation that is likely to have been echoed and amplified by the real-life mother or governess reading the books aloud to children; just as Joanna Baillie's colleagues, the lady 'examiners' or visitors, were urged to interpret and enforce the message of her *Lesson* in the schoolroom. For Mrs Barbauld, 'Education, in its largest sense ... includes the whole process by which a human being is formed to be what he is, in habits, principles, and cultivation of every kind'.[40] In particular, works like her much-praised *Hymns in Prose for Children* and Trimmer's *Easy Introduction to the Knowledge of Nature* – the standard childhood reading of the Victorians – emphasised first-hand obser-vation of nature as the book of God, which would teach children the worth of animals and their entitlement to happiness.[41] As late as the 1820s and 1830s, the pious Quaker Mary Sewell (mother of Anna, the future author of *Black Beauty*) raised her children on the teaching principles embedded in Maria and Richard Lovell Edgeworth's *Practical Education* of 1798.[42] The Edgeworths' work, while not religious in tone, had explained the moral importance of setting children to draw or cut out the forms of animals, and to study nature in the field or through the microscope. In this way, they believed, the natural sensibility of the young could be disciplined by reason, knowledge and insight, so that capricious likes and dislikes gave way to a wider appreciation of animals' characters and needs, and habits of benevolence to *all* living creatures, whether appealing or not, took root.[43]

The prevailing tendency to condone boys' destructiveness was a particular target of female writers. In story after story, little girls remonstrate with their brothers over wanton cruelties to animals, and try to rescue their victims. Girls' own sins seldom go beyond weak connivance with these wrongdoers, neglect of caged birds, or ignorant if well-intentioned forms of care that are against an animal's true interests. In *The Sister's Gift* of 1786 (reprinted in the 1820s), Kitty – a significant name – admonishes her brother severely for his habit of tying kettles to dogs' tails, goading cattle with a nail on a stick, throwing a girl's cat off a church tower and other such deeds, while in Mary Martha Sherwood's *Soffrona and Her Cat Muff* (1828), two little girls save a kitten that some boys have stolen and are trying to drown.[44] *The Looking-Glass for the Mind*, first published in 1787, was a translation of Berquin's *L'ami des enfans*, which, as we have seen, was mentioned by Coleridge as helping to promote a new vogue for sympathy with animals at the turn of the eighteenth century. 'Louisa's tenderness to the little birds in winter' (figure 3) tells of how the birds' distress 'seemed to afflict the tender-hearted maid very much'. When she feeds them with corn, 'It is impossible to describe the pleasure and satisfaction' expressed in her countenance, and this is only a preliminary to her solicitous acquisition of a bird trapped by 'a little boy ... whose heart was not of so tender a nature as

Louisa's'. Papa is so moved by this evidence of her compassion for animals that he 'tenderly embraced her, and shed tears of joy on her blooming cheeks'.[45] But if fictional episodes of this kind smack of the kind of self-indulgent solipsism, sensibility for prettiness's sake, that was increasingly discredited, it is clear that, in real life, girls were indeed tasked with restraining male cruelties, and becoming the conscience of society. In Joanna Baillie's *Lesson for the Use of the Hampstead School*, the female pupils were exhorted to restrain their brothers from 'bad practices': not only for the sake of the animals involved, but as a means of preserving the boys 'from after disgrace, and even from a shameful end', to which habits of cruelty must inevitably lead.[46] Yet a continuing de facto approval of boyish 'spirit', a fear of breeding milksops, flew in the face of such exhortations. For example, *The Boy's Own Book*, published in 1828, contained detailed, unabashed instructions for birds-nesting and bird-catching, using nets, traps or limed twigs. Captured nightingales and skylarks are to have their wings tied initially, and are to be confined in 'a cage about a foot square', in tacit defiance of a hundred poems and stories written by women that deplored such imprisonment of wild songbirds.[47] Such defiance or indifference seems to have persisted: as late as the 1890s, in pamphlets published by the newly established Society for the Protection of Birds (SPB), boys were still being exhorted to abandon these practices, as though for the first time.

LOUISA'S TENDERNESS TO THE
LITTLE BIRDS IN WINTER.

However long the winter may appear, the spring will naturally succeed it. A gentle breeze began to warm the air, the snow gradually vanished, the fields put on their enamelled livery, the flowers shot forth their buds, and the birds began to send forth their harmony from every bough.

Little Louisa and her father left the city, to partake of the pleasures of the country.—

3 John Bewick, illustration of 'Louisa's Tenderness to the Little Birds in Winter' wood engraving in a translation of Arnaud Berquin's *The Looking-Glass for the Mind; Or, Intellectual Mirror*, 15th edition, 1821.

It becomes evident that the constant exhortations in children's books to be merciful to all animals represented a strategy to inculcate a feminised gentleness of character that was intended to counterbalance the cult of virility embedded in public discourse, and to redefine 'manliness' as wholly compatible with such sensitivity. It was the symptom of a gendered divide in values that, as we shall see, deepened significantly in the Victorian period. Thus these books typically teach children to shun actions that, as the authors must have realised, formed a normal part of the pursuits and habits of the real adult world. Jane and Ann Taylor, in their *Original Poems for Infant Minds* (1804–1805), which in Britain alone went through some fifty editions down to the 1880s, described the sufferings of domestic and working animals in harrowing detail that might well upset a young child. But beside the pathos of descriptions of overladen and abused horses, abandoned old dogs and stolen nestlings, there are hard words for those who hunt hares, shoot, fish, drown kittens, or kill insects, spiders and household pests – practices that were likely to endure unchallenged.[48] On the nursery slopes of a lifelong process of moral education, domestic animals – the only living beings that children *could* have power over – provided a useful 'instrument', in Christopher Smart's words, for them 'to learn benevolence upon'.[49] Such animals are to be understood, a modern author has suggested, as 'didactic devices', rather than creatures whose treatment was ever likely to be ameliorated. The gentling of the human subject, not the relief of the animal object, was here the main purpose.[50]

The difficulty of establishing a proper, reasonable level of compunction over animal suffering was confronted head-on in a famous book, Sarah Trimmer's *Fabulous Histories. Designed for the Instruction of Children, respecting their Treatment of Animals.* First published in 1786, it was many times reissued down to the end of the nineteenth century, eventually being known simply as *The History of the Robins.*[51] Trimmer, a political and religious conservative, was anxious that animals should not be given the same status as humans, nor invested with human qualities of mind, for she perceived any assertion of animal 'rights' as an extension of moves for the levelling of British society. Yet an appeal to child readers, who often 'express a wish that their birds, cats, dogs &c. could *talk*' demanded an element of make-believe and anthropomorphism in the birds portrayed in *Fabulous Histories.*[52] Trimmer's family of robins replicates the virtues of a well-governed human family, conveying, in the manner of a fable, 'moral instruction' applicable to the children themselves, and naturalising a principle of subordination; but *as* robins, the children's 'little pensioners', they also 'excite compassion and tenderness for those interesting and delightful creatures, on which such wanton cruelties are frequently inflicted, and recommend *universal benevolence*' – a benevolence inspired by Christian teaching.[53] The birds' combination of roles gives the clue to Trimmer's intentions: kindness to domestic beasts and birds should be tempered by consciousness of natural hierarchy, linking, in Burkean fashion, the family and the nation, and relegating animals to a lower, dependent situation. In accordance with this conceptual framework, a compassionate but sensible treatment of domestic animals, avoiding both '*immoderate tenderness*' and callous cruelties, is itself a hallmark of right-minded people who are respectful and observant of social rank. Such people recognise that needy humans of the lower classes have a claim on their attention superior to that of irrational animals.[54] In this play of opposing forces and moral pressures, a fictional Mr Jenkins condones his son's terrible cruelties to cats and dogs, and his throwing at cocks, as the actions of 'a lad of life and spirit … fit to go through the world'; and, as a result, Master Jenkins predictably comes to a bad end.[55] But, at the other end of the spectrum, undue female devotion to animals, displacing human attachments and concerns, was itself liable to serious opprobrium, as 'unnatural affection'.[56]

Women's speculations on the problem of cruelty to animals: the genesis of a more comprehensive vision

How could women's distinctive sympathy with oppressed animals be recognised as a *reasonable* and principled attitude, deserving of influence in the public sphere? This was the problem tackled by various leading female thinkers at the turn of the eighteenth century, and it continued to surface throughout the Victorian era, becoming an important aspect of feminist polemics. Firstly, many writers now challenged the prevailing assumption that women were themselves akin to animals in their reliance on passion and intuition rather than on rationality, and this intention both informed and tempered the arguments they put forward for a new relationship with other species. Here Mary Wollstonecraft's writings are a particularly instructive example.

Wollstonecraft's early books for children such as *Elements of Morality* of 1790 are, like those of other female authors of the period, replete with exhortations to treat animals kindly.[57] *Original Stories from Real Life* of 1788, in particular, devotes the first three chapters to this subject: animals are God's creatures, wonderfully made, and intended to be happy according to their capabilities, while cruelty towards them is a sin which has lifelong, baneful effects on the sinner. As usual, the fictional woman and girls in the story are moved by their 'emotions of humanity' to plead for the release of various animals tormented by incorrigibly cruel boys; but the claims of 'some sick people' in the neighbourhood rightfully take precedence. The girls' mentor Mrs Mason congratulates them for acting 'like rational creatures', in both respects: 'every part of the creation affords an exercise for virtue', but humans are superior to animals – indeed, nearer to the angels than they are to the beasts.[58]

Thus far, Wollstonecraft's sentiments are virtually indistinguishable from those of Mrs Trimmer, at the opposite end of the political spectrum. However, the French revolution gave a sharper, more polemical edge to her thoughts on animals and their relations with humans. In *A Vindication of the Rights of Men* (1790), her riposte to Burke's *Reflections on the Revolution in France*, Wollstonecraft attacked Burke's passionate justification of the British constitutional tradition and status quo, with all their social inequities. She argued that his reliance on what he called 'untaught feelings' manifested all the irrationality and 'pampered sensibility' with which *women* were often taxed. 'In what respect are we superior to the brute creation, if intellect is not allowed to be the guide of passion? Brutes hope and fear, love and hate; but, without a capacity to improve … they neither acquire virtue nor wisdom.' She quoted Burke's own words ironically back at him: in a state where the mystique of royalty has been destroyed by godless revolutionaries, 'a king *is* but a man; a queen *is* but a woman; a woman *is* but an animal, and an animal not of the highest order'.[59] Wollstonecraft referred back to the strongly gendered characterisations of the sublime and the beautiful in Burke's *Philosophical Enquiry* of 1757. There the sublime was associated with the power, authority, intellectual strenuousness and grandeur of ideas that Burke attributes to the noblest males. In contrast, beauty, a quality highest in women, is 'no creature of our reason'. It arises from impressions of 'weakness and imperfection', and the 'softer virtues' of 'less dignity'. Furthermore, it depends on purely 'sensible qualities' of delicacy and apparent vulnerability, of a kind which attract us to songbirds and the cuddlier kinds of small mammals, as well as to women. Wollstonecraft was indignant that women were, on this analysis, debarred by 'nature' and by the requirements of physical beauty from the cultivation of 'truth, fortitude and humanity', which Burke had represented as being confined 'within the rigid pale of manly morals'. It was as if 'Nature has made an eternal distinction between the qualities that dignify a rational being and this animal perfection'.[60]

In *Vindication of the Rights of Woman* of 1792, Wollstonecraft raged again and again that female sensibility, mere sensation, was viewed as the antithesis of male rationality, with the effect of excluding women from all pursuits of the mind, and all virtuous actions in the public sphere. 'And if the dignity of the female soul be as disputable as that of animals' – if women were equivocal creatures, lacking both reason to guide their conduct *and* the 'unerring instinct' traditionally attributed to animals – 'they are surely of all creatures the most miserable! and, bent beneath the iron hand of destiny, must submit to be a *fair defect* in creation', or perhaps 'the link which unites man with brutes'.[61] Wollstonecraft's suspicion of the cult of sensibility, her need to affirm the rationality of women, and thus to distinguish their minds absolutely from those of animals (as then understood), seems to have deterred her from expressing support for the idea of animal rights, then being canvassed by many radical thinkers.[62] However, feminism did not exclude sympathy with animals' sufferings – for these sufferings, like those of women themselves, arose from a combination of sexual and societal injustice. Habits of cruelty to animals were taught to schoolboys, giving rise to future 'domestic tyranny over wives, children, and servants'. Labouring-class men inflicted cruelties on their beasts of burden, in 'revenge' or compensation for their own degraded condition, 'trodden under foot by the rich'. Therefore only political reform and national education could ultimately protect animals from harm; for 'Justice, or even benevolence, will not be a powerful spring of action unless it extend to the whole creation'.[63]

A few years earlier, a writer whom Wollstonecraft greatly admired, the historian Catharine Macaulay, had written more extensively on the intellectual problems raised by humans' relations with other species.[64] Her *Letters on Education* of 1790, which takes the form of an imaginary correspondence between the author and a female friend, is ostensibly a treatise concerned with moral principles, especially as applied to the education of girls.[65] However, the book opens, as though in mid-conversation: 'So you approve, Hortensia, of what I have advanced in favour of the future existence of brute animals'. Macaulay feels nothing but 'contempt and anger' when man addresses the deity as 'the god of all perfection, yet dealing out a severe and short mortality to the various tribes of his fellow animals, and assigning to himself an eternity of happiness' – 'what motive, worthy of divine wisdom, could influence the deity to draw the line of separation thus wide between his creatures?' Yet some modern philosophers, seeking to explain 'the introduction of moral and natural evil' into the world, 'limit the power and the benevolence of God' to what they can observe in the operations of nature; and nature is a 'monster' which is 'continually devouring and regorging itself, with rapture and delight'. A 'scoffer' among these philosophers may even ask 'why an omnipotent and infinitely wise being, should permit one order of his creatures', human beings, 'to abuse their superior powers, in ensnaring into the train of perdition other of his creatures of inferior endowments; for this … seems to infer a notion more derogatory to absolute moral perfection, than the manichean system'; the latter having suggested 'an impotence in power, rather than a deficiency in the benevolence or wisdom in the good deity'.[66] Macaulay thus wrestles with an age-old theological problem that would become more pressing in the nineteenth century: that of reconciling the cruelties of the natural order with belief that the deity is both benevolent *and* omnipotent, and hence of finding a logical basis for human morality. The treatment of animals is a crucial aspect of this complex disquisition. 'If brutes were to draw a character of man, Hortensia, do you think they would call him a benevolent being? No; their representations would be somewhat of the same kind as the fabled furies and other infernals in ancient mythology': for men, though uniquely gifted with reason and imagination, differ little in their behaviour from the 'relentless' animal predators that, for reasons we cannot yet understand, are licensed by God to haunt the natural world. Our animal victims, being instinctive and dumb creatures, cannot complain of man's cruelties;

> and being our own panegyrists, we can give ourselves what attributes we please, and call our confined and partial sympathy, the sublime virtue of benevolence. Goodness to man, and mercy to brutes, is all that is taught by the moralist; and this mercy is of a nature which if properly defined, can only be distinguished by the inferiority of its degree from the vice of cruelty.[67]

Incorrigible habits of abusing animals, including hunting, can only be corrected by a new consciousness of the claims of other species to happiness and fulfilment. As things stand, anthropocentrism and specious, self-interested reasoning blind us to the limits of our vaunted humanity. Men should therefore strive to attain that *true* benevolence which is manifested in dealings with animals and fellow-humans alike. It cannot be considered as such if it admits discrimination between individuals or species; and in fact there is no natural, inborn sympathy or benignity in the characters of human beings even to prevent *intra*-species violence, as slaves know to their cost.[68]

How, then, can this universal benevolence be attained, when human instincts are those of the beast of prey? Sensibility has a role, certainly, and should be cultivated.[69] Yet considerations of 'utility', invariably meaning human advantage, will tend to restrict sympathies, which are subject to 'inconsistency and mutability', as in 'every system of morals founded on human sentiment'. Only the power of reasoning – that same power which, when perverted, is a main cause of cruelty to animals – can redeem humankind and enable us to 'discern … an immutable and abstract fitness' in our dealings with other species, 'in a more satisfactory manner than what is called a moral consciousness from innate principles'.[70] Such reasoning should be expressed in protective legislation: 'were government to act on so liberal a sentiment of benevolence, as to take under the protection of law the happiness of the brute species, so far as to punish in offenders that … barbarous treatment they meet with in the course of their useful services, would it not tend to encrease sympathy?'[71] In this searching analysis of the psychology of cruelty, and of the conditions in which a supposedly civilised society continues to tolerate and excuse it, Catharine Macaulay's *Letters on Education* anticipates the debates of a century later; and her plea for moral conditioning through legal restraints – rational action built on 'a sentiment of benevolence' – was equally a pointer to the future.

As we have seen in the Introduction, the succession of bills concerned with anti-cruelty measures that were brought before parliament from 1800 onwards, especially Lord Erskine's of 1809, did indeed spark a national debate on the feasibility and legitimacy of controlling human behaviour towards animals through protective legislation. One of the most interesting responses to this debate was contained, not in a moral treatise or press article, but in a triple-decker novel, *Mornton* (1814), by a now forgotten writer, Margaret Cullen. Her background lay in the Scottish enlightenment: her father was the distinguished physician Dr William Cullen, and one of her sisters, Robina Craig Millar, was a noted radical intellectual; Margaret herself was known in her circle as 'the Good Spirit'.[72] The plot of *Mornton* involves the usual romantic entanglements, deceptions, misunderstandings and *éclaircissements*, before the heroine, Rosalind Fontroy, escaping from all moral snares, marries a man of true integrity. However, within the story there is a succession of episodes and resulting conversations in which cruelty to animals is extensively discussed; the virtuous and magnanimous characters invariably identifying themselves with the cause of greater kindness, while the loutish, unscrupulous and worldly people either practise or condone cruelty. The book was sympathetically reviewed in the *Monthly Magazine*, which, reflecting the views of its owner Richard Phillips, attempted to promote animal protection initiatives. Here *Mornton*'s storyline is treated simply as a frame for the disquisitions on cruelty to animals, which are nevertheless made more palatable to 'the young and volatile' by being presented as imaginary conversations rather than as a dry treatise. The reviewers go so far as to claim, perhaps wishfully, that by raising readers' awareness of the *real* abuses it describes, *Mornton* has already 'in various instances, had great effect in restraining cruelty', and helped to pave the way for the establishment of a society working for legal protection of animals, such as contributors to the *Monthly Magazine* often proposed.[73]

Cullen, like Catharine Macaulay, suggests that concern for animals is not, as many eighteenth-century writers had suggested, a contemptible female foible or a distraction from the proper business of philanthropy, but, rather, an expression of a person's essential goodness and benevolence, extended to all living creatures; and cruelty is likewise the outcome of thought processes that are woven into the whole social and political fabric of the nation. Hence in *Mornton*, expressions of sympathy with animals are not confined to passive weeping for crushed insects or deceased lapdogs – that melting tenderness supposedly inculcated in the nursery and retained as an attractive accomplishment by grown women. Genuine sympathy involves brave physical interventions – by women as well as men – to prevent and reprimand the many cruelties which Cullen describes in a footnote as terrible 'facts' of life in early nineteenth-century Britain. Thus Rosalind stops some brutal boys abusing a donkey, and others from robbing birds' nests; tries to dissuade coachmen and carters, encountered on the road, from beating their horses; and, most daringly, snatches up and protects a hunted hare.[74]

Like Macaulay, Cullen wrestles with the problem of connecting the kind of sensibility that recoils at the sight of animal suffering, and the kind of rational right-mindedness that public men will need in acting to prevent it. Certainly the human 'moral sense' (guilefully invoked by opponents of Erskine's bill of 1809 in the Commons as a sufficient guarantee of proper treatment of animals) in truth avails little without legal sanctions.[75] As one of Cullen's fictional characters, a Mrs Edgeville, points out, and as Macaulay had already noted, the 'moral sense' does not even protect human beings from one another; and 'I should think persons must walk through life with both their eyes and heart shut, if they are not aware how little the moral sense influences the unfeeling and vulgar of all ranks', in their dealings with animals.[76] The argument has, of course, strongly gendered implications: Cullen's whole book is an attempt to correct the belief that masculinity entails belligerence and a taste for blood, such as Windham had associated with bull- and bear-baiting, or that 'habits of the world' – the competitive male world – are an inevitable, indeed a desirable curb on womanish sentiment. On the contrary, Cullen's gentlest men and boys are shown to be also the bravest: and only cowards and bullies indulge in cruelties to defenceless humans or animals.[77] The boorish youth Dartrey tells Rosalind, after her rescue of the hare, that 'women's feelings always run away with them', and, in response, she defensively falls back on the old warnings about the corrupting effects of cruelty to animals on the human character and on society:

> 'It is not for a hare,' replied Rosalind, 'but for the want [of] feeling to which it leads. – Yet it is for a hare!' cried Rosalind, eagerly clasping her hands, as if seized by a sudden emotion; 'it is for that very identical, little, trembling creature, I saw in such agonies! – Oh! I can never forget it!'[78]

Identification and sympathy with animals *for themselves*, albeit prompted by the actual sight of suffering, rather than distant reports of its infliction, would become a vital feature of women's advocacy. However, the means by which such feelings could sway public opinion at large – when all tradition, custom, prejudice and commercial interest favoured the status quo – were far from clear. It was necessary to work against the grain, and to endure the ridicule and obloquy that were still directed against those who pressed for greater human-ity than it suited society to grant. Some of the imaginary company in *Mornton* stigmatise such would-be reformers as cranks, who should pay greater atten-tion to the views of their circle; to which Mrs Edgeville replies: 'our circle is the universe'.[79]

Sensitivity to animal suffering, once associated principally with over-refined ladies or whimsical eccentrics, could now be viewed, in defiance of current practices, as an essential aspect of civilised Christian behaviour. Indeed, for a growing number of Britons, continuing cruelty to animals was an inexcusable blot on the country's reputation. Like the continuance of slavery in the West Indies and the savagery of the penal code, it gave the lie to the idea that Britain was a truly humane country, advancing in high culture and enlightened atti-tudes as fast as it was advancing in industrial technology and wealth. To many observers, cruelty actually seemed to be getting worse. A dark thought then arose: was the heartless exploitation of animals an *effect* of the country's growing capitalist might, rather than an anomaly that further progress would rectify?

The playwright Joanna Baillie, whom we have encountered as the author of a pamphlet on cruelty to animals for use in charity schools, certainly wrestled with this enigma. She wrote some exquisite poems in which, without false sentiment, she tried to put into words a perception of animals' characteristics, and these are not irrelevant to her larger purposes. A kitten's 'clutching feet' rhythmically 'bepat the ground,/ And all their harmless claws disclose/ Like prickles of an early rose'.[80] Such acute delight in animals *as* animals, not as mere prompts to grander human themes, seems especially typical of female writers;

yet it inspired Baillie and others to ponder the wider dimensions of cruelty towards them. In 'Verses written in February, 1827', she imagines Britain as a landscape in shadow. Sunbeams streaming down through some breaks in the cloud light up 'verdant islet-spots': 'So in a land where Mammon's cares prevail' do 'deeds of gentle charity/ Refresh the moral gazer's mental eye'. However, these are only isolated points of reassurance. Britain's superiority in 'arms and commerce' is, admittedly, graced by 'many generous acts':

> And may we not say truthfully of thee,
> Thou art a land of mercy? – May it be!

Domestic cats and dogs and fighting cocks are 'hard-fated mates in woeful plight'; but the terrible abuse of horses, beaten and worked to death by 'thank-less, heartless owners', is the most flagrant example of endemic brutality.

> Ah no! A land of mercy is a name
> Which thou in all thy glory mayest not claim!
> But yet there dwell in thee the good, the bold,
> Who in thy streets, courts, senates bravely hold
> Contention with thy wayward cruelty,
> And shall subdue it ere this age glide by.[81]

Elizabeth Heyrick, Susanna Watts and the rise of female activism

In Joanna Baillie's view, the 'manly power' of legislators, already put in evidence by Richard Martin's act against cruelties to horses and livestock of 1822, was the key to national redemption. However, as in the case of the campaign for the abolition of slavery in the British dominions, which was going forward in the same years, extra-parliamentary pressure for measures to protect animals played a vital role in the transformation of public opinion, paving the way for more comprehensive and effective legislation. Two Leicester women in particular, Elizabeth Heyrick and Susanna Watts, who are now remembered principally for their anti-slavery activism, saw cruelty to slaves and cruelty to animals as associated sins, of equal gravity.[82] This mental association did not imply that they viewed African slaves as being somehow less than fully human, but rather that both slaves and animals were victims of tyranny, denied the freedom to which every living creature was entitled, and treated with a cru-elty that was offensive to every Christian precept. If not quite appealing to the universe, like Margaret Cullen's Mrs Edgeville, Watts and Heyrick certainly interpreted the mistreatment of both animals and slaves in a deeply religious light: conscientious Christians should act to prevent both kinds of cruelty by any means that offered. In fact, the British people's passive acquiescence in abuse (especially when they themselves had indirectly caused it, for example by the demand for slave-produced sugar) was a sin equal to that of the actual perpetrators.

However, if women were to become 'moral agents' in the public sphere, they must first be recognised as beings who were capable of analytical thought and rational action, not simply of heightened feeling. In their short-lived journal *The Humming Bird* (1824–1825), which was intended to be 'devoted to the cause of suffering animals as well as to that of suffering men', Heyrick, Watts and an unnamed female co-editor call themselves 'Truth', 'Common Sense' and 'Philanthropy': in thus rebutting the charges of '*Sophistry, Ignorance*, and *Quixotism*' levelled against them, they seek to place their twin causes on a firm philosophical footing.[83] In one issue of the journal they combat the ideas of John Bowdler as expressed in his 'Thoughts on the proposed improvement of female education'. Bowdler, it will be remembered, feared that schooling in logical thought would destroy women's distinctive sensibility, while exposure to the sight of extreme suffering and evil would endanger their mental balance. On the contrary, Heyrick and Watts argue, only 'solid judgment … exalted piety' and serious study of the 'great moral science' of duty, will earn women respect, and make them useful members of society.[84] Therefore female readers are not to close their eyes to the appalling cruelties to slaves detailed in the pages of the *Humming Bird*. 'With the delicate sensibility of modern refine-ment, we have nothing to do; if the susceptible be disgusted by the revolting object of a *flayed negro woman devoured by maggots*', they must remember that the sweet dishes they eat are 'the *single* cause of these agonising tortures … Our address is to that genuine sensibility, which is inseparably united with fortitude … it is not *impulses* that we seek to excite, but PRINCIPLES'.[85] In the event, cruelty to animals took up much less space in the *Humming Bird* than did the abominable sufferings of enslaved people, but those principles were as pertinent in the one case as in the other. An account of the notorious baiting of a captive lion by six dogs at Warwick in 1825 prompts the thought, akin to Baillie's, that Britain is '*brutified* amid the tasteful ARTS', and in danger of divine judgement.

> Call on thy Senate! wake thy slumb'ring laws!
> Redeem thy name! and show thou still canst feel!
> Protect the race of brutes, support their cause! –
> A cause well worthy of the Patriot's zeal.[86]

When slaves in British ownership were, at least nominally, given their freedom in 1834, the names of Heyrick and Watts were illuminated in Leicester, as the 'undaunted, persevering and eloquent' advocates of abolition; but it was Watts, rather than her already-deceased friend, who was additionally praised as 'the Succourer of the destitute, and the Animal's friend'.[87] The phrase alludes to her little book for young people published in the early 1830s, *The Animals' Friend*. It is an anthology of anecdotes and verses, some by Watts herself, which represents a genre of growing popularity: by demonstrating the sagacity and moral virtues of animals, especially their devotion to man – often in hearsay tales that stretch credulity – Watts recommends them to the kind protection of her readers.[88] This is the work of an affectionate, indeed doting, pet owner, as her scrapbook, full of prints and poems about dogs and cats, reveals.[89] As a single woman, she might have been satirised for an alleged *over*-fondness for these domestic companions; but the description of her as 'Succourer of the destitute' recognised the host of philanthropic projects that Watts initiated or supported in her native city, in addition to her passionate campaigning against slavery.[90]

The taproot of all these benevolent deeds was that very traditional form of Christian belief described in our Introduction, which taught the obligations, as well as the privileges conferred by natural hierarchy. In *The Insects in Council* (1828), Watts described the wonders of the natural world as proof of God's love for all his creatures, even those often deemed noxious or worthless. Yet men abuse the divine trust of dominion over the lower creatures: '*Here* the relation is not acknowledged of *master* and *servant*; – it is *owner* and *slave*; absolute power and absolute subjection.'[91] Thus fallen man, afflicted by 'original depravity', was like 'a wall of adamant' that obstructed God's loving attentions to His 'brute creation'; and such cruelty to animals was, as Joanna Baillie also observed at just this time, a source of shame for a country that boasted of being 'highly enlightened, refined, and as far removed from barbarism as science, art, and literature can make it'.[92] Once again, a reform in attitudes, such as to produce *true* refinement in the habits of the nation, was seen to depend on the efforts of women. In her poem 'To the young of both sexes', Watts calls on 'the softer sex' to restrain, by example and exhortation, the propensity of boys 'To hunt, distress, torment, ensnare', and to teach them that such behaviour is no part of true manliness. The female spirit is 'quiet, meek', suited to a life of retired domesticity, yet of superior morality, and uniquely capable of inculcating 'the Law of LOVE'.[93]

It should be noted that this law of love is fully consistent with the principle of subordination in nature and human society. Although Susanna Watts was no narrow sectarian (she, like many others in Leicester, fell under the spell of the charismatic Baptist preacher Robert Hall), her thinking reflects her personal contacts with conservative evangelical Anglicans, such as Thomas Gisborne and Wilberforce, and indeed her scrapbook includes engravings of the latter and of Hannah More and Sarah Trimmer.[94] The thinking of Elizabeth Heyrick, in contrast, involved a fundamental critique of the structures of economic power and of the public mores of the nation. As fellow-victims of the existing system, *all* oppressed groups – starving industrial workers and casual labourers, vagrants and mendicants, wrongly or harshly imprisoned men, slaves on West Indian plantations and working animals – seemed equally to cry out for her passionate advocacy.

Elizabeth Heyrick (figure 4) was born in 1769, the daughter of bookish, high-minded Unitarian parents; her father, John Coltman, being a worsted manufacturer in Leicester.[95] Even as a child, it was recorded, she evinced an urge to self-denial and a sympathy with underdogs; but a disastrous marriage and the early death of her dissolute husband brought on a religious crisis in the late

4 Silhouette portrait of Elizabeth Heyrick, from an album of 'Some Memories of John Eliot Hodgkin'. This modest and reticent form of portraiture was popular among Quakers. However, the lack of any other authentic portrait of Heyrick may reflect contemporaries' slighting of her importance as an author and activist.

1790s that shaped the rest of her life. It generated a sense of mission – 'holier purposes' in her brother's phrase – and a psychological need to sacrifice all material comforts and indulgences to the service of God through labours for his suffering creatures.[96] She was drawn to the Quakers, although she was not formally accepted into their community until 1807.[97] A close friend of the family, Catherine Hutton, bluntly suggested to her that this conversion was motivated not just by the opportunities open to Quaker women to become preachers, but also by the sect's emphasis on the urgent promptings of conscience: 'enjoining a more *savage* renunciation' of all Heyrick's 'taste and elegant accomplishments'. She had 'the most earnest desire to do *right*; but instead of obeying a natural impulse, which would probably lead to it, she reasons about it, and puzzles herself, till right is lost in a labyrinth'.[98] But what seemed to Hutton to be self-torturing perversity can now be seen as a search for principles of action that could direct, or that went beyond, good works in the locality. Like George Eliot's Dorothea in *Middlemarch*, Heyrick had a 'theoretic' mind, which 'yearned by its nature after some lofty conception of the world ... she was enamoured of intensity and greatness ... likely to seek martyrdom', while lacking both direction and scope for such heroism.[99] Like Dorothea, too, she was 'beset with so much obstruction and disappointment' in all her enterprises. Indeed, in her later years, the experience of immovable apathy and corruption, and of the disdain evinced by leaders of opinion, engendered periods of depression when all seemed hopeless.[100] Nothing could reveal more clearly the frustrations suffered by intelligent women seeking to influence public policy in the early nineteenth century than Heyrick's lifelong efforts as a writer and activist, and the oblivion into which they have fallen.

In a poem by her husband John Heyrick (calling himself Palemon), her fondness for animals had been prettily celebrated:

> Eliza oft forbade in vain
> The cruel pleasures of the plain;
> Palemon his allegiance broke,
> And still pursued the feather'd folk.[101]

This image of her tenderness for wild birds – appropriately feminine, and just as appropriately unavailing in its conflict with the masculine will of the sportsman – wholly conforms to eighteenth-century tropes, such as we have found in Mundy's chivalrous celebration of Julia Curzon. We take a leap into a new era, when the widowed Elizabeth Heyrick became a bold, independent operator, and impulsively intervened to attempt rescues of abused animals, anticipating the exploits of the fictional Rosalind in *Mornton*: and it was probably this experience of direct action (recorded by two nineteenth-century writers on Heyrick and her family) that spurred her into polemical writing for publication. In 1809 she was staying at Bonsall in Derbyshire with her sister Mary Ann Coltman, another passionate animal lover who, we are told, became a vegetarian due to thoughts of the 'suffering inflicted on the dumb creation'.[102] Their stay coincided with the annual bull-baiting in the village, and they 'resolved to leave no effort unaccomplished to secure its suppression'. Heyrick set out at three in the morning to call on 'some of the more influential persons in the neighbourhood, with a view of inducing them to unite their efforts with hers in so good a cause', but all were predictably 'disinclined, thinking it utterly unavailing, to render any active assistance', or perhaps motivated by a political caution and expediency which she would have despised.

> Mrs. Heyrick, therefore, hastened back to Bonsall, and after every effort to procure the rescue of the unfortunate animal, by remonstrance and by appeals to the better feeling and humanity of the villagers, had proved fruitless, she procured an interview with the owner of the bull ... secretly purchased the proposed victim, and had the satisfaction of seeing him led a peaceful captive into a parlour of a sequestered cottage (whose inhabitants shared her feelings on the subject), where he was quietly and securely detained until the rage and disappointment of the populace had subsided.[103]

Later the sisters visited 'from cottage to cottage, distributing tracts on the subject', which had been written and published by Heyrick herself: *A Christmas-Box for the Advocates of Bull-baiting* and *Bull-baiting: A Village Dialogue, between Tom Brown and John Sims*.[104] The format of the latter, in particular, recalls pamphlets of the 1790s, which sought to convince labouring-class readers of the evils of political revolution through imagined conversations between men of their own kind. However, the message that Heyrick sought to convey differed greatly from that of such government-sponsored loyalists. 1809 was the year of the famous debate in parliament between supporters of Lord Erskine's bill for a law against cruelty to animals and opponents led by William Windham. The latter had, as discussed in our Introduction, enraged reformers by his resistance to any law that would ban the blood sports of the lower orders, while protecting the equally cruel sports of the upper classes: such a law would, he thought, be full of political dangers. Heyrick, too, believed that cruelties were endemic to every social class, but (addressing the villagers directly) 'I should think it a much easier task to convince *your* understandings, and to soften *your* hearts, than to produce the same impression on the *rich* and *great*'. All human beings are the rational children of

God, capable of apprehending the marvels of nature and of embracing 'a religion of universal love' for His creatures of every species; but habits of selfishness and unchecked power are obstacles to the conversion of the rich. 'It is too evident that the great majority of persons of rank and fashion', even 'persons of education, taste, and refinement', 'pay little attention to the sufferings of that part of the creation over which Providence has given them such unlimited power'. Not only do they overwork and mutilate horses, sponsor cockfights, pursue *'mean* and *cruel'* field sports, and approve the infliction of *'lingering* tortures' in the slaughter of livestock: they also fail in their duty of educating the poor, over whom their authority is as absolute as it is over animals. The leaders of society, even men of practical enterprise, decline to interfere in the moral sphere. Yet 'Here is a sublimer field of action, a wider theatre for the exercise of the noblest talents; in which angels are the invisible spectators, and God himself is the strength and reward of the faithful labourer'.[105]

Such arguments apparently left the bull-baiters of Bonsall unmoved; but Heyrick, undeterred, continued to seek this 'sublimer field of action' at some personal danger. When she visited London for the Quakers' annual gathering, she was appalled by the brutal treatment of cattle at Smithfield (see figure 5), which it was the principal object of Richard Martin's act of 1822 to prevent; and she corresponded with Martin and other 'friends of humanity' about their campaign of prosecution and moral persuasion in the years that followed.[106] In her *Cursory Remarks on the Evil Tendency of Unrestrained Cruelty; Particularly on that Practised in Smithfield Market*, 1823, she remembered how she had longed to intervene when she saw an animal stunned 'under the infuriated passion of its tormentor'. She looked, but did not speak, her feelings, 'aware that it would be the extreme of folly to attempt it. But the remonstrance conveyed in the pleading of my countenance caught the eye of a drover ... who instantly lifted his weapon against me with such a savage, vindictive menace, as if he would, had he dared, have felled me to the ground'.

Even Heyrick was baulked by this aggression; but those 'who have no power themselves, may endeavour to stimulate others to its exertion'.[107] Hence, in *Cursory Remarks*, she described the physical and mental sufferings of the cattle at the hands of such men in horrific detail, just as she would describe the agonies of slaves in the West Indies, for the shock effect on her apathetic fellow-citizens, and in the hope of spurring them to action. However, she was not concerned only for the pain of the animals. In arguments familiar from many eighteenth-century sources, she insisted that cruelty to animals has malign effects on the characters of the perpetrators, and hence on society at large; but this analysis goes much beyond the usual homilies on proper education of the young. Rather, Heyrick sought to present *all* cruelties as the effects of a mindset characterised by selfish greed and disregard of Christian teaching. Like the many heads of the Hydra, its effects may be seen equally in 'the lowest possible remuneration' of industrial workers *and* in the mistreatment of carriage horses; and, as Britain's imperial power and industrial wealth grew, cruelty actually seemed to be increasing, 'in opposition to the boasted humanity of the present age'.[108] In words that seem to echo those of Catharine Macaulay, Heyrick complained that any powerful man 'has the vanity, the preposterous arrogance, to fancy himself the only worthy object of Divine regard ... authorized to despise, oppress, and torment all the creatures which he regards as inferiors'.

> Nay, he ... imagines that men of his own country, of his own colour, of his own rank in society, are the distinguished favourites of Heaven. Thus, an American republican, a zealot for the rights of man ... disclaims his relationship to his sable brethren ... whom he may, with impunity, buy and sell, and lash as beasts of burden. And thus the proud and voluptuous in the higher ranks of society too often regard the humble and laborious classes as beings of a different cast [*sic*] ... whom, whenever they interfere with their pleasures [by poaching game] ... they may persecute, oppress and imprison ... Of this self-preference, self-adulation, *cruelty* is the legitimate offspring.[109]

Through her mustering of unpalatable facts about the treatment of animals, and her examination of the systemic causes of all cruelties in contemporary society, Heyrick decisively distinguished herself from the ladies whose impulsive sensibility had been celebrated by eighteenth-century poets – that clichéd image of femininity which she and Susanna Watts attacked in the *Humming Bird*. In all Heyrick's projects there was the same moral urgency; the same anxiety to persuade and rouse others through a combination of direct action and publicity; and the same consciousness that financial and class interests were the root cause of the exploitation of all subaltern beings. Often the shared victimhood of animals and powerless humans would be suggested by the use of metaphor or analogy. In her *Exposition of One Principal Cause of the National Distress, particularly in the Manufacturing Districts* (1817), 'the greedy spirit of avarice and monopoly, which has pervaded the whole nation', reducing industrial labourers to helpless pauperism, is likened to the habits of beekeepers who, 'when the industrious bees have well filled their ingenious store-houses, with equal justice and humanity ... light the match, dismiss the workmen, and take possession of the ambrosial spoils'. Political reform, she goes on, is disingenuously proposed as a cure for the evils that are actually caused by 'mammon'; in this way, she tells the industrial magnates, 'You threw out the tub to the whale, to divert his attention from yourselves, some of whom had been foremost in piercing his sides'.[110] Heyrick's *Enquiry into the Consequences of the Present Depreciated Value of Human Labour*, published two years later, was an even more comprehensive indictment of Malthusian economics. Wages were lowered stage by stage, to the point where actual starvation threatened to set in: thus 'the miserable workmen resemble animals placed for experiment under the exhauster of an air pump ... the system of exhaustion would have been fatal had it proceeded any further'.[111]

In the case of her anti-slavery writings, Heyrick, like many other writers of this time, made direct comparisons between the condition of enslaved humans and working animals. *No British Slavery; Or, An Invitation to the People to Put a Speedy End to It* (1825) is one of several pamphlets which sought to mobilise public opinion, and to end slavery through a boycott of West Indian sugar, a strategy which she also promoted through door-to-door canvassing and small neighbourhood meetings. Slaves, she explains, are treated like animals by their owners – '*worked down, or killed off, like over-driven coach horses!!*' Only the intervention of those who have themselves known hardship and oppression will free slaves from tyranny, and raise them 'from the condition of a brute to that of a christian'.[112] Heyrick's most famous work, *Immediate, not Gradual Abolition* (1824), published anonymously, was an impassioned argument for immediate freeing of the slaves by the British parliament, in defiance of the temporising policies of the leaders of the abolitionist movement, and the obstructions of those with a commercial stake in slavery. But although this pamphlet was apparently quoted in the Commons and certainly influenced the policies of women's anti-slavery associations across the country, contributing indirectly to the passing of the emancipation act which Heyrick did not live to see, her powerful critique of British society made little impact.[113] She remained an obscure figure, written off as, in the abolitionist Joseph Sturge's words, an 'amiable enthusiast and visionary', or else ignored altogether. Even her writings on cruelty to animals were seemingly overlooked.[114]

The anonymous author of *A Brief Sketch of the Life and Labours of Mrs Elizabeth Heyrick* (1862) remarked that, in the earlier nineteenth century, there were 'no systematic plans for relieving distress', and hence little scope for specialisation in particular fields of philanthropy. Consequently, Heyrick's 'benevolence was marked by the universality of its aims ... she was compelled by the fearful amount of unrelieved suffering and oppression, that forced itself upon her attention', whether inflicted 'upon man or brute', 'to engage in a variety of attempts to alleviate or suppress it'.[115] Such 'universality' anyway reflects the fact that, for Heyrick, all forms of cruelty and injustice have a common origin, and therefore could not be viewed in isolation from one another. The connection lay not in men's 'original depravity', as cited by Susanna Watts, but rather in the avarice and selfishness of capitalist society, and in the arrogant exercise of power to which it gave rise. Thus she thought of Christianity, not as an institutionalised religion that governed public and private conduct in Britain, but as a set of beliefs with radical implications, perpetually at war with the forces of darkness. In her last pamphlet, *Letters of a Recluse* of 1830, she even told her brothers, who were worsted and hosiery manufacturers in Leicester, that they should measure their conduct by the uncomfortable 'standard of gospel truth', and not succumb to the 'spirit of accommodation' in religious observance that was prevalent among their business colleagues.[116] As Heyrick had expressed it in her *Apology for Ladies' Anti-Slavery Associations* of 1828, 'Christianity is not a voluminous code of arbitrary commands and prohibitions; – it is a system of principles, few in number, but of universal application': 'the love of our fellow-creatures' is essential to it, and failure to attack the evils that harm them alienates us from a loving God, making us 'moral suicides'.[117]

In this analysis of religious duty, no half-measures could be countenanced: the absolute values of right and wrong, whether in the treatment of humans or of animals, admitted no accommodations with the status quo or with vested interests, and placed virtuous aspiration before realism.[118] Heyrick's *Appeal to the Hearts and Consciences of British Women* (1828) represented this attitude as a female hallmark, arising not just from women's peculiar sensitivities to the plight of the suffering, but from their social situation: 'happily excluded from the great theatre of public business, from the turmoils of ambition, the strife of debate, and the cares of legislation', they apprehended the moral failings and subterfuges of that masculine world more clearly than their male counterparts, and could co-operate with one another in seeking to end the evils it generated. 'No cruel institutions or ferocious practices could long withstand' women's 'avowed and persevering censure'.[119] From their pedestal of idealism, women could refuse to condone compromise with those they perceived as disobeying the teachings of Christ; they could even seek to impress their views on the wider public through canvassing, pamphleteering and petitioning, an unwomanly 'presumption' excused by the greatness and altruism of the abolitionist cause. The experience of all-female association and of proselytising initiatives arising from the anti-slavery campaign had important implications for women's activism in many fields in the Victorian era. However, a fear that female supporters of animal protection, often the same people as the abolitionists, might display a similar fundamentalist zeal in the pursuit of their objects could well alarm the male leaders of bodies such as the RSPCA. The history of that institution and its attitude to female engagement in the protectionist cause is the subject of the next chapter.

Notes

1   Among many discussions of constructs of gender characteristics: Carol P. MacCormack and Marilyn Strathern (eds), *Nature, Culture and Gender* (Cambridge: Cambridge University Press, 1980). Penelope Brown and Ludmilla Jordanova, 'Oppressive dichotomies: the nature/culture debate', in the Cambridge Women's Study Group's *Women in Society: Interdisciplinary Essays* (London: Virago Press, 1981). Ludmilla Jordanova, *Sexual Visions: Images of Gender in Science and Medicine* (New York and London: Harvester Wheatsheaf, 1989), pp. 19f. Londa Schiebinger, *Nature's Body: Sexual Politics and the Making of Modern Science* (London: HarperCollins, 1994), pp. 9–10, 37f.

2   Priscilla Wakefield, *Instinct Displayed, in a Collection of Well-Authenticated Facts, Exemplifying the Extraordinary Sagacity of Various Species of the Animal Creation* (London: Darton, Harvey and Darton, 1811), pp. 288–9. William Howitt, *The Rural Life of England* (London: Longman, Orme, Brown, Green and Longmans, 2nd edn, 1840), pp. 45–6.

3   Aristotle, *Politics*, Book I, v, xiii; *Generation of Animals*, Book IV.vi, 775a. Genevieve Lloyd, *The Man of Reason: 'Male' and 'Female' in Western Philosophy* (London: Routledge, 2nd edn, 1993). Barbara T. Gates, *Kindred Nature: Victorian and Edwardian Women Embrace the Living World* (Chicago and London: University of Chicago Press, 1998), pp. 3f., 13f.

4   John Milton, *Paradise Lost* (2nd edn, 1674): Book VIII, lines 540–46; Book IX, lines 494f.

5   *The Satires of Decimus Junius Juvenalis*, trans. William Gifford (London: G. and W. Nichol, 2nd edn, 1806), Satire VI, lines 188, 192–3. Swift, 'The lady's dressing room', 1730, published 1732, in Robert A. Greenberg and William Bowman Piper (eds), *The Writings of Jonathan Swift* (New York and London: W.W. Norton, 1973), p. 536. Felicity A. Nussbaum, *The Brink of All We Hate: English Satires on Women 1660–1750* (Lexington: University Press of Kentucky, 1984), pp. 77–99.

6   Theresa Braunschneider, 'The lady and the lapdog: mixed ethnicity in Constantinople, fashionable pets in Britain', in Frank Palmeri (ed.), *Humans and Other Animals in Eighteenth-Century British Culture* (Aldershot: Ashgate, 2006). Markman Ellis, 'Suffering things: lapdogs, slaves, and counter-sensibility', in Mark Blackwell (ed.), *The Secret Life of Things: Animals, Objects, and It-Narratives in Eighteenth-Century England* (Lewisburg: Bucknell University Press, 2007). Laura Brown, *Homeless Dogs and Melancholy Apes: Humans and Other Animals in the Modern Literary Imagination* (Ithaca: Cornell University Press, 2010), pp. 65–77. In 1892, Linley Sambourne pictured a feathered lady as 'A bird of prey' in a *Punch* cartoon (see our chapter 6, figure 28).

7   Henry Fielding, *The History of the Adventures of Joseph Andrews* (1742), Book III, chapters 6 and 7.

8   Anon., *An Essay on Hunting. By a Country Squire* (London: J. Roberts, 1733), pp. 18, 28–39, 53, 60. John Smallman Gardiner, *The Art and the Pleasures of Hare Hunting* (London: R. Griffiths, 1750): especially pp. 3–5, 19–24. Maureen Duffy, 'Beasts for

pleasure', in Stanley and Roslind Godlovitch and John Harris (eds), *Animals, Men and Morals: An Enquiry into the Maltreatment of Non-Humans* (London: Gollancz, 1971), pp. 116–18. Matt Cartmill, *A View to a Death in the Morning: Hunting and Nature through History* (Cambridge, MA: Harvard University Press, 1993), pp. 238–40. Diana Donald, *Picturing Animals in Britain, 1750–1850* (New Haven and London: Yale University Press, 2007), pp. 250–1.

9   Alfred E. Pease, *Hunting Reminiscences* (London: W. Thacker, 1898), pp. 160–1.

10   Donald F. Bond (ed.), *The Spectator* (Oxford: Clarendon Press, 1965), 1:57 (5 May 1711), 241–4. Anon. [Hannah More], *Coelebs in Search of a Wife. Comprehending Observations on Domestic Habits and Manners, Religion and Morals*, 2 vols (London: T. Cadell and W. Davies, 11th edn, 1809), vol. 2, pp. 84–6, 96–9, 169, 175, 182, 184–6, 190–5.

11   William Alexander, *The History of Women, From the Earliest Antiquity to the Present Time*, 2 vols (London: C. Dilly and Stockton: R. Christopher, 3rd edn, 1782), vol. 1, p. 323.

12   Revd Humphry Primatt, *A Dissertation on the Duty of Mercy and Sin of Cruelty to Brute Animals* (London: T. Cadell, J. Dodsley, J. Johnson, 1776), pp. 161–2.

13   Francis Noel Clarke Mundy, *Needwood Forest, and The Fall of Needwood, with Other Poems* (Derby: Thomas Richardson, 1830), pp. 129–31.

14   William Wordsworth, 'To a butterfly', 1802, published in *Poems, in Two Volumes* (1807), in Alun R. Jones (ed.), *Wordsworth's Poems of 1807* (Basingstoke and London: Macmillan, 1987), p. 88. Compare his *The Prelude* (1805 text), Book XI, lines 214–21.

15   Sarah Trimmer, *An Easy Introduction to the Knowledge of Nature, and Reading the Holy Scriptures. Adapted to the Capacities of Children* (London: T. Longman, G. Robinson, J. Johnson, 5th edn, 1787), pp. 49, 50, 52.

16   There is a large literature on notions of sensibility in the eighteenth century, for example, Janet Todd, *Sensibility: An Introduction* (London and New York: Methuen, 1986); G.J. Barker-Benfield, *The Culture of Sensibility: Sex and Society in Eighteenth-Century Britain* (Chicago and London: University of Chicago Press, 1992). Ildiko Csengei, *Sympathy, Sensibility and the Literature of Feeling in the Eighteenth Century* (Basingstoke: Palgrave Macmillan, 2012). Donald, *Picturing Animals*, pp. 18–26.

17   'Thoughts on the proposed improvement of female education', 1808, in *Select Pieces in Verse and Prose. By the Late John Bowdler*, 2 vols (London: G. Davidson, 1816), vol. 1, pp. 96–7, 103, 107–8.

18   Hannah More, 'Sensibility: a poetical epistle to the Hon. Mrs. Boscawen', in *Sacred Dramas: Chiefly Intended for Young Persons: The Subjects Taken from the Bible* (London: T. Cadell, 2nd edn, 1782), p. 284.

19   Hannah More, *Strictures on the Modern System of Female Education*, 2 vols (London: T. Cadell jnr. and W. Davies, 1799), vol. 2, p. 8.

20   More, *Coelebs*, vol. 1, pp. 153–4.

21   Anon. [Jonas Hanway], *A Journal Of Eight Days Journey from Portsmouth to Kingston upon Thames … Addressed to two Ladies of the Partie* (London: H. Woodfall, 1756), p. 70.

22   Typical examples are F.G. Byron's *Old Maids at a Cat's Funeral*, 1789; C. Goodnight's *Old Tabbies attending a favorite Cat's Funeral*, 1794; and Isaac and George Cruikshank's *Tabies & Tom Cat, or Old Maids examining an Unique Male Tortiose* [*sic*] *Shell subject*, 1808. M. Dorothy George, *Catalogue of Political and Personal Satires in the British Museum*, 11 vols (London: British Museum, 1978), nos. 8558 and 11126. Cindy McCreery, 'Lustful widows and old maids in late eighteenth-century English caricatures', in Katharine Kittredge (ed.), *Lewd & Notorious: Female Transgression in the Eighteenth Century* (Ann

Arbor: University of Michigan Press, 2003), pp. 112–32. Cindy McCreery, *The Satirical Gaze: Prints of Women in Late Eighteenth-Century England* (Oxford: Clarendon Press, 2004), pp. 216–18.

23 *Engravings from Drawings by Landseer* (London: E. Gambart, 1848): no. 13, dated 1823. William Lauder Lindsay, *Mind in the Lower Animals in Health and Disease*, 2 vols (London: C. Kegan Paul, 1879), vol. 1, pp. 268, 482; vol. 2, pp. 322–3, 328.

24 Edward Payson Evans, *Evolutionary Ethics and Animal Psychology* (New York: D. Appleton, 1898), p. 147. Brian Luke, 'Taming ourselves or going feral? Toward a nonpatriarchal metaethic of animal liberation', in Carol J. Adams and Josephine Donovan (eds), *Animal and Women: Feminist Theoretical Explorations* (Durham, NC and London: Duke University Press, 1995), p. 293.

25 Laurence Sterne, *Tristram Shandy* (1759–1767), vol. 7, chapter 32; *A Sentimental Journey* (1768): vol. 2, 'The Passport, The Hotel de Paris'.

26 Anon. [Sarah Scott], *A Description of Millenium Hall ... Together with ... such Historical Anecdotes and Reflections As May excite in the Reader proper Sentiments of Humanity, and lead the Mind to the Love of Virtue* (London: J. Newbery, 1762), pp. 21–4, 76, 226. Lisa Lynne Moore, *Dangerous Intimacies: Toward a Sapphic History of the British Novel* (Durham, NC and London: Duke University Press, 1997), pp. 18, 22–48.

27 'Epitaph on a goldfinch', in Lucy Aikin (ed.), *A Legacy for Young Ladies, Consisting of Miscellaneous Pieces, in Prose and Verse, by the late Mrs Barbauld* (London: Longman, Hurst, Rees, Orme, Brown, & Green, 1826), pp. 183–4.

28 Barbauld's 'The mouse's petition', first published in her *Poems* (London: Joseph Johnson, 1773). William McCarthy and Elizabeth Kraft (eds), *The Poems of Anna Letitia Barbauld* (Athens, GA and London: University of Georgia Press, 1994), pp. 36–7, and 'The caterpillar', pp. 172–3.

29 Samuel Taylor Coleridge, 'Analysis of an "Essay on the public merits of Mr Pitt, by Thomas Beddoes, MD"', *The Watchman*, 9 (5 May 1796), 268.

30 Anthony Ashley Cooper, Lord Shaftesbury, 'An inquiry concerning virtue, or merit', 1699, in *Characteristicks*, vol. 2 (1714), pp. 163–5. John Locke, 'Some thoughts concerning education', 1693, in James L. Axtell (ed.), *The Educational Writings of John Locke* (Cambridge: Cambridge University Press, 1968), pp. 225–6.

31 Thomas Young, *An Essay on Humanity to Animals* (London: T. Cadell et al., and Cambridge: J. Deighton, 1798), pp. 41–2.

32 Revd Henry Crowe, *Zoophilos; Or, Considerations on the Moral Treatment of Inferior Animals* (published by the author, 2nd edn, 1820), pp. 4, 104–6.

33 Harriet Ritvo, *The Animal Estate: The English and Other Creatures in the Victorian Age* (Cambridge, MA: Harvard University Press, 1987), p. 131. Mary V. Jackson, *Engines of Instruction, Mischief, and Magic: Children's Literature in England from its Beginnings to 1839* (Aldershot: Scolar Press, 1989), pp. 99f., 139, 141–4, 159–60, 166–8, 180–1. Mary Hilton, *Women and the Shaping of the Nation's Young: Education and Public Doctrine in Britain 1750–1850* (Aldershot: Ashgate, 2007), pp. 90–112.

34 Anon., *The History of Little Goody Two-Shoes; Otherwise called, Mrs Margery Two-shoes* (London: J. Newbery, 3rd edn, 1766).

35 Maria Edgeworth, *The Parent's Assistant* (London: J. Johnson, 2nd edn, 1796). Anna Laetitia Barbauld's *Lessons for Children from Two to Three Years Old*, 4 vols (London: J. Johnson, 1778–1779) were geared to children's stages of development in reading.

36 Caroline ('Cara') Bray, writing as Mrs Charles Bray, *Our Duty to Animals* (1871); *Richard Barton: Or, The Wounded Bird* (c.1873); *Paul Bradley: A Village Tale,*

Inculcating Kindness to Animals (c.1876). Anna Maria Hall, writing as Mrs S.C. Hall, *Animal Sagacity* (c.1867–1868). All these works were published in London by S.W. Partridge. See also Hall's numerous articles in *The Juvenile Forget-Me-Not* and the RSPCA's journal *Animal World*.

37 Barker-Benfield, *Culture of Sensibility*, p. 236.

38 Sarah Trimmer, *The Two Farmers, an Exemplary Tale: Designed to Recommend the Practice of Benevolence towards Mankind, and All Other Living Creatures; and the Religious Observance of the Sabbath Day* (London: T. Longman, G.G.J. and J. Robinson, and J. Johnson, 2nd edn, 1787). Sarah Trimmer, *The Oeconomy of Charity; Or, An Address to Ladies concerning Sunday-Schools*, 2 vols (London: T. Longman, G.G.J. and J. Robinson, and J. Johnson, 1787), vol. 1, p. 174.

39 Anon. [Joanna Baillie], *A Lesson Intended for the Use of the Hampstead School. To be read to the Children occasionally, by the Ladies who are kind enough to examine them*, pamphlet dated 1826; copy in the Houghton Library, Harvard University. Judith Bailey Slagle, *Joanna Baillie: A Literary Life* (Madison: Fairleigh Dickinson University Press, 2002), pp. 214–15. Judith Bailey Slagle, 'John Hunter and Joanna Baillie: veterinary science, animal rights, and the pathology of cruelty', *European Romantic Review*, 22:5 (October 2011), 625–39. David Perkins, *Romanticism and Animal Rights* (Cambridge: Cambridge University Press, 2003), p. 132.

40 Anna Letitia Barbauld, 'What is education?', *The Monthly Magazine*, 5 (March 1798), 167–71, in William McCarthy and Elizabeth Kraft (eds), *Anna Letitia Barbauld: Selected Poetry and Prose* (Peterborough, Ontario: Broadview Press, 2002), pp. 321–32 (322).

41 Anna Letitia Barbauld, *Hymns in Prose for Children* (London: J. Johnson, 1781), with numerous later editions. Joanna Wharton, 'Inscribing on the mind: Anna Letitia Barbauld's "Sensible objects"', *Journal for Eighteenth-Century Studies*, 35:4 (December 2012), 535–50.

42 Adrienne E. Gavin, *Dark Horse: A Life of Anna Sewell* (Stroud: Sutton Publishing, 2004), p. 21.

43 Maria Edgeworth and Richard Lovell Edgeworth, *Practical Education*, 2 vols (London: J. Johnson, 1798), vol. 1, pp. 13, 28–30, 282–6.

44 Anon., *The Sister's Gift; Or, The Bad Boy Reformed*, originally a Newbery publication of 1786, pirated by Thomas Saint of Newcastle upon Tyne, c.1820. Nigel Tattersfield, *Thomas Bewick: The Complete Illustrative Work*, 3 vols (London: The British Library and New Castle DE: Oak Knoll Press, 2011), vol. 2, p. 641.

45 Arnaud Berquin, trans. Richard Johnson, *The Looking-Glass for the Mind; Or, Intellectual Mirror; being an Elegant Collection of the Most Delightful Little Stories and Interesting Tales, Chiefly Translated from … 'L'Ami des Enfans'*, 1787, 1792 (London: E. Newbery, 5th edn, 1796), pp. 21–7. Nigel Tattersfield, *John Bewick, Engraver on Wood, 1760–1795* (London: The British Library and New Castle: Oak Knoll Press, 2001), pp. 46, 62, 122–4, 228.

46 Baillie, *Lesson*, p. 10.

47 Anon., *The Boy's Own Book; A Complete Encyclopedia of All the Diversions, Athletic, Scientific, and Recreative, of Boyhood and Youth* (London: Vizetelly, Branston, 1828), pp. 147–61. Ernest Sackville Turner, *All Heaven in a Rage* (London: Michael Joseph, 1964), pp. 147–8.

48 Jane and Ann Taylor, *Original Poems for Infant Minds. By Several Young Persons*, 2 vols (London: Darton and Harvey, 1804–1805).

49 *The Poetical Works of Christopher Smart*, ed. Karina Williamson, vol. 1, *Jubilate agno* (Oxford: Clarendon Press, 1980), p. 88. The poem was written c.1759–1763.

50 Samuel F. Pickering jnr., *John Locke and Children's Books in Eighteenth-Century England* (Knoxville: University of Tennessee Press, 1981), p. 12.

51 Sarah Trimmer, *Fabulous Histories: Designed for the Instruction of Children, Respecting their Treatment of Animals* (London: J. Johnson, F. & C. Rivington, G. & J. Robinson, Longman & Rees, J. Hatchard, B. Tabart, 7th edn, 1802). Tess Cosslett, *Talking Animals in British Children's Fiction, 1786–1914* (Aldershot: Ashgate, 2006), pp. 37–49.

52 Trimmer, *Fabulous Histories*, pp. vii–viii.

53 Ibid., pp. viii, 16.

54 Ibid., pp. v–vi, 12, 14, 20, 57, 59, 88–9, 119–20, 164.

55 Ibid., pp. 48–9, 52–6, 168.

56 Ibid., p. 89.

57 Mary Wollstonecraft, *Elements of Morality, for the Use of Children; With an Introductory Address to Parents. Translated from the German of the Rev. C.G. Salzmann*, 1790; 3rd edn 1792 of 3 vols, in Janet Todd and Marilyn Butler (eds), *The Works of Mary Wollstonecraft*, 7 vols, vol. 2 (London: William Pickering, 1989).

58 Mary Wollstonecraft, *Original Stories from Real Life; With Conversations, Calculated to Regulate the Affections, and Form the Mind to Truth and Goodness* (London: J. Johnson, 1788; facsimile reprint of 1791 edition illustrated by William Blake, Oxford and New York: Woodstock Books, 1990), pp. 7–19.

59 *A Vindication of the Rights of Men, in a Letter to the Rt. Hon. Edmund Burke*, in Todd and Butler (eds), *Works of Wollstonecraft*, vol. 5, pp. 9, 14, 25, 31, 33. Susan Khin Zaw, '"Appealing to the head and heart": Wollstonecraft and Burke on taste, morals and human nature', in Gill Perry and Michael Rossington (eds), *Femininity and Masculinity in Eighteenth-Century Art and Culture* (Manchester and New York: Manchester University Press, 1994).

60 Edmund Burke, *A Philosophical Enquiry into the Origin of our Ideas of the Sublime and Beautiful* (1757), ed. J.T. Boulton (London: Routledge and Kegan Paul, 1958), pp. 110–16. Wollstonecraft, *Vindication of the Rights of Men*, in Todd and Butler (eds), *Works of Wollstonecraft*, pp. 45–6.

61 Mary Wollstonecraft, *A Vindication of the Rights of Woman: With Strictures on Political and Moral Subjects* (London: J. Johnson, 1792), ed. Miriam Brody (London: Penguin Books, 1992), pp. 118–20, 132, 154–5.

62 For example, John Oswald, 'Member of the Club des Jacobines', *The Cry of Nature; Or, An Appeal to Mercy and to Justice, On Behalf of the Persecuted Animals* (London: J. Johnson, 1791). Anon. [George Nicholson], *Remarks on Cruelty to Animals* (Manchester: Nicholson, 1795).

63 Wollstonecraft, *Vindication of the Rights of Woman*, pp. 291–2.

64 In ibid., pp. 206–7, Wollstonecraft praised Macaulay as 'The woman of the greatest abilities, undoubtedly, that this country has ever produced'. She reviewed Macaulay's *Letters on Education* in the *Analytical Review*, 8 (November 1790): Todd and Butler (eds), *Works*, vol. 7, pp. 309–22. Barbara Taylor, *Mary Wollstonecraft and the Feminist Imagination* (Cambridge: Cambridge University Press, 2003), pp. 48–9.

65 Catharine Macaulay, *Letters on Education, with Observations on Religious and Metaphysical Subjects* (London: C. Dilly, 1790), reprinted as vol. 3 of Janet Todd (ed.), *Female Education in the Age of Enlightenment* (London: William Pickering, 1996). Bridget Hill, *The Republican Virago: The Life and Times of Catharine Macaulay*,

Historian (Oxford: Clarendon, 1992), pp. 142–3, 146–7, 149f., 158–63. Hilton, *Women and the Shaping of the Nation's Young*, pp. 66–73.

66 Macaulay, *Letters*, pp. 1–6, 341.

67 Ibid., p. 121.

68 Ibid., pp. 9, 112–13, 189–94.

69 Macaulay rather surprisingly praised Berquin's sentimental *L'ami des enfans* (cf. note 45) and the poetry of Helen Maria Williams, such as 'Edwin and Eltruda' and 'To sensibility': *Letters*, pp. 54–5, 123.

70 Ibid., pp. 193–4.

71 Ibid., pp. 11–12, 20, 119, 276–7.

72 *Memoirs of the Life of the Late Mrs. Catharine Cappe. Written by Herself* (London: Longman, Hurst, Rees, Orme and Brown, 1822), pp. 296–7, 371. John Thomson, William Thomson and David Craigie, *An Account of the Life, Lectures and Writings of William Cullen*, 2 vols (Edinburgh and London: Blackwood, 1859), vol. 2, p. 684. Celia Morris, *Fanny Wright, Rebel in America* (Urbana and Chicago: University of Illinois Press, 1992), p. 14. Margaret Cullen apparently died unmarried, c.1840.

73 *Monthly Magazine*, 44:304 (1 November 1817), 290–1; 45:309 (1 March 1818), 118–20; 47:322 (1 February 1819), 17.

74 Margaret Cullen, *Mornton. A Novel in Three Volumes* (London: J. Mawman and York: Wilson & Sons, 1814), vol. 1, pp. 119–22, 224–5, 260; vol. 2, pp. 156, 327–32; vol. 3, pp. 5–7, 243.

75 Cullen's characters discuss Erskine's bill and Windham's opposition to it at length: *Mornton*, vol. 2, pp. 40–4; vol. 3, pp. 17–31, 247–9.

76 Ibid., vol. 3, p. 20.

77 Ibid., vol. 1, pp. 224–8; vol. 2, pp. 42–3; vol. 3, pp. 221–8.

78 Ibid., vol. 3, pp. 246–7.

79 Ibid., vol. 3, pp. 14–15.

80 Joanna Baillie's 'The kitten', first published in the *Edinburgh Annual Register for 1808*, was included in Sir Walter Scott's *English Minstrelsy. Being a Selection of Fugitive Poetry from the Best English Authors*, 2 vols (Edinburgh: John Ballantyne et al., and London: John Murray, 1810), vol. 2. Jennifer Breen (ed.), *The Selected Poems of Joanna Baillie 1762–1851* (Manchester and New York: Manchester University Press, 1999), pp. 77–8. Margaret Sprague Carhart, *The Life and Work of Joanna Baillie* (New Haven: Yale University Press; London: Humphrey Milford; and Oxford: Oxford University Press, 1923), p. 27. Slagle, *Baillie: A Literary Life*, p. 176.

81 Baillie, 'Verses written in February, 1827', in her *Fugitive Verses* (London: Edward Moxon, 1840). Breen (ed.), *Selected Poems*, pp. 121–2.

82 Kenneth Corfield, 'Elizabeth Heyrick, radical Quaker', in Gail Malmgreen (ed.), *Religion in the Lives of English Women, 1760–1930* (London and Sydney: Croom Helm, 1986). Moira Ferguson, *Animal Advocacy and Englishwomen, 1780–1900: Patriots, Nation, and Empire* (Ann Arbor: University of Michigan Press, 1998), pp. 27f., 53f. Shirley Aucott, *Susanna Watts, 1768–1842* (self-published, 2004). Aucott, *Elizabeth Heyrick 1769–1831* (self-published, 2007). Sarah Richardson, *The Political Worlds of Women: Gender and Politics in Nineteenth Century Britain* (New York and London: Routledge, 2013), pp. 10–11, 76–9.

83 *The Humming Bird; Or, Morsels of Information, on the Subject of Slavery: With Various Miscellaneous Articles* (Leicester: A. Cockshaw, 1824–5); 1:1 (December 1824), 7–8, 34.

84 'Friendly hints to the ladies, occasioned by reading Mr. Bowdler's thoughts on the

proposed improvement of female education', *Humming Bird*, 1:3 (February 1825), 86–93. Bowdler, 'Thoughts on the proposed improvement of female education', in *Select Pieces*, as cited in note 17.

85 Note on a report by 'A friend to truth' on 'Physical and penal sufferings of the Negro slaves', *Humming Bird*, 1:2 (January 1825), 56.

86 'Lines, on the fight between the lion Nero and six dogs, at Warwick, July 26, 1825', in *Humming Bird*, 1:10 (September 1825), 300–3.

87 Susanna Watts's scrapbook in the Leicestershire Record Office, DE 8170/1: manuscript biographical note by Clara Parkes, dated 1865, pp. 1–3.

88 Susanna Watts, *The Animals' Friend; A Collection of Observations and Facts tending to Restrain Cruelty, and to Inculcate Kindness Towards Animals* (London: Simpkin and Marshall, and C. Tilt, dateable on internal evidence to c.1831–1834). A rare surviving copy is in the Leicestershire Record Office, ref. LA.

89 The scrapbook includes a faint pencil self-portrait of Watts herself, inscribed 'I & Dash my Dog. SW' (p. 429).

90 *Hymns and Poems of the late Mrs. Susanna Watts, with a Few Recollections of Her Life* (Leicester: J. Waddington, 1842), pp. 53–68. Clara Parkes's note in the scrapbook. Aucott, *Susanna Watts*, pp. 23f.

91 Susanna Watts, *The Insects in Council, Addressed to Entomologists, with Other Poems* (London: J. Hatchard and Son; Hurst, Chance; Simpkin and Marshall, and Leicester: A. Cockshaw, 1828), pp. iii–xii.

92 Watts, *Animals' Friend*, pp. 1–3, 17.

93 Ibid., pp. 71–5.

94 Watts's scrapbook, pp. 183, 434, 460–3. She often stayed with Revd Gisborne, a member of the Clapham sect, at Yoxall Lodge: Aucott, *Susanna Watts*, pp. 12, 31, 37.

95 The main primary source on Elizabeth Heyrick is her brother Samuel Coltman's unfinished family memoir, 'Time's stepping stones – or some memorials of four generations of a family – by an octogenarian member of the same', pp. 104f. It was dictated c.1852–1854 to his wife Anne Byerley, whose manuscript has been copied as a typescript (both now in the Leicestershire Record Office, RO Misc. 1153). See also *A Brief Sketch of the Life and Labours of Mrs Elizabeth Heyrick* (Leicester, 1862), an anonymous pamphlet circulated by the Birmingham Ladies' Anti-slavery Society, and Catherine Hutton Beale, *Catherine Hutton and Her Friends* (Birmingham: Cornish Brothers, 1895), especially pp. 186–217.

96 Coltman, 'Time's stepping stones', pp. 148–50, 170–82.

97 Leicestershire Record Office, Leicester, 12D39/12B, Quaker minute book, minutes of women's meetings between 23 March and 11 June 1807, recording Heyrick's formal acceptance as a Quaker (3r, 5r, 5v, 6r).

98 Leicestershire Record Office, 15D57/387, anon. manuscript [written by Catherine Hutton], 'Hasty sketch of the Coltman family 1802'; addressed to Elizabeth Heyrick, who is nevertheless referred to in the third person.

99 George Eliot, *Middlemarch* (1871–2), opening chapter.

100 Beale, *Catherine Hutton and Her Friends*, p. 215. In a revealing letter of 28 December 1826 to Lucy Townsend (Bodleian Library MSS Brit. Emp. s.5: 102), Heyrick wrote of 'plunging deeper and deeper' into 'despairing torpor'. Among other discouragements, the influential preacher Revd Robert Hall, then in Bristol, had failed even to acknowledge receipt of her recently published pamphlet, *Letters on the Necessity of a Prompt Extinction of British Colonial Slavery*.

101 John Heyrick Jnr., 'On the author's gun missing fire at a black-bird', in *First Flights ... containing Pieces in Verse on Various Occasions*, posthumous publication (London: C. Dilly, 1797), pp. 7–9.

102 Beale, *Catherine Hutton and Her Friends*, pp. 156, 232–4.

103 Ibid., pp. 199–200. Anon., *A Brief Sketch*, pp. 12–15.

104 Anon. [Elizabeth Heyrick], *A Christmas-Box for the Advocates of Bull-baiting* (London: Darton and Harvey, 1809). Elizabeth Heyrick, *Bull-baiting: A Village Dialogue, between Tom Brown and John Sims* (London: Darton and Harvey, 1809).

105 Heyrick, *A Christmas-Box*, pp. 5–12.

106 Beale, *Catherine Hutton and Her Friends*, pp. 205–6. Diana Donald, ' "Beastly sights": the treatment of animals as a moral theme in representations of London, c.1820–1850', in Dana Arnold (ed.), *The Metropolis and Its Image* (Oxford: Blackwell, 1999).

107 Anon. [Elizabeth Heyrick], *Cursory Remarks on the Evil Tendency of Unrestrained Cruelty; Particularly on that Practised in Smithfield Market* (London: Harvey and Darton, 1823), pp. 8, 18.

108 Ibid., p. 22.

109 Ibid., pp. 12–13. In the letter to Lucy Townsend cited in note 100, Heyrick suggested that the condition of the labouring poor in Britain was little better than that of slaves in the West Indies.

110 Anon. [Elizabeth Heyrick], *Exposition of One Principal Cause of the National Distress, particularly in the Manufacturing Districts: With Some Suggestions for Its Removal* (London: the author, and sold by Darton, Harvey, and Darton, 1817), pp. 2–3, 11–12.

111 Anon. [Elizabeth Heyrick], *Enquiry into the Consequences of the Present Depreciated Value of Human Labour ... in Letters to Thomas Fowell Buxton Esq.* (London: Longman, Hurst, Rees, Orme and Brown, 1819) pp. 37–8.

112 Anon. [Elizabeth Heyrick], *No British Slavery; Or, An Invitation to the People to Put a Speedy End to It* (Bradford: printed by W.H. Blackburn, 1825), pp. 3–4, 5, 7–8. On her anti-slavery work: Corfield, 'Elizabeth Heyrick, radical Quaker'. Clare Midgley, *Women Against Slavery: The British Campaigns, 1780–1870* (London and New York: Routledge, 1992), pp. 49, 55, 58–9, 61, 75–6. Moira Ferguson, *Subject to Others: British Women Writers and Colonial Slavery, 1670–1834* (New York and London: Routledge, 1992), pp. 249f. Adam Hochschild, *Bury the Chains: Prophets and Rebels in the Fight to Free an Empire's Slaves* (Boston and New York: Houghton Mifflin, 2005), pp. 324–8. A letter from Heyrick to Lucy Townsend of 18 March 1829 (Bodleian Library MSS Brit. Emp. s.5: 94) reveals that she convened home meetings of women from poorer districts of Leicester, urging them to boycott imported sugar.

113 Anon. [Elizabeth Heyrick], *Immediate, not Gradual Abolition; Or, An Inquiry into the Shortest, Safest, and Most Effectual Means of Getting Rid of West Indian Slavery* (London: Hatchard et al., 1824). Anon., *A Brief Sketch*, pp. 17–20.

114 Sturge quoted in Corfield, 'Elizabeth Heyrick, radical Quaker', p. 47. On Heyrick's anti-slavery work and its 'impracticality', see also M.J.D. Roberts, *Making English Morals: Voluntary Association and Moral Reform in England, 1787–1886* (Cambridge and New York: Cambridge University Press, 2004), pp. 130–1. In *Animal World*, 1:8 (2 May 1870), 139, the RSPCA did briefly pay tribute to Heyrick's efforts to put down bull-baiting.

115 Anon., *A Brief Sketch*, pp. 16–17, 20–1.

116 Anon. [Elizabeth Heyrick], *Letters of a Recluse* (London: Hamilton, Adams & Co. and Liverpool: D. Marples, 1830), pp. 50, 66. I attribute this pamphlet to Heyrick because

a work with this title, 'addressed to Mrs. Heyrick's two brothers', is listed among her productions in Beale, *Catherine Hutton and Her Friends*, p. 214; but there it is said to have been published posthumously (i.e. after 1831) 'by her especial request'. However, the pamphlet of 1830 takes the form of letters to intimate family members, and the views expressed are characteristic of Heyrick.

117 Anon. [Elizabeth Heyrick], *Apology for Ladies' Anti-Slavery Associations. By the Author of 'Immediate Not Gradual Abolition' &c. &c.* (London: J. Hatchard and Leicester: Albert Cockshaw, 1828), p. 10.

118 Corfield in 'Elizabeth Heyrick, radical Quaker', p. 44, writes of her 'moral absolutism'.

119 Anon. [Elizabeth Heyrick], *Appeal to the Hearts and Consciences of British Women* (Leicester: A. Cockshaw, 1828), p. 3.

2

The early history of the RSPCA:
its culture and its conflicts

I n 1865 the historian William Lecky published his thoughts on the 'rise of rationalism' in Europe, and tried to relate this to the distinctive qualities of society in his own day. The hallmark of Victorian Britain was, he thought, a new spirit of humanity. In earlier centuries the baiting of bulls and bears and cockfighting were enjoyed 'by all classes, even the most refined and the most humane', and any expression of sympathy for the animals would have been 'incomprehensible'. But now such cruelty – like enslavement or torture of humans – disgusted right-thinking British people. This change in public opinion was 'effected much less by any intellectual process than by a certain quickening of the emotions, and consequently of the moral judgments', which Lecky associated with 'the silent pressure of civilisation'. 'Amusements that were once universal' were gradually rejected, in a change of heart that was transmitted 'from the women to the men, from the upper to the lower classes, from the virtuous to the vicious, till at last the Legislature interposed to suppress them', and a 'thrill of indignation' was now felt whenever cruelty to animals came to light.[1] A few years later Charles Darwin in *The Descent of Man* gave such progressivist notions a scientific gloss: as human culture evolved from a state of savagery to high civilisation, the sphere of benevolence was extended. 'Sympathy beyond the confines of man, that is, humanity to the lower animals seems to be one of the latest moral acquisitions ... This virtue, one of the noblest with which man is endowed, seems to arise incidentally from our sympathies becoming more tender and more widely diffused, until they are extended to all sentient beings.'[2]

This notion of ever-increasing sympathies with animals was challenged even in the Victorian era, and Lecky's claim that any remaining cruelties were residual – an effect of the backward mentality of the lower orders – was, though common at the time, increasingly open to question. What is particularly significant for us, however, is his positioning of women as forerunners or agents in the change in attitudes to animal suffering that he perceived in nineteenth-century Britain; for he believed that this apparent mutation in the collective psychology had arisen not from 'any process of definite reasoning', in which men would, according to the assumptions of the time, be superior, but in emotional refinement and in the 'moral standard' which civilised women were thought to set for the rest of society. Herbert Spencer, too, identified 'love of the helpless' and skill in 'interpreting the natural language of feeling' as leading feminine traits.[3] As we have seen, women had traditionally been viewed as more tender-hearted and sympathising, more alive to the plight of working and domestic animals than their male counterparts were. But how far could such qualities be brought into play in the public sphere, where women had as yet so little scope for the expression of independent opinions, let alone for positions of influence, and where hard-headed business calculations no less than the barbarity of street life and the demoralisation of the slums obstructed the efforts of humanitarian reformers? In this chapter I trace the emergence of an organised animal protection movement in Victorian Britain, and examine how far women were able to shape and further its development.

The formation and character of the animal protection movement

After many fruitless parliamentary debates of the kind described in my Introduction, an anti-cruelty bill introduced by Richard Martin MP finally became law in 1822. It imposed fines of up to five pounds, or prison terms of up to three months in default, for those who 'wantonly and cruelly beat, abuse, or ill treat' horses, mules, donkeys, cows, oxen or sheep. However, it did not cover cruelties to domestic animals, nor (as a test case established) did it apply to bulls and bull-baiting, let alone to the 'wild' creatures hunted by the upper classes.[4] Moreover, despite its limited and relatively uncontroversial nature, the new law stood only a slim chance of being enforced, and this was perhaps the main reason why it was allowed to slip through the legislative process. As Roswell McCrea later noted, 'The situation approximated the familiar one in which the public conscience is sufficiently stirred to pass a law, which, however, is ineffective perhaps by intent'.[5] Seven years before the creation of a metropolitan police force, implementation of any such law depended on 'delegated responsibility' – the voluntary efforts of private citizens, acting as prosecutors and court witnesses, and often subjecting themselves to the risk of public odium or even violence; and such individual efforts could anyway have little impact, when measured against the scale of customary abuses.

In these circumstances, the Society for the Prevention of Cruelty to Animals came into being in 1824; it was a voluntary body, but invested with quasi-policing powers in the apprehension and prosecution of offenders.[6] Despite initial struggles with financial problems, schismatic tendencies and public hostility, the Society began to win the battle for stronger animal protection. A more comprehensive anti-cruelty law of 1835 provided protection for domestic as well as working animals, and banned both baiting and animal fights, thus enhancing the Society's credibility.[7] With Queen Victoria's enthusiastic patronage, it became the *Royal* Society for the Prevention of Cruelty to Animals in 1840 (hereafter, for convenience, I call it the RSPCA, even in references to the pre-1840 period of its history). The Queen's favour was attributed to her love of animals – for where, asked a grateful speaker at the 1841 annual meeting of the Society, 'can woman, with all her loveliness and all her grace, display herself to more effect than when she exercises acts of mercy and humanity?'[8] Victoria's endorsement was followed by that of other royals and aristocrats, and the Society gained steadily in prestige over the decades, becoming a revered national institution.

From the very start, however, it was clear that this organisation – the first of its kind anywhere – faced peculiar difficulties. Whatever the real motives that impelled people to devote their thoughts, time and money to an apparently thankless cause in the early days, they could only win over a hostile press and magistracy by offering a rationale for their actions that went beyond the relief of 'dumb' and 'irrational' beasts. As Sir Roland Knyvet Wilson pointed out in his *History of Modern English Law* (1875), a law penalising cruelty to animals represented 'an entirely new principle of legislation ... not admitted without considerable hesitation'; but sceptics might, he thought, have been expected to yield to the suggestion that it promised collateral benefits for civilised people in raising standards of public behaviour.[9] Virtually all protectionists accordingly stressed that habits of kindness to animals would foster a more general benevolence in society, especially in mending the ways of the young, the ignorant and the feckless. As we have seen, this was a traditional view with a venerable history, and it would be endlessly reiterated throughout the Victorian era, in bids for public support.

Modern historians have often suggested that reform of lower-class morals was the *primary* object of the early RSPCA.[10] Certainly, the presence of several reformist Members of Parliament at the inaugural meeting of the Society in June 1824, and their appointment as nominal committee members, signalled close links with the ameliorative political causes of the day. Thomas Fowell

A Scene in Smithfield, including about 25 Oxen out of 2500 at Market, (and often more.)

The statement of the Society as regards the management of the Cattle being supposed by some persons to be exaggerated, the present representation is respectfully offered to the Public, and humane individuals are earnestly entreated, for once, to visit the Market about eight o'clock on a Monday Morning to be convinced of the truth of the Print.

The Print depicts the mode of forcing from 15 to 25 oxen to stand in circles, called " off-droves," with their horns conflicting in the centre of the circle. The beating at first is to form the circle, and then when one poor animal is selected for inspection, or for sale, it becomes necessary to hit it over the head and nose repeatedly to cause it to back out, and the others can only be kept in their position by

5 'A scene in Smithfield', anonymous wood engraving from the RSPCA's ninth annual report for 1835.

Buxton (in the Chair), William Wilberforce and Sir James Mackintosh were all associated with the campaign for the abolition of slavery (leadership of which had passed from Wilberforce to Buxton in 1821), and with moves for a reform of the criminal code.[11] Indeed, the beginnings of animal advocacy can only be understood as part of the wave of such 'humane' moral impulses. However, Buxton and his parliamentary associates played little direct part in the new group's work, and there is certainly little evidence that it aspired to a grand social or correctional purpose beyond the mitigation of cruelty to animals. As one journalist who attended that first 'thin meeting' later recalled, Richard Martin himself was 'entirely without influence, social or political', as was the co-founder of the Society, the Revd Arthur Broome. Moreover, by the later 1820s the Society's committee was for a time reduced to a very few active members, of no public prominence or status. It was uncertain in its policies, unpopular with many magistrates, insolvent and fissiparous. A speaker at the RSPCA's annual meeting of 1842 recalled that its leaders 'used to be opposed by unsparing ridicule and obloquy … represented as chimerical speculators, and called in the House of Commons a knot of "petty legislators"'. The pioneers had persisted in their work only from a strong (but perhaps not fully rationalised) conviction that cruelty to animals was a great wrong.[12]

It is, therefore, mistaken to represent the early RSPCA as an authoritarian, single-minded, univocal body, activated from its inception by a purposive ideology. Cruelty to animals was a phenomenon open to widely varying definitions and explanations, and responses to it might be mildly reproving and propitiatory or coercive, drastic, even (in the eyes of some) fanatical. Members represented a spectrum of viewpoints arising from political and religious affiliations, social class and (importantly) gender; and these differences were frequently articulated in the Society's debates and plans of action. At the inaugural meeting of 16 June 1824, as reported in the *Times*, it was evident that the cruelties of the London streets, markets and shambles, the main targets of the 1822 Act, preoccupied speakers; they were the most visible offences, and those most likely to distress or corrupt onlookers (figure 5).[13] According to the *Times* report, the Society's chairman, Thomas Fowell Buxton, observed that it was 'desirable, not only to prevent the exercise of cruelty towards animals, but to spread amongst the lower orders of the people, especially amongst those to whom the care of animals was intrusted, a degree of moral feeling which would compel them to think and act like those of a superior class, instead of sinking into a comparison (in which their inferiority was now unfortunately acknowledged) with the poor brute over which they exercised a brutal authority'. However, to be punishable under the Act, cruelty had to be 'wanton' or gratuitous. The law, as interpreted by magistrates of that time, did not penalise *customary* practices in managing and slaughtering animals, however painful in their effects; nor did it, at this stage, allow for prosecution of employers whose avarice and commercial competition might have been the original cause of their servants' cruelties to working animals. Indeed, the reformers themselves were as yet unprepared to ponder these wider social ramifications of the problem. Yet even as early as 1824, there was a consciousness of endemic upper-class cruelties, as well as of the sins of the lower orders. At this first meeting of the founding group, Richard Martin referred to the callousness of wealthy men who surreptitiously sold off their hunters, when no longer fit for the chase, thereby condemning them to an end-life of heavy draught labour in low trades.[14] Crying shame on these traitors (traitors both to their social class and to their faithful horses) was assumed to be a sufficient disincentive to such heartless conduct; but in the case of ignorant, demoralised labourers, appeals to their better nature seemed a less promising approach. A lawyer present, John Gilbert Meymott, insisted that men of this class were 'altogether unassailable by such weapons as tracts or sermons, because they never read nor went to church': nothing but prosecution, or the threat of it, would cause them to desist from cruelty.

However, a punitive policy carried its own risks: the Revd Broome reminded the meeting that prosecuting societies 'looked like powerful, and of course most objectionable and unconstitutional confederacies', reliant on paid agents or informers to bring their victims to court. Here the reputation of an existing 'confederacy', the Society for the Suppression of Vice, founded in 1802, would have been in his listeners' minds. This very conservative, indeed politically reactionary, Anglican association had included cruelty to animals – notably baiting, animal fights and cruelty to livestock – among the plebeian practices in need of suppression, largely because they led to drunkenness, social indiscipline and disorder in the streets.[15] A famous article in the *Edinburgh Review* of 1809 by Sydney Smith pilloried the Society for the Suppression of Vice's leaders as hypocrites who censured the amusements of the poor, while overlooking 'high-life cruelties' such as hunting, shooting and angling, and the agonies inflicted on animals in the course of producing culinary delights for rich epicures. Such men 'should denominate themselves a Society for suppressing the vices of persons whose income does not exceed £500 *per annum*'.[16] At just this time, as we have seen, William Windham directed equally biting sarcasm against Lord Erskine's bill for an anti-cruelty law, on similar grounds.[17] Nevertheless, the RSPCA founders concluded with some reluctance in 1824 that, despite the likelihood of public resentment and satirical flak, prosecutions for blatant cruelty would sometimes be necessary; but they were to be accompanied by a programme of enlightenment and persuasion, such as to effect 'a revolution in morals'. This process of persuasion initially depended on the contents of the Society's voluminous annual reports, together with the publication of informative pamphlets, sponsored sermons and prize-winning essays. Only after 1870 did the appearance of the RSPCA's journal *Animal World* and the educational activities of its ladies' committee give a high profile to the task of converting the public to the animal-protection cause – complementing and offsetting a steady rise in prosecutions for cruelty. Thus, according to a bald statement in a prospectus circulated in the 1870s, the RSPCA was 'an educational and punitive agency' – twinned functions that involved a strongly gendered division of labour.[18]

At an early stage the tensions which arose in trying to attain an acceptable balance between exhortation and prosecution very nearly shipwrecked the Society. In 1831 John Ludd Fenner seceded from the RSPCA committee, taking with him a recently established journal, the *Voice of Humanity*. In partnership with a clergyman, Thomas Greenwood, he then set up the Association for Promoting Rational Humanity (APRH) towards the Animal Creation, which existed to publish the *Voice*. This journal – the first to be entirely devoted to the subject of animal cruelty – exposed the horrors of private slaughterhouses, horse-knackers' yards and pits for fighting dogs through eyewitness accounts and engravings, adopting the kind of shock tactics that had often been used in propaganda against West Indian slavery. The Association's leaders believed that working on public opinion in this way would prevent the abuse of animals, and obviate the need for the prosecution of offending individuals.[19] However, the opposite approach was taken by the honorary secretary of the RSPCA, Lewis Gompertz, who insisted that reformist law-making always initially '*forced* its benefits upon an unwilling public' through surveillance and exemplary punishments.[20] Believing as he did that animals have minds and sensibilities equivalent to those of humans, he viewed cruelty towards them as a crime strictly analogous to the murder or serious injury of men and women, and thought it should be treated just as seriously.[21] Personal animosities as well as anti-Semitism were involved in this bitter dispute (Gompertz was Jewish), but for the residual members of the RSPCA committee, it could have only one outcome. A declaration in 1832 that 'the proceedings of this Society are entirely based on the Christian Faith, and on Christian Principles' and a temporary stop to the use of paid agents in bringing prosecutions, quickly secured a reunion with the APRH and forced Gompertz out.[22] He then started a rival group, the Animals' Friend Society, with its own hard-hitting illustrated journal, the *Animals' Friend*; but after this petered out in the 1840s, the RSPCA was confirmed as the undisputed leader of the animal protection movement – not to be challenged again until the damaging rifts over the vivisection issue in the mid-1870s. The Society soon resumed the employment of paid agents or constables, of whom there were over a hundred by the 1890s, and grew steadily in status and wealth.

The public avowal of Christian principles made in 1832 was more than a bid for respectability or a ploy to oust an unpopular secretary. Gompertz's heterodox, allegedly 'Pythagorean' beliefs about the fate of animal souls, his espousal of veganism and his conviction that animals should be treated as man's equals, not as his slaves, certainly might have had uncomfortable echoes of the wave of egalitarian radicalism and talk of animal rights that had followed the French revolution.[23] However, the RSPCA was not about to retreat into the kind of narrow sectarianism for which the Society for the Suppression of Vice was notorious. Rather, it sought to foreground Christianity as the only compelling basis for its admonitions. As we have seen, cruelty to animals was traditionally treated as a sin that stigmatised or fatally corrupted the moral nature of the perpetrator, leading on to greater evils. John Stuart Mill deplored the fact that objections to government interference in the 'domestic life of domestic tyrants' – in this case, interventions to prevent abuse of animals occurring on private premises – had made that line of argument necessary: 'many warm supporters of laws against cruelty to animals … seek for a justification of such laws in the incidental consequences of the indulgence of ferocious habits, to the interests of human beings, rather than in the intrinsic merits of the case itself'.[24] It will be noted that, unlike many modern historians of the animal protection movement, Mill presumed that animal suffering per se was the real, primary concern of the activists, and that claims for the social or political benefits of anti-cruelty laws were merely a stratagem for winning over a sceptical public. The American scholar Roswell McCrea, in his intelligent history of the humane movement, published in 1910, likewise observed that most nineteenth-century animal advocacy was 'based on a "faith" rather than on any rationalistic scheme of fundamentals. The emotional basis is the common one, and the kind treatment of animals is assumed to be a thing desirable in itself, as well as in its effects on animals and in its reflex bearings on man himself … a religion rather than the foundation of a logical scheme of uplift or reform'.[25]

Emotions and impulses were always open to challenge by those who did not feel them, but here again religious teaching could, as we saw in the Introduction, lend authority to animal protectionists. It may be true, as Dix Harwood later claimed, that 'It takes a pious and earnest lover of beasts to get much humanitarian comfort out of the Bible'.[26] Indeed, in the later nineteenth century, agnostics and atheists would challenge the notion that conventional Christian belief was a necessary concomitant of kindness to animals.[27] Nevertheless, many of those who consistently supported laws against cruelty, such as the Wesleyan Methodists, understood them as 'another approximation of our political institutions to the wisdom and benevolence of the Divine … the principle in the laws of MOSES'.[28] Scriptural texts that seemed to enjoin kindness and consideration towards animals were still regularly collected together for the edification of the reading public, as they had been in the eighteenth century, and children were encouraged to make their own collections.[29] According to the Old Testament, God had entrusted His cherished creation to the care of man, who was to exercise a benign dominion over the 'lower' animals. Christ's message of mercy in the gospels was taken to mean that benevolence should be extended to all living things – always remembering, however, that man, with his superior intelligence and immortal destiny, was 'of more value than many sparrows'.[30] The patron saint of this compassionate but hierarchical tradition of thought, which lingered on in the discourse of animal protectionists well into the Victorian era, was the eighteenth-century poet William Cowper. He was venerated for his affectionate care of animals and for his anathemas pronounced on the cruel, but he was valued just as much for the *limitations* that he had placed on animals' entitlements. His lines in *The Task*, encapsulating a Christian basis for human–animal relationships, were often quoted:

The sum is this: if man's convenience, health,
Or safety interfere, his rights and claims
Are paramount, and must extinguish theirs.
Else they are all – the meanest things that are,
As free to live and to enjoy that life,
As God was free to form them at the first.[31]

The value and convenience of this formulation may be seen in a review of Gompertz's *Animals' Friend* journal, which appeared in the *Monthly Review* in 1839. The writer took exception to Gompertz's claim that animals were on a level with humans, indeed closely allied to man in all their faculties, and that they therefore had strong claims to a fair share in the world's resources and in the pleasures of life. He was 'perfectly at a loss' to know whether the editor of the *Animals' Friend* approved 'of ever making use of animals in any one shape or not', and contrasted Gompertz's 'pervading sentimentality' with Cowper's more reasonable approach. 'We must not forget that the claims and necessities of man are paramount, and the toils and distresses of multitudes of our fellow beings surpass the average pains and deprivations of the brute creation.' No doubt, wanton cruelty of the kind seen in the streets, which was an 'outrage ... against the feelings of the community', should be checked; but the interests of 'so many thousands of the people' were bound up in the speed and strength of their working animals, and criticism of harsh treatment should be tempered accordingly. In the opinion of this reviewer, Gompertz's kind of 'sentimentality' or fundamentalism actually impeded the steady 'advance of intelligence, and the general improvement of manners of the age', which it was the business of humanitarians to foster.[32] In 1842, Earl Grosvenor, chairing the RSPCA's annual meeting, took a similar view, blaming the Society's early difficulties on Gompertz's 'morbid and misguided feelings of humanity'. Now there was 'a wise caution in not pushing extreme opinions, nor running counter to public feeling'.[33]

The RSPCA learnt, perhaps over-learnt, the lessons of this episode in its history; and as membership increased over the decades, there was a growing need to retain the support of this wider and more heterogeneous swathe of the public through moderation in the framing of policies. Indeed, for modern historians like Brian Harrison, a policy of 'wise caution' and restraint, distancing the Society from animal-protection fanatics, was the key to its enduring success – a success, which can, however, easily be overestimated.[34] At its annual meeting of 1879, amid the dissensions of the anti-vivisection campaign (in which the RSPCA was effectively sidelined), the president, Lord Aberdare, summed up the approach which had always guided the Society:

> The Committee do not represent extreme persons on this subject. (Hear, hear.) This Society has obtained its high position very greatly by the discretion, prudence and moderation which has characterised all its proceedings ... the voice of the country must be its governing power. (Cheers.) ... the best course in the main is to educate public opinion, while not getting too much in advance of it.[35]

The role of women in the early years of the RSPCA

When punitive policies and negotiation with powerful interest groups both failed to protect animals, such efforts to 'educate public opinion' might provide an answer. This educational mission of the RSPCA differentiated it strongly from the Society for the Suppression of Vice, and indeed has no exact parallel among other Victorian philanthropic bodies. As women were, by tradition, so closely associated with teaching and writing that was intended to inculcate kindness to animals (see chapter 1), it might have been expected that they would immediately take on a key role in this important aspect of the Society's work. Yet any such initiative would need to comply with the RSPCA's policy of coaxing the public into a supportive stance, rather than trying to impose unwelcome, 'extreme' views and measures upon it; and it was feared, with some justification, that the distinctive mindset of many of the Society's eager female supporters might make such compliance difficult.

As early as 1829, it was decided to set up a ladies' committee, 'to forward the objects of the institution', particularly in promoting sermons by sympathetic clergymen.[36] As both Mrs Fenner and Mrs Gompertz were members of this small 'corresponding and subordinate committee', it could not have survived the hostilities between their husbands that broke out a year or two later; but its functions were anyway strictly circumscribed from the start. In April 1830, it was decided by the (men's) executive committee, for reasons undisclosed in the minutes, that 'No proposition submitted by any sub-committee … be acted upon and considered as binding' unless ratified by a vote of the executive committee; and in the reunited, increasingly successful organisation that the Society became in the 1830s, there was apparently no thought of reviving the women's group in any form.[37] Not until 1870 was a regular ladies' committee established, with the limited remit of circulating RSPCA publications, notably its new periodical *Animal World*, and of promoting the humane education of the young.

The significance of this reluctance to admit women to decision-making tiers of the RSPCA hierarchy becomes apparent when it is compared with the practices of other philanthropic and moral-reform institutions of the time. The Society for the Suppression of Vice and the British and Foreign Bible Society (BFBS) both encouraged the participation of women in their activities.[38] Women also played an important part in the anti-slavery movement, though often encountering male resistance.[39] The BFBS, an interdenominational body, sold Bibles and New Testaments by small weekly payments in the poorer areas of British towns, as well as operating in the colonies, and from 1811 onwards an army of middle-class women was recruited (some ten thousand of them countrywide by c.1820) to carry out this door-to-door visiting. Although never free from controversy, the practice was believed to have many incidental benefits: according to Charles Stoke Dudley in his *Analysis of the System of the Bible Society* (1821), it tended to 'soften and humanize the manners and sentiments of the lower orders', and formed a much-needed 'bond of union … between the higher and lower classes of the community'. The philanthropic ladies themselves were also gainers: through participation in the Society's 'extensive plans of mercy and benevolence ... a great and important change has gradually taken place in the Female character ... the intellectual powers have been more ... assiduously cultivated', yet without any loss of feminine 'delicacy'.[40] Dudley might have added that the women gained experience in directing public work without male interference. The local BFBS female associations were autonomous, both financially and administratively, bringing together women of different religious affiliations – notably Anglican evangelicals and Quakers – in many communities. Indeed, the Revd John Owen believed that the BFBS was ushering in 'a new aera in the history of religion', marked by 'unanimity' and common endeavour in spreading the gospel message.[41]

This experience proved invaluable for the women's anti-slavery groups which sprung up in the 1820s, involving many of the same people. The Birmingham Ladies' Negro's Friend Society (it went under several differing names in the course of its history) was established in 1825 by Lucy Townsend, who was also active in the BFBS. She was the wife of the perpetual curate of West Bromwich, and shared his passionate engagement not only with the anti-slavery cause, but also with the suppression of blood sports, which were rife in the Black Country.[42] Her genius for leadership and organisation, and for enthusing others, is clear in the rapid growth of a network of branches or 'auxiliaries' of the Birmingham ladies' anti-slavery society in towns across the country, with 'district treasurers' forwarding subscriptions to Birmingham. While some of this considerable sum of money was sent on to the leaders of the anti-slavery movement in London, much of it was devoted to the production of publications, edited or authored by the women themselves.[43] Among their other ingenious means of awakening 'the public mind' was 'the manufacture and sale of work-bags' containing anti-slavery literature, samples of which were presented to the Duchess of Kent and Princess Victoria in 1831 by Elizabeth Fry.[44] The disarming femininity of this resort to needlework in the good cause was, however, offset by the more daring project of canvassing women to boycott West Indian sugar – no doubt building on the experience of knocking at doors with bibles. It was a move which marked the transition of the Birmingham society, under the influence of Elizabeth Heyrick (see chapter 1), from a 'gradualist' to an 'immediatist' position on abolition of slavery, and the women even threatened to withhold money from London unless the parliamentary campaign, too, was based on a demand for immediate abolition. The astonishing effectiveness of their network of communication and collaboration was made evident in 1833, when an anti-slavery petition to parliament from the women of England garnered over 187,000 signatures within about ten days – the women being, they said, 'impelled ... to step out of their usual sphere' by 'a painful and indignant sense of the injuries offered to their own sex' in the abuse of slave women.[45]

There is evidence that many of these female campaigners – not only Elizabeth Heyrick and Susanna Watts – felt as passionately about cruelty to animals as they did about the sufferings of human slaves. Lucy Townsend helped to organise the South Staffordshire Association for the Suppression of Bull-baiting, led by her husband in partnership with the wealthy Quaker industrialist Samuel Lloyd.[46] These men fought a very bitter, protracted and high-profile campaign against bull-baiting in the West Midlands. The *Voice of Humanity*, the *Animals' Friend* and sometimes the national press published their horrific descriptions of bulls being tortured with boiling water or fire to make them fight (in one case, in 1828, a bull's tongue was allegedly torn out and eaten in a nearby public house before the animal had died), and of dogs being mutilated or killed in falls when tossed by the bull.[47] However exaggerated these accounts may have been (and there seems no way of ascertaining the truth one way or the other), the disgust felt by women like Lucy Townsend about cruelty to animals is beyond doubt. Family correspondence reveals that on at least one occasion she sent a donation of two pounds to the RSPCA through an intermediary, and the Society's minutes for 1829 note that she had written a letter to the Committee, 'relative to Bull baiting'.[48]

Townsend's friend Sarah Wedgwood, a fellow-member of the ladies' anti-slavery society, author of *British Slavery Described* (1828) and a passionate 'immediatist', also wrote to the RSPCA in 1829, 'on the subject of sending a person to Birmingham to witness the Bull baitings'.[49] She was advised to recruit a witness locally – the Society would pay his expenses, and publicise his account. However, in the case of Miss Wedgwood – independently wealthy after inheriting part of the family fortune – action on behalf of animals went beyond such pleas. She sent very generous subscriptions and donations to the various anti-cruelty societies over a period of years; but she was also associated more directly with interventions in cases of mistreatment of animals – apparently acting in concert with her kinswoman Catherine ('Kitty') Mackintosh. The latter was the wife of the RSPCA co-founder and leading slave-abolitionist Sir James Mackintosh, and Kitty herself spent much time in furthering humanitarian causes, for example writing letters to the *Times* about abuse of cattle in Smithfield market.[50] A letter of 1826 from Elizabeth Wedgwood, Sarah's niece, to her (Elizabeth's) sister Emma, the future wife of Charles Darwin, reveals that Sarah and Kitty had started a local 'anticruelty society, of which they are almost the only remaining members I think'. Elizabeth mentioned an incident involving Kitty:

> Aunt M. had a man sent to Bedford jail for a month for ill treating his ass – his wife seemed rather glad to be so rid of him, & indeed it turned out a good thing for her, besides losing such a brute of a husband, for she got blankets clothes & money from Aunt M. and the poor ass was taken into the stable and nursed, for it could not stand at first – but one morning nobody can tell how, it was found drowned in the mud of a pool in the park whether it fell in or was thrown in nobody knew.[51]

The latter seems much the most likely: an act of defiance and revenge by friends of the accused man, in the face of a high-handedness and assertion of moral superiority that no quantity of free blankets could reconcile them to. This record has been preserved because of the eminence of the families concerned; but perhaps it may have been common for people of social position and local influence, including women, to prosecute offenders in their neighbourhoods under the laws of 1822 and 1835, or to get cruel practices suppressed by diktat, exerting a power that was almost independent of the policies of national bodies such as the RSPCA. Yet it was true idealism, not merely an assertion of magisterial authority, which gave strength to many women's actions. In 1839, for example, the *Animals' Friend* reported that the writer Sarah Hoare, daughter of the eminent Quaker merchant and abolitionist Samuel Hoare Junior, had 'used every personal exertion' to end dog-fighting in Bath, in compliance with the 1835 Act – 'Miss H. having made it her business to interfere herself and stop the combats about the town whenever she found them occur'. The fact that an agent employed by the Animals' Friend Society was roughed up as he left the police office in Bath suggests the determination and pluck that such interventions involved.[52] Later another Quaker, Elizabeth Pease Nichol (cousin of Joseph Pease MP, who introduced the 1835 anti-cruelty bill into parliament) moved on from passionate campaigning against slavery to equally passionate activism in a range of animal causes. She was 'the dauntless volunteer inspector of shambles, and of labour which employed horses', invoking the aid of the police and the press in putting down cruelty wherever she encountered it. When opposition to vivisection arose, this too 'roused her indignant advocacy and untiring energy'. For her, as for many religious women, all humanitarian causes seemed to be one: 'if needless pain were inflicted on the helpless, whether it were a subject race, or a child, or but a dog, her wrath blazed'.[53]

It is clear, then, that if the RSPCA had chosen to activate a network of female auxiliaries across the country, or to invite women onto its committee, it would have greatly augmented the ardour, mental energies, proselytising and fundraising skills, networks of communication and flair for publicity available to it, and would have mobilised a female enthusiasm for the cause that was already in evidence. However, the Society's policy of reasonableness and conciliation of antagonists, including hostile magistrates, evidently gave pause to any such idea. As was noted in the case of Elizabeth Heyrick, the campaigning fervour of women, inspired by a sense of moral imperatives, often made them impatient of compromise and dismissive of the *realpolitik* of public affairs. In the case of anti-slavery, this fundamentalist tendency had often set the women's groups at loggerheads with their male counterparts – not just the battle-weary leaders of the movement in parliament but also many of their own menfolk; and something of this religiously inspired zeal and militancy was carried over into their approach to the ending of cruelty to animals. If they were to become active participants in the animal protection movement, they would have to be closely supervised by male colleagues – men versed in the ways of the world and determined to limit the Society's ambitions to the small incremental gains that public opinion allowed. Yet despite a lack of active encouragement from the leaders of the RSPCA, the financial contributions of women became vital to its support base at grassroots level. Already in 1832, the list of subscribers and donors shows that 43 per cent of them were women, and of course more, not listed under their own names, would have contributed through their husbands – or might have petitioned the head of the household unsuccessfully for permission to send money. The resulting preponderance of independent single women in the membership lists in itself played into the old stereotype of the spinster who preferred animals to her fellow-humans. They included Sarah Wedgwood, who in 1832 gave the RSPCA ten pounds; and from 1836 onwards she increased her gift to sixty-five or even seventy pounds per annum, astonishing sums.[54]

Besides donating to the Society and raising funds from others in their respective circles, increasing numbers of upper- and middle-class women (including many Quakers) attended the RSPCA's annual meetings from the 1830s onwards. This development was in line with national trends: as many philanthropic societies' meetings became both more formal and more decorous, taking place in halls rather than in public houses, ladies could properly be admitted as spectators. However, in the case of the RSPCA, it evidently created some nervousness in the leadership. In 1832 speakers referred to 'such a large majority' or 'the great number' of ladies present; in 1834 it was 'the great proportion … of the fair, in comparison to the male sex', and similar comments were reiterated annually, suggesting that women represented well over half of the audience.[55]

The opinions of this silent majority (there is no record of any woman speaking at the public meetings) with respect to the matters under debate cannot be known. It is clear, however, that the men whose speeches are given in the annual reports of the 1830s–1840s strained to *construct* the attitudes and roles that the Society saw fit to attribute to these female enthusiasts. Members of the 'tender sex', always 'the first to promote humanity to the brute creation', 'evince a readiness ... to desert the privacy of their chamber, and sacrifice their feelings of retirement to promote feelings which do honour to human nature'. Such were the 'fine impulses', exquisite sensibilities and capacity for melting pity of these ladies, that speakers refrained from detailing the worst cruelties to animals in their presence. In 1835 J.G. Meymott assured them that 'although from *your* station in society you cannot assist at our various meetings, or personally interfere in the prevention or punishment of offences, yet by your influence in society ... you can do much in promoting the cause of humanity', through educational means. Viscount Mahon too thought that 'Even from within the domestic sphere', women's 'pure example' gave 'the tone to public feeling', through instruction of their own children in kindness to animals, and through their moral influence on the men of the family. This influence was worth more than public campaigning, law-making or prosecution, for 'Legislation is always more effectual when it *follows*, than when it *precedes* public opinion'. Nathaniel Goldsmid went further: in an anticipation of Lecky's views on the role of women as pioneers in the growth of humane feeling through the century, he credited them with being able to effect a 'gradual amelioration of society ... not only in matters connected with humanity to our fellow-creatures, but in all that relates to its exercise amongst all created beings'. There was much more every year in the same strain.[56]

Those who have studied the construction of gender roles in nineteenth-century Britain will have no difficulty in recognising here another manifestation of 'separate spheres' ideology, which impeded women's efforts to contribute publicly to altruistic causes – or arguably was designed to justify their exclusion from leading positions. At the international convention organised in London in 1840 by the British and Foreign Anti-Slavery Society, women who attended as delegates found themselves relegated to the audience area of the hall, debarred from speaking or taking any active part in the proceedings – a rebuff that caused great controversy. 'From that meeting', wrote the biographer of the abolitionist Elizabeth Pease Nichol, whom we have already encountered as a campaigner against cruelty to animals, 'the rise of the women's franchise movement may be dated'.[57] The episode was an extreme example of that conflict between the sexes about which Anna Jameson, in her *Sisters of Charity and the Communion of Labour* (1855–1856) complained bitterly: women fulfilled key roles as donors and visitors to institutions such as hospitals and workhouses, yet were denied partnership with men in their management. 'One half of the human community ... presses forward, striving ... for a more equal distribution of labour and its privileges. The other half resist.'[58] In the mid-century, the prevailing view – in the RSPCA as in other charitable organisations – was that women's reforming energies were best expended in the private sphere, and in inconspicuous supportive functions. As expressed by Lord Carnarvon, the RSPCA president, in 1843, women could make kindness to animals 'the rule of action within the limits of your blessed household homes ... silken ties are more strong and binding than links of iron'; but these ties, he implied, would be severed if women themselves were to invade the public sphere, and become hardened or corrupted by it.[59] Their principal office was moral persuasion within their immediate circles; and as grassroots supporters and generous benefactors (in 1841, a typical year, ten out of fifteen legacies to the RSPCA came from women) they might counterbalance the asperities of the Society's interactions with offenders, and soften its image.[60] One speaker at the Society's meeting in 1840 had 'oftentimes ... known one of the most rough and sturdy of the butcher race yield civilly, to gentle remonstrances – uttered by lady lips'. Thus the many references to moneyed women's existing philanthropic and religious good works among the poor give the eulogies of RSPCA speakers a class inflection. Such characteristic, condescending attention to the needs of indigent human beings was merely to extend 'a little lower in the scale of creation' to the protection of helpless animals.[61]

Women's responses to their exclusion from any share in the governance of the RSPCA obviously varied according to character and circumstances. Generally speaking, devotion to the animal-protection cause seems to have overridden any resentment, as it also overrode factional loyalties with regard to the various competing animal-protection bodies. The Association for Promoting Rational Humanity and the Animals' Friend Society – the breakaway groups – had significant support from women, and seem to have given them a wider role than that granted by the RSPCA. In 1832 the *Standard* reported that the 'principal portion' of those present at the first annual meeting of the APRH 'were ladies, very fashionably attired', and there is evidence that women started several local branches of the Association.[62] More surprisingly, a perusal of subscription and donation lists published by the warring groups reveals that many individual women (and quite a few men) made liberal gifts to all of the societies simultaneously. A Mrs Frances Maria Thompson, who evidently had the disposal of a large independent income, was one of the members of the short-lived RSPCA ladies' committee set up in 1829, and sometimes attended meetings of the executive committee as a 'visitor'.[63] In 1837–1838 she established a branch of the RSPCA in Dublin with the support of the London office.[64] However, she also gave lavish amounts of money (over forty-six pounds in one year) and collected funds from others towards the APRH's costs in running the *Voice of Humanity*, and often had letters published in its pages. She rejoiced that this journal now existed to expose cruelties and provide a channel for the expression of the public's sentiments. 'The increasing instances of cruelty in our streets have now arisen to such a height that it is impossible to go any distance from home without encountering something to wound our feelings.'[65] The focus of animal protectionists on the elimination of street cruelties owed more to the psychology of observers like Thompson than it did to any programme of disciplining the lower orders: to see and hear the sufferings of animals without power to prevent them was infinitely more upsetting and shaming than to learn of cruelties at second hand – those that occurred in the field, on the farm, in distant hunting grounds or trapping territories.

Frances Thompson was especially distressed by 'the cruel treatment of dogs, and leaving them to starve about the streets. They are made to perform the labour of drawing trucks … panting with exhaustion … without the possibility of getting a drop of water to quench their thirst'. Performing animals were routinely mutilated and abused; cattle and sheep were maltreated in Smithfield market, and driven to slaughter in a 'pitiable state'; and tired donkeys were brutally beaten with heavy sticks to make them go. Worst of all, omnibus horses were generally 'out of condition from being over-worked and over-loaded in drawing these cumbrous vehicles, with their necks quite raw under the collars', while 'The shocking state of the hackney-coach horses leads me to conclude that the Society for the Prevention of Cruelty to Animals cannot be in existence'.[66] Informative publications like the *Voice of Humanity* served a valuable purpose, she believed, but only if they generated action to end these horrible and entrenched cruelties, involving the regular police when necessary; and this conviction that publicity must be complemented by prosecution led her to support Gompertz's Animals' Friend Society as well as its deadly rivals. Her donations to the Animals' Friend Society are recorded down to 1841: in 1835 she met this Society's costs in connection with attempts to suppress the annual bull-running at Stamford, and in sending agents to London dog-pits to witness the fights there, leading to successful prosecutions of the owners.[67] Her letters to the *Animals' Friend* reveal that she also intervened personally to prevent cruelties. On one occasion, she directed her manservant to run for water when an old horse, 'glandered, with its thigh broken, starved, and totally unable to stir', was seen being dragged and flogged on the long road to the knacker's yard: 'After much abuse to the gentleman, police, &c., present, it was finally killed on the spot to end its tortures, perhaps owing to my interference.' She even sometimes sent her servant to appear as a witness, testifying in court against the perpetrators of cruelties they had seen in the streets.[68] However, through such passionate, single-minded activism she exposed herself to accusations of folly, such as would not, probably, have been made against a man. A reviewer of the *Voice of Humanity* in the *London Literary Gazette* picked out Thompson's letters for special criticism: her protest about the use of dogs to draw carts typified the 'weak panoply of morbid sensibility. Let us strive to correct real grievances … not encumber our exertions with mawkish affectations'.[69]

It appears from these examples that animal protection activities undertaken by women went far beyond the modest auxiliary and educational roles within the limits of their 'blessed household homes' that the RSPCA thought suitable for the sex, but in doing so they risked not only ridicule but also controversy and violent confrontations. The reputational risks become clear from the records of a short-lived 'Ladies' Association for the More Effectual Suppression of Cruelty to Animals', which was established by Charles Wheeler in the early 1830s. Wheeler had been an inspector for the RSPCA in the 1820s; when he was laid off during the period in which the Society temporarily ceased to employ agents in bringing prosecutions, he evidently saw an opportunity to garner and exploit the contributions of women who were similarly dissatisfied by an appearance of inaction, and he fraudulently boasted of achieving numerous successes in the courts on their behalf.[70] He also claimed to be undertaking ambitious projects to relieve animal suffering: Frances Maria Thompson (again) advanced Wheeler over fifty pounds 'to establish an *Omnibus with four horses*, to be called "The Humanity Omnibus"': but he neither produced the vehicle nor refunded the money.[71]

Such ill-judged, misplaced generosity was a propaganda gift to that segment of public opinion opposed to anti-cruelty measures, and an attack on Wheeler's society in *John Bull* of 8 March 1835 found the female membership a particularly easy target for its sarcasms. 'Our fair countrywomen' deserved credit not only for all their pious tracts against bull-baiting and cockfighting, but for their employment of 'constables, overseers, and inspectors', whose reports were 'replete with the most horrible and frightful anecdotes'. The writer disbelieved and ridiculed accounts of the sufferings of horses in knack-ers' yards and of livestock being hurled down from street level into subter-ranean slaughterhouses: abuses which had also been described in the *Voice of Humanity* and the *Animals' Friend*. The ladies' idea of providing wooden ramps and straw to break the animals' fall in the latter case 'suggests a most luxurious mode of mitigating the barbarity of the proceeding, by tenderly *chaperoning* a Lincolnshire ram down an inclined *chaise longue* with a pillow at its end … its innocent throat cut in order to provide an *entrée* of *côtelettes* for the dinner of the sympathizing lady, the kind inventress of the mitigator of its sufferings'. Accusations of false sensibility, born of a self-indulgent, sybaritic lifestyle, were still as potent a means of attacking female animal-lovers as they had been in the eighteenth century. The women's proposals to acquire sup-plies of grit to spread on roads and thus assist horses working in icy weather, and to buy old horses in order to put them down mercifully, were dismissed by *John Bull* as illogical and absurd, 'the very extravagance of humanity'. They exposed the women's gullibility, lack of knowledge of real-life conditions, and crying need for 'some better councillor' – a man, clearly – 'as to the channels through which their bounty should flow'. But the writer's main quarrel with the women arose from their alleged victimisation of the lower orders. In the report of prosecutions supplied by Wheeler, it was 'as if the omnibus-drivers, cab-drivers, carters, butchers', and the costermongers selling 'apples and tur-nips – monsters!' – were themselves 'so many *vegetables*', incapable of moral feeling. The ladies conveniently forgot the equal hardships of their own over-worked carriage horses, just as they ignored the part played by the gustatory demands of the wealthy in the brutal methods used to slaughter animals for their tables; and in truth, the cruelty of 'correcting an unruly horse', as these working men necessarily did, was as nothing compared to the cruelty of 'fining a poor "ruffian" with a large family, or sending a "recreant" omnibus-driver to prison while his wife and children are left to starve at home'.[72]

The social complexion of the RSPCA and its work in the Victorian era

Accusations of pharisaic hypocrisy and oppression of the helpless poor pursued the RSPCA, too, throughout the nineteenth century – the accusers often being those who had an interest in preventing *any* extension of anti-cruelty legisla-tion. The attacks that had been made by William Windham and Sydney Smith on the opponents of plebeian blood sports offered a useful precedent; and when the Act introduced by the Quaker Joseph Pease in 1835 made bull-baiting illegal, these culture wars were briefly resumed. Historians have given much attention to the class discrimination involved in the campaign to suppress animal baiting, which reveals, in their view, the ulterior motives of moneyed animal protectionists: their desire to impose social order and work discipline on labourers in an era of rapid industrialisation. However, this thesis underplays various factors: the participation of many members of the privileged classes themselves in popular blood sports like cockfighting and dog fights, and – more importantly – the groundswell of revulsion against cruel sports coming from sectors of the shop-keeping, artisan and labouring classes themselves. Members of Methodist and other chapel congregations were especially horrified by the presence of women among the onlookers and indeed by the warped notion of 'manliness' that the popularity of such sports signified.[73]

The cessation of the annual bull-running at Stamford in 1839 marked the moment when majority public opinion decisively shifted in favour of abolition of baiting and animal fights. In any case, the RSPCA's central concern had always been, and remained, the abuse of working animals and livestock, especially horses, as is evident in any analysis of the pattern of prosecutions tabulated in the RSPCA's annual reports. In 1869 and 1873, for example, cruelties to horses, donkeys and mules accounted for 88 per cent of all court convictions, with cruelties to sheep and cattle as the next largest category, and these are typical figures both for London and for the provincial branches of the Society.[74] Some of the offences listed in the first printed report of 1832 remained discouragingly prevalent for the rest of the century: 'Beating a half starved horse on wounds … Whipping a horse till the blood came … Cruelly beating an overloaded horse … Beating and kicking a horse which could not rise so that it was obliged to be killed on the spot, and the hip bones of which protruded the skin.' A report on the annual meeting of the Manchester branch of the RSPCA in 1889 exemplifies a typical pattern of surveillance by the Society's inspectors, adapting traditional work patterns to the conditions of a new age: local officers were deployed principally in inspecting the condition of cattle in transit at railway sidings, the treatment of barge horses and of ponies employed in coal mines. Such activities had been augmented by the massive growth of industry and urban populations, but in the focus on working animals they did not differ essentially from those that Richard Martin and the infant RSPCA had undertaken in the 1820s.[75]

If controlling the lower orders was never per se the primary aim of the RSPCA, the Society's focus on the most egregious and demoralising instances of cruelty witnessed in the streets inevitably brought to book men who worked directly with animals, such as hackney coachmen, cart and coal-wagon drivers, omnibus and cab drivers and cattle drovers. The offences of the wealthy classes might be equally grave, but they were less visible than those of such men, and hence aroused less spontaneous public revulsion. Most occurred on private property, where the RSPCA had no right of access, and where witnesses willing to testify in court were difficult to obtain. Moreover, upper-class cruelties often involved the pursuit of 'wild' animals (even carted stags kept in captivity for hunting and the hares and rabbits used in coursing competitions were thus designated), and these were not protected by the existing anti-cruelty laws.[76] Hunting was anyway treated as a special case, hedged round with ancient traditions that supposedly extenuated its cruelties. On one occasion in 1870–1871 the RSPCA – stirred by the indignation expressed in local newspaper reports and by the protests against field sports in the correspondence columns of its own journal *Animal World* – did venture to prosecute a hunt. However, this was for cruelty to the horses (two had died of exhaustion) rather than cruelty to a fox; the Society insisted nervously that it was 'endeavouring to suppress an excess and not to put down "sport"'. The magistrate nevertheless dismissed the case on the grounds that 'there was not sufficient cruelty shown to incur the penalties of the Act of Parliament' … 'If cruelty were exercised in this case, every day and every week cruelty was exercised in the hunting field, and the Society would have to prosecute a great many persons'. The grandees involved would, furthermore, often be closely connected with the local magistracy.[77] Many other cruelties imputed to moneyed people were indirect, or they were sins of omission rather than commission – for example, passive acquiescence in the behaviour of coachmen or cab drivers, who lashed tired horses without hindrance or reproof. 'Wanton' cruelty within the terms of the Act was then difficult to prove. Furthermore, the privileged classes were well represented among the committee members, patrons and patronesses of the RSPCA itself, as well as in the Lords and Commons. When the political radical Flora Tristan visited London in 1842, she expressed her contempt for such people and for their philanthropic pretensions, in a reference to the Society:

> People … deceived by its title and prospectus might easily believe that the members … were universal benefactors. Fancy considering the welfare of horses, donkeys and dogs! Think how generous they must be towards their fellow men! … Just another piece of humbug; this Society consists of members of the riding, hunting, horse-dealing and carriage-owning confraternity, whose aim is to keep a *closer watch* on the menials employed to tend their precious animals.[78]

In his *Manifesto of the Communist Party* (1848), Karl Marx characterised 'members of societies for the prevention of cruelty to animals' as types of the left-leaning bourgeoisie, anxious to preserve the status quo by 'redressing social grievances'.[79] Among leaders of the progressive intelligentsia, John Stuart Mill was notably more sympathetic to the RSPCA, of which he was a lifelong member and benefactor. As we have seen, Mill, while generally resistant to any interference of government in the private sphere, made an exception in the case of 'those unfortunate slaves and victims of the most brutal part of mankind, the lower animals'. However, when he was invited to take on the honorific post of an RSPCA vice president in 1868, he declined, feeling that it was inconsistent with his 'principles of action' to identify himself 'to any greater extent with the management, while it is thought necessary or advisable to limit the Society's operations to the offences committed by the uninfluential classes of society'.[80]

In this 'respect of persons', as Mill called it, the Society was evincing once again the pragmatism and caution it had made *its* 'principles of action'. Respect for public opinion meant, in practice, respect for the utterances of the articulate classes who dominated parliament, the judiciary, landed society, the business world, the columns of the *Times* – and RSPCA membership rolls: without the financial and moral support of the wealthy classes no action against cruelty of *any* kind would have been possible. The opinions of lower-class people about abuse of animals and about the activities of the Society were little regarded by the reformers, and are therefore, alas, very difficult for the historian to establish. Attitudes must have varied widely, however, not only between men and women, but between the 'respectable', often chapel-going people in working communities and the desperately downtrodden and demoralised. The poor *needed* to over-exert their animals, if they were to scratch a living; but this bitter truth was not always evident to their accusers. Certainly the people who set the direction of the animal protection movement – high-minded and moneyed evangelicals, together with Quaker and Unitarian merchants and bankers and their wives and daughters, had much difficulty in comprehending or even becoming acquainted at first hand with the intricate symbiotic relationships between the poor and their animals, dwelling in the closest physical proximity with one another in the modern city.[81] As picturesquely described by writers like Henry Mayhew and James Greenwood, it was a partnership in toil and often in suffering and privation, variously encompassing affectionate intimacy, callous exploitation and disregard, and downright cruelty.[82]

Horses and donkeys were worked to the limit of their strength and beyond it, but so were their handlers. Even a diseased or lame draught horse might still

72

TO THE

FRIENDS OF HUMANITY.

Suffer me to call your attention to the dreadful cruelty
exercised on horses in our dust-carts, in our water carts, in
our light vans, and in the carts which carry the wash for
cows. The vans are light in themselves, but when loaded
with heavy goods, the weight is very considerable, and in
general, the poor animals condemned to draw them are old
and weak. They are sadly beaten at the first setting off, if
not afterwards; and when they return unloaded, the men
get into the van to rest themselves, but the poor horses are
made to trot, although ready to drop with fatigue.

As to the dust-cart horses, it is dreadful to see them,—
weak, old, lame: some, if they have a second horse, very
small, put to such heavy work; for the dust-carts are large,
and the load is great when they are full.

Next, I name the water-carts. The horses put to these
are as wretched as to the dust-carts; they get sadly beaten,

6 'The dreadful cruelty exercised on horses in our dust-carts', anonymous wood engraving
from the RSPCA's tenth annual report for 1836.

keep a family from destitution. A leaflet addressed *To the Friends of Humanity* that was inserted in the RSPCA's annual reports featured a wood engraving of a skeletal dust-cart horse – 'weak, old, lame' – but mercilessly beaten to make it drag its heavy load (figure 6).[83] Yet an engraving of a London dust-yard in Greenwood's *Unsentimental Journeys* (figure 7) shows ragged female 'cinder-pickers' alongside such broken-down horses – women who laboured in all weathers, picking through 'great mounds of ordinary dustbin muck' for sale-able items, just as many women collected the faeces of dogs for sale to tanners.[84] Even in cities, pigs, dairy cows and poultry lived in the back yards or tenements of their owners, and were fed on waste products such as domestic garbage.[85] Dogs pulled heavy trucks or carts through the streets, or fought to the death in taverns to earn money for their owners, or wore skirts and danced on their hind legs to extract halfpennies from the crowd, or were turned loose to forage for survival as best they could. Pauper children, almost as houseless as stray dogs, caught wild birds, reptiles and small mammals to sell in the street; and most of these animals quickly died.[86]

Worst of all were the facts revealed in the press and in evidence to a Commons select committee in 1832, relative to the treatment of domestic animals. The appalling mutilation of fighting dogs in one establishment was only stopped when, according to the owner (who had a side line as a brothel keeper), 'A gentleman got a parcel of ladies to sign a petition against them'. Meanwhile women of another caste – the poorest of the poor – were the main operators in the trade of stealing cats, stunning and skinning them alive in back alleys, in order to sell their coats, apparently at threepence each, for processing and marketing by 'respectable' furriers. At one London Magistrates' Court in 1832, it was reported that a young woman 'of mild aspect' had been found 'with thirteen cat-skins in her possession'; fifty flayed bodies blocked a nearby drain and five still-living animals had been thrown into a privy.[87] Only the affluent could afford to sympathise greatly with their sufferings, and were horrified by what they took to be the callousness or indifference of the poor. However, Mary Bayly (friend of Mary Sewell and of her daughter Anna, author of *Black Beauty*), in *Ragged Homes and How to Mend Them* (1859) described the shanty towns of west London as a 'Slough of Despond' where the human inhabitants, deprived of moral and religious instruction, could hardly be expected to rise above the level of their own grimy pigs and poultry.[88]

Many of the barbaric practices which were described in 1832, and out-lawed in the more comprehensive anti-cruelty Act of 1835, were evidently functions of economic necessity. They were linked by complex patterns of

MR. DODD'S DUST-YARD.

7 'Mr. Dodd's dust-yard', anonymous wood engraving from James Greenwood's *Unsentimental Journeys*, 1867.

interdependence to the commercial life of London, salvaging and recycling its waste products, and catering to the amusements and luxuries of the privileged classes. Unconscious of these circumstances, many reformers could see only the revolting cruelties of an ignorant and savage underclass, which wounded their sensibilities on every foray into the streets. They were unable to understand a form of interaction with animals that differed absolutely from their own religious and paternalist solicitude for dependent creatures. However, the RSPCA was certainly alive to these difficulties, and anxious to justify its own policies with respect to the behaviour of different social classes. At virtually every annual meeting of the 1830s and 1840s, the question of primary responsibility for cruelty was raised – if not by official speakers on the platform, then by dissenting voices from the floor. William Mackinnon MP, a RSPCA committee member, had chaired the parliamentary enquiry on animal cruelty referred to above, and in 1832 had introduced a bill to extend the 1822 Act (it was temporarily halted by loss of his seat in the Commons, but its provisions were embodied in Pease's Act of 1835). In his speeches, Mackinnon was always confident, like Lecky, that cruelty to animals was steadily diminishing under the influence of Christianity, 'the progress of civilisation' and the 'benevolence and philanthropy' of the educated classes, especially of his 'fair countrywomen' in the audience. However, barbaric behaviour still persisted among the ignorant lower orders, and it was they who needed both education and the restraint of the laws. Viscount Mahon, a noted sportsman, agreed; the business of the Society was to prosecute street cruelties, not to institute an 'inquisition into domestic life', or to infringe the rights of property, which would not be tolerated by public opinion. In any case, field sports were 'innocent amusements', if 'needless cruelty be not inflicted'.[89]

Other speakers disagreed, querying Mackinnon's assertions as to the social locus of cruelty and its steady diminution. Several thought that abuse of animals was neither limited to the labouring classes, nor showing any sign of decline. Revd John Styles believed that cruelty arose out of 'the depravity of human nature', which was not class-specific; and, alarmingly, 'in this country, which boasts of its humanity and its police, there is more cruelty exercised towards the brute creation than was ever exhibited or tolerated in the ages of acknowledged barbarism' – a thought that was expressed by many others.[90] Styles's book, *The Animal Creation: Its Claims on Our Humanity Stated and Enforced* (1839), developed out of an essay that had won the prize in a competition organised and judged by the RSPCA itself; yet in this work he did not hesitate to point out the cruelties of the rich, including hunting and racing, which, he alleged, *grew* with civilisation rather than diminishing.[91] Indeed, a focus on the sins of the wealthy classes – especially cruelty to horses and culinary practices involving avoidable pain to live animals – was common to all the competition essays, in striking contrast to the social slant of the RSPCA's prosecutions.[92] This pointed emphasis was perhaps a tacit acknowledgement that the offences in question were beyond the reach of the law; but the consciences of educated and cultured men – supposed to be tenderer than those of the poor – might yet respond to peer pressure and public obloquy. At the RSPCA's 1835 and 1836 annual meetings, Thomas Butts Junior mentioned the cruelty of subjecting horses and ponies to road races against time for a 'wretched wager', 'wanton furious riding or driving' and steeplechasing, such as was often reported disapprovingly in the *New Sporting Magazine*. 'These with many similar cruelties, which harrow our feelings, and make the gentler class of society', that is, women, 'hate their opposite fellow creatures, may be repressed, nay even exterminated, by that one powerful engine – the force of public opinion'. Other forms of cruel conduct were less tractable, however, because they arose from hard-nosed commercial greed, notably that of the rival coaching companies.[93] John Wilks similarly blamed business interests, 'operating in the House of Commons', for the failure of successive attempts to reform or remove Smithfield market, where the cramped and chaotic conditions necessitated violent goading of the animals; and Robert Batson thought that cruelty was actually increasing, due to 'the *competition* which exists in every quarter ... poor people are driven to make greater exertions to earn a subsistence, and these exertions are principally obtained from the animals under their charge'.[94]

More was involved in these debates, published in the Society's annual reports, than self-justifying responses to the routine accusations of social bias raised by journalists and correspondents in the press. The differing analyses of the causes of cruelty to animals exposed a political divide. Mackinnon was the author of a book *On the Rise, Progress, and Present State of Public Opinion* (1828), which defined public opinion as 'a sentiment that depends on the degree of information and wealth, which together may be styled civilization' ... 'that sentiment on any given subject which is entertained by the best informed, most intelligent, and most moral persons in the community'. For Mackinnon this association of enlightenment with wealth obviated the old distinctions between people of inherited rank and the commercial or middle classes enriched by industrialisation: and the growing importance of the latter was, he believed, the key to Britain's social and political superiority to other nations. Public opinion, thus defined, was wholly distinct from the 'popular clamour' arising from the passions of the ignorant labouring classes, who must be rigorously excluded from the franchise.[95] Mackinnon's pronouncements at the RSPCA's meetings, as to the progress in kindness to animals that might be expected – that was indeed evident – from the growing moral influence of the prosperous middle orders, were of a piece with his general political views, and attuned to the historical theories of writers like Lecky. They were generally cheered and echoed by many others connected with the RSPCA, from the president downwards. But how far did the experience of the Society bear them out?

From the mid-century, it became increasingly clear that, as Wilks and Batson had argued, the main obstacles to progress in the humane treatment of animals were neither original sin nor the benighted state of the lower orders, but rather the effects of uncontrolled urbanisation and a fast-developing capitalist society. Those conditions were recognised as inexorable. Indeed, many recent historians, following in the footsteps of Flora Tristan and Karl Marx, have accused nineteenth-century animal defenders of ritual breast-beating: a wish to palliate the crueller effects of capitalism in a marginal and harmless way – 'smoothing the rougher features of laissez-faire' – as a means of protecting and maintaining an economic system from which they profited. Expressions of concern for animals could, they allege, even be a ploy to distract attention from the unmitigated hardships of exploited industrial workers.[96] However, as Michael Pollan has suggested, to witness the fearful suffering of animals used in intensive, industrialised farming is to be offered 'a nightmarish glimpse of what capitalism can look like in the absence of moral or regulatory constraint'.[97] In the nineteenth century as much as in the twenty-first, the cruel exploitation of animals could embody and painfully bring home the malign effects of untrammelled business competition for humans and animals alike. Moreover, the fact that such abuses could be widely condoned as societal conventions or commercial necessities – could coexist with the decencies of civilised behaviour – raised uncomfortable thoughts about the very nature and causation of cruelty to animals, which could no longer be treated as simply a product of ignorance, or as the hallmark of a *wholly* evil and unregenerate persona. A writer of 1865 remarked that an individual's 'instinct of cruelty' to animals, or even just indifference to their suffering, was entirely compatible with acts of kindness to fellow-humans: and a reputation for such kindness could (on the supposition of consistency in character) make many cruelties to animals seem unobjectionable.[98] Nevertheless, Victorians shocked and often genuinely moved by the sorry state of livestock and working animals that they saw around them were led to question the assumption that public morality and humane feelings were progressing in step with 'the march of mind', technological advances and wealth creation. Indeed, at the RSPCA's annual meeting in 1841, its president, the Earl of Carnarvon, who had recently travelled in the near East, remarked that animals were treated more kindly in Moslem peasant societies than in supposedly Christian, civilised Britain.[99]

There were many egregious examples of failings specific to a capitalist and increasingly technological society. Horses were cruelly exploited in large-scale engineering projects such as the embankment of the Thames and the construction of railway viaducts, as well as in the increased traffic in freight along canals and to and from railway stations.[100] The demand for speed on the high roads and in urban transport also put excessive demands on carriage horses, especially those used in hired chaises. Henry Curling in his *Lashing for the Lashers* (1851) detected a steady deterioration in the treatment of London cab and omnibus horses, due to the greed of the firms or gang-masters employing the drivers – 'their cry is only for money'. Yet wealthy passengers turned a blind eye: even 'delicate and tender-hearted ladies … 'sit smiling'.[101] So also the vested interests of wholesale meat traders and of the City of London Corporation, which profited from tolls and dues levied on users of the Smithfield site, were now recognised as the fundamental cause of the cruelties committed there. As 'John Bull' wrote, in *An Enquiry into the Present State of Smithfield Cattle Market* (1848), the 'clinging pertinacity of an avaricious monopoly' was chiefly responsible for 'the furious blow, the choking rope, and unrelenting punishment' of the animals penned into that congested space on market days.[102]

In 1849, awareness of such indirect cruelties led to an emendation of the animal protection laws, making employers answerable for offences which they caused to be committed by their staff; but the difficulties of establishing a consciously cruel intent remained.[103] Men 'of wealth, name, and position' were outwardly respectable – '"all that could be desired"' in a civilised country, and thus their agency in the infliction of cruelty was not readily apparent.[104] This was especially the case when live cattle, sheep and poultry suffered during transportation. In order to supply the meat markets of the major cities, they were now imported in ever larger numbers from Ireland, mainland Europe and the United States, packed tightly into trains and boats for their long journeys without food or water, so that they arrived exhausted, fractured or bruised, and sometimes died on the way. Anonymous eyewitnesses of cruel behaviour were always ready to write to the *Times* with complaints of RSPCA inaction, but much less ready to respond to the Society's pleas to identify themselves, appear in court and give evidence. Indeed, throughout the nineteenth century, RSPCA prosecutions depended far more on the agency of the Society's inspectors and the regular police than it did on that of private individuals, who were often unwilling to offend interested parties by their testimony, especially when the accused were high-ranking men; and the inspectors and constables, who were relatively few in number and still had no general right to enter private premises, were very restricted in what they could accomplish.

Just as such cruelties originating in industrialisation and urbanisation emerged, the demands that the cities made on the countryside also became evident in greatly increased trapping of wild songbirds to supply the market for caged pets, and in wholesale shooting of seabirds for the plumage trade.[105] Such developments must be set alongside the continuing reluctance of Mackinnon's 'most moral persons in the community' to curb the more notorious cruelties of the moneyed classes, such as trap pigeon shooting, steeplechasing, and road racing of horses and ponies for wagers. Since all these upper-class pursuits involved heavy gambling, they lacked the unassailable prestige of traditional field sports, but still proved resistant to press criticism – and to the pleas of the RSPCA, which felt unable to act against the powerfully-placed organisers. The manifestation of double standards was especially embarrassing at a time when popular revolutions abroad and pressure for a widening of the franchise in Britain (partly achieved in the Representation of the People Act 1867) exacerbated class feeling. Trap pigeon shooting, in particular, was, according to the *Times*, 'battue shooting of the poorest type', its offensiveness 'aggravated rather than redeemed by the attendance of ladies' who seemingly had no concern for the acute suffering of wounded birds.[106] But even the commercialisation of shooting on the great estates, in particular the growing fashion for aristocratic battues with huge kills of game species, notoriously involved a painful and lingering death for the many birds left wounded in the field. There were also many acknowledged cruelties in the trapping and destruction of 'vermin' by gamekeepers. Emma and Charles Darwin produced a pamphlet on the subject, and Emma approached the RSPCA in 1863 with the idea of sponsoring a competition for the design of a more humane trap, but she was later very disappointed to learn that none of the exhibited models proved acceptable to the sporting lobby. The existing steel-toothed traps, which condemned animals to hours of terror, agony and crushed limbs before the gamekeeper finished them off, remained a 'necessity', which the Society was apparently unwilling or unable to challenge, and indeed their use continued into the twentieth century.[107] Meanwhile the growing power of the scientific community made itself felt in a bold expansion of vivisection for physiological research, leading to sharp divisions in public opinion and a deep crisis in the animal protection movement. The RSPCA continued

8 'Distribution of Prizes, and Presentation of Delegates, at the late Jubilee Meeting' of the RSPCA, wood-engraved illustration in *Animal World* (1 September 1874).

to prosecute offenders whose cruelties were straightforwardly covered by the animal protection laws, but even offences committed by working men showed little sign of diminution: the golden age of universal benevolence foreseen by Lecky, Mackinnon and many others had failed to materialise.

In 1874, nevertheless, the RSPCA celebrated its jubilee in a triumphant spirit by hosting an international congress of societies established in various countries for the prevention of cruelty to animals, among which it claimed both primacy and moral leadership. The annual meeting of the Society coincided with this event, and was a particularly grandiose affair, held in the Royal Albert Hall and attended by some ten thousand people. Coming soon after the Society's move to a more prestigious building in Jermyn Street, the launch of a new journal, *Animal World*, and the establishment of a ladies' committee to oversee an expanded educational programme (discussed in chapter 3), the ceremony marked a key moment in the Society's history. Several platform speakers noted the change of fortune since the difficult and obscure early days. Now public opinion was on the Society's side; prosecutions for cruelty had laid a stigma on its perpetrators, while the march of mind had produced 'a kind of triumph to the humane principles'. That triumph was symbolised by the presence of royalty: the Grand Duchess Maria Alexandrovna of Russia had become a daughter-in-law of Queen Victoria by her marriage to the Duke of Edinburgh, and presented prizes to over four hundred metropolitan schoolchildren who had produced the best essays on kindness to animals in the Society's newly established annual competition (figure 8). There was organ-playing, hymn-singing and interminable (apparently often inaudible) addresses, including lavish tributes to the lady-organisers; luckily the children were provided with refreshments. But no amount of stirring rhetoric, mutual congratulation, clapping and cheering, buns and oranges, could disguise the fact that many cruel practices remained stubbornly endemic to British society. This became evident when the Society's secretary, John Colam, read out a long list of successful prosecutions. So large a number of convictions spoke well of the Society's 'watchfulness', and people clapped accordingly:

> but at the same time it was clear that the more numerous convictions implied continuance or increase of cruelty to animals, and that could hardly be applauded by an assembly of philanthropists, and many, seeing this, broke up their applause into bits, and it died away curiously.[108]

'Philanthropists' had come to the painful realisation that cruelty to animals would not be eliminated by civilising or punishing the lower classes: it was intrinsic to the systems of production and commercial competition that provided the prosperity of the nation, and was unlikely to yield to moral persuasion. Yet it seemed like a blot, an anomaly, in a country that prided itself on high culture and programmes of political and social reform; the very visible sufferings of animals, like the squalor of the slums, discredited the notion that material and ethical progress were associated, or even compatible.

Work for the RSPCA as a springboard for women's independent initiatives

In this situation, reformers began to think that women had a key part to play in animal protection, the part that Lecky had attributed or allotted to them. Only women, traditionally more sympathetic to animals and solicitous for their well-being than men were, could provide a counterweight or corrective to the cruelties arising from the competitiveness and aggression of the male-dominated public sphere. They were to seek forms of intervention on behalf of animals that sidestepped, rather than confronted, business interests, notably by establishing various forms of animal welfare and 'humane education'. Nevertheless, the female originators of these enterprises remained greatly dependent on the RSPCA's resources, experience and guidance; though often criticised or challenged, the Society continued to form the institutional backbone of animal protection in Britain.[109] As we shall see, the RSPCA's Ladies' Committee in London, and similar women's committees attached to RSPCA regional branches, often provided a moral lead on contentious animal protection issues that went beyond their prescribed educative functions. Moreover, nearly all the female pioneers of Victorian animal charities whom I discuss in later chapters – Mary Tealby of the Battersea Dogs' Home, Catherine Smithies of the Band of Mercy, Eliza Phillips and Margaretta Lemon of the SPB and a great many others – were veteran volunteer workers for the RSPCA, and in return they were fully supported by the latter in their new ventures. The London offices of the RSPCA were made available for their meetings, and the Society's secretary John Colam often joined their committees or collected subscriptions on their behalf, giving them credibility in the eyes of the public. Indeed, RSPCA annual reports tracked their progress in the manner of an encouraging and proud parent. In 1897, for example, Colam reminded the audience at the RSPCA's annual meeting that the SPB, 'This excellent association ... was established in your Board Room, your Secretary occupying the chair on the occasion', and had since been 'wisely developed, mainly by the excellent and indefatigable services of the honorary secretary, Mrs Lemon'.[110] The RSPCA report for 1898–1899 carried a more general review by Colam of 'the work of kindred associations, offshoots of your Society'; 'it may be said that the satisfactory results attained by them amply confirms the wisdom of dividing labour which is found to be necessary for the securing the reasonable protection of animals', and he therefore commended 'all to the benevolent support of animal lovers'.[111] Through such friendly collaborations, women gradually took on more prominent roles in the animal protection movement as a whole than the (then) exclusively male senior hierarchy of the RSPCA itself would lead one to expect.

In this process of growth and diversification, the relationship between the London headquarters of the RSPCA and its countrywide network of members and affiliates was of critical importance, and sometimes under considerable strain. Female supporters of the Society – already conspicuous in the early years, as we have seen – grew steadily in numbers and influence over the century; by the late 1890s they represented nearly 70 per cent of all subscribers, and, as far as is ascertainable, this ratio was fairly typical of the membership of individual provincial branches, with women often taking on the role of local honorary secretaries.[112] The distinctive and often outspoken views of women on matters of animal cruelty therefore had greater scope for expression at the grassroots than they had at the national level; and not all their initiatives fell within uncontroversial areas of animal welfare and protection, of a kind that the RSPCA could unhesitatingly support and adopt. It is clear that there was a degree of friction over especially sensitive questions such as vivisection and blood sports, where women's antipathy tended to be more 'extreme' or vehement than that of the men who comprised the RSPCA's executive committee. Enthusiastic regional activists evidently became frustrated by their lack of influence on the Society's policies as formulated in London, and they wanted a stronger voice in the conduct of affairs.[113] After several years of resistance to their pressure for enlargement of the executive committee's membership, the RSPCA capitulated: it was agreed in 1906 that the committee should become a council, which was to include representatives of RSPCA branches. The branches were grouped into sixteen regional clusters for the purpose of electing their representatives, and eight of the chosen delegates, half the total, were women.[114] In this way, almost inadvertently, women finally gained admission to the policy-forming body of the RSPCA, over eighty years after its foundation.

In the following chapters, I trace the course of women's immense efforts to relieve the suffering of animals in the later Victorian period, efforts which led up to this epochal change in the prevailing institutional culture. Through the educational activities of the RSPCA's ladies' committee and the Band of Mercy, the founding of welfare charities, authorship of polemical and imaginative literature and open militancy in animal causes, women arguably became the moving force in the animal protection movement in Britain; but, as we shall see, their peculiar difficulties when operating in the public sphere did not go away.

Notes

1 William Edward Hartpole Lecky, *History of the Rise and Influence of the Spirit of Rationalism in Europe*, 2 vols (London: Longmans, Green, 3rd edn, 1866), vol. 1, pp. 331–4.

2 Charles Darwin, *The Descent of Man, and Selection in Relation to Sex*, 1871; 2nd edn 1879, ed. James Moore and Adrian Desmond (London: Penguin, 2004), p. 147.

3 Herbert Spencer, 'Psychology of the sexes', *Popular Science Monthly*, 4 (November 1873), 30–8, corresponding to part of ch. XV in Spencer's *The Study of Sociology* (1873).

4 *Statutes*, 3 Geo. IV, Cap. 71, 22 July 1822, 'Act to Prevent the Cruel and Improper Treatment of Cattle'. Shevawn Lynam, *Humanity Dick: A Biography of Richard Martin, M.P. 1754–1834* (London: Hamish Hamilton, 1975), pp. 197f. Hilda Kean, *Animal Rights: Political and Social Change in Britain since 1800* (London: Reaktion Books, 1998), pp. 33–5. Robert W. Malcolmson, *Popular Recreations in English Society 1700–1850* (Cambridge: Cambridge University Press, 1973), p. 124. Frederick William Hackwood, *A History of West Bromwich*, ed. Alan A. Vernon (Studley: Brewin Books, 2001), p. 291.

5 Roswell Cheney McCrea, *The Humane Movement: A Descriptive Survey* (New York: Columbia University Press, 1910), p. 5.

6 Edward G. Fairholme and Wellesley Pain, *A Century of Work for Animals* (London: John Murray, 1924), pp. 49f. Arthur W. Moss, *Valiant Crusade: The History of the R.S.P.C.A* (London: Cassell, 1961), pp. 22–3. James Turner, *Reckoning with the Beast: Animals, Pain, and Humanity in the Victorian Mind* (Baltimore and London: Johns Hopkins University Press, 1980), pp. 40f.

7 *Statutes*, 5 & 6 William IV, Cap. 59, 9 September 1835; 'Act to Consolidate and Amend the Several Laws Relating to the Cruel and Improper Treatment of Animals', introduced by Joseph Pease. J.E.G. Montmorency, 'State protection of animals at home and abroad', *Law Quarterly Review*, 18:69 (January 1902), 34–5.

8 RSPCA *Report* (1841), p. 56, speech of Montague Bere. Fairholme and Pain, *Century of Work*, pp. 89–90.

9 Roland Knyvet Wilson, *History of Modern English Law* (London, Oxford and Cambridge: Rivingtons, 1875), pp. 234–5.

10 Brian Harrison in *Peaceable Kingdom: Stability and Change in Modern Britain* (Oxford: Clarendon Press, 1982), pp. 116, 127, 137, refers to the RSPCA's 'ultimate aim' as being to 'convert the masses' and 'civilize manners', thereby buttressing the moral authority of the wealthy classes, and privileging their 'sentimental' attitude to animals, which he associates especially with women. Cf. Keith Thomas, *Man and the Natural World: Changing Attitudes in England 1500–1800*, first published 1983 (London: Penguin

Books, 1984), pp. 185–6. Harriet Ritvo, in *The Animal Estate: the English and Other Creatures in the Victorian Age* (Cambridge, MA: Harvard University Press, 1987), chapter 3, refines and develops this argument.

11 Michael J.D. Roberts, *Making English Morals: Voluntary Association and Moral Reform in England, 1787–1886* (Cambridge and New York: Cambridge University Press, 2004), pp. 109–111, 113–14.

12 Samuel Carter Hall, *Retrospect of a Long Life*, 2 vols (London: Richard Bentley and Son, 1883), vol. 1, pp. 228–9. RSPCA *Report* (1836), p. 18, speech of George Raymond, and (1842), pp. 31–2, speech of J.A. Warre. Even in the 1830s many magistrates were evidently unwilling to convict men brought before their courts by the RSPCA: see for example *Report* (1836), pp. 55f., 62.

13 'Society for the Prevention of Cruelty to Animals', *The Times* (17 June 1824), p. 3.

14 Ibid. Martin believed that the 1822 Act had already lessened this practice.

15 *Part the First, of an Address to the Public, from the Society for the Suppression of Vice* (London: The Society, 1803), p. 44; Part II, pp. 3, 68–72, 91. Michael J.D. Roberts, 'The Society for the Suppression of Vice and its early critics, 1802–1812', *Historical Journal*, 26:1 (1983), 159–76, and *Making English Morals*, pp. 109–10.

16 Sydney Smith, review of *Statement of the Proceedings of the Society for the Suppression of Vice* and the Society's *Address to the Public*, both of 1804, in *Edinburgh Review*, 13:26 (January 1809), 333–43.

17 Windham's speech, discussed in our Introduction, quoted Sydney Smith's article, which may actually have been prompted by the debate on an anti-cruelty law: *The Parliamentary Debates from the Year 1803* (London: T.C. Hansard, 1812), vol. XIV for 1809, col. 1028.

18 Prospectus inserted in the reports of the Liverpool RSPCA from 1872 onwards. On this combination of law-enforcement and education, see 'A.H.', 'On cruelty to animals', Letter 1, *Gentleman's Magazine* (May 1825), 397–400.

19 *The Voice of Humanity: for the Communication and Discussion of All Subjects relative to the Conduct of Man towards the Inferior Animal Creation*, 3 vols, 1830–1833; prospectus prefacing vol. 2. See also RSPCA *Records* (vol. 5 for 1830–1846), pp. 1–21.

20 Lewis Gompertz, 'Legislation to animals', *The Animals' Friend, or the Progress of Humanity*, 6 (1838), p. 2.

21 Lewis Gompertz, *Moral Inquiries on the Situation of Man and of Brutes*, 1824, ed. Peter Singer (Fontwell: Centaur Press, 1992), and *Fragments in Defence of Animals, and Essays on Morals, Soul, and Future State* (London: W. Horsell, 1852).

22 RSPCA *Report* (1832), pp. 5, 58. Details of the preceding dispute emerged in *Report of an Extra Meeting of the Society for the Prevention of Cruelty to Animals January 13th 1832*. See also the Wesleyan Methodist *Christian Advocate*, 3 (1832), pp. 29, 52, 140, 237 (strongly partisan for the APRH). Gompertz gave his version of events in 'Sketch of the societies for the prevention of cruelty to animals'. *Fragments*, pp. 173–80. Turner, *Reckoning with the Beast*, pp. 41–3.

23 For Gompertz's notion of the eternal 'personal identity' of every animal, and his arguments against consumption of meat, dairy products and eggs: *Moral Inquiries*, pp. 69f., 83f., 97f.

24 John Stuart Mill, *Principles of Political Economy, with Some of Their Applications to Social Philosophy*, 2 vols (London: John W. Parker, 1848), vol. 2, p. 534.

25 McCrea, *Humane Movement*, p. 117.

26 Dix Harwood, *Love for Animals and How It Developed in Great Britain*, first published

1928, ed. Rod Preece and David Fraser (Lewiston, Queenston, Lampeter: Mellen Animal Rights Library Series, vol. 10, c.2002), pp. x, 368.

27 For example, Thomas Ellis, 'The Royal Society for the Prevention of Cruelty to Animals. To John Colam', *The National Reformer, Secular Advocate and Freethought Journal*, new series 6:3 (15 January 1865), 35.

28 'Christian retrospect no. VII. Close of the session of Parliament', *Wesleyan Methodist Magazine for the Year 1822*, 3rd series, 1 (September 1822), 582.

29 Anon. [David Edwards], *Our Moral Relation to the Animal Kingdom: Being a Digest of the Statements of the Bible in Respect Thereto* (London: Morgan and Chase, c.1862), and Revd Arthur Penrhyn Stanley, Dean of Westminster, *The Creation of Man: A Sermon* (Oxford and London: Parker, 1865): both works sponsored by the RSPCA. The ladies of the Liverpool RSPCA offered children a prize for the best collection of biblical texts bearing on kindness to animals (Liverpool Record Office 179 ANI 6/1 minutes of the ladies' committee meeting, 27 March 1874). Chien-hui Li, 'A union of Christianity, humanity, and philanthropy: the Christian tradition and the prevention of cruelty to animals in nineteenth-century England', *Society & Animals*, 8:3 (2000), 265–85, and her *Mobilizing Traditions in the First Wave of the British Animal Defence Movement* (London: Palgrave Macmillan, 2019), pp. 32–6.

30 Genesis, 1:26. Matthew's gospel, 10:31.

31 William Cowper, *The Task*, 1785, Book VI, 'The Winter Walk at Noon', lines 581–6. On Cowper's 'most beloved writer' status in the early nineteenth century: Leonore Davidoff and Catherine Hall, *Family Fortunes: Men and Women of the English Middle Class, 1780–1850* (London and New York: Routledge, revised edn, 2002), pp. 157–8.

32 Review of *Animals' Friend*, 7 (1839) and of Grantley Berkeley's *Reply to Dr. Styles's Prize Essay*, in *Monthly Review*, new series, 3:1 (September–December 1839), 77–92.

33 RSPCA, *Report* (1842), pp. 15–16.

34 Harrison, *Peaceable Kingdom*, pp. 103f.

35 RSPCA, *Report* (1879), p. 92.

36 RSPCA executive committee minutes, book 1, p. 100, meeting of 20 July 1829. It is unclear whether a proposal (28 January 1830, pp. 113–16) for a subcommittee of ladies and gentlemen 'to obtain sermons from clergymen of various denominations' refers to the same initiative. Moss, *Valiant Crusade*, p. 24.

37 RSPCA executive committee minutes, book 1, p. 117, meeting of 5 April 1830. This resolution immediately followed a vote of thanks to the ladies for their efforts.

38 *Address to the Public, from the Society for the Suppression of Vice*, Part 1, p. 39. Charles Stokes Dudley, *An Analysis of the System of the Bible Society, throughout Its Various Parts* (London: R. Watts, 1821), especially pp. 343–9, 352, 357, 362–3, 374. Roberts, *Making English Morals*, p. 76.

39 Speech of Sir James Mackintosh at a 'General Meeting of the Anti-Slavery Society and Its Friends', 23 April 1831, in *The Anti-Slavery Reporter*, 80 (9 May 1831), 257. George Stephen, *Antislavery Recollections: In a Series of Letters, Addressed to Mrs Beecher Stowe* (London: Thomas Hatchard, 1854), pp. 196–8. Louis Billington and Rosamund Billington, '"A burning zeal for righteousness": women in the British anti-slavery movement, 1820–1860', in Jane Rendall (ed.), *Equal or Different: Women's Politics 1800–1914* (Oxford: Blackwell, 1987). Moira Ferguson, *Subject to Others: British Women Writers and Colonial Slavery, 1670–1834* (London and New York: Routledge, 1992). Clare Midgley, *Women Against Slavery: The British Campaigns, 1780–1870* (London and New York: Routledge, 1992).

40 Dudley, *Analysis*, pp. 343, 348, 382.

41 Revd John Owen, *The History of the Origin and First Ten Years of the British and Foreign Bible Society*, 2 vols (London: Tilling and Hughes, 1816), vol. 1, p. 468. Maurice James Quinlan, *Victorian Prelude: A History of English Manners 1700–1830* (New York: Columbia University Press, 1941, 1965), pp. 127–32.

42 'Memorial of Lucy Townsend' in *The Twenty-Second Report of the Ladies' Negro's Friend Society, for Birmingham, West Bromwich* [etc.] (1847), pp. 12–20. Midgley, *Women Against Slavery*, pp. 43f., 73, and her article on Lucy Townsend in the *Oxford Dictionary of National Biography* (British Academy and Oxford: Oxford University Press, 2004).

43 Library of Birmingham, MS 3173, records of the Birmingham and West Bromwich ladies' anti-slavery group. Bodleian Library, Oxford, MSS Brit. Emp. s.4,5, Lucy Townsend's scrap book and 'Autographs' album, containing drawings, prints, letters etc.

44 Bodleian Library, Oxford, MSS Brit. Emp. s.4, containing a printed *Card explanatory of the Contents of the Society's Work Bags*, these contents being extracts from the *Jamaica Gazette* etc. 'Memorial of Lucy Townsend', pp. 15–16. Midgley, *Women Against Slavery*, p. 57.

45 Susanna Watts's scrapbook in the Leicestershire Record Office, DE 8170/1, pp. 301–3 contains details of the countrywide petition; the Leicester ladies collected 3,025 signatures in little over a week, 'time not allowing more'. Charles Buxton (ed.), *Memoirs of Sir Thomas Fowell Buxton, Baronet* (London: John Murray, 1848), pp. 320–1. Stephen, *Antislavery Recollections*, pp. 196–7. Midgley, *Women Against Slavery*, pp. 65–9.

46 'Memorial of Lucy Townsend', p. 19.

47 'Society for the Suppression [*sic*] of Cruelty to Animals', *The Times* (4 July 1828), p. 4; the Society had received a letter from Revd Charles Townsend, describing this 'horrible barbarity'. RSPCA executive committee minutes, book 1, p. 94, meeting of 4 May 1829. RSPCA *Records* (vol. 3 for 1827–1830), pp. 26–7, indicates that four petitions against bull-baiting were sent to the Commons from Staffordshire in 1828, and one from West Bromwich. *Voice of Humanity*, 1 (1830), 50. *Animals' Friend*, 2 (1834), 19; 3 (1835), 6; 4 (1836), 4–5, 24; 5 (1837), 17. Gompertz, *Fragments*, p. 179. John F. Ede, *History of Wednesbury* (Wednesbury: Wednesbury Corporation, 1962), p. 155. Douglas A. Reid, 'Beasts and brutes: popular blood sports c.1780–1860', in Richard Holt (ed.), *Sport and the Working Class in Modern Britain* (Manchester and New York: Manchester University Press, 1990), pp. 12–28. Emma Griffin, *England's Revelry: A History of Popular Sports and Pastimes, 1660–1830* (Oxford and New York: Oxford University Press, 2005), pp. 146f., 224, 237f.

48 Bodleian Library, MSS Brit. Emp. s.5: 85, undated letter to Lucy Townsend from her daughter, saying she had paid a Mrs Heale '*the two Anti-cruelty sovereigns* you desired'. Heale collected subscriptions for the RSPCA; see *Report* (1832), p. 26. RSPCA executive committee minutes, book 1, p. 107, meeting of 22 September 1829: Lucy Townsend had written 'relative to Bull baiting'.

49 RSPCA executive committee minutes, book 1, p. 102, meeting of 20 August 1829.

50 Edna Healey, *Emma Darwin: The Inspirational Wife of a Genius* (London: Headline Book Publishing, 2002), p. 107. Adrian Desmond and James Moore, *Darwin's Sacred Cause: Race, Slavery and the Quest for Human Origins* (London: Allen Lane, 2009), pp. 60–1. Sarah Wedgwood was sister-in-law to Elizabeth (Bessy) Wedgwood, née Allen, who was the sister of Catherine (Kitty) Mackintosh.

51 Wedgwood Museum, Barlaston, Mosley Archive manuscript W/M 182: letter from Elizabeth Wedgwood to Emma Wedgwood, 19 December 1826.

52 *Animals' Friend*, 7 (1839), 25.

53 Anna M. Stoddart, *Elizabeth Pease Nichol* (London: J.M. Dent, 1899), pp. 215, 255, 279–81.

54 RSPCA *Reports* (1832), pp. 26–7; (1836), p. 111; (1837), p. 146. A MS notebook of 1909 in the RSPCA archive, CM/167, 'The history of the Society, summary of chief events in each year', records several important legacies from women in the early years.

55 RSPCA *Reports* (1832), pp. 11, 15; (1834), p. 22; (1835), p. 19. On the problems of women's admission to the meetings of philanthropic bodies: Davidoff and Hall, *Family Fortunes*, pp. 433–4.

56 RSPCA *Reports* (1832), pp. 14–15; (1833), pp. 17, 20; (1834), pp. 15, 22; (1835), p. 17; (1837), p. 30; (1840), p. 43.

57 Stoddart, *Elizabeth Pease Nichol*, pp. 107–8.

58 Anna Jameson, *Sisters of Charity, and The Communion of Labour: Two Lectures on the Social Employments of Women* (London: Longman, Brown, Green, Longmans, and Roberts, new edn, 1859), p. xvi.

59 RSPCA *Report* (1843), p. 21.

60 RSPCA *Report* (1841), p. 173. Brian Harrison calculates (*Peaceable Kingdom*, p. 137) that 470 out of 739 legacies to the RSPCA in the nineteenth century came from women – about 64 per cent.

61 RSPCA *Reports* (1840), p. 54; (1841), p. 56.

62 *Standard* (24 May 1832), in RSPCA *Records* (vol. 5 for 1830–1846), p. 18. 'Review of report of proceedings at the annual meeting of the Association for Promoting Rational Humanity [etc.]', *Baptist Magazine and Literary Review*, 24 (October 1832), 440. Kean, *Animal Rights*, pp. 66–7.

63 RSPCA executive committee minutes, book 1, pp. 98–100, meeting of 6 July 1829; pp. 112–13, 117, meeting of 28 January 1830.

64 RSPCA *Report* (1838), p. 37.

65 *Prospectus of the Association for Promoting Rational Humanity* (inserted in *Voice of Humanity* before vol. 3, c.1832), 7, and cf. vol. 3, 24. *Voice of Humanity*, 1 (1830), 37.

66 *Voice of Humanity*, 1 (1830), 37, 102–3.

67 *Animals' Friend*, 3 (1835), 6.

68 Ibid., 18–19, 30. Similarly, a Mrs Livingstone of Pentonville enabled the Animals' Friend Society to prosecute a knacker's yard guilty of gross cruelties: Kean, *Animal Rights*, p. 53.

69 Review of the *Voice of Humanity* in *London Literary Gazette*, 751 (11 June 1831), 369–70.

70 The RSPCA accused Wheeler of deceitfully establishing a rival organisation, and trying to divert funds to it for his own gain: RSPCA *Report* (1832), pp. 18–22. Gompertz believed that all Wheeler's accounts of successful prosecutions were bogus: *Animals' Friend*, 3 (1835), 8–9 and 4 (1836), 22.

71 *Animals' Friend*, 3 (1835), 19.

72 *John Bull*, 15:743 (8 March 1835), 77–8.

73 RSPCA *Report* (1839), pp. 10, 29, 39. Malcolmson, *Popular Recreations*, pp. 127–34. Kean, *Animal Rights*, p. 32. Griffin, *England's Revelry*, pp. 223f. The *Christian Advocate* promulgated the Wesleyan Methodists' opposition to baiting, especially in the many articles and letters in vol. 1 (1830).

74 RSPCA *Reports* (1869), p. 23; (1873), p. 21. Liverpool Record Office 179 ANI/9, Liverpool RSPCA *Report* (1873), pp. 9–10: cruelties to horses and mules accounted for 93 per cent of all successful prosecutions.

75 RSPCA *Report* (1832), pp. 28f. 'Royal Society for the Prevention of Cruelty to Animals', *Manchester Guardian* (26 March 1889), p. 12.

76 There was no legal protection for native wild mammals in Britain throughout the nineteenth century. Wild species in a captive state, such as menagerie and circus animals, were partly protected from cruelty by an Act of 1900.

77 RSPCA executive committee minutes, book 12, p. 20, meeting of 13 December 1870. RSPCA *Records* (vol. 12 for 1870–1872), pp. 57–63; action against Lord Middleton's hunt in Yorkshire. It transpired that one of the local magistrates, who declined to act, was the Hunt Secretary.

78 Jean Hawkes (ed.), *The London Journal of Flora Tristan 1842: The Aristocracy and the Working Class of England: A Translation of 'Promenades dans Londres'* (London: Virago, 1982), pp. 161–2. Kean, *Animal Rights*, p. 66.

79 Karl Marx, *Manifesto of the Communist Party* 1848, ed. Friedrich Engels (London: William Reeves, 1888): chapter 3, 'Socialist and communist Literature' (2), 'Conservative or bourgeois socialism'.

80 Francis E. Mineka and Dwight N. Lindley (eds), *The Later Letters of John Stuart Mill 1849–1873*, vol. 16 of *The Collected Works of John Stuart Mill* (London: Routledge and Kegan Paul, 1972), pp. 1423–4; letter 1271 to the RSPCA Secretary John Colam, 26 July 1868. There are frequent instances of press criticism of the RSPCA for class bias: for example 'A looker on', *The Times* (1 April 1844), p. 6; 'Cruel match Windsor, Wednesday April 24', *The Times* (25 April 1844), p. 6.

81 Cf. Kean, *Animal Rights*, pp. 30, 73f. Diana Donald, '"Beastly sights": the treatment of animals as a moral theme in representations of London, c.1820–1850', in Dana Arnold (ed.), *The Metropolis and Its Image: Constructing Identities for London, c.1750–1950* (Oxford: Blackwell, 1999).

82 Henry Mayhew, *London Labour and the London Poor*, 1851–1852; enlarged 4-vol. edn, 1861–1862; modern 4-vol. facsimile edn (London: Frank Cass, 1967). James Greenwood, *Unsentimental Journeys: Or, Byways of the Modern Babylon* (London: Ward, Lock, & Tyler, 1867).

83 RSPCA *Report* (1836), pp. 72–3. Mayhew also mentioned the gross overworking of rubbish carters' horses: *London Labour* (1967 edn), vol. 2, p. 292.

84 'Mr Dodd's dust-yard', Greenwood, *Unsentimental Journeys*, pp. 64f. A similar scene in Mayhew, *London Labour*, vol. 2, facing p. 208, shows a sow, ducks and a dog beside the piles of refuse.

85 Edwin Chadwick, ed. M.W. Flinn, *Report on the Sanitary Condition of the Labouring Population of Great Britain*, 1842 (Edinburgh: Edinburgh University Press, 1965), pp. 87, 108, 115, 189. Kean, *Animal Rights*, pp. 48–9, 74–5. Hannah Velten, *Beastly London: A History of Animals in the City* (London: Reaktion Books, 2013), pp. 27–8.

86 Mayhew, *London Labour* (1967 edn), vol. 2, p. 72.

87 *Reports from Committees* (Session 6 December 1831 to 16 August 1832), No. 667: *Report from the Committee on the 'Bill to consolidate and amend several Laws relating to the cruel and improper Treatment of Animals … .' with the Minutes of Evidence … Printed, 1 August 1832*, pp. 10, 13, 21. 'Guildhall' and 'State of the Law for the Prevention of Cruelty', on cases of cat skinning, *Christian Advocate*, 3:143 (24 September 1832), p. 310, and 3:145 (8 October 1832), p. 327. Fairholme and Pain, *Century of Work for Animals*, pp. 83–5.

88 Mary Bayly, *Ragged Homes and How to Mend Them*, 1859 (London: James Nisbet, 1860 edn), pp. 28, 35.

89 RSPCA *Reports* (1833), pp. 23–4; (1834), pp. 14–15, 33–5; (1835), pp. 25–6, 46–7; (1839), pp. 24, 31–2. Cf. RSPCA *Report* (1840), pp. 40, 45–6.

90 RSPCA *Reports* (1833), pp. 30–3; (1839), p. 50.

91 Revd John Styles, *The Animal Creation: Its Claims on Our Humanity Stated and Enforced* (London: Thomas Ward, 1839), pp. 22–58.

92 For example, David Mushet, in *The Wrongs of the Animal World* (London: Hatchard, 1839), condemns upper-class cruelties such as hunting, steeplechasing, trotting matches and overworking of stagecoach horses (pp. 91–101, 117, 121–3). William H. Drummond, in *The Rights of Animals, and Man's Obligation to Treat Them with Humanity* (London: John Mardon, Smallfield, Green and Dublin: Hodges and Smith, 1838), p. 94, blames cruelty on 'Gambling and the love of gain … love of sport … luxury and gluttony … love of science perverted' – i.e. vivisection.

93 RSPCA *Reports* (1835), pp. 43–4; (1836), pp. 33–5.

94 RSPCA *Reports* (1834), p. 44; (1836), p. 40.

95 William Alexander Mackinnon, *On the Rise, Progress, and Present State of Public Opinion, in Great Britain, and Other Parts of the World* (London: Saunders and Otley, 1828), pp. 1, 15, 184. Kean *Animal Rights*, pp. 64–5.

96 Thomas, *Man and the Natural World*, p. 187; Harrison, *Peaceable Kingdom*, p. 151; Turner, *Reckoning with the Beast*, pp. 56–7. Kathleen Kete (ed.), *A Cultural History of Animals* vol. 5: *In the Age of Empire* (Oxford and New York: Berg, 2007), Kete's introduction, p. 15.

97 Michael Pollan, 'An animal's place', *New York Times Magazine* (10 November 2002), reprinted in Anne Fadiman (ed.), *The Best American Essays 2003* (Boston and New York: Houghton Mifflin, 2003), pp. 190–211.

98 Anon., *Some Remarks on Cruelty to Animals, and the Principles in Human Nature from which That Vice Proceeds. In a Letter to a Friend* (London: S. Low, Son, & Marston, and Birmingham: Josiah Allen junior, 1865), pp. 19, 25, 35, 38.

99 RSPCA *Report* (1841), pp. 36–7.

100 Letter from the RSPCA Secretary John Colam about 'Ill-treatment of horses on the Thames embankment', *The Times* (6 July 1865), p. 10. On the abuse of draught horses on canal towpaths: Liverpool Record Office 179 ANI/9, RSPCA Liverpool branch, *Report* (1877), p. 12.

101 Henry Curling, *A Lashing for the Lashers; Being an Exposition of the Cruelties Practised Upon the Cab and Omnibus Horses of London* (London: W.N. Wright, 1851), pp. 14–15.

102 *An Enquiry into the Present State of Smithfield Cattle Market … by John Bull*, 2nd edn (London: James Ridgway, 1848), p. 10.

103 *Statutes*, 12 & 13 Victoria, Cap. 92, 'Act for the More Effectual Prevention of Cruelty to Animals'.

104 *The Times* (8 September 1869), p. 7.

105 Growing concern over the trapping and shooting of wild birds is discussed in our chapter 6.

106 Leading article in the *Times* (21 June 1871), p. 9. Velten, *Beastly London*, p. 95.

107 Emma and Charles Darwin, *An Appeal* (1863), privately printed leaflet from a text originally published in the *Bromley Record* and in *Gardeners' Chronicle and Agricultural Gazette* (29 August 1863), 821–2. The latter was signed 'C.D.', but correspondence reveals that it was Emma who raised the issue and suggested a RSPCA competition for an improved trap. Darwin Correspondence Project: letters 4294, 4355 and 4497 from Emma to William Darwin Fox (undated [September 1863]; 8 December 1863; 16 May

1864). See later reports on this issue in the *Times* (25 June 1869), p. 5; RSPCA *Reports* (1876), p. 26; (1878), p. 76; (1879), p 74; *Animal World*, 1:4 (1 January 1870), 65–6, 75. Henrietta Litchfield (ed.), *Emma Darwin: A Century of Family Letters 1792–1896*, 2 vols (New York: Appleton, 1915), vol. 2, pp. 178–80. Healey, *Emma Darwin*, pp. 265–8. Janet Browne, *Charles Darwin: The Power of Place* (London: Jonathan Cape, 2002), pp. 420–1.

108 *Illustrated London News*, 64:1818 (27 June 1874), 610. RSPCA *Report* (1874), pp. 17f., quoting *Saturday Review* and *Good Words*. Leading article on the Congress, *The Times* (22 June 1874), p. 11. 'Prevention of cruelty to animals', *The Times* (23 June 1874), p. 11.

109 McCrea, *Humane Movement*, p. 8.

110 RSPCA *Report* (1897), pp. 129–30; (1898–9), p. 133; (1899–1900), p. 127. An obituary of Colam in the RSPB's *Bird Notes and News*, 4:2 (24 June 1910), 19, spoke warmly of his 'cordial sympathy' for the Society's work, and the practical assistance he had given.

111 RSPCA *Report* (1898–9), pp. 119–20.

112 For the subscription statistics, see my Introduction, note 4: 69 per cent of named subscribers to the RSPCA were women.

113 RSPCA *Report* (1896), p. 134.

114 RSPCA executive committee minutes, meetings of 15 January, 28 March, 30 April, 14 May, 9 July and 12 November 1906. *Report* (1906), pp. 45–7, 107. It is often incorrectly stated that women gained admission to the RSPCA executive committee in 1896.

3

Animal welfare and 'humane education': new roles for women

In nineteenth-century Britain, the astonishing growth of organised charities offered middle- and upper-class women opportunities to venture out of the home, to comprehend more fully the nature of the society in which they lived, and slowly to change it. Through voluntary work in ragged schools, hospitals, workhouses and reformatories, they not only encountered at first hand the realities of destitution, but also became more conversant with the functioning of the official bodies that were established to regulate the life of the poor.[1] Frank Prochaska has shown how women's remarkable contributions to Victorian philanthropy have often been overlooked due to the inconspicuous local nature of many of their activities and a lack of acknowledgement by men of the time.[2] Nevertheless, the formation of institutions such as the National Association for the Promotion of Social Science (1857) and the Ladies' National Association for the Diffusion of Sanitary Knowledge (1858) enabled female participants to speak and debate publicly, and to set their work in a wider context of ideas and practices.[3] As the century progressed, so women grew more knowledgeable, experienced and confident in their participation in public life. They gained greater recognition of their achievements, and took on leading positions as administrators of charities, members of School Boards and Poor Law Guardians: developments which in turn furthered demands for female suffrage and access to higher education and professional training for women.[4]

Attention to animals' welfare can certainly be seen as an extension of Victorian philanthropic endeavours, and charitable institutions designed to assist poor and needy people often have direct counterparts in those established for the benefit of animals. As early as 1846, Ralph Fletcher, Consulting Surgeon to the Gloucester General Hospital, urged that there should also be 'Hospitals for the Dumb Creation'. William Lauder Lindsay similarly thought that, 'if it be desirable or incumbent to maintain aged men and women in comfort in their declining years', then equal support was due to working animals that had given their lives to the service of man.[5] The Home of Rest for Horses, now the Horse Trust, which offered veterinary treatment, was established by Ann Lindo in 1886. Our Dumb Friends' League, now the Blue Cross, began in 1897; its first president was Mrs George R. Mathews, followed by Lady Olive Smith-Dorrien.[6] In the same spirit, refuges set up by various rescue societies to redeem homeless and 'fallen' women find a parallel in Mary Tealby's Home for Lost and Starving Dogs of 1860.[7] John Hollingshead, writing in the *Morning Post* in February 1861, thought that this Home's address to the public 'may sound to many people like a parody of an ordinary appeal on behalf of a reformatory, or some refuge for lost and repentant outcasts'; it was thus 'trembling upon the verge of absurdity', and yet, 'a process of reasoning' showed it to be 'founded on a sound principle'.[8] That principle was developed in the National Canine Defence League, now the Dogs' Trust, initiated by Lady Gertrude Stock in 1891. Miss Swifte's Dublin Home for Starving and Forsaken Cats opened in 1885, and there were several similar homes in London, all started and run by women, the first (1895) being Mrs W. Gordon's. A Society for the Protection of Cats, run by women with Lady William (Maria Jane) Lennox as its president, also rescued London strays in the late 1890s.[9] Other enterprises, such as benevolent societies to help cabmen, answered the needs of humans and working animals together.[10] The problems encountered by these charities, human and animal, also have various common features; for example, they involved considerable expense in the provision of staffing, premises, installations and supplies, such as to require extensive fundraising and often an eventual partnership with public bodies. In the case of animal charities, the availability of funding was also a measure of the degree to which the public now sympathised with animal suffering, in a process of gradual conversion of opinion that continued through the nineteenth century.

What is particularly striking in our context is the large number of cases in which women took the initiative in animal welfare, as the examples above demonstrate. We have seen the beginnings of the welfare concept in the 1830s, when members of the ill-fated ladies' society started by Charles Wheeler contemplated action for the gritting of slippery roads, and for buying up old horses to put them down, thus sparing the animals further painful toil without financial loss to labouring-class owners. Both these ideas were taken up by others – again largely women: in the case of the RSPCA's Fund for the Purchase of Worn-out Horses, the annual reports show that in 1838 twenty-one out of twenty-five listed contributors were women; in 1841 and 1842 all were women.[11] Not until the second half of the century did women actually found and lead autonomous animal charities, but from the early years of the animal protection movement, their moral pressure for the amelioration of conditions for horses, cattle and dogs, and in particular their generous donations and bequests for this purpose, were of critical importance.

The Metropolitan Drinking Fountain and Cattle Trough Association: women's charitable giving on a grand scale

Wealthy ladies' contributions were certainly essential to the viability of the Metropolitan Drinking Fountain and Cattle Trough Association (MDFCTA), established in 1859. This organisation aimed to provide clean drinking water for wayfarers, drovers and slum-dwellers, and also for their animals – at a time when no free supply of pure water was otherwise available in the London streets.[12] The Association was founded by the Quaker banker and independent MP Samuel Gurney Junior, a nephew of Elizabeth Fry, with support from other Quaker businessmen. He had succeeded his father as honorary treasurer of the RSPCA and his mother had also worked enthusiastically for that Society, which awarded her a medal in 1833 for her attempts to get agreement for the removal of Smithfield cattle market to the London suburbs.[13] Although the Drinking Fountain Association started providing troughs for animals only in the mid-1860s, this development in fact owed much to the RSPCA's earlier initiatives, and its attempts to call attention to the 'crying evil' of animal thirst.[14] In the 1840s the RSPCA was already installing pumps and tanks in the west end of London for watering horses, and in 1852 it negotiated with various parish authorities over the erection of troughs.[15] In Liverpool, where working men and their horses were also in great need of a free water supply in the streets, and where imported livestock arrived at the docks in a dehydrated condition, fountains and troughs were erected with both private and municipal support from the early 1850s onwards.[16] In the 1870s and 1880s, the ladies' committee of the Liverpool RSPCA made this one of their special responsibilities; they petitioned the men's committees both in London and Liverpool to supply funds for a trough at Lime Street Station, 'for the benefit of Cab horses & other Cattle entering or arriving at that Terminus', and successfully chivvied the town council into renewing the water supply to existing troughs.[17] Thus the emergence of Gurney's Association with support from the RSPCA is a good example of the openness of the latter, which throughout the nineteenth century acted as parent or midwife to groups concerned with special aspects of animal protection in tune with its own concerns, while adopting others that had originally been separate.[18]

9 A trough costing £80, erected by the Metropolitan Drinking Fountain and Cattle Trough Association in 1868, illustrated in a wood engraving by W. Palmer in *Animal World* (1 July 1870). It was one of four 'presented by a lady' who was 'an old and staunch supporter' of the RSPCA.

Signs of extreme thirst and distress in animals being driven into London and other cities – 'constantly seen with their tongues hanging from their mouths' – had long caused 'anxiety and grief' to humane onlookers.[19] By 1882, some five hundred troughs had been erected by the MDFCTA in the London area alone, in addition to roughly the same number of fountains for humans, and all were in heavy use: an article in the RSPCA's *Animal World* estimated that 'more than 250,000,000' animals drank from the troughs annually.[20] The annual running costs for troughs were higher than those for fountains, due to the great quantities of water consumed and the wear and tear on the fixtures. In 1872 the annual cost of maintenance alone for all fountains and troughs was computed as £3,450, and this figure rose steadily in the years that followed. Yet most vestries and Boards of Works were loath to provide support out of the public purse.[21] The MDFCTA, lacking an endowment or an adequate subscriber base, therefore depended heavily on munificent one-off gifts from individual benefactors; and although its vice-presidents, chief functionaries and committee were exclusively male, a majority of these benefactors were women (figure 9). Some wished to erect elaborate memorial fountains in public parks, but others were willing to underwrite the less glamorous business of constructing and repairing purely functional fountains and troughs, especially by replacing decayed materials with more durable granite.[22] In 1869, Queen Victoria set an example by donating £100, and in 1872, Mrs Elizabeth Hambleton and the Dowager Marchioness of Westminster bailed out the Association with gifts of £100 and £200 respectively.[23]

Information given in the Association's annual reports strongly suggests that this female engagement with the cause was strengthened, if not actually prompted, by the decision to build troughs for horses, cattle, sheep and dogs as well as fountains for humans. From the mid-1860s onwards, donations from women significantly exceeded those from men, and were often specifically intended for animal provision. In 1867, Mrs Phillipson of Lyndhurst in Hampshire – one of the 'considerable number of ladies' who now attended the Association's annual meetings – pledged to subscribe twenty pounds a year for five years towards the maintenance of the troughs.[24] Mrs Hambleton, who, as a 'lover of animals', was a passionate supporter of the Association's work, eagerly observing 'the poor creatures round the troughs', gave at least £600 down to 1872, and bequeathed £3,000 in 1874.[25] A Miss Wasey of Newbury anonymously donated £4,000 in total between 1866 and 1874, to be 'appropriated at once for the benefit of animals'.[26] Baroness Burdett-Coutts was also a constant and generous contributor from c.1869 onwards, and speeches given in Manchester, when a fountain and trough she had donated were officially unveiled, make it clear that promotion of kindness to animals was the prime motive for the gift. Indeed, it was reported that, at the ceremony, 'rough-looking … working men' held up their dogs for her to stroke and bless.[27] Whether, as critics might have alleged, this bias manifested a greater concern for animals than for humans, or whether it stemmed from a perception that animals would otherwise not be provided for, is impossible to determine; certainly these women would have felt that they were, in the words of the 1867 Association report, 'pleading for those who cannot plead for themselves'.[28]

The experience of the Association typifies that of many nineteenth-century animal welfare bodies. Firstly, the costliness and planning implications of its work strained resources, and made it greatly reliant on a few wealthy donors – in this case, overwhelmingly women. The *Graphic* thought it was 'nothing less than a disgrace to a so-called civilised city of such enormous wealth as London' that the public relied on 'private effort and beneficence' for such a vital amenity.[29] In fact, provision of clean water in the streets ultimately became the responsibility of London's local authorities and the municipalities of other British cities. Secondly, animal protection was now linked with wider social concerns. There was a growing need for pure drinking water to replace the polluted wells and pumps that had caused outbreaks of cholera, and the Association was especially anxious to keep working men out of public houses, which provided water for animals only on the understanding that the men in charge of them would drink alcohol there.[30] Temperance was conducive to what one of the founders of the Association called 'habits of good order and subordination' among drivers and drovers, while inducing a kinder and more patient treatment of the animals in their charge.[31] However, a perception that animals in cities *increasingly* suffered from human indifference and brutality went much beyond the need for water, and, once again, women were in the forefront of initiatives for reform.

The Home for Lost and Starving Dogs and its disputed *raison d'être*

In 1860 another institution for animal welfare came to birth in London, the Temporary Home for Lost and Starving Dogs – now known as the Battersea Dogs' Home, in reference to the site to which the institution moved in 1871; cats were also admitted from 1882 onwards.[32] It was the first such animal refuge, which provided a prototype for many similar institutions in Europe, the United States and elsewhere; and it was also the first animal charity started by a woman – Mrs Mary Tealby. Little is known about Tealby, who, according to the inscription on her grave in Biggleswade churchyard, was born in 1801 and died in 1865, only a few years after the Home's foundation.[33] She too was a long-time supporter of the RSPCA, and had begun to succour stray dogs in her local area of Islington. Becoming conscious of the 'aggregate amount of suffering among these faithful creatures' that there must be across London, she wrote to the *Standard* and other papers in September 1860 with a proposal for the 'Home'.[34] The London streets, even in the wealthy West End, were then full of such lost or abandoned dogs – some fifty thousand were wandering loose without identification of ownership, according to a *Times* correspondent of 1865 – and 'humanity' was unpleasantly 'shocked' by seeing so many of them 'in a state of semi-starvation'.[35] Their pathetic supplications for food and shelter as they trailed people along the street, their occasional aggression and their filthy, diseased state provoked confused reactions in passers-by, as human derelicts often did and still do: pity, compunction, shame, fear, revulsion or outright hostility. As one lady wrote to the *Times* to explain, 'our sympathy for their misery is mixed with terror'.[36] Both sexes experienced such feelings, but only males, apparently, turned to violence: the animals were frequently chased, stoned, kicked or beaten to death by men and boys, especially when outbreaks of rabies occurred or were wrongly suspected. The idea of providing safe accommodation for these creatures may have been entirely novel, but the need for it was undeniable, and, once established, the Home expanded rapidly, taking on a quasi-official role that Tealby could never have anticipated.

Her choice of the word 'Home' for the proposed institution was highly significant: what she had in mind was not a comfortless pound of the kind used to confine trespassing cattle or horses, much less a place of extermination, but rather a refuge where Christian charity and compassion could be expressed in affectionate care of the 'foundlings', until they were reclaimed by their owners or rehomed. The dogs were to be individually registered and even, according to an article in *Leisure Hour*, given names.[37] Moreover, the idea of a 'Home', a haven of shelter and comfort, legitimated the role of women in administering it, as an extension of, or a parallel to, the domestic sphere.[38] Tealby specifically addressed her appeal in the *Standard* to 'the humanity of the ladies of London and its environs' – perhaps intending to forestall charges of unfeminine presumption by suggesting an acceptable parallel to the female auxiliary committees of existing charities. However, she was certainly conscious of the epochal nature of her project:

> The establishment of a Home for such a purpose would be an example to all ladies throughout the kingdom and even throughout the Christian world ... We would not refuse any subscriptions or donations from kind-hearted and humane gentlemen, but we hope they would allow us the proud privilege of calling the Society our own.

According to a pamphlet *Appeal for the Home for Lost and Starving Dogs* of 1861, Tealby's letter was 'immediately answered by three ladies, promising most liberal pecuniary help and active personal exertion'.[39] A committee was formed, unusually comprising both men and women, with the latter initially in the majority: the female co-founders included Tealby's friend Mrs Sarah Major; Mrs Hambleton, whom we have already encountered as a provider of cattle troughs; and a Miss Morgan, who, according to an obituary of 1874, had worked for the RSPCA since the 1820s, and founded a branch of the Society for Streatham and Brixton in south London.[40] Tealby's and Morgan's long connections with the RSPCA were honoured and sustained: the Society took a risk in supporting this unorthodox project and its female leadership. The recently appointed RSPCA Secretary John Colam followed the lead of his predecessor by agreeing to take in subscriptions for the Home, giving it a status it might not otherwise have enjoyed; Colam later joined the Home's committee and his son Charles became its secretary.[41] Furthermore, the RSPCA itself made donations to the Home, and offered the use of its own offices for committee meetings in the early days, establishing a pattern of co-operation between the two institutions that lasted the century. As Hollingshead noted, the Home 'begins precisely where the Society for the Prevention of Cruelty to Animals leaves off', being concerned not with the pursuit of cruel men through the courts, but with the nurture and care of their potential victims.[42]

Despite such respectable sponsorship, the idea of a *ladies'* independent enterprise – to save unwanted mongrels that many regarded only as a public nuisance and a danger to human health – immediately sparked a critical reaction on sexist lines. 'MK' in a letter to the *Standard*, chose to attribute the spurious enterprise to a charlatan of the Charles Wheeler type – 'the very prince of humbugs … he knows the world and I should not be surprised to find his ridiculous appeal answered by a great many old maids who love dogs and whose sympathies can easily be moved by reference to the miseries of the canine race to sending him subscriptions to a large amount'. Why not a 'Butterfly and Caterpillar Protection Society'?[43] A charge of female gullibility, a *reductio ad absurdum* and a revival of the ancient typology of the animal-doting spinster were all to be expected, and a letter to the *Times* made the equally predictable objection that suffering humans should have come first: 'Surely charity can be better bestowed by thinking of homes for starving and wandering children?'[44]

The writer of a *Times* article on the same day agreed: 'One might … have expected that human benevolence would have its limits … marked somewhere within the regions of humanity, so far as mere sentimental interference was concerned'. RSPCA-sponsored legislation to prevent 'unnecessary' cruelty had produced a welcome change in public attitudes. However, the Dogs' Home project marked a transition 'from the sublime to the ridiculous – from the reasonable inspirations of humanity to the fantastic exhibitions of ridiculous sentimentalism … when we hear of a "Home for Dogs" we venture to doubt if the originators and supporters of such an institution have not taken leave of their sober senses'. The writer falsely suggested that these female 'originators and supporters' intended to prioritise valuable pedigree dogs, which were unlikely to need such assistance. Thus traditional accusations of illogicality, snobbery and ignorance of the world on the part of upper-class women could be added to the charge sheet. At the core of the argument was women's alleged tendency to extreme emotional sympathy with animals, set in antithesis to the restrained and well-considered actions of 'humane men'. Only the latter could judge where praiseworthy, feasible action against 'unnecessary' cruelty ended, and arrant folly began; but from one to the other 'there is but a single step'.[45]

Sober 'reason' could, however, be equated in this context with worldly calculation and emotional distance, even with callousness; and for many commentators, 'feeling', as an expression of spiritual values, seemed greatly preferable. According to the anonymous author of the 1861 *Appeal for the Home*, true sympathy and Christian love were never restrictive in their objects; those observers who were indifferent to the suffering of dogs left to die in the streets – those who even poured scorn on the efforts of people who tried to help them – must have rejected 'the blessed Saviour's most merciful religion' … 'the necessity of wielding with thought and kindness that dominion which God in His providence has given us over the brute creation'.[46] James Greenwood, in a sympathetic account of the dogs' home published in 1866, remembered how people had at first 'sneeringly demanded to be informed whether the very last little boy or girl had been fished out of the kennel [street gutter] to which the vice or poverty of its parents had consigned it', before 'these humanitarians felt at liberty to extend a succouring hand to mangy little puppy dogs and prowling curs generally orphaned and in distress'. This was an attack on the Home which Greenwood thought was shamefully at odds with the effusive tributes to dogs in much popular literature of the day.[47] Nevertheless, the founders had – heroically in his view – persisted in their efforts and won over a majority of the public, thus establishing the home on a firm foundation.

The moral debates thrown up by this episode recur throughout the history of nineteenth-century animal welfare, involving a series of linked antitheses: heart against head; a notion of Christian teaching that embraced the compelling duty of kindness to animals, as against a down-to-earth, more or less principled prioritisation of human interests; and an accepted contrast between the attitudes of women and men that aligned them – in imagination and often in fact – with these polarities. In a letter to the *Daily News* in 1872, the Shakespearian actress Isabella Dallas-Glyn wrote that she could not sleep after visiting the home, and she urged readers passionately to help the dogs there: 'It is a piteous sight to see their big earnest eyes, filled with tears, and heart-breaking to hear their cries and wailings for those they have lost.'[48] In contrast to effusions of this kind, a writer in the *Illustrated London News* in 1868 rehearsed all the old arguments against humanitarian treatment of animals, with all the old misogynistic prejudices that, as we have seen, were rife in the Georgian era. He thought it would be 'unjustifiable, as a matter of social and political economy … to undertake to support all the idle dogs in London as long as they chose to live at the public expense'.

> Oh dear! the Philocynic is not a philanthropic Institution. It must have been founded (in 1860, by an elderly lady, now deceased, we are told) more in the interests of dogs than of mankind ... There are people in London, and even women – or rather ladies, not women – who are not ashamed to say they like dogs better than children. Neither the children nor the dogs like *them*, and the men like them least of all.[49]

Despite such attacks, a large section of the press was soon describing the Home with sympathetic interest. It offered a perfect subject for the journalist and the illustrator in its novelty, in the picturesque variety of the dogs, and in the opportunities they afforded for humour, sentiment and anthropomorphism – especially the possibility of witty analogies with social caste and the problems of pauperism among humans. It was easy to enter into the feelings of the dogs, a species already so thoroughly anthropomorphised in books of anecdotes and personal reminiscences, children's stories and the immensely popular paintings of Edwin Landseer. Some of the accounts of the Home were 'written' by dogs in the first person, to heighten this sense of identification. In *The Queen*, a journal aimed at women (figure 10), the canine author begs the reader to imagine the plight of a 'houseless, abandoned creature – the sort of dog that the 'midnight pedestrian finds softly pattering after his heels', as though to say ' "pray don't drive me away when we get to the street-door." "Go home!" says you, trying to speak as much like a ruffian as possible, and making a tremendous flourish with your umbrella. But ... he can't; he hasn't got a home'.[50]

Frances Power Cobbe, soon to become the leading opponent of vivisection, published her *Confessions of a Lost Dog* to assist the Home; Cobbe's close friend Mary Lloyd being its chief financial benefactor. In the *Confessions*, Cobbe's own Pomeranian or Spitz dog Hajjin recounts the experience of becoming separated from her mistress in the street, and being chased and injured by cruel men and boys until near death. Finally, an imagined kind lady – one of several in the story – arranges for Hajjin to be taken to the refuge of the Dogs' Home, with a happy outcome.[51] Cobbe's title – the 'confessions' of a 'lost' being – wittily alludes to the idea of a *human* fall from grace and respectability: as Charles Dickens wrote to Baroness Burdett-Coutts in 1846, apropos of the home for reformed prostitutes that they were jointly setting up, each applicant should be told 'that she is degraded and fallen, but not lost, having this shelter'.[52] Uncertain or divided views of such girls – were they hardened profligates or pathetic victims, more sinned against than sinning? – find a parallel

10 An early depiction of the dogs' home, signed by the artist Harden Sidney Melville. It reveals cramped conditions and the pathetic state of some of the dogs, one of which is having its leg bandaged. Wood-engraving on the front page of *The Queen, An Illustrated Journal and Review*, No. 4 (28 September 1861).

in journalists' descriptions of the inmates of the dogs' home. The persecution of street dogs suspected of being rabid creates an especially close connection with social attitudes in the human sphere.[53] In the 1860s, when the Contagious Diseases Acts authorised the compulsory examination of suspected prostitutes and the incarceration in 'lock hospitals' of those found to be suffering from venereal diseases, the identification of dogs with human outcasts must have had special resonance.[54]

Dickens himself, in an article in *All the Year Round* in 1862, set up an antithesis between the pampered pedigree exhibits at a recent dogs' show and the 'poor vagrant homeless curs' in the Home, who, 'flattening their poor snouts against the wires, ask in their own peculiar and most forcible language whether you are their master come at last to claim them?' Solicitude for the unwanted dogs was an extension of concern for their human counterparts, in a nation sharply divided between haves and have-nots. Thus Dickens wanted those readers prepared to acknowledge in themselves 'a certain weakness called pity' to rescue the Home from ridicule, as an 'institution in this practical country founded on a sentiment' ... 'evidence of that hidden fund of feeling which survives in some hearts even the rough ordeal of London life in the nineteenth century'.[55] In that hard-headed country and era, it was quickly evident, however, that pity must reach an understanding with financial realities. As early as 1861 there was, according to Hollingshead, a 'dissension' among the committee members, between the 'humane' and the 'practical' tendencies: the women on the Home's committee consented only with 'utmost reluctance', to the suggestion of their male colleagues, who were soon in the ascendant, that unclaimed and unsaleable dogs would, after a certain time, have to be put down.[56] The passing of the Metropolitan Streets Act (1867), which authorised the police to seize any dog not led by its owner nor wearing a muzzle, resulted in an accommodation between the police and the Home which further compromised Mrs Tealby's original vision. In 1868 the Home agreed to take in such dogs, most of which were necessarily killed there; a writer in the *Morning Post* even referred to the institution as 'the great slaughter-house'. Periodic outbreaks of rabies, or rabies scares, massively increased both admissions to the Home and the proportion of dogs that went to the lethal chamber. In 1885 alone the Home accepted over 25,000 dogs, and in 1886 over 40,000: of these, well over three-quarters were destroyed. Sarah Major, a co-founder of the Home in 1860, was reported as being present at the annual meeting in 1886: one wonders how she felt about these statistics.[57] The novelist Ouida at least described the extermination policy bitterly as the 'profitable manufacture of sensitive living creatures into manure': in her eyes, Battersea had no right to call itself a 'Home', suggesting 'peace and safety' for the animals, nor to appeal to the dog-loving public rather than to the government for its funding.[58] In fact, 'Good Samaritan' enterprises, as Roswell McCrea called them – expressions of the personal kindness and sympathy of their originators – often proved unable to cope with the scale of need for their services, and were increasingly obliged to enter into partnerships with more impersonal, hard-headed public bodies.[59] In the circumstances of the Victorian era, when women were only beginning to be admitted to the membership of such decision-making bodies, this transition also had gendered implications. The tension between male pragmatism, based on a view of general policy, and female 'sentiment' or compassion for *individual* creatures, was reinforced. Reactions to abuses in the cattle trade provide a particularly striking example.

The transit of animals, and the gendered element in
solitude for their sufferings

Reference has already been made in chapter 2 to the mounting anxieties of animal protectionists and many members of the public over the way in which live cattle and sheep were imported to Britain from continental Europe and Ireland, or sent from Scotland to London by train. Many animals were landed at the ports of Liverpool, Hull and London after painfully cramped journeys without food or water, and often arrived badly injured by trampling.[60] Moreover, supplies of food and water for cattle and sheep in transit by train were very seldom provided by any railway company, even over two-day journeys.[61] In the case of livestock coming from Germany and the Low Countries, the ships used by consignors were generally passenger or merchant vessels that had not been adapted for the carriage of animals, which were consequently packed together on the lower decks or in the stifling holds, with no pens or tethers to prevent their being thrown together and suffocated in rough weather. Worse even than these shortcomings was the indifference of ships' crews and port officials to the animals' suffering: shocked passengers reported gratuitous cruelties such as sailors walking over the backs of tightly packed sheep, or drovers flogging dazed and frightened cattle to get them up the gangways when they reached port.[62] Yet the root cause of the cruelties lay elsewhere: the writer of a *Times* editorial in 1869 noted that 'It is easy to denounce the untrained natures of the sailors and drovers, and to say that they need not merely education, but some kind of moral discipline; but what is to be expected of them under the circumstances?'

> If employers – men of wealth, name, and position, – see nothing amiss in taking aboard a cargo of animals under conditions which necessitate cruelty and filth, how can men comparatively ignorant and unrefined indulge any feelings of gentleness and humanity?[63]

To secure a conviction under the anti-cruelty laws, it was necessary to prove deliberate and 'unnecessary' cruelty by the individuals concerned. However, in the case of customary practices which were well understood to hinge on 'pounds, shillings, and pence', all denied responsibility, while the power of business interests in parliament effectively prevented any major reforms. A central paradox was pointed out: if dead meat were the cargo being transported – a commodity that quickly deteriorated – it would be delivered more carefully and expeditiously than the living animals were: their animate, sentient state was the key to their cruel mistreatment.[64]

Stung by criticisms of its seeming inaction and emboldened by the evidence of public support for reform, the RSPCA in 1868 sent a deputation to the Lord President of the Privy Council, the Duke of Marlborough, requesting him to introduce measures protecting animals in transit by steamboat or railway.[65] In the following year, the Contagious Diseases (Animals) Act, which was mainly concerned with halting the spread of cattle plague from imported animals to home-reared stock, included a few clauses relating to animal welfare, and empowered the Privy Council to implement them.[66] Amid much public outrage about cruelty expressed in letters to the *Times*, the Privy Council set up a committee, chaired by its clerk, Arthur Helps, which sought information from anyone willing to give it, and deliberated on what could be done. Seventy leading veterinary surgeons advised, at the RSPCA's instigation, that animals in transit should be given water every ten or twelve hours, not the thirty hours stipulated in the Act.[67] But Helps warned the press that people should not expect too much: the committee 'must proceed with great circumspection … Otherwise, what we might recommend might be very humane in the abstract, but might be practically almost impossible to carry out'.[68]

The outcome announced in 1870 was in fact a severe disappointment. Helps's committee proposed some minor improvements to existing conditions – especially the provision of food and water for the animals at some ports and railway stations; but the privations and abuse they suffered while in transit by boat or train were otherwise untouched.[69] Helps explained that any more stringent Orders in Council would be unenforceable; and the committee was mindful of the interests of British meat traders – nothing should be done that restricted the supply of animals or raised prices, causing them to lose out to foreign competitors. In the event, even the measures suggested by the committee proved ineffective: in the decades that followed, the same complaints of cruelty would repeatedly be made, without stirring the government into any more decisive action. In 1875 one observer noted that, for the eager reformer, 'There are few things more irritating than the imperturbable type of officialdom'. The force of enthusiasm 'is beaten into foam against the rocky stiffness of those who administer existing systems' … 'In these days humanitarian principles are quickened to a restless sensitiveness; here is a field in which they may find abundance of work'.[70]

The most influential champion of such 'humanitarian principles' was Angela Burdett-Coutts, whose benefactions to the MDFCTA have already been mentioned. In September 1869 she wrote a letter to the *Times* which had considerable impact on public opinion. Like many women concerned with animal protection in the past – one thinks again of Elizabeth Heyrick – being humane 'in the abstract', as Helps put it, was for her a moral and religious imperative that transcended worldly considerations. Yet, while chiding the RSPCA for its failure to prosecute those guilty of 'the detestable treatment of live stock', she tacitly acknowledged that such prosecutions were fraught with difficulties. Only 'systematic teaching of the absolute duty of man towards the lower animals' would provide a solution.[71] John Colam, secretary of the RSPCA, agreed. Although the Society had been 'energetically ... prosecuting offenders' for forty years past, cruelty was still rife. 'It is wiser and easier, surely, to humanize the heart when it is young'; and such humanisation was a 'glorious enterprise' which should be entrusted to ladies.[72] On this analysis, education was not so much the complement of legal sanctions as an admission of the latter's almost complete failure.

It might be assumed that Arthur Helps, functionary of the Privy Council, was a 'business as usual' politician, principally concerned not to alienate wealthy interest groups, or to waste his time on a hopeless cause. But this is not the view of him that emerges from a reading of his book *Some Talk about Animals and Their Masters*, published in 1873.[73] It is actually dedicated to Burdett-Coutts, 'whose efforts to promote the humane treatment of animals have been earnest and unremitting'. Like Helps's *Friends in Council*, it consists of a series of imagined conversations, and is one of the most thoughtful works on man's treatment of animals to have been written in the Victorian era. One of the public men featured in it, Milverton, represents Helps himself: he is a member of the 'Transit of Animals Committee' but also an author who plans a book on 'the treatment of the lower animals by man'.[74] Drawing on the works of respected thinkers from Montaigne to Anna Jameson, the friends ponder the intelligence and virtues of animals and the rights that these qualities should confer: yet sheep, cattle and geese that are consigned to boats and trains on their way to slaughter, suffer as much as Africans did in the 'fearful and wicked' transit of slaves.[75] The pressure of public feeling and a programme of governmental 'supervision and inspection' should do 'something for the general good'. However, any attempts at preventive legislation are met by objections, as being 'contrary to the laws of political economy' and an unwarranted intrusion on the rights of property; and in any case, given the 'thousands of transactions' involving animals that now occur in the course of trade, effective policing is impossible.[76]

In this discussion of the conflict between conscience and 'political economy', women are implicitly left on the sidelines. Indeed, the imaginary ladies present are the objects of routine jokes about female unsuitability for professional occupations and even about women's supposed likeness to butterflies.[77] Nevertheless, Milverton and a fictional Lord Ellesmere both suggest that animal advocacy could well be delegated to women: they 'could do a great deal in this matter, as indeed they can in most social affairs', and their natural qualities of sympathy give them a special aptitude for the task, if not for the more combative aspects of public life. Lady Ellesmere welcomes the suggestion: for her, 'It would be quite enough reason for refusing to marry any man, if one knew that he practised any needless cruelties upon animals'.[78] However, the sexes have different approaches to the prevention of such cruelties, as becomes clear in Helps's allusion to a real-life case. The RSPCA received a complaint that a consignment of imported geese, bound for Leadenhall Market, had been left at Waterloo Station for over twenty-four hours. The birds were packed tightly into crates, without food or water: 'Some … were screaming, many were lying down with heads and necks extended, seemingly quite exhausted; several were dead … It was painful to see.' The men, including Milverton, are duly concerned by such reports, but rule out the possibility of legislating for so insignificant a species as geese. Any attempt to do so would be greeted with howls of derision: only a very mild, general stipulation that animals in transit should be carried in compartments suited to their respective sizes would stand any chance of passing into law. The women, in contrast, can hardly bear to think of such *specific* and acute physical distress: their empathy with the birds makes continuation of such treatment intolerable. 'Imagine their nights of suffering! Think only of one thing, the want of water!!' Lady Ellesmere berates the men for their untroubled acceptance of political and commercial realities:

> It is all very well to speak scornfully of us women; but I do seriously think, that if we had more voice in the management of affairs, these things which you call minor matters would be very differently managed. Say what you like, we are more humane. To feel deeply for these creatures is just the sort of thing that many men would laugh at, and call it sentimental, and a spurious kind of humanity.[79]

There was only one way of bridging this divide between male pragmatism and impassioned female identification with animal suffering. According to Milverton, 'Our object should be to get a better spirit introduced' … 'You ask for practical remedies, for things to do. Well, I say, follow the example of Lady Burdett Coutts', who rewards kindness to animals and has undertaken the moral education of the young.[80] Here was a form of activism that was peculiarly suited to women, and they were soon to be given many opportunities to develop it.

The RSPCA ladies' committee and other women's groups: struggles for usefulness

Burdett-Coutts's 1869 letter to the *Times*, complaining of the 'hideous ... depravity' of the cattle trade, proposed action that would, she hoped, get to the root of the problem of cruelty: a programme of humane education 'among all classes'. As we have seen, the notion that education should complement prosecution in a two-pronged attack on habits of cruelty dates back to the inception of the RSPCA's work in the 1820s; but only now, in the face of seemingly intractable problems in eradicating cruelty at every level of modern industrial society, did the Society put it on an organised footing. An important stimulus came from America in the person of the dynamic Bostonian George Thorndike Angell. He was president of the Massachusetts Society for the Prevention of Cruelty to Animals, which he had co-founded in 1868, and later he also directed the American Humane Education Society. Angell was in London in 1869 and 1870, and had several meetings with Burdett-Coutts and with RSPCA personnel. Members of the Society's executive committee had already mooted the production of a journal to inform the public about its activities, but Angell, who was invited to visit and address a committee meeting in June 1869, suggested something more popular and broad-ranging in its contents. The model he had in mind was *Our Dumb Friends*, an illustrated monthly which he himself edited and distributed very widely in the United States. Angell was bemused that the 'fine-looking ... elderly gentlemen' of the RSPCA executive committee seemed more preoccupied with procedural niceties (which of them should propose a vote of thanks to their American visitor?), than with absorbing his ideas, but this impression proved to be mistaken. Before the end of the year the committee's discussions resulted in the launch of the RSPCA's *Animal World*, which became a highly successful illustrated journal with a wide appeal.[81]

At this time and again in the summer of 1870, Angell also passionately urged Colam and Burdett-Coutts to establish a 'Ladies' Humane Education Society' on the model of the one at Boston, 'which should enlist the best and foremost women of Great Britain, and ... lead perhaps to the forming of similar societies among the influential women of other nations'. In Angell's vision of the progress of civilisation, it was women who were to usher in an age of peace and reconciliation – for both human nations and the animal kingdom. His words fell on receptive ears. In her letter to the *Times* of September 1869, Burdett-Coutts proposed the formation of a ladies' society to further the RSPCA's educational mission, particularly in promoting and distributing *Animal World*, and Colam supported the idea, appealing to female readers to assist in form-ing such a group. Some fifty women responded; but since then the idea had, Angell noted, 'hung fire'. It will be remembered that, from very early days, the RSPCA's directors had been averse to the institution of all-women groups, and Angell's renewed pressure, including some verbal bullying of the RSPCA president, the Earl of Harrowby, led to a 'lengthy' and, one imagines, fraught discussion. The outcome was a decision to form a *men's* 'Education and litera-ture sub-committee', 'empowered to consider and prepare the basis of a Ladies' Auxiliary' and to communicate with Burdett-Coutts and 'the other Ladies said to be interested in such matter'.[82] In 1870, these moves at length resulted in the establishment of the 'Ladies' humane education committee' (significantly, not a semi-independent 'Society' of the kind Angell envisaged), with strictly circumscribed functions.

Burdett-Coutts had been a loyal and generous patron of the RSPCA since 1840, and as a friend and family connection of Lord Harrowby, she counted as an insider. She was also a philanthropist of wide experience and high reputa-tion. In these circumstances, the elaborate precautions that were still thought necessary to limit and monitor the activities of the ladies' committee, and if necessary to overrule its proposals, give the measure of the men's anxiety not to be hustled into rash decisions that might compromise the Society's policy of judicious moderation. It was as if the practical advantages of women's par-ticipation had to be balanced against the disadvantages of any public percep-tion that the Society was beginning to be dominated by women's 'sentimental' views. The all-male executive committee and the ladies' committee were sepa-rately constituted, communicating only through the Secretary, who attended the women's discussions and reported back on any ideas needing the men's approval; but the ladies' leader, Burdett-Coutts, had no *ex officio* right to attend meetings of the main committee, and the Society publicly stressed that she had 'no voice or power to interfere' with the conduct of its publications, despite her many benefactions.[83] When the Earl of Harrowby retired from the presi-dency of the Society in 1877, the minutes of the executive committee record a letter from him, 'suggesting that the Ladies' Committee be consulted' about the choice of his successor. Tellingly, the secretary has here crossed out 'consulted' and substituted 'communicated with'.[84] There is thus, it appears, a striking dis-connect between the public highlighting of the ladies' purely social or educative role – one speaker at the annual meeting of 1874 described them as the 'main-stay' of the Society – and their actual powerlessness when it came to decisions on policy. As we saw in chapter 2, it was only in 1906 that women finally gained admission to membership of the executive committee itself. In 1879 Sydney Buxton found an elegant way of putting the situation as it then existed in a positive light: the ladies' committee through its educational mission was 'steadily attacking the roots of cruelty', while the executive committee in its punitive actions was merely 'lopping off the branches'.[85]

Editorial articles in *Animal World* in 1870 express clearly the gendered mental constructs that lay behind all these restrictions on the women's work, revealing that, in this respect at least, little had changed since the 1830s. Ladies are to play no part in the 'political' and prosecuting functions of the RSPCA, as these, it was claimed, might alarm, perplex or annoy them. However, men are preoccupied with 'business or political cares – from which, happily in this country, ladies are exempt at present'; and these cares leave the men little time or inclination for 'the minutiae of humane education', which therefore naturally fall to women. 'Perhaps, too, in view of the tendencies of the age, it would be well ... on political and social grounds alone, to provide women with suitable work', and thus stem their endless complaints of being excluded from the field of public action. However, the God-given vocation of ladies of the 'influential classes' lies not in political but in social work, as a natural extension of their existing charities among the poor and ignorant, and their moral education of children: they can 'awaken minds and soften hearts' as 'missionaries of humanity'.

This 'astonishing argument' prompted a furious riposte from one reader of *Animal World*, Frances Power Cobbe, who would soon herself, as leader of the anti-vivisection movement, demonstrate the inseparability of animal advocacy, politics and feminism:

> Women have already, it seems to me, since the world began, endeavoured to train their young to compassion, both for human sufferers and for those harmless brutes which nearly all women love and nearly all men delight to destroy. Their efforts, however, never being backed by the possession of any direct legislative power, have done but half the good they might have effected.

If the writer of the offending article had worked as earnestly as the 'energetic ladies' he mocked to relieve poor and sick people and to 'protect animals from their masculine tormentors, he would understand how the more such objects are dear to women's hearts, the more they must necessarily desire the natural and direct means of promoting them through Parliamentary representation'.[86]

It is difficult to gauge how far the RSPCA ladies' committee, with its circumscribed functions, experienced the kind of frustration that Cobbe described.

The minutes of its meetings from early in 1871 to late 1891 are missing, and this is possibly significant.[87] The period in question was marked by constant strife both within and beyond the RSPCA over the question of vivisection. As we shall see, women tended to be among the most passionate and uncompromising opponents of the practice, as Burdett-Coutts certainly was; so it is telling that there were no women on the committee appointed by the Society in January 1875 to advise the Royal Commission on the regulation of experiments on live animals.[88] Already in August 1870, according to the minutes of the RSPCA executive committee, 'Miss Coutts had suggested that a Paper should be written against Vivisection and read by the writer at the forthcoming Meeting of the British Association [for the Advancement of Science], and it was Resolved that it would be inexpedient to force a discussion on that subject on the occasion referred to'.[89] Attitudes to hunting were another potential flash-point. In October 1869, Professor Edward Freeman had published a long article in the *Fortnightly Review* attacking field sports, which prompted a rejoinder from Anthony Trollope and then an onslaught on Trollope by Helen Taylor, stepdaughter of John Stuart Mill.[90] Both Burdett-Coutts and a Miss Wemyss wrote to the RSPCA executive committee to suggest giving Freeman's essay further circulation and publicity, but this was refused. Indeed, a discussion of the hunting issue prompted by Miss Wemyss's letter led to a resolution by the male leaders of the RSPCA not to publish *any* letters critical of field sports in *Animal World* – a policy which the strenuous opposition of many correspondents soon forced them to abandon.[91]

What, then, was the complexion and permitted scope of the RSPCA ladies' committee which held its first meetings in 1870? The nominal membership was to include all the titled patronesses of the Society, presumably with the idea of giving the committee a safely conservative and formal character. However, few of these grandees attended meetings.[92] The active members, besides Burdett-Coutts and her companion Mrs Hannah Brown, were often the wives of men who were members of the RSPCA executive committee or its offshoots, such as Mrs Samuel Gurney, Constantia Ann Ellicott, wife of the Bishop of Gloucester and Bristol, and Mary Anne Jackson, wife of the Bishop of London. Georgina, wife of William Francis Cowper-Temple, later Baron Mount-Temple, shared with her husband a passionate, religiously inspired and lifelong commitment to animal protection – the couple later emerged as members of Frances Power Cobbe's Victoria Street Society, opposing vivisection. Mrs Catherine Smithies, another RSPCA ladies' committee member, co-founded, with Lady Mount-Temple, the countrywide Band of Mercy movement, through which children, gathered in local groups, were taught kindness to animals.[93] It is clear, then, that the committee was not simply a coterie of Lady Bountifuls: these were women whose Christian beliefs and moral convictions spurred them to action on behalf of animals, as they spurred them also to several other charitable causes.

The 1870s was the decade when women at last began to gain a stake in public life as voters in local government elections, as members of the new school boards and as poor law guardians. At this time, too, Josephine Butler – already actively involved in groups pressing for higher education for women – took the lead in campaigning for the repeal of the Contagious Diseases Acts, which victimised prostitutes and implicitly condoned the sexual promiscuity of men. Now, too, the movement for women's suffrage got under way.[94] In these circumstances it is difficult not to feel that the more enterprising women on the RSPCA ladies' committee must have chafed at the purely 'auxiliary' if time-consuming duties allotted to them by the men. As defined in the prospectus of the ladies' committee, drafted by Colam in 1870, these duties centred on the distribution of *Animal World* and other RSPCA publications to 'schools, village libraries, clubs, reading rooms, public houses, railway stations, hospitals, work-houses, prisons, and cottages', with an emphasis on reaching lower-class men, such as grooms, drovers and railway employees, who worked directly with animals.[95] The ladies also circulated various short tracts on the care of animals and natural history; they published a song based on Sir Edwin Landseer's famous painting *The Old Shepherd's Chief Mourner*, and gave out 'beautifully printed copies of Cowper's lines on cruelty' on linen sheets for display in schoolrooms and 'other public places'. The organisation of sermons, 'penny readings', lectures and magic lantern shows and Sunday school classes also fell within their educational remit.[96] In particular, they began to liaise with national schools in order to obtain teachers' interest and co-operation in the moral education of the young, and this activity developed into essay competitions for children, in which many hundreds of schools participated – the presentation of prizes taking place at the RSPCA's annual meetings, which the ladies also organised.

Where records survive, it is possible to make interesting comparisons between the activities of the RSPCA ladies' committee in London, and those of its counterparts in provincial branches of the Society. There had been many abortive or transient projects for an anti-cruelty society in Liverpool since the first decade of the nineteenth century, including a women's group in the early 1830s led by Jane Roscoe, presumably the person of that name who was a daughter of William Roscoe, the great Unitarian polymath, anti-slavery campaigner, writer and art collector.[97] In 1871 the London office of the RSPCA set up a branch in Liverpool which had better success, and a ladies' committee patterned on the London one was active from the following year. The membership of the network of little 'auxiliary' groups established in the environs of Liverpool was also overwhelmingly female, as it may have been in other such local groups across the country.[98] It was reported in 1874 that the Liverpool RSPCA ladies' committee had 'circulated the *Animal World*, pictorial placards', and other 'humane' literature, 'amongst all classes in their respective districts', set up school essay competitions, and rewarded kind donkey drivers and carters. Such exhortations and incentives to good behaviour counterbalanced the Liverpool society's legal actions against the perpetrators of cruelties to horses and cattle at the Liverpool docks and on the steep, congested roads through the town. The Revd Gardner noted at the annual meeting in 1874 that 'we cannot get on without ladies':

> We have been generally accused in times gone by of being entirely a prosecuting Society ... always taking the rough side. But it has often struck me that ... a little reward for kindness to animals as well as punishment for cruelty would be a good thing ... the ladies very soon smoothed a way. (Hear, hear, and applause.)[99]

However, the Liverpool women's efforts soon went beyond this traditionally feminine, conciliatory role. They 'personally interfered' when they witnessed cruelties in the streets, using 'kind persuasion and remonstrance', or demanding that employers correct the behaviour of their men. Sometimes the women brought reports of such cruelties to the secretary of the Liverpool branch, Jesse Motum, for further action – in many cases leading to successful prosecutions: they were, in a sense, the eyes and ears of the Society.[100] They negotiated very successfully with the municipal authorities, either by a direct approach or via the men's committee, to get slippery roads sanded and, as we have seen, to ensure a supply of fresh water via standpipes and troughs.[101] They were also the driving force behind the establishment of the Liverpool dogs' home in 1883, and supplied a majority of its committee members and subscribers.[102]

Some other animal welfare causes developed into moral crusades. Thus the Liverpool ladies campaigned tirelessly, in the face of much apathy and discouragement, and with scant success, to get local drivers to leave off the use of bearing reins on their horses – especially on draught horses, which were particularly distressed and harmed by these cruel devices. They circulated Edward Fordham Flower's pamphlet *Bits and Bearing Reins* (1874) (see figure 19), which also inspired Anna Sewell at this time; and they gave financial rewards to men who relinquished them.[103] They even pleaded with the mayor of Liverpool and civic officials to discontinue use of bearing reins on horses that they themselves employed, in order to set a good example to the public.[104] However, in 1877 the Liverpool women's plans to organise a grand *conversazione* on the subject of bearing reins in St George's Hall, to be addressed by Flower, were scotched by the men's committee: 'while wishing to carry out the suggestions from time to time made to them by the Ladies, the Committee feel that the matter in itself is not of sufficient importance to insure a successful gathering'.[105] While they could not 'get on without ladies', these local worthies evidently felt, like the RSPCA's managers in London, that the discretion and judgement acquired by men of the world were needed to control the women's more extravagant enthusiasms.

No such male control and limitation was acceptable to many women's anti-cruelty groups in America, whose stance was noticeably more militant than that of their British counterparts. Research by Diane Beers has revealed the fundamental contribution made by these women to animal advocacy in the later nineteenth century, as writers, campaigners and fundraisers.[106] The Philadelphian Caroline Earl White in particular, took on a leading role in the movement – equal in importance to that of Henry Bergh, founder of the American Society for the Prevention of Cruelty to Animals in New York, or of George Angell in Boston. In a gendered pattern that is now becoming familiar, she was in fact more intransigent and radical in battling for animals' interests than either of these men were, especially over the issue of vivisection.[107] White was the daughter of a leading Quaker lawyer and married an attorney from a powerful Catholic family, giving her connections to the centres of power in Philadelphia. She started an anti-cruelty society in the town in 1868, and when it adopted the normal policy of excluding women from its management committee, she formed in 1869 an autonomous 'Women's Branch' which was later renamed the Women's Pennsylvania Society for the Prevention of Cruelty to Animals (WPSPCA, now the Women's Animal Center). In order to be able to receive bequests directly, rather than being funded through the men's organisation, 'the Women's Branch solicited and obtained from the State Legislature a charter, and by this action constituted itself an independent society'. It shrewdly invested its considerable income, and was able to employ its own team of inspectors or agents (five of them by the 1880s, with many 'honorary' coadjutors) to patrol the streets of Philadelphia and the interstate railroads to watch for instances of cruelty that were actionable under existing anti-cruelty laws. In 1883, these agents even acquired the statutory right to make arrests on the women's behalf.[108] In a manner that the women themselves described as 'aggressive', their Society prosecuted railroad companies for cruelty to cattle in interstate transportation, and repeatedly petitioned the state and federal governments for extensions of the legislation protecting these animals – Caroline Earl White herself representing the Society in interviews with senators.[109] The public authorities of Philadelphia and the directors of local 'railways' or tram companies were also harried with demands for a better treatment of their horses, for example by limiting passenger loads and the number of stops.[110] As an offshoot from the WPSPCA, White in 1883 established the American Anti-Vivisection Society, supported by the *Journal of Zoophily*. The Society's policy of aiming for a complete ban on vivisection was framed in close partnership with British allies such as Frances Power Cobbe, and White controversially maintained this position to the end of her life.

There were few outright victories in these struggles, but the Philadelphian women's campaigns were dauntless and unremitting, despite the trouble and expense of legal actions. However, in recognition of the limits of the achievable in a ruthlessly commercial society, White and her colleagues turned – as British women had done – to solutions for the problem of cruelty that depended on their own vigorous welfare measures: the opening of a dogs' home; the provision of drinking troughs and animal ambulances; an attempt to develop more humane slaughtering instruments, and so on. The education and moral conditioning of the young – believed to be the only hope for the future – was undertaken on a grand scale through 'Bands of Mercy', with which Angell was also deeply involved, and various school-based societies that amalgamated in 1883 to become the Young American Humane Union.[111] In 1877 Caroline Earl White was a leading figure in the establishment of the American Humane Association, initially called the International Humane Society, which brought together the disparate groups concerned with the protection of both animals and children. Despite a tendency to safe conservatism and conciliation of business interests, it became a platform for challenges to bodies operating across state boundaries, such as railroad companies – challenges which White herself never relinquished.[112] Developing from its local roots in Philadelphia, the Women's Pennsylvania Society – funded though it was by commercial wealth – gradually assumed national importance in the struggle against cruelties arising from corporate power.

The mission of Angela Burdett-Coutts

The remarkable record of the WPSPCA raises an interesting question: why did Burdett-Coutts, whose wealth, intellect, experience of public work, social standing and political connections were certainly as impressive as those of Caroline Earl White, never see fit to challenge the RSPCA's restriction of the ladies' committee to purely supportive functions? Why did she never establish her own autonomous group of women in the anti-cruelty cause? Visits to London by White and other Philadelphians had certainly familiarised her with the work of the WPSPCA, and she also knew, through Angell, about the vigorous women's group at Boston.[113] The answer lies in Burdett-Coutts's personality and world view, which generated a quite different vision of the role of women as moral agents in society.

Angela Burdett-Coutts (1814–1906) (figure 11) was the daughter of Sir Francis Burdett, the liberal-minded MP for Westminster, himself an animal lover.[114] In 1837, at the age of twenty-three, she inherited a vast banking fortune from her maternal grandfather, Thomas Coutts, through the will of his second wife, and was given complete discretion in the disposal of it.[115] Thenceforth she devoted her long life to charities of various kinds; her benefactions ranged from the private relief of individuals to huge public projects of a kind that one might expect to be undertaken by government bodies. The character of a woman who was simultaneously the intimate friend of both the aged Duke of Wellington and of Charles Dickens is not to be easily pigeonholed.[116] In fact Burdett-Coutts combined devout Anglican churchmanship and a very conservative kind of morality with 'a generous and ready sympathy' for suffering humans and animals: an earnest desire to do good – to carry out Christ's injunction to 'feed my sheep' – that, while founded in traditional notions of *noblesse oblige*, was generally free of haughty condescension or bigotry.[117] For a popular writer of 1900 on *Noble Work by Noble Women*, she typified a 'lady of the old school', to stand in contrast to the adventurous 'new' women represented by the suffragist Millicent Fawcett.[118] Burdett-Coutts was opposed to female suffrage and careers for women, as being prejudicial to their 'quiet but potent influence of good'. She even declined invitations to serve as a Guardian of the Poor and as a member of the London School Board: 'she did not think it advisable, under present circumstances, for women to hold such an office'.[119] Yet through her speeches across the country, her letters to the press and philanthropic activities – all the products of strong personal convictions – she became one of the most famous and revered women in Britain. Large-scale patronage gave her a freedom, even an autocratic wilfulness, in pursuing her goals that could never have been attained by committee work. She was, however, genuinely loved by those she championed and assisted; in 1871 she was made a Baroness in her own right – an unprecedented honour.[120]

11 Angela Burdett-Coutts, photograph by Francis Henry Hart for the firm of Elliott & Fry,
albumen print, 1882.

While Burdett-Coutts financed religious and humanitarian projects world-wide, including missionary work and the creation of Anglican bishoprics in Africa and elsewhere, her patronage was focused principally on London. Dickens's influence and information had given her a particular interest in the impoverished East End – in its appalling lack of decent housing and sanitation, the destitution of unemployed textile workers, the social abandonment of street-walkers, and the total neglect of children. One result of this engagement was her energetic support for organised child protection, which started strangely as an outgrowth of the RSPCA.[121] In America, 'humane' associations had long worked for the protection of both animals and children, with no apparent sense of inappropriateness in the combination.[122] Conscious of this precedent, in 1883 Samuel Smith, MP for Liverpool, spoke at the annual meeting of the Liverpool branch of the RSPCA: 'while they were looking so very carefully after the inter-ests of dumb animals they should not forget another class of animals' – children of their own species. A society for the purpose of helping neglected and cruelly treated children was accordingly started in the city.[123] The momentum of this initiative prompted similar developments in London, with the involvement of the RSPCA. Many people contributed to the birth of the movement that became the London Society (later the National Society) for the Prevention of Cruelty to Children, which continued to be closely associated with the RSPCA in its early years; but contemporaries gave Burdett-Coutts much credit for her part in it. She hosted the initial meetings, canvassed support behind the scenes, wrote publicly to the Home Secretary on the need for protective legislation, and became a trustee of the infant London Society for the Prevention of Cruelty to Children.[124] The link between human and animal causes was, as we shall see, highly characteristic of her thinking.

According to her great niece, Burdett-Coutts realised 'the connection she might have with all that mass of the poor, the wretched and the obscure … whom she ultimately assisted and comforted to so great an extent' in the London slums, compensating for 'the inhuman features of the Poor Law System' for which she had 'a great hatred'.[125] In the 1860s she relieved those suffering during an outbreak of cholera with plentiful supplies of food, nursing care and medi-cation. She commissioned the building of model tenements in Bethnal Green, an elaborate fountain in Victoria Park and a huge market hall with the appear-ance of a Gothic cathedral. This Columbia market was intended to provide Eastenders with a source of wholesome cheap food, but the active hostility of monopolists in the existing London markets meant that it was never viable.[126] This was a bitter lesson for Burdett-Coutts on the power of vested interests to thwart humanitarian projects – just as they had impeded measures to improve conditions for cattle in transit and rejected the improved cattle truck design she had sponsored, as being commercially unfeasible.[127] She was, however, successful in defending costermongers from the threat of a legal ban on street vending, and provided stabling for their donkeys; and this was just one of her many charities to assist working men and their animals.[128] Her support for the fund to buy up old horses past work for humane destruction, her payments for the installation of brakes on trams and omnibuses and for the construction of street drinking troughs are other examples.[129] In *Baroness Burdett-Coutts: A Sketch of Her Public Life* (1893) we read of her co-founding of the Cart Horse Parade Society, which awarded prizes to cart and wagon drivers whose horses 'give evidence of kind and careful attention'. Its success justified the view that 'more can be done to ensure good treatment of these animals by rewarding their attendants for good care than by prosecuting them for isolated cases of cruelty and neglect'. In Newcastle upon Tyne in 1882, thousands of people attended Burdett-Coutts's presentation of prizes, in a parade that included colliers and their pit ponies as well as heavy draught horses and donkeys. The crowd was requested to be quiet so as not to frighten the animals, but spontaneous 'loud cheers, and a cry of "God bless you," were evoked by her concluding remark that, "in this life man and beast are held together by God's own chain under one law"'.[130]

Burdett-Coutts's efforts to help lower-class men and their animals together was a reflection of the Victorian tendency to elide the two groups mentally, as joint recipients of the guidance and charity bestowed by their superiors. As the popular writer quoted earlier remarked, 'From the coster[monger] to his donkey the transition is natural'.[131] However, Burdett-Coutts's own words, quoted above, provide a deeper reason for her holistic approach to philanthropy. Kind stewardship of working and domestic animals, man's servants and loving friends, would complement that reconciliation between social classes which was her objective in the human sphere, ensuring order and concord in the whole – 'God's own chain' binding together all his creatures. In the many letters she wrote to the press, either as spokesperson for the RSPCA ladies' committee or on her own account, a need to respect the bond between humans and animals was always uppermost in her mind. When she was in Edinburgh in 1873, the sight of tramway horses – 'miserable skeletons' that were made to 'toil and sweat up the incline of Leith Walk and the North Bridge' under the lash – filled her with despair; such cruelty was a 'flagrant violation' of 'the right of every creature to good and fair treatment from the hands of man'. 'It is impossible for me to express what I feel when seeing these animals … Knowing that a horse would rather die than not do its work', she believed that duress added mental torment to their physical suffering. Burdett-Coutts felt for the horses, but she also felt for the 'lads' who were required to goad them up the steep hill: they received 'an evil education' in 'habits of active cruelty' to sentient beings, and 'even a nature originally kindly must become hard and callous when daily compelled to exercise cruelty in order to earn a living'.[132]

As we have seen, the argument that habitual cruelty to animals demoralised the perpetrator, conditioning him to commit crimes of violence on fellow-humans, had been put forward by virtually all animal advocates over the centuries; but here there is a difference. It is not the innate malignity of the individuals concerned that has to be corrected, but rather the social and economic system which necessitates cruelty 'in order to earn a living': the selfishness and mercenary spirit of those who wield power. 'Have we' asked Burdett-Coutts, 'in our respective situations done all, or even done what we could, to humanize that seething mass of both brutal and unreclaimed self-indulgent living which is round and about us, whether in town or country?' Steeplechasing and trap pigeon shooting, both sports of the wealthy, said little for the 'humanity or refinement' that might be expected of the educated classes; but 'the shameless cruelties perpetrated either to pander to the gourmand's depraved tastes, or to the intellectual curiosity which seeks to discover the mystery of life through the phenomena of death by torture' in vivisection were worse. Such permitted, even relished cruelties bore 'loathsome fruit' in instances of heartlessness towards 'women, old, helpless, or sick, young children, and animals, which curdle the blood' ... 'God only knows now, but man may, to his cost, know on some future day, where the germ of cruelty may with retributive justice develop'.[133]

This fear of 'retribution', deriving from Burdett-Coutts's sense of rottenness at the core of British society, took on an almost superstitious dimension: the abuse of God's creatures was revenged by Him through seemingly natural processes of cause and effect. Ruthless commercialism and the cruelties it engendered came at a price, in the 'recoil of suffering': the 'tainted breath and fevered blood' of abused cattle 'carry with the tread of their lacerated feet ... the germs of retributive disease', infecting even 'wholesome farms and pastures'.[134] So too the fate of a lost retriever puppy, beaten and knocked about by men and boys in Piccadilly until it was rescued – too late – by 'a brave woman', typified the prevailing cruel harassment of stray dogs, that in Burdett-Coutts's (mistaken) opinion, shared by many of her contemporaries, brought on epidemics of rabies. 'But while all that relates to animal life affects indirectly the welfare and safety of man, and the close connexion should never be lost sight of, yet, even apart from and beyond all this, the inhuman treatment of animals should be held to be a wrong and a sin.'[135]

Burdett-Coutts's actions were inspired by a traditional, hierarchical kind of Christian belief, apparently little disturbed by Darwinism. She admitted that a principle of benevolence could not easily be discerned in wild nature; 'for though man might arrive at the virtue of justice' through 'nature's teaching' (in the form of an eye for an eye and a tooth for a tooth), yet the virtue of mercy, 'the "gentle dew" from heaven', was learnt only from Christ's gospel.[136] Her greatest emphasis, therefore, was on consideration for the working and domestic beasts which formed a bond with their owners. Like many Victorians, she was only beginning to become aware of the wholesale destruction of wild species through hunting, trapping and environmental degradation in other parts of the world. For example, the estate village she had built near to Holly Lodge, her Highgate home, made much use of fine quality teak wood, imported from Asian countries such as Burma, where habitats were being systematically destroyed by clear felling and a teak monoculture.[137] Similarly, her gift to a favourite great-niece was a sable fur muff and stole.[138] However, she protested powerfully against the fashion for feathered millinery, which threatened humming birds and other exotic species with extinction, at the same time as it put deserving British ribbon manufacturers and artificial-flower makers out of work. She was also greatly disturbed by the trapping of native wild birds for caging or consumption: a form of cruelty which became a special concern of the RSPCA ladies' committee.[139] English songbirds such as nightingales, 'represent to us song, poetry, childhood, summer, and home': they evoked an ideal, harmonious domestic ambience attuned to wild nature.[140] Burdett-Coutts herself lived surrounded by companion animals of all kinds, in a sort of little Eden. A journalist from the *Strand Magazine* who visited Holly Lodge in 1894 encountered not just her adored dogs but also a pet cockatoo, donkeys that had been presented by grateful costermongers, horses, prize goats, cows, pigs and poultry.[141] The artist Edmund Caldwell depicted the cockatoo in the manner of Landseer's portraits of the royal family's pets, and even designed a humorous Christmas card where 'Cocky' and the dogs drink the Baroness's health.[142] Sentimental anthropomorphism was the fashion, and Burdett-Coutts had no embarrassment in subscribing to it.

The most remarkable example of this tendency to invest animals with emotional and moral characteristics was the monument to a dog, 'Greyfriars Bobby', which Burdett-Coutts commissioned from the sculptor William Brodie; it was constructed at her expense and unveiled in 1873 (figure 12).[143] Bobby, a Skye

GREYFRIARS BOBBY, EDINBURGH
THE DOG WHICH WOULD NOT LEAVE HIS MASTER'S GRAVE
STATUE ERECTED BY THE BARONESS BURDETT COUTTS

SUTHERLAND

12 'Greyfriars Bobby' monument, Edinburgh, 1873, undated photographic postcard, showing William Brodie's bronze statue of Bobby, the drinking fountain and trough, donated by Baroness Burdett-Coutts.

terrier, had belonged (it was said) to a shepherd or farmer, who on market days had refreshed himself at Traill's Dining-Rooms, near Greyfriars churchyard in Edinburgh. When the man died in 1858 and was buried in this churchyard, the dog was found in the vicinity, and remained there, apparently keeping a vigil by his late master's grave, until his own death in 1872.[144] The fame of this animal – no doubt fostered by local people with an interest in attracting visitors to the spot – was such that, when Burdett-Coutts was in Edinburgh, she too made a pilgrimage to Greyfriars churchyard and met Bobby. She was apparently so moved by the experience that Brodie was given the task of sketching the dog 'From the life just before his death', as recorded on the plinth of the monument, with a view to commemorating his undying love for his master; the verisimilitude of this life-size portrayal seems intended to vouch for the veracity of the legends that had already grown up around him.[145] The monument is sited near the entrance to the churchyard, just where two routes into the centre of old Edinburgh converge at George IV bridge, and Candlemaker Row plunges down the hill to the left. Poised at this dramatic intersection, the dog turns to face the throng of travellers approaching the bridge, as he might often have done in life. The little bronze figure sits on a granite column, below which a plaque pays tribute to his 'affectionate fidelity', while a fountain and a trough for thirsty dogs encourage the passer-by to linger, look and read. Such is the continuing popularity of the memorial that, although the water no longer flows, the dog's nose is bright from repeated touching by fond or superstitious admirers.

It is noteworthy that this memorial is not a tribute of affection and mourning for a deceased favourite, such as might have been erected by its owner, but rather a monument to an ideal which Bobby supposedly embodied. Stories of the undying devotion of dogs to their masters or mistresses are legion in nineteenth-century Britain, both in poetry and in much-reprinted collections of anecdotes – in striking contrast to the shunning and persecution of stray animals.[146] As in the case of the circumstantial storytelling about Greyfriars Bobby and Brodie's realistic sculpture of him, these anecdotes, which attribute almost preternatural insight, resourcefulness and self-sacrifice to their canine heroes, are always claimed to be strictly factual. Lady Julia Lockwood, in her *Instinct; Or Reason?* of 1861, told her young grandson that God in his 'tender providence' had endowed dogs with mental qualities that both resembled and mysteriously transcended reason, in order for them to love and serve mankind.[147] Edwin Landseer created many famous visual expressions of this ideal in his paintings, notably *The Old Shepherd's Chief Mourner* (1837); as we have seen, the RSPCA ladies' committee even arranged the publication of an anthem based on the story of Landseer's picture for all to sing. Likewise, the Society's book on *Claims of Animals* (c.1875) recorded that 'A lady has written a song for this interesting little creature', Greyfriars Bobby himself, addressed to his 'friends'.[148]

It is easy to dismiss such fictions as mere crowd-pleasing Victorian senti-mentalism, of a kind to discredit the animal-protection cause, and indeed they stand in contrast to the more combative, comprehensive and philosophical protests against cruelty to animals put forward by many women in the later decades of the nineteenth century. However, as the workings of nature were gradually understood to embody a principle of 'survival of the fittest', 'each for itself', the idea that *some* creatures shared man's moral impulses – indeed, possessed them in a higher, exemplary degree – was very comforting. In fact Darwin himself, believing in an evolutionary continuity between humans and other species, gave credence to the notion that dogs were capable of quasi-human emotions of loyalty and devotion. Thus the animal psychologist William Lindsay reported that the cult of Greyfriars Bobby was sometimes attributed to 'the tendency of imaginative men and women to idolise their ideals of animal virtue'.[149] The assurance that animals reciprocated human affection provided the strongest argument for their protection, and it is this that Burdett-Coutts intended to impress on the public by her monument. In the later nineteenth and early twentieth centuries there would be many documentary or fictional-ised re-tellings of Bobby's story, which emphasised its ethical dimension. In Eleanor Atkinson's novel *Greyfriars Bobby* of 1912, Burdett-Coutts is made to say '"Our society for the prevention of cruelty to animals is finding it so hard to get people even to admit the sacredness of life in dumb creatures, the brutal-izing effects of abuse of them on human beings, and the moral and practical worth to us of kindness"'; but Greyfriars Bobby '"seems to have brought out the best qualities of the people who have known him"', including hundreds of deprived children.[150]

We have seen that Burdett-Coutts's response to the revelations of systemic cruelty to cattle and other animals had been to press repeatedly for education of the young in the need for kindness. This objective took on considerable importance in the 1870s and 1880s: in 1870 the Elementary Education Act made it mandatory to provide places for all children up to the age of thirteen, either in existing voluntary (mainly Church of England) schools or in new state schools; elected regional school boards, which women were eligible to join, became responsible for implementing the Act. The principal intention was to improve the competence of working-class children in literacy and numeracy, and thus to satisfy the needs of employers and to fit the young for the responsibility of voting in national elections; the Representation of the People Act of 1867 had extended the franchise to all male householders.[151] However, Burdett-Coutts, like many others, was anxious that the government should also acknowledge the spiritual needs of a demoralised nation, both in the conduct of public affairs and in the framing of curricula for use in the secular state schools. The sufferings of Edinburgh's tramway horses led her to reflect that 'when the Imperial Parliament rules that a large expenditure of the public money is incumbent upon the country for educational purposes, it becomes a manifest duty to see that there are no open violations of those legal, moral, and social obligations upon which the well-being of the Commonwealth hinges'.[152]

In her preface to *Woman's Mission*, the set of essays that accompanied British women's contribution to the World's Columbian Exposition at Chicago in 1893, Burdett-Coutts pondered a great historical transition. She looked back nostalgically to the pre-industrial period, to an imagined age of benign rural paternalism, when 'the ordinary domestic habitudes' of the manor house and the aristocrat's mansion included ladies' 'charitable duties' to the poor of the locality.[153] The growth of urban populations and vast changes in living and working conditions in the nineteenth century had made such piecemeal acts of charity quite inadequate to the task of relieving human misery. Reliance on the state – impersonal and secular as it was – had taken their place; and, although women would gradually begin to hold responsible positions in this public world, the immediate effect of a growth in governmental and municipal bodies was to supersede the stupendous individual efforts of women like Angela Burdett-Coutts. However, in the field of animal protection, the Christian conscience and women's distinctive sympathy for animals continued to find scope for personal expression: if not in law-making, then in moral education and in the production of literature that, as will be shown, powerfully contrasted with the prevailing masculine ethos.

Notes

1 M. Jeanne Peterson, *Family, Love, and Work in the Lives of Victorian Gentlewomen* (Bloomington and Indianapolis: Indiana University Press, 1989), pp. 132f.

2 Frank K. Prochaska, *Women and Philanthropy in Nineteenth-Century England* (Oxford: Clarendon Press, 1980), pp. 23f., 44–5.

3 Dorice Williams Elliott, *The Angel Out of the House: Philanthropy and Gender in Nineteenth-Century England* (Charlottesville and London: University Press of Virginia, 2002), pp. 114 (note 10), 133. Prochaska, *Women and Philanthropy*, pp. 175–6, 178. Michael J.D. Roberts, *Making English Morals: Voluntary Association and Moral Reform*

in England, 1787–1886 (Cambridge and New York: Cambridge University Press, 2004), p. 206. Sarah Richardson, 'Philanthropic economy: radicalism, women and charity', in *The Political Worlds of Women: Gender and Politics in Nineteenth Century Britain* (New York and London: Routledge, 2013), pp. 63–81.

4   Julia Wedgwood, 'Female suffrage, considered chiefly with regard to its indirect results', in Josephine Butler (ed.), *Woman's Work and Woman's Culture: A Series of Essays* (London: Macmillan, 1869). Dorothy Thompson, 'Women, work and politics in nineteenth-century England: the problem of authority' and Patricia Hollis, 'Women in council: separate spheres, public space', both in Jane Rendall (ed.), *Equal or Different: Women's Politics 1800–1914* (Oxford: Basil Blackwell, 1987).

5   Ralph Fletcher, *A Few Notes on Cruelty to Animals; On the Inadequacy of Penal Law; On General Hospitals for Animals* (London: Longman, 1846), pp. 59f. William Lauder Lindsay, *Mind in the Lower Animals in Health and Disease*, 2 vols (London: C. Kegan Paul, 1879), vol. 2, pp. 330–1.

6   'Shelters for stray cats', *The Times* (8 June 1910), p. 22, shows that Our Dumb Friends' League was also active in this field. Edward G. Fairholme and Wellesley Pain, *A Century of Work for Animals: The History of the R.S.P.C.A., 1824–1924* (London: John Murray, 1924), p. 281. Arthur W. Moss, *Valiant Crusade: The History of the R.S.P.C.A.* (London: Cassell, 1961), pp. 109–10. Hilda Kean, *Animal Rights: Political and Social Change in Britain since 1800* (London: Reaktion Books, 1998), pp. 137–8. Chien-hui Li, *Mobilizing Traditions in the First Wave of the British Animal Defense Movement* (London: Palgrave Macmillan, 2019), p. 40.

7   Judith R. Walkowitz, *Prostitution and Victorian Society: Women, Class and the State* (Cambridge: Cambridge University Press, 1980), pp. 16–18, 42, 133.

8   John Hollingshead in *Morning Post* (27 February 1861), p. 4; reprinted with slight modifications as 'Happy dogs' in Hollingshead's *Miscellanies: Stories and Essays*, 3 vols (London: Tinsley Bros., 1874), vol. 2, pp. 201–5.

9   Peter Ballard, *A Dog Is For Life: Celebrating the First Hundred Years of the National Canine Defence League* (London: National Canine Defence League, 1990). Listing of 'Societies and homes for animals' in Emily Janes (ed.), *The Englishwoman's Yearbook and Directory* (London: Adam and Charles Black, 1899), pp. 138–9. RSPCA 'Sermons and reports', information on cat protection groups. Frances Simpson, 'Cat and dog London', in George Robert Sims (ed.), *Living London*, 3 vols (London: Cassell, 1902), vol. 1. Kate Cording, *Waifs of a Great City, Being More About the Beggar Cats of London* (London: Gilbert and Rivington: 1907) (untraced). Fairholme and Pain, *Century of Work*, p. 288. Kean, *Animal Rights*, pp. 138, 148–9.

10 University College London Bloomsbury Project, 'London Cabmen's Mission' (www.ucl.ac.uk/bloomsbury-project/institutions/london_cabmens_mission.htm, accessed July 2015).

11 RSPCA *Reports* (1838), p. 139; (1841), p. 172; (1842), p. 100.

12 Edgar Preston, *Half-a-Century of Good Work: A Jubilee History of the Metropolitan Drinking Fountain and Cattle Trough Association, 1859–1909* (London: The Association, 1909). Howard Malchow, 'Free water: the public drinking fountain movement and Victorian London', *London Journal*, 4:2 (1978), 181–203. Kean, *Animal Rights*, pp. 54–7. The MDFCTA's records are held at the London Metropolitan Archives.

13 RSPCA *Report* (1874), p. 24, quoting an article in *Good Words*.

14 MDFCTA *Report* (1865), pp. 10–11. John Lee, Secretary of the MDFCTA, announced the new initiative in the *Times* (20 May 1867), p. 11. The institution had originally

been named the 'Metropolitan Drinking Fountain Association'; the words 'and Cattle Trough' were added at this point.

15 RSPCA *Reports* (1842), p. 8; (1843), p. 12. 'Hydrophobia', a letter in the *Times* (10 July 1852), led to a special meeting of the RSPCA (12 July), and a request to the London parish authorities to provide troughs: RSPCA *Records* (vol. 7 for 1850–1857), pp. 66–7.

16 Preston, *Half-a-Century of Good Work*, pp. 7–8. Malchow, 'Free water', 183.

17 Liverpool Record Office, 179 ANI 9/1–2: Liverpool RSPCA *Reports* (1873), p. 11; (1882), p. 11. 179 ANI 1/2, Liverpool RSPCA minute book no. 2 (May 1881–April 1895), meetings of 31 May and 28 June 1882. 179 ANI/6/1–2, Liverpool RSPCA ladies' committee minute books (1873–1878), meetings of 25 June, 20 August and 19 November 1875; (1885–1891): meetings of 16 January, 13 March and 23 October 1885.

18 However, the MDFCTA committee later criticised the paucity of the RSPCA's contribution to its expenses, which had greatly increased when it took over responsibility for animal troughs: MDFCTA *Report* (1868), pp. 9–11.

19 MDFCTA *Reports* (1865), p. 5; (1867), p. 6. 'Drinking fountains', *The Times* (30 June 1880), p. 10.

20 'Metropolitan Drinking Fountain and Cattle Trough Association', *Animal World*, 13 (1 August 1882), 126–7.

21 MDFCTA *Reports* (1869), p. 7; (1870), pp. 7–8, 13–15. *The Times* (26 June 1872), p. 11.

22 Philip Davies, *Troughs & Drinking Fountains: Fountains of Life* (London: Chatto & Windus, 1989) shows some of the more elaborate designs, which were often costly to maintain.

23 MDFCTA *Report* (1869), p. 5. Letter from Samuel Gurney, chairman of the Association, forwarding one from Mrs Hambleton: 'Drinking fountains', *The Times* (7 March 1872), p. 6.

24 MDFCTA *Reports* (1867), p. 15; (1870), p. 20; (1871), p. 16.

25 MDFCTA *Reports* (1869), p. 9; (1870), p. 16. Preston, *Half-a-Century of Good Work*, p. 40.

26 MDFCTA *Reports* (1866), p. 12; (1867), p. 7; (1868), pp. 7–8, 13–14. 'Drinking fountains', *The Times* (30 June 1880), p. 10. Preston, *Half-a-Century of Good Work*, pp. 31, 38, 40.

27 MDFCTA *Reports* (1870), pp. 9, 16; (1871), p. 8. 'The luxury of doing good things', *Animal World*, 6:74 (1 November 1875), 162–3. Preston, *Half-a-Century of Good Work*, pp. 32, 42, 49. Malchow, 'Free water', 199–200. Diana Orton, *Made of Gold: A Biography of Angela Burdett Coutts* (London: Hamish Hamilton, 1980), p. 159. An article on 'Drinking fountains' by 'W.W.' in *Building News* (21 April 1871), pp. 292–3, described the fountain and trough commissioned by Burdett-Coutts that stood outside the Zoological Gardens in London. Her visit to Manchester was reported on 11 September 1875 by the *Times*, p. 3, and *Manchester Guardian*, p. 9.

28 MDFCTA *Report* (1867), p. 8.

29 *Graphic*, 24:608 (23 July 1881), 90.

30 MDFCTA *Reports* (1865), p. 7; (1866), p. 8. Preston, *Half-a-Century of Free Water*, pp. 5–7, 26–7. Malchow, 'Free water', 182–4.

31 Malchow, 'Free water', 195, quoting Edward Thomas Wakefield, *A Plea for Free Drinking Fountains in the Metropolis* (London: Hatchard, 2nd edn, 1859).

32 Gloria Cottesloe, *The Story of the Battersea Dogs' Home* (Newton Abbot: David & Charles, 1979). Kean, *Animal Rights*, pp. 88–90. Garry Jenkins, *A Home of Their Own: The Heart-Warming 150-Year History of Battersea Dogs & Cats Home* (London: Bantam

Books, 2010). Hannah Velten, *Beastly London: A History of Animals in the City* (London: Reaktion Books, 2013), pp. 208f. Battersea has plans to open its archive to researchers, but here my account is based only on published sources.

33 Mary Tealby was buried with her brother, Revd Edward Bates, who also worked for the Home in its early days. Cottesloe, *Story of the Battersea Dogs' Home*, pp. 18–19. Jenkins, *Home of Their Own*, pp. 20–30. Article on Tealby by Hilda Kean in the *Oxford Dictionary of National Biography* (British Academy and Oxford: Oxford University Press, 2004).

34 Mary Tealby, letter to the *Standard* (11 September 1860), signed 'A friend to all dumb animals'; in RSPCA *Records* (vol. 8 for 1858–1864), pp. 24–5. 'Home for lost and starving dogs', announcement in the *Times* (18 October 1860), p. 6.

35 'Dogs in London', letter from 'H.M.E.', *The Times* (15 May 1865), p. 8.

36 *The Times* (10 May 1866), p. 12.

37 William Kidd, 'The home for lost dogs', *Leisure Hour*, 506 (5 September 1861), 564–6; reprinted in the Quakers' *Friends' Review*, 15:23 (8 February 1862), 363–5. Cottesloe, *Story of the Battersea Dogs' Home*, p. 24.

38 Kean, *Animal Rights*, pp. 88–9. Philip Howell, *At Home and Astray: The Domestic Dog in Victorian Britain* (Charlottesville and London: University of Virginia Press, 2015), pp. 74–5.

39 Anon., *An Appeal for the Home for Lost and Starving Dogs, by a Member of the Society* (London: W.H. Dalton, 1861), p. 4.

40 Jenkins, *Home of Their Own*, pp. 49, 95. RSPCA archive (CM/167), manuscript 'History of the Society' dated 1909, with a note of the obituary of Miss Morgan, who died in April 1874. Moss, *Valiant Crusade*, pp. 198–9.

41 'Home for lost and starving dogs', announcement in the *Times* (18 October 1860), p. 6.

42 Hollingshead in *Morning Post* (27 February 1861), p. 4.

43 'M.K.', letter in the *Standard*, September 1860, in RSPCA *Records* (vol. 8 for 1858–1864), p. 26.

44 'A.B.', letter to the *Times* (18 October 1860), p. 6. Frances Power Cobbe remarked that such a self-righteous outcry over a supposed 'defrauding of human claims' never arose when gin palaces or casinos were built: *Studies New and Old of Ethical and Social Subjects* (London: Trübner, 1865), p. 245.

45 *The Times* (18 October 1860), p. 8.

46 Anon., *An Appeal for the Home*, pp. 5–7.

47 James Greenwood, *Going to the Dogs* (London: C. Beckett, 1866), pp. 3–4, reprinted from Greenwood's article in the *Star*.

48 Isabella Dallas-Glyn, 'The home for lost dogs', letter to the *Daily News* (20 July 1872).

49 'The home for lost dogs', *Illustrated London News*, 53:1498 (22 August 1868), 182.

50 'A dog's-eye view of the dog hospital', *The Queen*, 4 (28 September 1861), 50. Cf. 'The home for lost dogs', *Home Chronicler*, 7 (5 August 1876), 105–6.

51 *The Confessions of a Lost Dog. Reported by Her Mistress, Frances Power Cobbe* (London: Griffith and Farran, 1867). Cobbe and Lloyd resigned from the committee of the Dogs' Home in 1882 in protest at the membership of George Fleming, who had defended pathological research on live dogs. Jenkins, *Home of Their Own*, 95, 105–9. Sally Mitchell, *Frances Power Cobbe: Victorian Feminist, Journalist, Reformer* (Charlottesville and London: University of Virginia Press, 2004), p. 166.

52 Clare Tomalin, *Charles Dickens: A Life* (London: Viking, Penguin Books, 2011), p. 180.

53 Harriet Ritvo, *The Animal Estate: The English and Other Creatures in the Victorian Age*

(London: Penguin: 1990), pp. 167–202. Neil Pemberton and Michael Worboys, *Mad Dogs and Englishmen: Rabies in Britain, 1830–2000* (Basingstoke: Palgrave Macmillan, 2007), pp. 80f., 135f. Howell, *At Home and Astray*, pp. 153–73.

54 Walkowitz, *Prostitution and Victorian Society*. Paul McHugh, *Prostitution and Victorian Social Reform* (London: Croom Helm, 1980). Jane Jordan, *Josephine Butler* (London and New York: Hambledon Continuum, 2001).

55 Charles Dickens, 'Two dog-shows', *All the Year Round*, 171 (2 August 1862), 493–7. Grace Moore, 'Beastly criminals and criminal beasts: stray women and stray dogs in *Oliver Twist*', in Deborah Denenholz Morse and Martin A. Danahay (eds), *Victorian Animal Dreams: Representations of Animals in Victorian Literature and Culture* (Aldershot: Ashgate, 2007), pp. 209–11. The suggestion that 'Two dog-shows' was actually written by Dickens's colleague, John Hollingshead (Howell, *At Home and Astray*, p. 38, referring to an earlier source), seems unconvincing. Hollingshead's autobiography, *My Lifetime* (1895), referred (vol. 1, pp. 20–1) to his essay about the Home in *Morning Post*, which had reappeared in *Good Words* and subsequently in his *Miscellanies*. However, Hollingshead never claimed authorship of 'Two dog-shows', and it is not in *Miscellanies*. Moreover, its style is quintessentially Dickensian.

56 Hollingshead in *Morning Post* (27 February 1861), p. 4. Jenkins, *Home of Their Own*, p. 51.

57 'The fate of the dogs', *Morning Post* (1 July 1868), p. 6. 'Home for lost and starving dogs', *The Times* (2 April 1886), p. 13. Edward Bruce Hamley in *Our Poor Relations: A Philozoic Essay* (Edinburgh and London: William Blackwood & Sons, 1872), pp. 67–8, suggested that the Home tried to hide the extent of the killings. Susan Hamilton, 'Dogs' homes and lethal chambers, or, what was it like to be a Battersea dog?', in Laurence W. Mazzeno and Ronald D. Morrison (eds), *Animals in Victorian Literature and Culture: Contexts for Criticism* (London: Palgrave Macmillan, 2017).

58 'Home for lost dogs', letter from the Secretary of the Dogs' Home, Charles Colam, in the *Standard* (24 December 1886), p. 2. Ouida, 'Cure for rabies', letter to the *Times* (4 November 1886), p. 3, and 'The quality of mercy', in her *Critical Studies* (Leipzig: Bernhard Tauchnitz, 1901), p. 227. Kean, *Animal Rights*, pp. 91–5. Howell, *At Home and Astray*, pp. 85, 87, 96.

59 Roswell McCrea, *The Humane Movement: A Descriptive Survey* (New York: Columbia University Press, 1910), p. 89.

60 'The importation of cattle', letter from T.F. Hewitt, Secretary of the Hull and East Riding branch of the RSPCA to the *Times* (4 August 1865), p. 10. Liverpool RSPCA *Reports* (1873), p. 11; (1876), pp. 14–15; (1877), p. 12; (1878), p. 12; (1881), p. 13.

61 All these abuses were frequently discussed in the press, in connection with parliamentary reports on the Contagious Diseases (Animals) bill of Spring 1869. *The Times* (28 September 1866), p. 5; (29 July 1869), p. 9; (8 September 1869), pp. 5, 7; (9 September 1869), p. 9; (6 October 1869), p. 8; (9 November 1869), p. 3. *Hansard's Parliamentary Debates*, 3rd series, vol. 194: Commons debates on the Contagious Diseases (Animals) Acts; col. 90f. (17 February 1869); col. 672f. (4 March 1869); col. 996f. (10 March 1869). Velten, *Beastly London*, pp. 14f.

62 *The Times* (8 September 1869), p. 7.

63 *The Times* (11 September 1869), p. 7.

64 Ibid.

65 RSPCA *Records* (vol. 10 for 1868–1869), p. 11.

66 *The Times* (20 August 1869), p. 7.

67 RSPCA *Report* (1869), p. 20.

68 *The Times* (11 September 1869), pp. 7, 8.

69 RSPCA *Records* (vol. 11 for 1869–1870), pp. 96–149.

70 *The Times* (2 June 1875), p. 11.

71 Angela Burdett-Coutts, 'Systematic education for the humane treatment of animals', *The Times* (14 September 1869), p. 6. Burdett-Coutts's recommendations were strengthened by her sponsorship of a humane cattle truck designed by W. Reid; *The Times* (9 November 1869), p. 3. Cf. *Animal World*, 1:3 (1 December 1869), 61; RSPCA *Report* (1870), pp. 25–6.

72 Colam's letter in the *Times* (16 September 1869), p. 6. 'On board the Leo', *Animal World*, 1:1 (1 October 1870), 16.

73 Sir Arthur Helps, *Some Talk About Animals and Their Masters. By the Author of 'Friends in Council'* (London: Strahan, 1873). Helps, Clerk of the Privy Council from 1860 onwards, was a friend of the widowed Queen Victoria, having edited *The Principal Speeches and Addresses of His Royal Highness The Prince Consort* (1862) and *Leaves from the Journal of Our Life in the Highlands* (1868). John R. DeBruyn's article on Helps in the *Oxford Dictionary of National Biography*.

74 Helps, *Some Talk About Animals*, pp. 5, 14.

75 Ibid., pp. 15–18.

76 Ibid., pp. 44–5, 71, 158.

77 Ibid., pp. 117, 128–9.

78 Ibid., p. 43.

79 Ibid., pp. 113–17. See *The Times* (24 May 1866), p. 9; RSPCA *Report* (1874), p. 20; (1876), pp. 24–5. John Lilwall's letter to the *Times*, 'Cruelty to poultry *in transitu*' (17 October 1874), p. 10, was answered by Colam (19 October 1874), p. 11, who explained the difficulty of convicting consignors of the birds under existing laws.

80 Helps, *Some Talk About Animals*, pp. 158–9.

81 RSPCA executive committee minutes, book 11, pp. 210–12, meeting of 14 June 1869. George Thorndike Angell, *Autobiographical Sketches and Personal Reflections* (Boston: American Humane Education Society, undated [c.1898]), pp. 20–1. James Turner, *Reckoning with the Beast: Animals, Pain, and Humanity in the Victorian Mind* (Baltimore and London: Johns Hopkins University Press, 1980), pp. 49f.

82 RSPCA executive committee minutes, book 11, p. 375, meeting of 27 June 1870. Burdett-Coutts's and Colam's letters, as notes 71–2. Angell, *Autobiographical Sketches*, pp. 22–3, 33. *Animal World*, 1:10 (1 July 1870), 168, 182; 1:12, 216.

83 RSPCA ladies' committee minutes, inaugural meeting of 15 July, 1870, pp. 2–6. 'The luxury of doing good things', *Animal World* 1875, as note 27. Moss, *Valiant Crusade*, p. 199. RSPCA *Report* (1871), pp. 17–20.

84 RSPCA executive committee minutes, book 13, pp. 350–2, meeting of 13 November 1877.

85 RSPCA *Reports* (1874), p. 44; (1879), p. 112.

86 *Animal World*, 1:10 (1 July 1870), 168; 1:11 (1 August 1870), 200; 1:12 (1 September 1870), 216, 220.

87 The minutes of the Liverpool RSPCA ladies' committee are also missing from the beginning of 1879 to the end of 1884.

88 RSPCA executive committee minutes, book 13, pp. 100–2, meeting of 25 January 1875. Mary Ann Elston, 'Women and anti-vivisection in Victorian England, 1870–1900', in Nicolaas A. Rupke (ed.), *Vivisection in Historical Perspective* (London and New York: Routledge, 1987), p. 270.

89 RSPCA executive committee minutes, book 11, p. 398, meeting of 9 August 1870.

90 Edward A. Freeman, 'The morality of field sports', *Fortnightly Review*, n.s. 34 (1 October 1869), 353–85. Anthony Trollope, 'Mr Freeman on the morality of hunting', *Fortnightly Review*, n.s. 36 (1 December 1869), 616–25. Helen Taylor, 'A few words on Mr Trollope's defence of fox-hunting', *Fortnightly Review*, n.s. 37 (1 January 1870), 63–8.

91 RSPCA executive committee minutes, book 11, pp. 244, 284–6, meetings of 8 November 1869 and 24 January 1870. At a meeting on 11 April 1870, p. 330, 'A letter was read from Mrs Hargreaves severely commenting upon the Society for not actively opposing Field Sports'.

92 The men did concede that, as these patronesses of the Society were to be *ex officio* members of the ladies' committee, the latter should have a say in the patronesses' appointment: executive committee minutes, book 11, p. 400, meeting of 9 August 1870.

93 The work of Cowper-Temple and Smithies in founding the Band of Mercy is discussed in chapter 4.

94 Jane Jordan, *Josephine Butler* (London: Hambledon Continuum, 2001), pp. 85f., 106f. Until 1894, the female right to vote in local government elections was restricted to single women who were ratepayers.

95 A copy of the *Prospectus* is inserted in the ladies' committee minutes, pp. 20–2, meeting of 8 August 1870.

96 Ladies' committee minutes, meetings of 18 July 1870, p. 10; 7 November 1870, p. 28; 21 November 1870, p. 34; 12 December 1870, p. 36. *Animal World*, 1:10 (1 July 1870), 162. RSPCA *Report* (1876), pp. 27–8.

97 Samuel Jackson Pratt in *The Lower World: A Poem* (London: Sharpe and Hailes, 1810), pp. 128–9, described a short-lived animal protection society 'lately formed at Liverpool'. In 1833, William Fry reported on the group of ladies there led by Jane Roscoe. RSPCA *Report* (1841), pp. 8, 67–9. Moss, *Valiant Crusade*, pp. 20–2. After further vicissitudes, a new group was successfully established in 1871 – the first to leave minutes and printed records.

98 For example, the 'Auxiliary' in the Liverpool suburb of West Derby was run by a Miss Alice Houghton, and its membership was about 72 per cent female. Liverpool Record Office, 179 ANI 9/1–2, Liverpool RSPCA *Reports* (1880), p. 28; (1881), pp. 29–30.

99 Liverpool RSPCA *Report* (1874), pp. 8, 20. *Animal World*, 4:48 (1 September 1873), 140, reported that the Liverpool ladies' committee would undertake work 'mostly of a persuasive and educational' rather than a 'punitive' character, and was subordinate to 'the Gentlemen's Committee' there.

100 Liverpool RSPCA *Report* (1874), p. 8, and *Report* (1875), p. 13. Liverpool Record Office 179 ANI 6/1, Liverpool RSPCA ladies' committee minutes for 1873–1878, meeting of 21 August 1874. See also minutes for 24 October 1873; 20 August and 22 October 1875.

101 Liverpool RSPCA *Report* (1877), p. 12.

102 Early in its history, the ladies' committee mooted the idea of a dogs' home in Liverpool (minutes of the ladies' meeting of 24 October 1873), and it took the initiative in establishing one. 179 ANI 1/2, Liverpool RSPCA general committee minutes, book 2 (May 1881–April 1895): minutes of the meetings of 28 February and 21 March 1883. The *Reports* of the Liverpool Temporary Home for Lost and Starving Dogs, 1884 onwards, in the Liverpool Record Office (179 ANI 9/10), also indicate the predominant role of women. In 1887, for example, they were 75 per cent of the committee membership.

103 Liverpool RSPCA *Reports* (1876), p. 16; (1877), pp. 12–13; (1879), pp. 8, 14. The issue was raised at nearly every meeting of the ladies' committee. See especially minute book for

1873–1878, meetings of 22 May 1874; 25 June 1875; 6 October 1876; 23 March 1877. The women were still working for the abolition of bearing reins as late as 1896.

104 Liverpool RSPCA ladies' committee minute book for 1873–1878, meeting of 26 May 1876. *Liverpool Courier*, clipping pasted in the Liverpool RSPCA general committee minutes, book 2, with a report on speeches at the Society's annual meeting on 19 April 1884.

105 Liverpool RSPCA ladies' committee minute book for 1873–1878, meetings of 20 April and 25 May 1877.

106 McCrea, *Humane Movement*, pp. 78, 80, 85, 88. James Turner, *Reckoning with the Beast: Animals, Pain and Humanity in the Victorian Mind* (Baltimore and London: Johns Hopkins University Press, 1980), pp. 48, 51–2. Diane L. Beers, *For the Prevention of Cruelty: The History and Legacy of Animal Rights Activism in the United States* (Athens, OH: Swallow Press/Ohio University Press, 2006), especially pp. 9, 27, 40, 45–8, 53–8, 64, 69, 73–8, 84–6.

107 Susan E. Lederer, 'The controversy over animal experimentation in America, 1880–1914', in Rupke (ed.), *Vivisection in Historical Perspective*. Beers, *For the Prevention of Cruelty*, pp. 123f. Janet M. Davis, *The Gospel of Kindness: Animal Welfare and the Making of Modern America* (New York: Oxford University Press, 2016), pp. 44–5, 53–5. Flora Helm Krause, *Manual of Moral and Humane Education* (Boston, New York and Chicago: Atkinson, Mentzer [1910]), pp. 245f., 'A brief survey of the anti-cruelty movement', especially p. 254.

108 Mary F. Lovell, *Outline of the History of the Women's Pennsylvania Society for the Prevention of Cruelty to Animals from Its Foundation April 14, 1869, to December 31, 1899* (Philadelphia: Office of the Society, 1900), pp. 3–4, 27–8.

109 Ibid., pp. 7, 11, 13, 15, 19, 30–1, 41–2, 54, 56–7, 61, 63.

110 Ibid., pp. 5, 6, 7–8, 14, 16, 26, 29, 53.

111 Ibid., p. 27.

112 Ibid., pp. 17, 18–19. McCrea, *Humane Movement*, pp. 28–9.

113 In 1870 some visitors to Britain, the Chase family of Philadelphia, told the RSPCA ladies' committee about the Women's Pennsylvania Society, and in 1894 Caroline Earl White herself was the guest of the London ladies. RSPCA ladies' committee minutes, meetings of 7 November 1870 and 25 June 1894. Anon., *Baroness Burdett-Coutts: A Sketch of Her Public Life and Work. Prepared for the Lady Managers of the World's Columbian Exposition, by Command of Her Royal Highness, Princess Mary Adelaide, Duchess of Teck* (Chicago: A.C. McClurg, 1893), pp. 87–8.

114 Moss, *Valiant Crusade*, pp. 43–4. Edna Healey, *Lady Unknown: The Life of Angela Burdett-Coutts* (London: Sidgwick & Jackson, 1978), and her article on Burdett-Coutts in the *Oxford Dictionary of National Biography*. Orton, *Made of Gold*. Susan S. Lewis, 'The artistic and architectural patronage of Angela Burdett-Coutts' (PhD dissertation, Royal Holloway, University of London, 2012).

115 Orton, *Made of Gold*, pp. 45–8. According to Orton, Burdett-Coutts received gold to the value of nearly £600,000 and an income of £50,000 a year, beside houses and other goods.

116 Orton, *Made of Gold*, pp. 78f., 110f. Edgar Johnson (ed.), *Letters from Charles Dickens to Angela Burdett-Coutts 1841–1865. Selected and Edited from the Collection in the Pierpont-Morgan Library* (London: Jonathan Cape, 1953). Healey, *Lady Unknown*, pp. 116f. Tomalin, *Dickens*, pp. 202–10.

117 Anon., *Baroness Burdett-Coutts: A Sketch*, pp. 17, 189. Clara Burdett Patterson, *Angela*

Burdett-Coutts and the Victorians (London: John Murray, 1953), pp. 44, 151–2, 212. Healey, *Lady Unknown*, p. 77.

118 Jennie Chappell, *Noble Work by Noble Women* (London: S.W. Partridge, undated [1900]), pp. 5–6.

119 Anon., *Baroness Burdett-Coutts: A Sketch*, pp. 48, 103–4. Orton, *Made of Gold*, p. 160. Healey on Burdett-Coutts in *Oxford DNB*. Lewis, 'Artistic and architectural patronage', pp. 169–71.

120 Healey, *Lady Unknown*, pp. 177–8. Orton, *Made of Gold*, pp. 212–13.

121 George K. Behlmer in *Child Abuse and Moral Reform in England, 1870–1908* (Stanford: Stanford University Press, 1982) stresses the importance of the RSPCA, both as mentor and model, in the early history of the NSPCC: pp. 52–68, 82, 95–6, 138–9, 162–3, 188. Monica Flegel, *Conceptualizing Cruelty to Children in Nineteenth-Century England: Literature, Representation, and the NSPCC* (Farnham and Burlington: Ashgate, 2009), pp. 39f., 61f., 170–1. Roberts, *Making English Morals*, pp. 259–61.

122 McCrea, *Humane Movement*, pp. 14–15, 135–44.

123 *Daily Post*, clipping of 29 March 1883 in Liverpool RSPCA general committee minutes, book 2.

124 'Cruelty to children', letter from Burdett-Coutts to the Home Secretary William Vernon Harcourt, *The Times* (8 December 1883), p. 9. *Baroness Burdett-Coutts: A Sketch*, pp. 60–9. Hesba Stretton [pseud. of Sarah Smith], 'Women's work for children', in Burdett-Coutts (ed.), *Woman's Mission; A Series of Congress Papers on the Philanthropic Work of Women by Eminent Writers*, published for the Royal British Commission, Chicago International Exhibition (London: Sampson Low, Marston, 1893), pp. 4–11. Jeanie Douglas Cochrane, *Peerless Women: A Book for Girls* (London and Glasgow: Collins' Clear-Type Press, undated [1904]), p. 137. Chappell, *Noble Work*, p. 22.

125 Patterson, *Angela Burdett-Coutts*, pp. 44, 212.

126 Anon., *Baroness Burdett-Coutts: A Sketch*, pp. 118–19. Healey, *Lady Unknown*, pp. 166f. Orton, *Made of Gold*, pp. 206f., 262. Lewis, 'Artistic and architectural patronage', pp. 19–20, 248–60, 270f.

127 'Spirit of the journals … The transit of cattle', *The Examiner*, 3224 (13 November 1869). 'The story of the truck', *Animal World*, 1:3 (1 December 1869), 61. Anon., *Baroness Burdett-Coutts: A Sketch*, p. 82.

128 Anon., *Baroness Burdett-Coutts: A Sketch*, p. 83. Healey, *Lady Unknown*, pp. 165, 174.

129 Moss, *Valiant Crusade*, pp. 94, 97.

130 Anon., *Baroness Burdett-Coutts: A Sketch*, pp. 84–7. Moss, *Valiant Crusade*, p. 110.

131 Chappell, *Noble Work*, p. 23.

132 'Cruelty to animals in Edinburgh', letter from Burdett-Coutts, writing as 'President' of the RSPCA 'Ladies' Humane Education Committee' to the Secretary of the Scottish Society for the Prevention of Cruelty to Animals: *The Times* (5 December 1873), p. 9.

133 'Cruelty to animals', letter from Burdett-Coutts, then in Edinburgh, to the *Times* (24 December 1873), p. 6.

134 Burdett-Coutts, 'Systematic education for the humane treatment of animals', *The Times* (14 September 1869), p. 6.

135 Burdett-Coutts, 'Ugly pastime', *The Times* (7 April 1871), p. 5.

136 'Cruelty to animals', letter from Burdett-Coutts, then in Edinburgh, to the *Times* (24 December 1873), p. 6.

137 Lewis, 'Artistic and architectural patronage', p. 268. Raymond L. Bryant, 'Branding

natural resources: science, violence and marketing in the making of teak', *Transactions of the Institute of British Geographers*, 38:4 (2013), 517–30.

138   Patterson, *Angela Burdett-Coutts*, p. 8.

139   'Humming birds', letter from Burdett-Coutts in the *Times* (2 February 1875), p. 7. RSPCA *Report* (1872), p. 24. She had also led a petition for a law to stop the shooting of British sea birds: 'House of Commons', *The Times* (27 February 1869), p. 6.

140   'Protection of birds', letter from Burdett-Coutts, representing the RSPCA ladies' committee, *The Times* (6 June 1872), p. 12. Anon., *Baroness Burdett-Coutts: A Sketch*, pp. 75–7. Healey, *Lady Unknown*, p. 173.

141   Mary Spencer-Warren, 'The Baroness Burdett-Coutts', in the series 'Illustrated interviews', 32, *Strand Magazine*, 7:40 (April 1894), 348–60. Patterson, *Angela Burdett-Coutts*, p. 37.

142   Healey, *Lady Unknown*, pp. 163, 170–5, with photographs. Lewis, 'Artistic and architectural patronage', pp. 132–3, 267.

143   Hilda Kean, 'An exploration of the sculptures of Greyfriars Bobby, Edinburgh, Scotland, and the Brown Dog, Battersea, South London, England', *Society and Animals*, 11:4 (2003), 353–73. Hilda Kean, 'The moment of Greyfriars Bobby: the changing cultural position of animals, 1800–1920', in Kathleen Kete (ed.), *A Cultural History of Animals*, vol. 5, *In the Age of Empire* (Oxford and New York: Berg, 2007). Lewis, 'Artistic and architectural patronage', pp. 133–8. Sir Joseph Noel Paton also sketched the dog for Burdett-Coutts.

144   Among the many early versions of the story, some semi-fictionalised: Henry T. Hutton, *The True Story of 'Greyfriars Bobby'* (Edinburgh: Oliver and Boyd, 1902). Eleanor Stackhouse Atkinson, *Greyfriars Bobby* (New York: A.L. Burt, 1912).

145   *Animal World*, 1:4 (1 January 1870), 80, and 1:8 (2 May 1870), 129–30. Anon., *Baroness Burdett-Coutts: A Sketch*, pp. 79–80. Patterson, *Angela Burdett-Coutts*, pp. 37–8. Orton, *Made of Gold*, p. 159.

146   For example, Joseph Taylor, *Canine Gratitude; Or, A Collection of Anecdotes, Illustrative of the Faithful Attachment and Wonderful Sagacity of Dogs* (London: T. Hughes, undated [1806]). Edward Jesse, *Anecdotes of Dogs* (London: Henry G. Bohn, 1849, 1858). Thomas Bingley, *Stories About Dogs: Illustrative of Their Instinct, Sagacity and Fidelity. With Plates by Thomas Landseer*, new edn (London: T.J. Allman, 1864). Teresa Mangum, 'Dog years, human fears', in Nigel Rothfels (ed.), *Representing Animals* (Bloomington and Indianapolis: Indiana University Press, 2002), pp. 35–47. Diana Donald, *Picturing Animals in Britain, 1750–1850* (New Haven and London: Yale University Press, 2007), pp. 132–40.

147   Lady Julia Lockwood, *Instinct; Or Reason? Being Tales and Anecdotes of Animal Biography; Written for the Instruction and Entertainment of My Youngest Grandson, Mark Napier, and All Other Good Little Boys* (London: Saunders, Otley, 1861), pp. 47, 175. Lockwood's experience of physical abuse by her husband may have heightened her eagerness to teach gentleness to boys.

148   RSPCA ladies' committee minutes, pp. 28, 36, meetings of 7 November and 12 December 1870. RSPCA *Report* (1871), pp. 18–19. *Animal World* (1 February 1871), 68–9. Richard Ormond, *Sir Edwin Landseer* (Philadelphia: Philadelphia Museum of Art, 1981), pp. 110–11. Richard Ormond, *The Monarch of the Glen: Landseer in the Highlands* (Edinburgh: National Galleries of Scotland, 2005), pp. 68–9. Donald, *Picturing Animals*, pp. 154–8. J. Keri Cronin, '"Popular affection": Edwin Landseer and nineteenth-century animal advocacy campaigns', in Jodey Castricano and Lauren Corman (eds), *Animal*

Subjects 2.0 (Waterloo: Wilfrid Laurier University Press, 2016), pp. 81–108. Anon., *Claims of Animals: A Lecture ... On Behalf of the RSPCA* (London: S.W. Partridge, undated [c.1875]), pp. 45–8.

149 William Lauder Lindsay, *Mind in the Lower Animals in Health and Disease*, 2 vols (London: C. Kegan Paul, 1879), vol. 1, pp. 27–8.

150 Atkinson, *Greyfriars Bobby*, pp. 280–1.

151 Eric E. Rich, *The Education Act 1870: A Study of Public Opinion* (London and Harlow: Longmans, Green, 1970).

152 Burdett-Coutts, 'Cruelty to animals in Edinburgh'.

153 Burdett-Coutts, *Woman's Mission*, preface, pp. xiv–xx. Lewis, 'Artistic and architectural patronage', pp. 158–60.

4

The 'two religions':
a gendered divide in Victorian society

Two contrasting images expose a fault line that runs through attitudes to animals in Victorian Britain. In May 1873, the RSPCA's journal *Animal World* decorated its front page with an engraving of Queen Victoria and Princess Beatrice in the cottage of 'an old Highland woman' (figure 13). One of the Queen's many dogs, an adopted collie of 'doubtful character', is menacing the old woman's cat, but the Princess, graciously directed by her mother, wards off his attack with her parasol. The royal ladies 'deem it not derogatory to their high rank to prevent cruelty, and with the true instinct of women, eagerly interpose to mitigate the suffering of a terror-stricken little cat'. When dogs let their passions rise, they must be taught that 'God did *not* "make them so"' – they become 'brutal only by brutal training'.[1] The incident typified Victoria's well-known love for all animals: as chief patron of the RSPCA, she took a personal interest in the design of the 'Queen's Medal' presented to persons who had saved animals from suffering, and at her request a cat was included in the group of domestic and working animals pictured on the medal.[2] In 1874, she expressed her pleasure that a daughter of the Russian Tsar, who became her own daughter-in-law as the Duchess of Edinburgh, was to present the essay prizes at the RSPCA's grand annual meeting, honouring the Society's jubilee, and the Queen took this opportunity to convey her anxieties over the sufferings caused by vivisection (see figure 8). In 1887, the year of her own jubilee, she conferred a greater honour by herself attending the Society's meeting in the Albert Hall. In her address she expressed 'warm and entire sympathy' with the RSPCA's work, and 'real pleasure' in 'the growth of more humane feelings towards the lower animals' among her subjects. 'No civilization is complete which does not include the dumb and defenceless of God's creatures within the sphere of charity and mercy.'[3]

Very different was the concept of regality expressed in Major-General Bisset's

13 'The Queen and Princess protecting a cat', wood engraving signed 'IAT' in *Animal World* (May 1873).

Sport and War ... With a Narrative of HRH The Duke of Edinburgh's Visit to the Cape (1875). Prince Alfred, who as Duke of Edinburgh assisted his wife in presenting the RSPCA's prizes in 1874, had visited South Africa in 1860 with the Queen's blessing, and indulged there the taste for 'deeds of daring and danger' that was believed to distinguish aristocratic British manhood. On one 'glorious day' in 1860, there was a 'Grand Battue' of 'Royal Sport': a thousand or so native retainers corralled a great mass of panicking wild animals, so that the royal party was able to kill 'Six hundred head of large game'. 'The Prince fired as fast

THE CHARGE.

14 'The charge', anonymous wood engraving in Major-General Bisset's *Sport and War*, 1875, showing Prince Alfred, Duke of Edinburgh, shooting an elephant.

as guns could be handed to him ... It became very exciting to see great beasts larger than horses rolling over' ... 'most of the sportsmen looked more like butchers than sportsmen, from being so covered in blood'.[4] On a return visit to southern Africa in 1867, the Duke led – or was given the illusion of leading – an elephant hunt. As etiquette demanded, 'All those around HRH were holding their shots for him to fire first', as the great beast charged. An illustration in the book dramatises this exciting moment, and the Duke's 'cool bravery and nerve' is tellingly contrasted with the cowardice of a 'Hottentot after-rider' who bolts from the terrifying encounter (figure 14). Bisset's party also painfully wounded and ultimately killed a splendid lioness, whose skin was to be a wedding present to the Duke. Her body was laid at the feet of Bisset's daughters, who were with him in the bush. It turned out that 'she had two beautiful cat-like cubs inside her, which made me feel the more sorry for her death'. The emotions of his daughters on the occasion are not recorded.[5]

What is one to make of the polarity between these images of the royal mother and son, and between the patterns of behaviour they typify? An appearance of tender, familial solicitude for the most insignificant and defenceless of creatures is contrasted with bloody carnage of the grandest. Gentle fellow-feeling of a kind likely to harmonise social distinctions is opposed to a ruthless exercise of power, differentiating ranks, races and species. Of course, the Queen, who countenanced the hunting and shooting activities of Prince Albert and later of her sons, might stand accused of rank hypocrisy.[6] Yet a passionate attachment to her pets, revealed in private correspondence, was matched by her very public opposition to vivisection and other institutionalised cruelties.[7] Much here depended, it seems, on a mental separation between 'wild' and 'domestic' animals. One sees it even in the art patronage of the royal family: the paintings of Landseer present a stark contrast in types of subject matter – scenes of hunting and predation that exemplify the brutality of nature in the raw are set against sentimental portraits of dogs and other pets ensconced in the royal apartments.[8] However, attitudes were also conditioned by expectations of behaviour linked to gender. The Duke's zest for the hunt had established his masculinity and royal authority, whereas in the *Animal World* article, it is 'the true instinct of women' that makes Victoria and Beatrice rush to the defence of the cat. Indeed, the Queen was shocked to hear in 1880 that her granddaughter Princess Victoria of Hesse had been out on a shooting expedition: 'To look on is harmless but it is not lady like to kill animals … It might do you great harm if that was known.'[9] At a deeper level the supposedly antithetical natures of men and women were expressed in their respective views of animal nature. *Animal World* credits the Queen with a belief that dogs are not *naturally* aggressive; it is brutal men that make them so. Conversely, the hunters of big game in the British colonies of India and Africa were strikingly receptive to the darker lessons of Darwinism. Sir Samuel White Baker concluded his study of *Wild Beasts and Their Ways* (1890) with the thought that 'the strong predominate, and the weak must suffer' in the struggle for survival, and what was true of the natural world was true also of human society:

> We *hear* of love, and pity, and Christian charity; we *see* torpedoes and hellish inventions of incredible power to destroy our fellow-creatures … The civilised world boasts of its progress in civilisation … but those countries which command respect … are the possessors of the *big battalions*. 'Force,' the great law of nature, will assert its power and rule.[10]

Herbert Spencer in *The Study of Sociology*, first published in 1873, had given these ideas a more sophisticated expression and a more comprehensive frame of reference. Europe was, he thought, presently at a median stage of development between a state of brutishness and a more advanced stage of civilisation. At this historical juncture, competition between nations and imperial conquest demanded extreme aggression; but commercial and social progress demanded, contrarily, an ability to co-operate and conciliate, symbolised by the message of Christianity. These 'two religions' of 'enmity' and 'amity' were, seemingly, incompatible as rules of conduct, and existed only in a precarious balance or alternation; but their power over men's minds was actually far from equal. Like White Baker, Spencer concluded that 'The religion of enmity nearly all men actually believe. The religion of amity most of them merely believe they believe'.[11] The word 'men' here has a sexual force. Spencer thought too poorly of the mental capacity of women to envisage their securing a complete triumph for 'amity', which would anyway be against the nation's interests; nevertheless, their maternal instincts and their age-old need to bow to the will of more powerful men induced a characteristic 'love of the helpless' and pity for the suffering, based on intuition and religious faith: qualities that were the polar opposite of those required of males.[12]

The problems of 'manliness'

In the upbringing of the young, this contrast of values had a particular prominence. Spencer explained that mothers try to affect 'the thoughts and feelings of boys, and afterwards in domestic and social intercourse … the feminine sentiments sway men's public acts, both consciously and unconsciously'.[13] However, the countervailing process of toughening-up boys was far more powerful. In the wealthy family described by Anne Brontë in her novel *Agnes Grey* (1847), the father and uncle of a small boy encourage his brutal beating of a pony, and also his trapping and torture of wild birds and their nestlings: '"Damme, but the lad has some spunk in him, too! … He's beyond petticoat government already: – by G[od]!–he defies mother, granny, governess, and all!"', and, as his treatment of his sister shows, he is a bully of women in the making.[14] Spencer noted that the sons of the moneyed classes were soon removed from 'petticoat government' altogether, and sent away from home to public schools, where the future legislators, administrators and generals of the British Empire were thoroughly trained in 'enmity' – 'made callous, morally as well as physically'. Such schools allegedly paid only lip service to the teachings of Christianity. Instead, study of the bloodiest episodes of Roman history alternated with arbitrary and extreme corporal punishment of the boys, and there was unrestrained bullying and fighting between them, such as to inculcate a respect for naked power and a ruthless struggle for dominance.[15] The histories of these schools make it clear that hunting and sadistic abuse of animals were normal parts of the conditioning that Spencer described. *A History of Marlborough College* dating from 1893 recorded that the 'barbaric instinct of slaughter and adventure inherent in Englishmen' was fostered there by the hurling of 'squalers' (lead weights attached to cane handles) at birds and small mammals, 'occasionally even deer'. One typical boy was 'a "cock bird-nester" … He roasted squirrels … in coffee-pots'.[16] Birds-nesting in order to make collections of eggs was encouraged at Wellington: Charles Kingsley, lecturing there, called it a 'manly and excellent pursuit'.[17] At Eton College, boys organised illegal badger-baiting and cockfighting, and the school kept its own pack of dogs for hare hunting, a practice which lasted through the Victorian era, despite growing public disapproval. Henry Salt, future leader of the Humanitarian League, which waged war on aristocratic field sports, was a pupil at Eton in the 1860s, and subsequently taught there; he remembered it as a 'nursery of barbarism', in the 'twofold cult of sport and soldiership'. When hare hunting palled, the boys were allowed 'to pursue with beagles a mutilated fox deprived of one of his pads'. As a historian of Eton remarked, women were often distressed to learn of their sons' brutalised condition, but 'natural motherly kindness' had no place in institutions of this kind.[18]

The mentality fostered at the public schools prepared youths for an equally male-dominated life in the colonies, where enslavement of native peoples and appropriation of their land provided the conditions for reckless hunting and shooting of big game – another kind of warfare.[19] Its victims included vast numbers of the sportsmen's draught oxen, horses and dogs, which died by predation, exhaustion, thirst or disease, as well as the elephants, giraffes, big cats, boars and antelopes that were pursued. As we have already seen in the description of the Duke of Edinburgh's party, the gentlemanly 'hunting code' venerated in the home country had no purchase in the wilds of Africa and India. Animals of all species were killed in unlimited numbers – females and young ones as well as mature males; and in the conditions of trackless jungle, wounded animals often got away and suffered an agonisingly slow death. Hunters' memoirs describe the sensual exhilaration of the kill, and the freedom and irresponsibility *ultra vires* that a roving life conferred. William Charles Baldwin in his *African Hunting* (1863) reflected that he could wander 'wherever my restless fancy and my love of excitement and adventure may lead me'.[20] In the same spirit, Lord Baden Powell quoted with approval one writer's opinion that rash, unruly boys made the best imperial pioneers: 'they are the experimenting fringe of civilization'.[21]

Yet, for all their maverick qualities, one can discern characteristics in these men's pursuits that associate them with the active forces of capitalism and laissez-faire in the home country. Both were based on a desire for personal autonomy and an urge to dominate and control, based on a conviction that survival of the fittest was indeed the law of life. Both involved rivalry and fierce competition: in the case of the sportsmen, this centred on claims of precedence (the first successful shot or spearing of a particular animal), or of killing a greater range of species.[22] As in the business world, such successes were measured statistically, dignifying random slaughter with the appearance of a scientific pursuit. The dead animals' injuries (where a bullet had entered and left the body) were registered with precision worthy of a forensic patholo- gist, although White Baker thought his female readers might wish to 'pass over' these 'careful *post mortem*' analyses.[23] The lengths and circumferences of horns were also carefully tabulated for comparative purposes; the surviving game diaries of Baron Maurice Egerton of Tatton, and their more systematic equivalents in books published by the taxidermist Rowland Ward, are set out in columns like a ledger, with the trophies of each species listed in descending order of size against the names of their competing 'owners'.[24] Thus the feverish and often highly sexualised excitement of the kill is rationalised, transposed into calculation and distanced from emotion; the 'masculine' mind is victorious over merely sensuous and instinctive life, as though in conscious antithesis to the cult of sympathy with all living creatures which had been gaining ground in the home country.

Nevertheless, literature for boys sometimes betrays an uneasy conscious- ness of the imbalance of 'enmity' and 'amity' that resulted, threatening the requirements of good citizenship. The *Boy's Own Paper*, which was issued by the Religious Tract Society from 1879 onwards and aimed at a middle-class readership, featured many exciting encounters between youths and ferocious wild animals, in imitation of the memoirs of big game hunters that went through edition after edition in the second half of the nineteenth century.[25] However, such yarns were interspersed with articles of a very different com- plexion. 'The gravelling trustees' recounts a true episode: an elderly maiden lady, 'poorly-clad', journeyed daily to Tower Hill in London, to scatter sand or gravel in order to prevent the horses slipping, and she left money for the work to be continued after her death. There is a lesson here for readers: 'Boys of England, you are spirited, brave, and full of courage; be merciful also, and merciful to animals', for gratuitous cruelty is 'unmanly and despicable'.[26] James Greenwood, commissioned for a compendium of *Wild Sports of the World* (1862), opened with stirring thoughts on the British spirit of 'adven- ture' which, while it brings success in hunting, secures also 'the subjugation of territory, and the supplanting of less useful races', to the benefit of the whole world. Yet amidst all the tales of derring-do and carnage, Greenwood interpolates a 'pretty ... little poetic story' in verse by a Miss Crewdson (presumably one of the Quaker family of that name) about a young girl, ' "gentle, kind, and mild" ', who succours a chamois fawn orphaned by her father in the hunt.[27] Exemplars of kindness are *female*, but also pathetic or powerless, in unacknowledged conflict with the bellicose and commanding notions of masculinity; and that conflict of ideas would shape and arguably restrict the forms of animal advocacy that one finds recommended in women's writing. The care of the 'inferior' creation – domestic animals and any wild ones which it proved possible to tame – is the mission of the ideal woman, herself locked into a pattern of domesticity and social subordination that conforms to a greater hierarchy.

The expression of feminine virtues and religious belief in animal protection

The restrictions placed on women's scope for public activism in mid-Victorian Britain were often internalised and justified by women themselves, on the grounds that they reflected essential differences between the sexes in aptitudes and social roles, ordained by God. Whereas men were 'naturally' independent operators, women were self-denying and merely instrumental beings, defined by their varied auxiliary roles in support of the other sex. For modern feminists, Sarah Stickney Ellis's writings are a particularly notorious expression of this view.[28] A prolific author, born into a Quaker family but married to a Congregationalist missionary, she produced a series of very successful conduct books: *Wives of England*, *Mothers of England* and so on, the very titles of which expressed the familial relativity of women's functions.[29] *The Daughters of England: Their Position in Society, Character & Responsibilities*, published in 1842, is a *locus classicus* of so-called 'separate spheres' ideology.[30] The 'first thing of importance' for a young woman is to accept inferiority to men in intellectual ability. Yet 'in the softer touches of mental and spiritual beauty, her character may present a lovelier page than his', and hence what she lacks in power may be compensated by moral influence. Her 'distinct and separate sphere' within the home and family circle, is one which no 'right-minded' wife or mother would consider a restriction. In that sanctum of virtue, she is not called upon 'to calculate, to compete, to struggle' as men must do in those 'eager pecuniary speculations, and in that fierce conflict of worldly interests' which often 'stifle their best feelings'. Instead, a wife or daughter 'may love ... and serve', with a solicitude that reaches the lowliest members of the household, including all the domestic and working animals.[31]

The importance that Ellis gives to animals in this scheme of things is very remarkable, reflecting her own great fondness for them; and as she was the kins-woman and confidante of Mary Sewell and her daughter Anna – the future author of *Black Beauty* – her thoughts on the relations between humans and animals have a particular interest.[32] In the album of Ellis's drawings titled *Contrasts*, published in 1832, kind companionship with animals is shown to give rise to happiness on both sides, while cruelty leads to alienation. Anna Sewell must have been espe-cially interested in one pairing of scenes, captioned 'Necessity' and 'Free agency': a worn-out horse drags a cabriolet overloaded with fashionable pleasure-seekers, in expressive contrast with a scene of horses frisking happily together in their field (figures 15 and 16).[33] Two articles published anonymously in *Once A Week* in 1859–1860 reveal Ellis's consciousness, in her later years, of the extent of ani-mals' yearning for such 'free agency'. She affectionately recalled the assortment of animals that she had adopted as a child – 'sometimes savage creatures' which she attempted, not very successfully, to nurture and tame. They included a buzzard, a raven, a weasel, a snake and a monkey. The style of these articles is wryly down-to-earth, and might easily have been mistaken for that of a man of liberal opinions, even a freethinker. Thus Ellis was amused by the loathing she excited in some of her less amenable protégés; by her Quaker father's loss of confidence in natu-ral theology when he witnessed two robins fighting; and by her bachelor uncle's anthropomorphic fancies, like his 'history of a lady pigeon', who, in defiance of all the pious accounts of maternal devotion in nature, 'persuaded her husband to sit while she flew off from the nest to take her pleasure among the inmates of a neighbouring dovecote'.[34] In contrast, Ellis's *The Poetry of Life*, first published in 1835, is piously philosophical. The suffering of animals like donkeys at the hands of 'creation's lord' is a cause of grief and shame, if also of poetic inspiration, seeming to symbolise the travails of a fallen world: suffering 'borne with a meekness that looks so much like the Christian virtue, resignation, that ... the heart is softened with feelings of sorrow and compassion, and we long to rescue it from the yoke of the oppressor'.[35]

Inculcating such feelings of compassion was, Ellis thought, a task that devolved especially upon women, despite their restriction to the domestic sphere. In *The Wives of England* (1843), she noted among the trials of married life, 'the disposition evinced by some men to be inconsiderate and cruel to animals'. This was a tendency attributable to males' general lack of capacity for empathy, aggravated by the effects of their schooling, in which 'all regard to the

15 Sarah Stickney Ellis, 'Necessity and free agency', an overstrained carriage horse, in *Contrasts, A Series of Twenty Drawings designed by S. Stickney*, lithographed by George Smith, 1832.

16 Sarah Stickney Ellis, 'Necessity and free agency', horses enjoying their freedom in a field, on the facing page in *Contrasts*.

feelings of animals' is absent, and by the nature of their worldly avocations.[36] Ellis seems to go almost as far as to suggest that kindness to animals was, for the average man, incompatible with the general toughness that life in the public sphere required. Indeed, in her novel *Home, Or the Iron Rule*, published in 1836, a dreamily idealistic and unworldly youth called Allan, who 'seemed born to protect what was helpless, and to love what was capable of loving him', tries in vain to save a 'beautiful spaniel' from persecution, and later proves wholly unfitted to make his way in a harsh world.[37]

Middle-class women might be politically powerless, but they were, according to Ellis, superior to their menfolk in the sureness of their moral compass and their capacity for sympathy with all those around them.[38] In such women, indifference to cruelty towards animals would indeed be 'repulsive'.[39] In *Wives of England*, Ellis suggested that the enlightened mistress of a household, its 'presiding mind', should ensure that the 'rights' of every member of it, including the animals, were properly respected, and should teach the servants 'what they possibly will have had no means of learning at home, that these are creatures committed to our care by their Creator and ours'.[40] A mother could do more: counteracting the powerful influences that led boys into vicious cruelty, and conscious of husbands' tendency to be 'not quick-sighted or particularly scrupulous on these points', she should 'bring up her children ... with higher and more enlightened views of the requirements of Christian duty' with respect to animals: what Ellis called 'the law of kindness' or 'the law of love'.[41] Enmity and amity played out in the domestic sphere, no less than in the affairs of nations.

As we have seen, this sort of advice on the upbringing of children can be traced at least as far back as John Locke's *Thoughts Concerning Education*. However, Ellis was thinking of something greater and more inspiring than mere admonition in the nursery. Letting children look after domestic animals may certainly teach them 'to feel both pity, and sympathy for this portion of the creation. But then there are so very few animals capable of being made so happy in confinement, as they would be in their natural state, that there appears considerable danger, lest we should by this means be guilty of inflicting misery, for the sake of seeing it pitied'.[42] Better far to seek 'an intimate acquaintance with the nature and habits of the animal world' in the wild, and to impart it to the young. Such a distinctively feminine approach to natural philosophy was not to involve the kind of analytical or taxonomic research undertaken by male scientists and collectors, who killed and tabulated species of insects – a practice 'most revolting to the female mind'. 'I am not quite sure, that ... we have a right to make even a beetle struggle to death upon the point of a pin, or to crowd together boxes full of living creatures, who, in the agony of their pent-up sufferings, devour and destroy one another.'[43] Much less was she recommending the kind of knowledge that came from hunting animals, 'the sole pleasure of which consists in taking advantage of the weaker party'. Her objection to field sports was no merely womanish 'morbid sensibility': 'I still maintain that it is inconsistent with a noble and a truly generous nature, to find sport in what occasions unnecessary suffering to any living creature', and this licence to abuse animals has the worst effects on youths' treatment of other 'weaker parties', namely women and girls – a 'twofold' power which they relish.[44] Here Ellis was at one with women of more 'advanced' opinions. When Anthony Trollope sneered at critics of hunting as proponents of a 'soft-hearted, rose-leafed, velvet life', inimical to manliness, Helen Taylor, stepdaughter of John Stuart Mill, reacted with fury. For her, as for Ellis, hunting was simply an expression of the male 'desire to overcome, to exercise power, to domineer, to destroy', which had no place in the civilised modern world.[45]

For women at least, Ellis explained, intercourse with nature involved not destruction but communion or reconciliation. 'Yes, there is an acquaintance with the animal creation, which might be cultivated … an acquaintance which seems to absolve these helpless creatures from the curse of estrangement from their sovereign man … brings them near to us in all … their amazing instincts, and in the voiceless, and otherwise unintelligible secrets of their mysterious existence.'[46] In *Home, Or the Iron Rule*, the fictional Mrs Lee takes her young son on Sunday walks in the countryside, where he 'first learned to look for a pervading Spirit in the realms of nature – to welcome all the animated and joyous creatures of earth as members of his own wide brotherhood'.[47] A child thus instructed will gain 'a general impression that everything in nature and art has its particular use', which can be made palpable and memorable through close observation and careful sketching of live subjects.[48] At the same time, poetic imagination, which she represented as the antithesis of commercial utilitarianism, will 'lead our thoughts beyond the narrow limits of material existence, up to that higher region of wonder and of love, where to behold is to admire – to feel is to adore'.[49]

The 'humble sphere of minute observation' cultivated in the countryside (from which men are, according to Ellis, 'generally and very properly considered as excluded'), extended also to the city streets. Thus she directed the attention of England's daughters to the mass of poverty and human misery to be seen in such places, and no less to 'the droves of weary animals goaded, stupefied, or maddened' on the road to the slaughterhouse, or the horses – 'galled and lacer-ated victims of oppression, waiting for their round of agony to come again'.[50] But to what end were these observations made, when the business of the world was conducted exclusively by men? Despite her insistence on the propriety of women's exclusion from politics and even from political discussions, Ellis conceded that there were some public issues 'on which, neither to know, nor to feel', was 'disgraceful': 'the extinction of slavery, the abolition of war in general, cruelty to animals'; but she offered no suggestions as to how women could aid reform in any of these fields, other than by their guidance of the young.[51]

Charlotte Elizabeth Tonna – an anti-slavery activist, political conservative, Protestant zealot and fervent animal lover – faced the same dilemma.[52] As editor of *The Christian Lady's Magazine* in the 1830s, she introduced a series of imaginary conversations between a woman (representing herself) and her uncle, in which the proper limits of women's involvement in politics were dis-cussed. Uncle's thoughts were 'employed on a subject where mine frequently dwell with intensity of pain – the wrongs of the dumb and irrational creation'. Cruelty to animals was a national sin, such as to 'provoke the Lord to anger against us', and a failure to combat cruelty was itself a sin of which these two people accuse themselves. Charlotte Elizabeth vowed to 'assist the good work' of securing protective legislation, but such campaigning was necessarily, for her, of a literary and journalistic kind, rather than involving direct political engagement.[53]

As Leonore Davidoff and Catherine Hall have noted in their comments on 'separate spheres' ideology, 'The tension between subordination and influence, between moral power and political silence', was one which affected 'all the protagonists of "woman's mission"'.[54] Nowhere was this truer than in women's writing on the human relationship with animals, which often adopted a purely domestic and personal frame of reference: a sphere contracted intellectually as well as spatially, where biblical literalism and natural theology lingered on well into the Darwinian era. Charlotte Elizabeth herself produced 'a little book for boys', *Kindness to Animals: Or, The Sin of Cruelty Exposed and Rebuked* c.1844, which went through many editions. She writes about animals 'which have belonged to me'; her companions apparently included parrots and cockatoos, falcons, squirrels and mice, as well as the usual domestic species.[55] She writes too about Jack, a poor Irish deaf and dumb boy whom she adopted and guided into a religious view of the world. As she recorded in her *Personal Recollections* (1841), Jack had previously 'been rather teasing to the dog, and other inferior creatures ... but now he became most exquisitely tender towards every living thing, moving his hand over them in a caressing way, and saying, "God made" '. At the same time, 'The noble nature of man was struggling to assert its pre-eminence over the irrational brute' that, unlike Jack, has no immortal soul to save.[56] Charlotte Elizabeth's mental world is a social and spiritual hierarchy. Her aim is to conjure up and restore the harmonious relationship between God, humanity and the animals that existed before sin entered the world, when man was 'a careful and loving ruler over the poor dumb creatures'.[57]

One cannot imagine a more complete illustration of Spencer's antithetical principles of 'enmity' and 'amity' than the contrast between contemporary big game hunters' narratives and homilies like those of Charlotte Elizabeth. As we have seen, they involve not simply the distinction between violent and amicable relations with animals, but contrasting concepts of nature itself. Thus John Madden, in *The Wilderness and Its Tenants* (1897) dismissed notions of a future reign of peace – Heaven itself was probably 'an Empire', corresponding to the 'law of force' in the natural world.[58] For many female writers, in contrast, nature and society were, or should be, united by a 'law of love' under God, and almost any animal could be reconciled and tamed by human kindness. The typical male adventurer, like the typical capitalist, arrogated a right to personal license and freedom of manoeuvre; the conservative female moralist, persuaded of her own 'relativity', saw the world in terms of co-operation and interdependence within a stratified society, which embraced even the 'poor dumb animals' as objects of paternalistic concern. The commercial sphere and lawless colonial territories were the natural domains of the one; an idealised English country home of the other. One feature, however, unites the extremes of this gendered divide in nineteenth-century proclivities: a desire to *possess* animals, whether as trophies, or as adoptees. There is an assumption that humans have a right to dominate and appropriate an essentially passive natural world, just as the more powerful and propertied social classes assumed a right to direct their social inferiors.

Eliza Brightwen's immensely popular *Wild Nature Won by Kindness* (1890) and *More About Wild Nature* (1892) are quintessential examples of these tendencies in Victorian women's writing; especially of a genre of 'tales' about pet birds and other tamed creatures, told by their benefactresses.[59] A wealthy widow living 'sequestered' in a mansion at Stanmore with a large estate, Brightwen impressed her own personality and ambience on every page of her natural history books.[60] Her sketches of the house and gardens often appear among the illustrations, in proprietorial association with the menagerie she kept there. Charitable but condescending patronage of the local villagers and poor Londoners whom she invited to the house was of a piece with her moral direction of the 'good servants' at Stanmore (she described her household as 'one family "serving the Lord"'), and extended to the taming of her animal 'pensioners'.[61] In this way, the aura of superior social status, ideal domesticity and Christian precepts was inseparable from the notion of 'kindness' which Brightwen's books were intended to convey. Many of the animals she described were native species that inhabited her grounds or were 'redeemed' from less desirable owners, like Joey the kestrel, who had been living in cramped conditions in a local woman's cottage, and reacted with 'immense delight' to his 'present happy circumstances'.[62] Other birds had been taken as fledglings from their nests in the locality of Stanmore, to enjoy, as she thought, a more privileged existence.[63] However, Brightwen also frequented the 'dingy' London premises of Jamrach the animal dealer, where imported tropical creatures were kept in appalling conditions (those she bought there seldom survived for long).[64] All the animals thus acquired were given names and portrayed as quirky individuals. Once the 'little wild heart' of an animal had been 'won by kindness', as a young child's heart would be, its 'instincts and curious ways will be shown', to the delight of its human companion, and it will not pine for loss of liberty.[65] Less anxious than Sarah Stickney Ellis was to respect the autonomy of wild creatures, Brightwen claims that voluntary 'friendship' with humans, while admittedly 'artificial', lifts them to a superior state of wellbeing; for 'the tender dumb creatures' were given to mankind by 'our Heavenly Father' to be 'a solace and joy during our life on earth', and even Roman snails and an Indian fruit-eating bat proved capable of touching affection.[66]

There is here, once again, a reiteration of the old evangelical notion of 'reclaiming' the wild beasts alienated from man by original sin, and thus recreating a kind of paradise; but only when man is restored to grace at the millennium will animals resume their peaceful vegetarian ways.[67] Until that came to pass, it was sadly necessary to feed live prey to her water shrews, and it was 'a really painful sight' when her mole pounced on a worm 'with the fury of a tiger'.[68] Brightwen was in fact – like Charlotte Elizabeth – as resistant to modern scientific thought on the predatory and disruptive principles in nature as she was to the erosion of traditional class distinctions, now threatened by mass education and the rise of socialism.[69] Over thirty years after the publication of Darwin's *Origin of Species*, Brightwen rejected the implications of evolutionary theory, and maintained a strong belief in God's benign providence; according to her kinsman, the writer Edmund Gosse, 'the apparatus of pure science seemed to bewilder and depress her'.[70] Hunting was equally an affront to her pacific view of nature, though she hesitated to criticise the 'gentlemen' who participated in it, at least when she was writing for publication: 'a lady like myself cannot well appeal against it'. Nevertheless, actually seeing 'the anguish of a deer, a fox, or hare' at the end of a hunt was distressing, and in her private journal Brightwen especially deplored the involvement of women in the kill.[71] The 'useless slaughter' of birds in the name of sport was equally repugnant, and gamekeepers' ruthless extermination of birds of prey was 'a grievous pity', but even here Brightwen was harder on the plebeian trippers who took aim at sea birds than she was on the aristocratic owners of shooting estates.[72] As to 'books of sport and hunters' travels', she never read them – 'they make me so wretched'.[73]

Like Sarah Stickney Ellis and many others before her, Brightwen could see no answer to these endemic depravities other than setting a good example to the lower orders, for example by providing a trace horse to help the local draught horses up a hill, and exhorting drivers there to loosen the bearing reins.[74] The young especially should be schooled in humanity, through close, reverent study of the wonders of nature: for Brightwen, 'our Father's works' and the Christian gospel still conveyed a single, unproblematic lesson which children must learn in order to become kind to animals.[75] Despite her habit of taking a nestling or two from their nests for taming, she wrote and lectured frequently on the evils of trapping or caging wild birds, and was active in the local Band of Mercy, teaching children under its aegis in the village school.[76] This movement, which in a sense extended the reformative work of Victorian ladies into a broader sphere of operation, has been little studied until now, but its mission of teaching children to be kind to animals throws an interesting light on the gendered contrast in attitudes that is the subject of this chapter.

The Band of Mercy movement: problems of reforming masculine proclivities

In many ways the programme of the Band of Mercy, which established itself in the last quarter of the nineteenth century, typified the kind of devout, conservative didacticism that we have found in the works of many female authors of the Victorian age.[77] It originated in the informal 'humanity classes' for children organised by many supporters of the RSPCA in their own localities from the 1850s onwards: those given by Florence Horatia Suckling, who came from a gentry family at Romsey in Hampshire, proved to be particularly influential.[78] Suckling's friend Lady Georgina Mount-Temple (formerly Cowper-Temple), whom we have already encountered as a member of the

RSPCA ladies' committee, partnered her husband in initiating classes for local children at Broadlands, their mansion in Hampshire, and elsewhere, initially under the name of the 'Fellowship of Friends of Animals'. At Broadlands, too, religious conferences were held annually from 1874 onwards, embracing many denominations and heterodox creeds, notably spiritualism. In fact, the Mount-Temples' teaching of kindness to animals, which included fervent opposition to vivisection, had the same evangelical inspiration as their many other philanthropic activities.[79] There is an amusing account of a 'Band of Mercy Treat' for some three hundred children, held in Broadlands Park in 1880. The children entered the park 'singing a favourite Band of Mercy hymn, the composition of Miss Prout', before being regaled with 'a hearty tea'. Essay prizes were presented by Lady Mount-Temple, and then Frances Power Cobbe, 'who had come specially from London … gave a very amusing and instructive address … the little Mercy Bands went home delighted with their day'.[80]

There is an unmistakable element of *noblesse oblige* in these attempts to instil humane values in lower-class children, but the nascent Band of Mercy movement acquired a broader social and institutional base through the initiatives of the Smithies family, who were devout Methodists, Sabbatarians and teetotallers; the very name of the movement echoed that of the Band of Hope, a temperance organisation for children founded by Thomas Smithies.[81] His mother Catherine Smithies was the author of *A Mother's Lessons on Kindness to Animals*, which was published in several series in the 1860s. In 1875 Mrs Smithies (another member of the RSPCA ladies' committee) established the first Band of Mercy to bear that name at Wood Green near London. The ceremony was attended by John Colam and other representatives of the RSPCA, on whose executive committee Thomas Smithies served.[82] Mrs Smithies died a few years later, but her adoring son, conscious of the growth of the movement she had helped to found, started a monthly periodical in 1879, the *Band of Mercy Advocate*, which was distributed to the five or six hundred Bands scattered across the country. These groups were largely led by women, often the wives and daughters of the clergy, or wealthy local benefactors. Having arisen through individual initiatives, they were diverse in character and situation: some were attached to the Sunday schools of churches or chapels, others to day schools, regional branches of the RSPCA, or, as we have seen, even aristocratic households; local clusters of Bands occasionally formed unions.[83] The *Band of Mercy Advocate* gave all the groups a collective identity, and a more consistent, recognisable philosophy. In 1882–1883, direction of the movement as a whole and editorship of the journal were taken over by the RSPCA, and became the special responsibility of the ladies' committee under Angela Burdett-Coutts. While individual bands retained a large measure of autonomy, the RSPCA's issue of the journal, standard membership cards, registers, almanacs, pictures and lantern slides further integrated the movement.

At the time he launched the *Band of Mercy Advocate*, Thomas Smithies was already expert in the production of cheap religious magazines for a lower-class or child readership, the character of which he transformed through attractive journalism and illustrations – the latter often commissioned from the leading artists and wood engravers of the time.[84] However, it is the distinctive approach of the women who led the movement and contributed features to the *Band of Mercy Advocate* that stamped its character. As in Mrs Smithies's *A Mother's Lessons*, there is an evident preoccupation with the problem of converting and civilising *boys*, through impressing upon them the compatibility of tenderness for animals with true manliness. The very first cover illustration in 1879 pictured 'donkey boys', who were notorious for their cruelties, signing – under a lady's guidance – the Band of Mercy's membership pledge to be kind to all animals.[85] On the cover of another number, a village schoolmaster draws the attention of two boys, guiltily intent on bird trapping and egg collecting, to a Band of Mercy notice on the school wall, listing legally protected species – a girl also shows it to a younger boy, her arm affectionately round his shoulder.[86] The journal is full of chocolate-box images of pretty little girls caressing their pets, just as, in the stories themselves, animals are rendered preternaturally 'sagacious' and loving by their owners' 'persevering kindness'. In fact, the sentimentality of the illustrations in Smithies's publications often exceeded that of his authors' texts. George Eliot commiserated with her friend Cara Bray over the 'namby-pambiest' pictures provided in 1876 for Bray's *Paul Bradley: A Village Tale, Inculcating Kindness to Animals*.[87] Moreover, as in many late Georgian books for children, women and girls are represented, not only as gentle and kind themselves, but also as moral redeemers of the other sex. In 'Sylvia and the blackbird', Sylvia deters a rough village boy from birds-nesting, and finally enrols him in the Band of Mercy. In 'The merciless boy; or, "Oh! don't, don't, brother John"', mother and sister both remonstrate with John for torturing a butterfly – '"It was God's butterfly"'.[88]

The battle for boys' souls could, alternatively, be waged by a system of antitypes: cruel boys are constantly set against kind boys, often on facing pages. In 'Robert the stone-thrower', a boy stones birds on his way to church, and is duly admonished by his mother, but his father remarks carelessly that '"Lads *will* be lads"': a fictional example of the kind of parental contrast in attitudes that we

ROBERT, THE STONE-THROWER.

"SHAME upon you, Robert! You grieve me exceedingly by throwing stones at the poor little birds ; and then to do it on the *Sabbath-day* ! It is very sad."

Mrs. Wilson turned towards her husband, after having addressed these words to her little son, and with a sigh which evidenced a mother's deep concern, she said, "I fear that something *sad* will happen to Robert some day on account of his cruelty."

17 'Robert the stone-thrower', in the *Band of Mercy Advocate* (June 1880), with wood engraving by John Gilbert.

have found in Anne Brontë's and Sarah Stickney Ellis's books (figure 17). Robert predictably goes to the bad, and his father dies broken-hearted. However, in 'The pleasure van', a story that immediately follows, a kind boy, braving ridicule, declines to join a party on a trip to the countryside, because he perceives that the horses pulling the carriage are already overtaxed. A merchant, witnessing the boy's good judgement and moral courage, offers him employment, and he consequently rises to 'eminence and wealth'.[89]

> For boys may be merry in spirit,
> While gentle and thoughtful and kind;
> And to care for the weak and the helpless,
> Marks a noble and generous mind.[90]

A surfeit of such moralities would have become tedious even to converts, and offered little scope for entertainment at Band of Mercy meetings. Some notion of what these meetings were like may be gleaned from a novel by a female author published in the United States, Marshall Saunders's *Beautiful Joe: An Autobiography* (1894), the story of a dog. It had won a Humane Society competition for a successor to Anna Sewell's *Black Beauty*, instigated by George Angell, who also founded a very successful American Band of Mercy movement on the British model.[91] In Saunders's fictional description of an ideal Band meeting (run by the children themselves), hymn singing, recitation, and true stories about the cleverness and devotion of domestic animals are followed by the children's testimonies – redolent of religious witnessing – of what they had done for animals in fulfilment of their pledge of kindness. 'One girl had kept her brother from shooting two owls that came about their barnyard.' Another little girl had 'reasoned with different boys outside the village who were throwing stones at birds and frogs, and sticking butterflies, and had invited them to the Band of Mercy', as well as starting 'a petition to the village boys' not to go birds-nesting.[92] In such ways, Angell and his colleagues hoped, exhortation, fortified by 'the whole humane literature of the world', might pour into ignorant children's minds 'those noble, elevating, and merciful thoughts, which will make both them *and their parents* better in all the relations of this life, to say nothing of the life hereafter'.[93]

It may be doubted whether branches of the Band of Mercy in Britain offered children the kind of active, participatory role imagined by Saunders: indeed, there was consternation when George Bernard Shaw, addressing a Band meeting in 1899, encouraged the children to challenge received opinions.[94] However, a compilation by Florence Suckling, *The Humane Educator and Reciter ...*

A Selection of Ancient and Modern Poetry, Dialogues and Sketches for Little Performers at Entertainments (1891), dedicated to the RSPCA ladies' committee, offered a fund of materials for use at such meetings. Its inclusion of poems by Cowper, Burns, Clare, Wordsworth, Coleridge and many other famous writers was intended to provide the kind of uplift and cultural authority for kindness to animals envisaged by Angell. As so often, the meekness expected of the child audience by Suckling and other Band of Mercy organisers had its counterpart in the imagined humility and devotion to service evinced by animals themselves. In Mary Sewell's 'Bob, the fireman's dog', Bob risks his life to save those of humans; in Mary Howitt's 'The cry of the suffering creatures', the animals acknowledge that they were made to be man's servants ('we know it, and complain not'), and ask only for kindness in return. True, Julia Goddard's verse drama for child actors, 'The animals on strike', conjures up a vision of wronged animals staging a rebellion to establish their 'rights', but they quickly return to duty after receiving assurances of redress by a 'philanthropist' and the RSPCA committee.[95] In another of her publications, *The Humane Play-Book* (1900), Mrs Suckling explained that public performances of such tableaux and dramas would inspire parents – 'Hodge' the ploughman, 'Mrs Hodge' and their 'village neighbours' as well as the child actors themselves, 'tending to draw all classes and ages into a common bond of sympathy and of friendship for the "lower brethren"'. The children in Suckling's photographic plates look mystified by this allotted role, and girls certainly outnumber boys. Suckling admitted that, in one play about a mock trial of some cruel children, the part of the judge might need to be taken by a girl; but, making a virtue of necessity, her black robes were to be thrown off at the end, to reveal her in a white muslin dress as 'the Spirit of Mercy'.[96] This *coup de théâtre* nevertheless marked a failure to inspire and engage boys in the cause, which was painfully evident in the low numbers of those who entered the school essay competitions organised by the RSPCA ladies' committee.[97]

The records of the Band of Mercy and of kindred groups such as the Dicky Bird Society frequently hint at the inhibitions that prevented older boys from signing up publicly to animal protection bodies: inhibitions that arose fundamentally from the gendered contrast of attitudes and ideals of behaviour outlined in this chapter. Flora Thompson in *Lark Rise to Candleford* remembered village boys' compulsive birds-nesting as a pursuit by which they established a distinct masculine identity, separating themselves off from female society, and impervious to girls' pleas to desist.[98] In a typical *Humane Educator* story, some rough lads who have been chided by Band of Mercy boys for planning to set a dog on a cat call their accusers 'softies' and 'mollys' – the latter term signifying effeminacy or even homosexuality.[99] In fact, this problem of threatened masculinity was foremost among the 'perplexities', as Eliza Brightwen called them, of the Bands at grassroots level.[100] The minute book of the branch at Knutsford in Cheshire for the years 1896 to 1900 (a rare survival), shows a leadership and committee composed entirely of moneyed local ladies, with the town's Unitarian minister, Revd George Payne, serving as a rather unwilling secretary.[101] When they sent out a circular to local tradesmen, 'inviting their hearty cooperation' in a plan to enlist their young employees, the response was 'very poor', so that plans for a 'Senior Branch' of the Band, to be composed of youths who actually managed horses and livestock, had to be abandoned.[102]

It may be significant that the Lords of the Manor at Knutsford, the Egertons of nearby Tatton Park, held values that were the very antithesis of those of the Band of Mercy ladies. The big game hunting exploits of Baron Maurice Egerton have already been mentioned. At Knutsford, he organised a rifle and drill corps and a boys' club and taught their members to shoot (rabbits were used for target practice); the boys were also regularly invited to survey and admire the large collection of animal trophies at Tatton.[103] Moreover, the opposition of 'enmity' to the Band of Mercy's 'amity' was not restricted to the celebration of hunting prowess: the boys whom the Knutsford ladies tried in vain to recruit, and indeed working youths across the country, would have been habituated to practices that were an essential part of rural and commercial life, but were wholly incompatible with the feminised spirit of kindness celebrated in the *Band of Mercy Advocate* and in Mrs Suckling's books. Whatever affection might exist between farmworkers and their animals, it was normal for livestock to be castrated, docked, branded and transported for slaughter under cruel conditions, and horses were gelded, routinely overworked, and destroyed without compunction when no longer useful. Moles, rabbits, rooks, sparrows and other species perceived as agricultural pests were ruthlessly exterminated; and, as was shown in *The Keeper's Book* of 1903 (promoted as the favourite reading of 'schoolboys and the youth of the country'), gamekeepers trapped, poisoned or shot any animals classifiable as 'vermin' that might threaten populations of game birds, often inadvertently killing pet cats in the process.[104] The licensed cruelties of the London streets were equally persistent, and, like farming practices, often seemed to have the sanction of government and the general public. In 1886, Frances Power Cobbe wrote to the *Times*, to protest about the treatment of an injured and frightened dog. On the supposition that it might be rabid and therefore must be destroyed according to law, it had been beaten to death by a policeman, watched by a crowd of laughing and jeering young people. How could the RSPCA and its 'Royal and noble patrons and patronesses' tolerate such horrors? 'The inculcation of humanity to animals in pretty little tracts and illustrated magazines, and the formation of bands of mercy for the young, is simply a farce while the street boys and roughs of London are receiving such practical and lively lessons in cruelty' as the murder of the dog.[105] Could improving literature ever, indeed, transform attitudes on these subjects as many women writers hoped?

Anna Sewell's *Black Beauty*: transcendence of a fictional genre

Black Beauty: His Grooms and Companions. The Autobiography of a Horse. Translated from the Original Equine, by Anna Sewell was published in 1877 and quickly became a publishing sensation.[106] By 1888, some 86,000 copies had been sold in Britain, for family reading but also as a school reader or Sunday school prize, and the RSPCA noted in 1899 that it had 'proved of great service in inculcating the principles of the Society'.[107] George Angell, promoter of the Band of Mercy in America, was introduced to the work, and with characteristic impetuosity he immediately raised funds to produce a cheap pirated edition there. Carrying a significant new subtitle, *The Uncle Tom's Cabin of the Horse*, and Angell's hyperbolical recommendation, free or subsidised copies of the book were distributed across the States.[108] With the endorsement of the American Humane Education Society, *Black Beauty* became, in the words of Roswell McCrea, 'a veritable bible of the animal protective cause'.[109] 'Intensely practical in its suggestions' for the welfare of horses, 'it has at the same time a coloring and a lively and varied action that makes an intense appeal not only to children, but even to adults'. In other words, this was not a case of a sermonising work being distributed wholesale by charitable persons at their own expense for the improvement of the lower orders: the book was genuinely popular among readers of all ages and social classes, and, issued in countless editions, has maintained a high reputation down to the present day.

In many ways the impact of Anna Sewell's book is mysterious: far from offering novelty, it belonged to a well-established, even hackneyed genre. As we have seen, talking animals were commonplace in humane literature like the *Band of Mercy Advocate*, deriving from the ancient tradition of moral fables. Biographies and imagined autobiographies of animals had been written in profusion since the beginning of the nineteenth century, and in fact had their roots in earlier anthropomorphic fictions like those of Jonathan Swift, which aimed to make the sufferings of animals palpable to the reader.[110] There was a spate of such narratives c.1800 – one symptom of the stirring of notions of animal subjectivity at that time. They included the anonymous *Memoirs of Dick, the Little Poney* and Dorothy Kilner's *The Rational Brutes; Or, Talking Animals*, which Sarah Stickney Ellis mentioned as having profoundly affected her as a child, making her conscience-stricken about any acts of unkindness.[111] Nearer to the date of *Black Beauty*, Mrs Burrows's *Tuppy; Or, The Autobiography of a Donkey* (1860), an anonymous *Adventures of a Donkey, Written by Himself* (c.1870), *Poor Blossom: The Story of a Horse* (c.1876, reissued as an 'old favourite' among Ernest Bell's 'Animal Life Readers' in 1896) and many other works diversified this already-familiar vein; and Anna Sewell's variant in turn would have many successors.[112] Accounts of the declining fortunes of a horse's life also had a long history in poems, dramas, paintings and sets of prints, which was epitomised in the many versions of the story of 'The high-mettled racer'. This kind of narrative reflected the actual fate of most horses in the nineteenth century, giving it a particular poignancy. Even once-esteemed racehorses, hunters and fine carriage horses might be sold on many times in their declining years, to endure more and more backbreaking and menial labour as they were 'used up' before being consigned to the knackers.[113] As Dr Ralph Fletcher described it in *A Few Notes on Cruelty to Animals* (1846), the life of the horse was 'generally full of misery. Its spring is short and deceitful; its summer, uninterrupted slavery, cold and cheerless; its winter, long and bitter, a series of every kind of cruelty, neglect, and scorn, closed by a death of murderous and disgusting violence'.[114]

The plot of Anna Sewell's *Black Beauty*, as narrated by the horse himself, entirely followed this general pattern: as an enthusiast for Landseer's paintings, some of which she copied in oils, Sewell may well have read about his paired *Prosperity* and *Adversity* (1865), which pictured a noble lady's riding horse in its pampered prime, and then in its sad final state as a broken-down night cab horse with open sores.[115] Black Beauty too is a colt with a distinguished pedigree, who moves from the benign care of Squire Gordon to the grand mansion of an earl, where he first suffers pain and misfortune as an effect of the countess's use of the fashionable bearing rein. When recklessly ridden by a drunken groom, he stumbles and breaks (cuts and disfigures) his knees. It is the beginning of a downward trajectory which consigns him to the ownership of a London cabbie, and then of a brutal job-master; but at the nadir of his fortunes he is rescued by a gentleman farmer and his grandson, and is unexpectedly reunited with the kind country people he had known in his youth, who vow to keep him for the rest of his life.

The short episodic chapters of *Black Beauty* are rather like the shifting scenes of a play, or the separate frames of the many series of prints of the 'High-mettled racer', tracking the vicissitudes of the horse's life through a succession of experiences. They were well suited to the limited attention span of inexpert or child readers, and enabled Sewell to introduce a great many varied situations that are illustrative of the needs of horses and the ways they are abused.[116] Nevertheless, the constant changes that Beauty and his various owners endure give the book a disconcerting dreamlike quality: a sense of transience and insecurity, such that even the promise of a settled permanent home at the end seems precarious. As Beauty's mother warns him early on, 'a horse never knows who may buy him, or who may drive him; it is all a chance for us'.[117] The fatalistic mood of *Black Beauty* – the apparent lack of a benevolent guiding providence – already suggests a mental world that differs significantly from the comfortable certainties of Eliza Brightwen's *Wild Nature Won by Kindness* or the tales in the *Band of Mercy Advocate*.

While *Black Beauty* follows a traditional schema, it transcends it in every way: in the flow, balance and absorbing interest of the narrative, the gracefulness and economy of the language, and above all in the moral seriousness and passionate feeling for the suffering of animals that Sewell communicates to the reader. She noted on a scrap of paper that her 'special aim' was 'to induce kindness, sympathy and an understanding treatment of horses', and particularly to explain, 'in a correct and telling manner', the 'great difficulties' of cabmen and their horses, when forced to work for seven days a week without intermission.[118] The 'grooms' mentioned in her title, together with stable boys and cab drivers, are the central human protagonists in the book and their real-life counterparts were a key part of Sewell's target readership. Through *Black Beauty*, she intended to reach boys and men too oppressed by overwork, too ignorant, careless or brutal to understand the pain they inflicted on the acutely sentient animals under their control. In one incident, a cowardly boy who is cruel to a pony gets his comeuppance, while in another a kind boy bravely gives evidence of the cruelty committed by a brickmaker's driver. This was the kind of instructive moral contrast in boys' behaviour that might have been found in the pages of the *Band of Mercy Advocate*.[119] Sewell even used the archaic device of tag names ('John Manly' the wise and humane head groom; 'Mr Thoroughgood' the kind gentleman farmer etc.), with a demonstrative purpose as direct as that of Bunyan's *Pilgrim's Progress*, which the life journey of Black Beauty indeed somewhat resembles. However, merely instrumental or serviceable writing does not rank high in the literary canon, so scholarly interpreters of

Black Beauty have often tried to make it something more or other than a book that was intended to persuade people to be kind to horses.[120] It is, they insist, a meditation on slavery and imperialism, or a protest against mental and physical constraints on women, or even a symbolic autobiography of Sewell herself, rather than the life of a mere horse.[121]

It is ironic, then, that *Black Beauty* is actually a more single-minded work, and in a sense a simpler work than many of its prototypes. In Mrs Burrows's *Tuppy*, as in her *Neptune; Or the Autobiography of a Newfoundland Dog* (1869), cruelty to animals is certainly deplored, but the imaginary animal narrator also ponders his mistakes in life, especially rebelliousness arising from a 'self-willed, presumptuous spirit', as a cautionary lesson for the child reader.[122] In the anonymous *Adventures of a Donkey* of c.1870, the young people in the story discuss the extent of animal intelligence, and the differences between natural fact and anthropomorphic fiction.[123] The donkey-hero of yet another *Adventures of a Donkey*, this one by 'Arabella Argus' and published in many editions, becomes an absurdly self-conscious and fastidious author: 'I began in idea to polish my language, smooth my periods, and, according to Donkey taste, improve my style altogether.'[124] Such witty metafiction, and the endowment of the animal subject with a fully human (conscientious but morally fallible) persona, may divert the reader, but shifting registers detract from the self-consistency and emotive power of the narrative. Anna Sewell rendered Black Beauty capable of speech and of reflection on human character and society, as a familiar, well-understood and necessary convention, but she avoided any inessential artifice that would draw attention to her literary methods or to her own identity as an author: her 'translation from the original equine' is as faithful as possible, and her fine writing is wholly at the service of her didactic purpose.[125] Black Beauty never acts in a way that would be unnatural in horses: nothing was to detract from the conviction that *real* horses are routinely subjected to cruelties that cause intense suffering and that, through Sewell's strangely moving story, distress and appal the reader.

The rejection of mere cleverness and entertainment in *Black Beauty* reflects Sewell's lack of self-regard – her moral earnestness and concern for absolute truthfulness in all things. Her family remembered that, whenever she arranged a bowl of fruit, she took care that any blemishes faced *outwards*, and so it was in her picturing of contemporary society.[126] These character traits were closely connected with her Quaker family heritage and childhood conditioning.[127] As has been mentioned, her mother Mary Sewell was a confidante of Sarah Stickney Ellis, a relative by marriage who was also from a Quaker family.

Mary entirely shared Sarah's ideas on how to bring up children – encouraging a reverent love of nature as a lesson in divinity and a stimulus to affection towards all animals.[128] The Quakers' special feeling for animals, which we have already encountered in the work of Elizabeth Heyrick, Elizabeth Pease Nichol and the Gurney family, had a distinctive theological basis, explained by Thomas Clarkson in his *Portraiture of Quakerism* (1807). The 'spiritual vision' of fallen man is 'dim, short, and confused', so that he cannot perceive the true nature of animals, and as a result treats them as mere 'brute-machines'. Only the 'renovated' Christian is able to discern God's purposes in the creation, to see His animals in a 'sublime light', and hence to treat them lovingly.[129] So important was this moral imperative, that, for Quakers, even acquiescing in cruelty was a sin almost as terrible as committing it. In *Black Beauty*, bystanders often intervene to admonish or prevent cruel behaviour, as Anna Sewell apparently did herself.[130] Indeed, the whole project of writing the book – her only published work – during her last illness, seems to have been prompted by anxious solicitude to fulfil a religious duty.

Thus several aspects of Quaker thinking offer crucial insights into *Black Beauty*, and partly explain its differences from the general run of Victorian women's literature on the treatment of animals. As we have seen, such writers clung to the traditional doctrine of 'dominion', involving a chain of command stretching from God to man, and from him to the 'lower' creatures: man was God's viceroy on earth, entrusted with the merciful stewardship of animals that were created for his use and service. Moreover, 'mercy' towards them had an important additional motive, which the RSPCA and the Band of Mercy continually stressed – the corrupting effects of habitual cruelty on the character of the perpetrator and hence on society at large. The ideas of the Quakers largely lacked these hierarchical and reflexive emphases; rather, they trusted the 'inner light' of the mind to create a bond of sympathy with animals, as cherished offspring of the same Father, with their own divinely conferred rights. There could be no imagined sexual distinction in attitudes here – women's tenderness supposedly compensating for men's aggression – because amity between animals and humans was essential to a state of spiritual grace. In fact, the reactions of Sewell's first readers confirm that *Black Beauty* seemed to them to escape the clichéd, feminised homilies of the *Band of Mercy Advocate* and its ilk. One female cousin of Sewell's thought she had been 'doing angels' work in writing this book, bringing messages of peace and good-will from the Lord of all to these His poor dumb creatures'; but the book's message was, she noted, conveyed by a combination of extensive knowledge about horse management, such as only male authors ordinarily possessed, with a passionate sympathy for suffering animals – 'it is *so good*; &, forgive me, so unladylike that but for "Anna Sewell" on the title-page, and a certain gentle kindliness all through the story, no one, I think, would believe it to be written by a lady'.[131] An American reviewer simply remarked that the book was not 'namby-pamby'.[132]

Black Beauty is nevertheless a rather melancholy work, which in many ways suggests Sewell's rejection of the confident but simplistic beliefs of Victorian evangelicals, including published female writers in her own family circle. Her aunt Anne Wright wrote *What Is a Bird? The Forms of Birds, Their Instincts, and Use in Creation Considered* (1857) to show boys that 'Natural history is a kind of book in God's providence', although the workings of that benign providence admittedly seemed to involve violent conflict and predation, as a way of maintaining the healthiness of all species.[133] Anna's mother Mary Sewell, a popular author of sentimental and moralising ballads like *Mother's Last Words* (1860), had such an unshakeable belief in divine agency as to think that even Anna's lameness and final cruel illness had a spiritually purifying purpose. Mary wrote to her friend and distant kinswoman Eliza Brightwen that trees and flowers were 'always speaking to me in parables', showing what 'exquisite loveliness' the Christian character may gain 'by the infinite skill and tender patience of the great Husbandman'. Mary was, like Brightwen, 'almost frantic ... that good Mother Nature should not be left to stand only upon her scientific foot', at the mercy of Darwinian 'sceptics'.[134] Yet a belief that all things worked together for good was difficult to sustain when the fate of animals was considered. Mary's sympathies, like those of her daughter, 'flowed out to every living thing'; but such love of animals had 'a shadow side of horror in this evil world'.[135]

It was the shadow side that was uppermost in Anna Sewell's thoughts. Her life as a disabled and rather isolated woman involved, according to a family friend, constant 'repression' of all intellectual ambition and all thoughts of philanthropic or political action in the public sphere. She was often, her mother observed sadly, in Bunyan's 'Doubting Castle', and in fact seems to have endured years of religious anxiety or despair.[136] In these circumstances, she was quick to seize on any recent theological works that might offer solutions to the crises of faith that she and many other thoughtful Victorians experienced. Mary Bayly, in her biography of Mary Sewell, recalled a conversation she had with Anna on a visit to the Sewell family home. Bayly told the future author of *Black Beauty* about the ideas of the American Congregationalist theologian Horace Bushnell. In his *Moral Uses of Dark Things* (1868), Bushnell decisively rejected natural theology: a belief that the natural world, 'this constant scene of destruction', was created by a God who was both omnipotent and benevolent, could, in Bushnell's view, only be sustained by the notion that such evils were intended as strenuous 'moral training' for mankind – an instructive representation of 'the ferocity of man's sin'. Goodness 'is no such innocent, mawkishly insipid character, no such mollusc softness swimming in God's bosom as many affect to suppose'.[137] However, Bayly apparently gave Bushnell's 'grand symbolism' a gloss that was more favourable to the animal protection cause, quoting his ideas from memory. 'In creation, animals are so associated with man that they must fall or rise with him':

> I never see an animal bearing the marks of man's cruelty, without feeling that in its mute anguish it is saying, 'This is my body broken for you;' and perhaps no view of man's sin has impressed me so deeply as the fact, that its consequences have wrung this same cry both from the Highest in the universe and the lowest … There will be no 'breaking in' required when the promised days of universal peace and righteousness dawn upon the earth.

By Bayly's account, Anna wrote to her after the publication of *Black Beauty*, saying 'The thoughts you gave me from Horace Bushnell years ago have followed me entirely through the writing of my book, and have, more than anything else, helped me to feel it was worth a great effort to *try*, at least, to bring the thoughts of men more in harmony with the purposes of God on this subject'.[138] In the present degraded state of society, working animals were the abused slaves of their human owners; but did Anna Sewell believe that horses' servitude to man could ever represent God's will, or bring them happiness? When Black Beauty is broken in, he can barely reconcile himself to the intrusion of the heavy bit in his mouth – 'it is very bad! yes, very bad!'; he yearns for liberty, knowing that 'year after year, I must stand up in a stable night and day except when I am wanted … Straps here and straps there … blinkers over my eyes. Now, I am not complaining, for I know it must be so'.[139] But *must* it always be so? Beauty's resignation comes at a heavy price, especially when, later, he has to endure the agonies inflicted by the bearing rein. Much more does the tragic mare Ginger suffer for her refusal to submit to the will of her owners: she ends her life beaten, hungry and exhausted, pulling a cab for a job-master, whose voice was 'as harsh as the grinding of cart wheels over gravel stones'. In a chance meeting with Beauty, she concedes that '"men are strongest, and if they are cruel and have no feeling, there is nothing that we can do, but just bear it, bear it on and on to the end" … A short time after this, a cart with a dead horse in it passed our cab-stand' (figure 18).

18 'The head hung out of the cart tail' – Black Beauty's last sight of Ginger. Half-tone illustration from a pen drawing by John Beer, in the first illustrated edition of Anna Sewell's *Black Beauty*, published by Jarrold in 1894, reprinted 1898.

The head hung out of the cart-tail, the lifeless tongue was slowly dropping with blood; and the sunken eyes! but I can't speak of them, the sight was too dreadful … I believe it was Ginger.

The horses' conviction that 'men are strongest' recognises inescapable *force majeure*, but it is hardly an acceptance of the *justness* of man's dominion over the 'lower' species, a notion which the insights of Anna Sewell's talking horses call into question: '"What right had they to make me suffer like that?"' Ginger asks.[140] We are here far away from the conservative pattern of thought that imbued most Victorian women's writing on the treatment of animals. One famous example of the latter comes especially close to *Black Beauty* in its plot line: Margaret Gatty's hugely popular *Parables from Nature*, published in numerous editions from 1855 onwards, includes a story titled 'Kicking', about a rebellious young horse who ultimately learns that 'it was possible for submission and love and happiness to go hand in hand together … Animals under man – servants under masters – children under parents – wives under husbands – men under authorities – nations under rulers – all under God'.[141]

Anna Sewell, who identified with horses so intimately that the death of one in the street, a daily occurrence in Victorian London, seemed as 'dreadful' as a human passing, could hardly accept belief in this scale of subordination and relative consequence. In fact her book is full of episodes that – more in sorrow than anger – call into question the moral standing of the powerful classes in British society. In some famous eighteenth-century fictions such as Goldsmith's *Citizen of the World*, an oriental visitor to Britain provides a penetrating commentary on the country's social practices from across a cultural divide; *Black Beauty* critiques such practices from the imagined standpoint of another species – clear-eyed horse commentators who are more innocent but also wiser than the men they observe. Almost at the start of the book, the young Black Beauty is startled and distressed by seeing a hare hunt, which results not just in the death of the hare, but in that of Beauty's own brother and of the squire's son. Later the old cavalry horse Captain remembers the part he played in the charge of the Light Brigade in the Crimean war. It was a tragedy for the horses as well as for their riders – again the fates of animals and men hang together. 'Some of the horses had been so badly wounded that they could scarcely move from the loss of blood; other noble creatures were trying on three legs to drag themselves along … Their groans were piteous to hear, and the beseeching look in their eyes as those who escaped passed by, and left them to their fate, I shall never forget.' All this was 'more than a horse can understand, but the enemy must have been awfully wicked people, if it was right to go all that way over the sea on purpose to kill them'.[142]

Conscientious opposition to hunting and to militarism was part of the Quaker legacy, and, as we have seen, women writers in general, when pleading the cause of animals, often condemned field sports with particular vehemence. However, in *Black Beauty*, Anna Sewell related such assertions of mastery over animals to the deeper ills of Victorian society, believing them to be more nearly related to social privilege and avarice than to gender. Thus, while conservative moralists like Sewell's friend Sarah Stickney Ellis tended to assume that middle- and upper-class women had a mission to educate servants and the labouring classes in the principles of humanity to animals, Sewell makes a countess – a slave of fashion – a chief offender in ordering the use of cruelly tight bearing reins on her horses. In *Black Beauty*, it is the wealthy of both sexes who make unreasonable demands for speed when travelling or when awaiting tradesmen's deliveries; it is they who keep carriage horses waiting for hours in the cold and rain outside grand party venues.[143] Worst of all, it is they who carelessly dispose of blemished or broken-winded animals, condemning them to an end-life of increasing misery.

Conversely, at a time when men who worked with horses for a living were often accused of ignorance, moral degradation and brutality – they were, indeed, one of the groups most often prosecuted by the RSPCA – Anna Sewell describes their experiences with sympathy and insight. The 'poor old men' trying to buy worn-out horses at a sale 'looked not much better off than the poor beasts they were bargaining about'. As we have seen, she wished *Black Beauty* to draw attention in particular to the 'great difficulties' of London cabmen and their horses. She had heard about these difficulties from the cabbies themselves, but the subject was actually much discussed at the time she was writing, and had already been imaginatively treated in George MacDonald's novel, *At the Back of the North Wind* (1871). Many philanthropists of the mid-century sought to rescue cabmen from their reputation for drunkenness and dishonesty, to introduce them to Christian teaching, and to provide them with shelters near the cab ranks.[144] In 1859 *The Cabman's Chronicle* invited lay readers to pic- ture the physical hardships of a cabby's life in very much the same terms that Anna Sewell later employed, and already this journal – in partnership with the London Cabmen's Lord's-day Rest Association and Thomas Smithies' *British Workman* – promoted the idea of six-day licences, so that the drivers and their horses could rest on Sundays.[145] In Sewell's book, Black Beauty's cabman owner, Jerry Barker, risks offending a valued customer by holding out for this day of rest, but later his merits as a good family man who treats his horses kindly find their reward.[146] *The Cabman: A Monthly Journal and Review* (1874– 1876), another evangelical paper, dealt more specifically with the welfare of horses, and must have been an important source for *Black Beauty*. However, it was clear that the animals' sufferings had as much to do with commercial practices as with gratuitous cruelty.[147] The *Chronicle* described the unfair 'privi- lege' system operated by the big rail companies at the London termini, and the extortions of the job-masters, who had to be paid (at a steep rate) for the hire of cab and horse out of the driver's takings.[148] In *Black Beauty*, Seedy Sam is criticised by the other drivers for cruelly overworking and whipping a hired horse, but he protests that he could not otherwise make a meagre living from his fares. 'There's wrong lays somewhere' in the whole system of society, he reflects, shortly before dying of overwork. The horse proprietor who exploits Seedy Sam is the ruthless Nicholas Skinner, whose regime kills Ginger, and later nearly kills Black Beauty. Perhaps Sewell, in her anxiety to arouse the consciences of individual readers over their treatment of animals, failed to come to terms with the actual impersonality and huge scale of commercial stabling and horse hire in late nineteenth-century London.[149] Nevertheless, *Black Beauty* conveys – as ladies' homilies of the Band of Mercy type seldom did, the inequity that was endemic, not just in the behaviour of particular men and boys, but in the very structure of the Victorian economy.

For Anna Sewell, the cruelty of the times, stubbornly failing to fulfil reformers' hopes of progress in the treatment of animals, was epitomised in use of the bearing rein or check rein. *Black Beauty* is famous for its protest against this form of harness, which held the horse's head high and arched its neck, giving it a noble and spirited appearance – but at the cost of obstructing the windpipe, straining the neck muscles, damaging the eyes by exposure to the sun overhead, causing stumbles over unseen obstacles, and bringing on premature debility. The bearing rein was often combined with the curb bit, which worked on a lever principle, and caused great pain and damage to the horse's delicate mouth. In Sewell's story, the mare Ginger fiercely rebels against wearing these devices – in vain – and there is a moving description of the pain that Black Beauty, too, experiences from their use, especially when pulling a loaded cart uphill.[150] With its head strapped up in an unnatural position, a horse could not use all its muscular power to draw the weight, and the strain fell on its back and legs. In this respect, the malign practices of the *upper* classes were being imitated by tradesmen and even labouring men, to the dismay of successive leaders of the animal protection movement.

Anna Sewell was, in fact, just one of very many writers to expose the cruelties of these reins and bits, and she was not the last. Bitter reproaches continued to be published through the 1890s, still indicting women in particular; they suggest that *Black Beauty* had much less influence in this respect than has sometimes been suggested.[151] As early as 1835, the veterinary surgeon Bracy Clark, in *A Treatise on the Bits of Horses*, blamed their misguided use on the power of custom, fashion and vested commercial interests. As a Quaker, Clark deplored the 'bitter anguish' they caused, which was eloquently expressed in the horse's restless movements – 'How is this excellent creature, who is so full of feeling', and willingly gives up his 'natural rights' to become man's slave, 'used by those called Christians, in defiance of all the mild precepts they pretend to?'[152] Sewell may have known this work by her co-religionist, and she certainly read Edward Fordham Flower's impassioned tract, *Bits and Bearing Reins; With Observations on Horses and Harness*, which appeared in many editions from 1875 onwards (figure 19). Sewell sent Flower a copy of *Black Beauty* as soon as it was published, and he praised it enthusiastically as a key contribution to the humanitarian cause.[153] Flower often accused the RSPCA of being lukewarm on the issue, due to fears of offending its aristocratic patrons, but this was not quite fair.[154] He acknowledged that he had received warm support from the RSPCA ladies' committee led by Burdett-Coutts ('I believe that the ladies are more humane than the men'), and *Animal World* carried many articles attacking the bearing rein, that were written or endorsed by leading vets. The RSPCA also posted public notices at the foot of steep hills, begging drivers to loosen these reins and give the horse its head on the ascent. It even once prosecuted a wealthy man for 'cruelly torturing a horse' with a bearing rein – only to see this expensive test case dismissed out of hand by the presiding magistrate, who declared that he 'would not make that court an arena for ventilating sentimentality'.[155] Similar counter-arguments had been heard down the years, since 'Nimrod', writing in the *Sporting Review* in 1839, treated objections to the bearing rein as 'a sort of sickly and overstrained morality, carrying the affectation of fine feeling to the very borders of the burlesque', to the detriment of the 'bold and masculine character of the English people'.[156]

Such opinions seem to return us to the familiar territory of attitudinal contrasts between men and women, which have been the theme of this chapter. However, in this case, the opposing principles of 'enmity' and 'amity' were not so easily gendered, as Anna Sewell realised. Several writers on the bearing rein dissented from Flower by accusing women of being its greatest devotees: it prevented the horse from tugging on the reins, making it easier to drive, and it created a showy appearance which fashionable women were said to favour.[157] We have seen that in *Black Beauty*, it is the self-willed countess who defies the better judgement of both her husband and the head groom, and commands that the rein should be tightened to the maximum, inflicting excruciating and prolonged pain on Beauty and Ginger.[158] In the writing of Anna Sewell but also in the protests of many other women (including, it will be remembered, those of the Liverpool RSPCA ladies' committee), abolition of the bearing rein

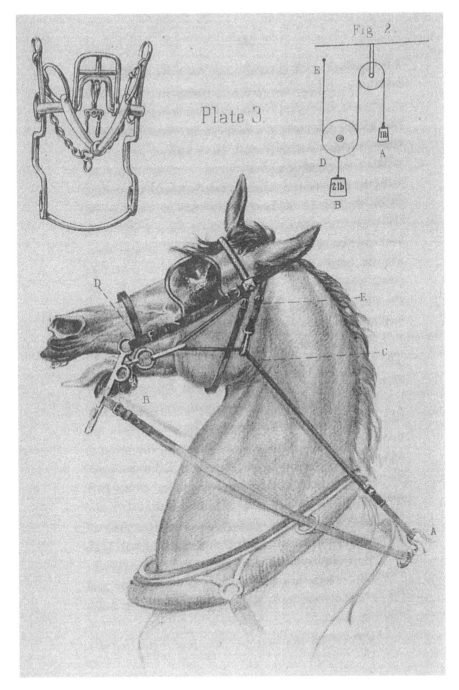

19 'Torture' of the bearing rein, lithographic illustration in Edward Fordham Flower's *Bits and Bearing Reins*, 1875.

became a crusade, just as the campaign against feathered millinery would make reform-minded women the accusers of their sisters.[159] In these circumstances it is difficult to construe *Black Beauty* as a feminist diatribe against the physical constrictions of women's dress or their confined lives, as has sometimes been done, or to interpret the bearing rein as a symbol of patriarchal oppression.[160] Rather, it is the most powerful example of the undeserved, gratuitous suffering of sentient animals, inflicted by mankind, which prompted the writing of the book in the first place.

When Beauty finds himself condemned to work for Skinner, he realises for the first time what Ginger must have endured. 'I have heard men say, that seeing is believing; but I should say that *feeling* is believing; for much as I had seen before, I never knew till now the utter misery of a cab-horse's life.'[161] The act of seeing is external to the thing seen, and requires an effort of imagination to interpret the outward signs of suffering. *Feeling* involves actually sharing the experience of other beings, and identifying with them wholly. Anna Sewell herself was undergoing severe pain as she wrote *Black Beauty* in her last years, pain that must have obtruded itself on her consciousness as the great leveller. The anonymous author of *Some Remarks on Cruelty to Animals* (1865) also claimed to be writing from his or her deathbed, and pondered, as Sewell must have done, the 'inexplicable' problem of why 'creatures ... incapable of sin or moral offence of any kind, should be called upon to suffer in the way they do'. We try to differentiate ourselves from them by claiming to be 'mental and spiritual more than ... animal beings', but acute *physical* pain is in truth more terrible than any suffering of the mind.[162] A capacity for pain is the existential bond between humanity and other species that reminds us of all the other faculties we have in common, and urges upon us the need for kind fellow-feeling: Anna Kingsford, in her description of the evils of vivisection, evoked a 'brotherhood of suffering' among all sentient beings.[163] Writing *Black Beauty* in the mid-1870s, Sewell must, in fact, have assimilated the furious arguments over the pain caused to animals by vivisection, which were then at their height. If her wonderful book never suggested such a fundamental re-examination of society's treatment of animals as did the writings of Frances Power Cobbe and many other female writers of the 1880s–1890s, it already escaped the confines of 'feminine' conventions in its fearless and impassioned assault on the cruelties of the times. The 'religion of amity' never had a finer prophet.

Notes

1   'The Queen and Princess protecting a cat', *Animal World*, 4:44 (May 1873), 65–6.
2   Edward G. Fairholme and Wellesley Pain, *A Century of Work for Animals: The History of the R.S.P.C.A., 1824–1924* (London: John Murray, 1924), pp. 94–5.
3   'Prevention of cruelty to animals', *Illustrated London News*, 64:1818 (27 June 1874), 610. Arthur W. Moss, *Valiant Crusade: The History of the R.S.P.C.A.* (London: Cassell, 1961), pp. 156, 163. 'Our Jubilee meeting', *Animal World*, 5:59 (1874), 114–17, and illustration in 5:60 (1874), 133. 'The Queen at our anniversary meeting', *Animal World*, 18:214 (1887), 97, and 18:215 (1887), 114–26. 'The Queen at the Albert-Hall', *The Times* (5 July 1887), p. 10. Fairholme and Pain, *Century of Work for Animals*, pp. 92–3.
4   Major-General John Jarvis Bisset, *Sport and War, Or Recollections of Fighting and Hunting in South Africa from the Years 1834 to 1867. With a Narrative of H.R.H. The Duke of Edinburgh's Visit to the Cape*, illustrated from sketches by Captain H.K. Wilson and G. Scanlan, M.D. (London: John Murray, 1875), pp. viii, 180–2, 194–7. Anon. [Professor Roderick Noble], *The Progress of His Royal Highness, Prince Alfred Ernest Albert through the Cape Colony, British Kaffraria, the Orange Free State, and Port Natal, in the Year 1860* (Cape Town: Saul Solomon, 1861), pp. 85–90.
5   Bisset, *Sport and War*, pp. 218–21, 235–53.
6   Prince Albert's battues in the Scottish Highlands in the 1840s were satirised in *Punch* cartoons. Diana Donald, *Picturing Animals in Britain, 1750–1850* (New Haven and London: Yale University Press, 2007), pp. 300–3. For the hunting enthusiasms of the Prince of Wales, later King Edward VII: Alfred E.T. Watson, *King Edward VII as a Sportsman* (London: Longmans, Green, 1911). Antony Taylor, '"Pig-sticking princes": royal hunting, moral outrage, and the republican opposition to animal abuse in nineteenth- and early twentieth-century Britain', *History*, 89:293 (January 2004), 30–48.
7   Christopher Hibbert (ed.), *Queen Victoria in Her Letters and Journals* (London: John Murray, 1984), pp. 1–2, 205, 239, 249, 263–4, 281, 340. Fairholme and Pain, *Century of Work for Animals*, pp. 96–7. Gloria Cottesloe, *The Story of the Battersea Dogs' Home* (Newton Abbot: David & Charles, 1979), pp. 65–8. Richard D. French, *Antivivisection and Medical Science in Victorian Society* (Princeton and London: Princeton University Press, 1975), pp. 123, 126–7, 145–6. Rod Preece (ed.), *Awe for the Tiger, Love for the Lamb: A Chronicle of Sensibility to Animals* (New York and London: Routledge, 2002), pp. 326–7.
8   Richard Ormond, *Sir Edwin Landseer* (Philadelphia: Philadelphia Museum of Art, and London: Tate Gallery, 1981), and Richard Ormond, *The Monarch of the Glen: Landseer in the Highlands* (Edinburgh: National Galleries of Scotland, 2005). Donald, *Picturing Animals*, pp. 94–100, 127–58.
9   Hibbert, *Queen Victoria in Her Letters*, p. 263.
10 Sir Samuel White Baker, *Wild Beasts and Their Ways: Reminiscences of Europe, Asia, Africa and America* (London and New York: Macmillan, 1890), pp. 453–4.
11 Herbert Spencer, *The Study of Sociology* (London: Henry S. King, 3rd edn, 1874), pp. 178–202; quote from p. 179.
12 Ibid., pp. 375f.
13 Ibid., p. 381.
14 Anne Brontë, *Agnes Grey*, ed. Hilda Marsden and Robert Inglesfield (Oxford: Clarendon

Press, 1988), pp. 20–3, 47–9. The novel was first published with Emily Brontë's *Wuthering Heights* in 1847.

15 Spencer, *Study of Sociology*, pp. 179–80, 190.

16 A.G. Bradley, A.C. Champneys and J.W. Baines, *A History of Marlborough College during Fifty Years, From Its Foundation to the Present Time* (London: John Murray, 1893), pp. 78, 93–6, 134, 150, 152, 174–6.

17 *Charles Kingsley: His Letters and Memories of His Life. Edited by His Wife*, 2 vols (London and New York: Macmillan, 1894), vol. 2, p. 148.

18 Henry S. Salt, *Seventy Years Among Savages* (London: Allen & Unwin, 1921), pp. 16, 27, 154, 175. Revd C. Allix Wilkinson, *Reminiscences of Eton (Keate's Time)* (London: Hurst and Blackett, 1888), pp. 23, 26, 31–2, 148, 319–21. 'Blood-sports at schools: the Eton hare-hunt', by 'An Old Etonian', in Salt (ed.), *Killing for Sport: Essays by Various Writers* (London: G. Bell & Sons for the Humanitarian League, 1915), pp. 116–29. A.C. Crossley, *The Eton College Hunt: A Short History of Beagling at Eton* (Eton College: Spottiswoode, Ballantyne, 1922).

19 John M. MacKenzie, 'Chivalry, social Darwinism, and ritualised killing: the hunting ethos in Central Africa up to 1914', in David Anderson and Richard Grove (eds), *Conservation in Africa: People, Policies and Practice* (Cambridge: Cambridge University Press, 1987), and MacKenzie's *The Empire of Nature: Hunting, Conservation and British Imperialism* (Manchester and New York: Manchester University Press, 1988). J.A. Mangan and Callum McKenzie, *Militarism, Hunting, Imperialism: 'Blooding' the Martial Male* (London and New York: Routledge, 2010). John Miller, *Empire and the Animal Body: Violence, Identity and Ecology in Victorian Adventure Fiction* (London, New York and Delhi: Anthem Press, 2012).

20 William Charles Baldwin, *African Hunting, from Natal to the Zambesi … From 1852 to 1860* (London: Richard Bentley, 1863), pp. 58, 236.

21 Lieut.-General Sir Robert Stephenson Smyth Baden-Powell, *Yarns for Boy Scouts, Told Round the Camp Fire* (London: C. Arthur Pearson, 1910), p. 202. The bloodthirsty sporting ebullience manifested in Baden-Powell's *Pigsticking or Hoghunting* (London: Harrison and Sons, 1889) was largely absent from his scouting books. Shefali Rajamannar, *Reading the Animal in the Literature of the British Raj* (Basingstoke: Palgrave Macmillan, 2012), pp. 82–108.

22 For example, Baldwin, *African Hunting*, pp. 36, 55, 188, 197, 200, 211, 281–2.

23 White Baker, *Wild Beasts*, pp. 275, 287.

24 Cheshire Archives, Chester, DET 3229/60/2 (5), Egerton's manuscript hunting diary headed 'Sardinia/ Big Bar Klondyke 1900'. Rowland Ward, *Records of Big Game, with the Distribution, Characteristics, Dimensions, Weights, and Horn and Tusk Measurements of the Different Species* (London: Rowland Ward, 4th edn, 1903).

25 J.S. Bratton, 'Of England, home and duty: the image of England in Victorian and Edwardian juvenile fiction', in John M. MacKenzie (ed.), *Imperialism and Popular Culture* (Manchester: Manchester University Press, 1986). Joseph Bristow, *Empire Boys: Adventures in a Man's World* (London: HarperCollins, 1991), pp. 20–1, 37–41. Kelly Boyd, *Manliness and the Boys' Story Paper in Britain: A Cultural History, 1855–1940* (Basingstoke: Palgrave Macmillan, 2003), pp. 2–4, 31, 34, 45. Miller, *Empire and the Animal Body*, pp. 68–73.

26 'The gravelling trustees', *Boys' Own Paper*, 1 (1879), 227–8; prize essay on the theme of 'Kindness to animals', 240, 543–4. For the 'gravelling' lady, Miss Lisetta Rist, see 'A humane bequest', *The Times* (6 February 1879), p. 8.

27 James Greenwood, *Wild Sports of the World: A Boy's Book of Natural History and Adventure* (London: S.O. Beeton, 1862), pp. v–vi, 358–9, 404. Greenwood mistakenly renders 'Crewdson' as 'Crewdner'.

28 Sarah Stickney Ellis's comment in *The Daughters of England: Their Position in Society, Character and Responsibilities* (London: Fisher, 1842), p. 133, that women's 'highest duty is so often to suffer, and be still' was quoted in the title of Martha Vicinus's *Suffer and Be Still: Women in the Victorian Age* (London: Methuen, 1980).

29 Elizabeth Langland, *Nobody's Angels: Middle-Class Women and Domestic Ideology in Victorian Culture* (Ithaca: Cornell University Press, 1995), pp. 65–76. Henrietta Twycross-Martin, 'The drunkard, the brute and the paterfamilias: the temperance fiction of the early Victorian writer Sarah Stickney Ellis', in Anne Hogan and Andrew Bradstock (eds), *Women of Faith in Victorian Culture: Reassessing the Angel in the House* (Basingstoke and London: Macmillan, 1998), and Twycross-Martin's article on Ellis in the *Oxford Dictionary of National Biography* (British Academy and Oxford: Oxford University Press, 2004). Leonore Davidoff and Catherine Hall, *Family Fortunes: Men and Women of the English Middle Class, 1780–1850* (London and New York: Routledge, revised edn, 2002), pp. 180–4.

30 Differing views on this topic are given by Amanda Vickery, in 'Golden age to separate spheres? A review of the categories and chronology of English women's history', *Historical Journal*, 36:2 (1993), 383–414, and by Davidoff and Hall, in *Family Fortunes*, pp. xxi, 115, 30, 114–15, 450–1.

31 Ellis, *Daughters of England*, pp. 11–12, 15, 18–20.

32 Ellis's sister, Dorothy Stickney, had married Abraham Sewell, Anna Sewell's uncle.

33 *Contrasts, A Series of Twenty Drawings, designed by S. Stickney*, lithographed by George Smith (London: R. Ackermann, 1832): National Art Library, London.

34 'S.S.' [Sarah Stickney Ellis], 'Our pets', *Once a Week. An Illustrated Miscellany*, 2 (1859–1860), 15–18, 55–8, 89–92. Ellis's authorship is confirmed in *The Home Life and Letters of Mrs Ellis. Compiled by Her Nieces* (London: J. Nisbet, undated [1893]), pp. 4–5, 206–7.

35 Sarah Stickney Ellis, *The Poetry of Life*, 2 vols (London: Saunders and Otley, 1835), vol. 1, pp. 110–11.

36 Sarah Stickney Ellis, *The Wives of England: Their Relative Duties, Domestic Influence, and Social Obligations* (London: Fisher, 1843), pp. 172–3, 177–8.

37 Sarah Stickney Ellis, *Home, Or the Iron Rule: A Domestic Story*, 3 vols (London: Saunders and Otley, 1836), vol. 1, pp. 71–4.

38 Sarah Stickney Ellis, *Education of the Heart: Woman's Best Work* (London: William Tegg, 1876), pp. 58–9. This work (preface dated 1869), was based on a series of articles in the Religious Tract Society's *The Leisure Hour*.

39 Ellis, *Daughters of England*, p. 86.

40 Ellis, *Wives of England*, p. 273.

41 Ibid., p. 173. Sarah Stickney Ellis, *The Mothers of England: Their Influence and Responsibility* (London: Fisher, 1843), pp. 298–305; *Daughters of England*, pp. 85–7; *Education of the Heart*, p. 120.

42 Ellis, *Mothers of England*, p. 103.

43 Ellis, *Daughters of England*, pp. 79–87, 127.

44 Ellis, *Mothers of England*, pp. 301–5.

45 Anthony Trollope, 'Mr Freeman on the morality of hunting', *Fortnightly Review*, new series 36 (1 December 1869), 616–25 (625); Helen Taylor, 'A few words on Mr Trollope's defence of fox-hunting', 37 (1 January 1870), 63–8 (67). Both were responding

to Edward A. Freeman's essay on 'The morality of field sports', *Fortnightly Review*, 34 (1 October 1869), 353–85. On the gendered mystique of hunting: Philip Howell, 'Hunting and animal-human history', in Hilda Kean and Philip Howell (eds), *The Routledge Companion to Animal-Human History* (London and New York: Routledge, 2019).

46 Ellis, *Daughters of England*, p. 81.

47 Ellis, *Home, Or the Iron Rule*, vol. 1, p. 22.

48 Ellis, *Mothers of England*, p. 78.

49 Ellis, *Daughters of England*, p. 89.

50 Ibid., pp. 154–5, 166.

51 Ibid., p. 92.

52 Lewis Hippolytus Joseph Tonna, *A Memoir of Charlotte Elizabeth; Embracing the Period from the Close of Her Personal Recollections to Her Death* (New York: M.W. Dodd, 1847). Clara Lucas Balfour, *A Sketch of Charlotte Elizabeth* (London: W. & F.G. Cash, 1854). Kathryn Gleadle, 'Charlotte Elizabeth Tonna and the mobilization of Tory women in early Victorian England', *Historical Journal*, 50:1 (2007), 97–117. Her surname is sometimes given as Phelan, that of her estranged first husband. She allegedly used the pen name 'Charlotte Elizabeth' to prevent Phelan from claiming her earnings.

53 Charlotte Elizabeth, 'Politics', *Christian Lady's Magazine*, 3 (January–June 1835), 366–74. Gleadle, 'Charlotte Elizabeth Tonna', 105. Sarah Richardson, 'Women, philanthropy, and imperialism in early nineteenth-century Britain', in Helen Gilbert and Chris Tiffin (eds), *Burden or Benefit? Imperial Benevolence and Its Legacies* (Bloomington and Indianapolis: Indiana University Press, 2008), pp. 92–6, and *The Political Worlds of Women: Gender and Politics in Nineteenth Century Britain* (New York and London: Routledge, 2013), pp. 8, 79–80.

54 Davidoff and Hall, *Family Fortunes*, p. 183.

55 Charlotte Elizabeth, *Kindness to Animals* (London: The Religious Tract Society, undated), chapter 1. Tonna, *A Memoir*, pp. 20–1.

56 Charlotte Elizabeth, *Personal Recollections* (London: R.B. Seeley and W. Burnside, 1841), pp. 181, 185.

57 *Kindness to Animals*, chapter 1. Tonna, *A Memoir*, p. 20.

58 John Madden, *The Wilderness and Its Tenants: A Series of Geographical and Other Essays Illustrative of Life in a Wild Country*, 3 vols (London: Simpkin, Marshall, Hamilton, Kent, 1897), vol. 3, p. 176, quoting Winwood Reade's *Savage Africa*.

59 On Brightwen: Barbara T. Gates, *Kindred Nature: Victorian and Edwardian Women Embrace the Living World* (Chicago and London: University of Chicago Press, 1998), pp. 222–9. Barbara T. Gates, 'Ordering nature: revisioning Victorian science culture', and Bernard Lightman, '"The voices of nature": popularizing Victorian science', both in Bernard Lightman (ed.), *Victorian Science in Context* (Chicago and London: University of Chicago Press, 1997). Gates's article on Brightwen in the *Oxford Dictionary of National Biography*.

60 Eliza Brightwen, *The Life and Thoughts of a Naturalist. Edited by W.H. Chesson. With Introduction and Epilogue by Edmund Gosse* (London: T. Fisher Unwin, 1909), pp. x–xi. The leading literary critic Edmund Gosse was the stepson of Brightwen's sister-in-law.

61 Eliza Brightwen, *More About Wild Nature ... With Illustrations by the Author* (London: T. Fisher Unwin, 2nd edn, 1893), pp. 188–9, 194, and *Inmates of My House and Garden* (New York and London: Macmillan, 1895), pp. 30–2, 55, 108. *Life and Thoughts*, pp. 133–4, 141, 190–6.

62 Brightwen, *More About Wild Nature*, pp. 47–57. *Inmates*, p. 94.

63 Eliza Brightwen, *Wild Nature Won by Kindness* (London: T. Fisher Unwin, 1890), pp. 18–19. *More About Wild Nature*, p. 61.

64 Brightwen, *Wild Nature*, pp. 197–200. *More About Wild Nature*, pp. 37–41.

65 Brightwen, *Wild Nature*, pp. 12–13.

66 Ibid., pp. 40, 73, 145–6. *More About Wild Nature*, pp. 37–40.

67 Brightwen, *Life and Thoughts*, pp. 130–1.

68 Brightwen, *Wild Nature*, pp. 123, 132–3.

69 She deplored the fact that popular resentment over aristocratic field sports fomented socialism, and was 'scared' by evidence of 'unlooked-for intelligence' and knowledge of Darwinism among her own servants and villagers: *Inmates*, pp. 32–3; *Life and Thoughts*, pp. 103, 128, 133–4.

70 Brightwen, *More About Wild Nature*, pp. 185–6, 197, 210–15. *Life and Thoughts*, pp. xxiv, 174–6.

71 Brightwen, *Wild Nature*, pp. 214–15. *More About Wild Nature*, pp. 96–9. *Life and Thoughts*, pp. 102, 178.

72 Brightwen, *More About Wild Nature*, pp. 55–6, 234–5.

73 Brightwen, *Life and Thoughts*, p. 135.

74 Ibid., pp. 144–5.

75 Brightwen, *Inmates*, 'Teaching village children to be humane', pp. 127f. *Life and Thoughts*, p. 174.

76 Brightwen, *Wild Nature*, p. 118. *Life and Thoughts*, pp. 112–13, 142–3, 146, 180, 188–9.

77 Fairholme and Pain, *Century of Work for Animals*, pp. 166–72. Frederick S. Milton, 'Taking the pledge: a study of children's societies for the prevention of cruelty to birds and animals in Britain, c.1870–1914' (PhD dissertation, Newcastle University, 2008), pp. 81–117.

78 Fairholme and Pain, *Century of Work for Animals*, p. 166. Moss, *Valiant Crusade*, pp. 198–9.

79 Anon. [Georgina Mount-Temple], *Memorials*, printed for private circulation, 1890, pp. 88–9. Rt. Hon. George W.E. Russell, *Portraits of the Seventies* (New York: Charles Scribner's Sons, 1916), pp. 278–84. James Gregory, *Reformers, Patrons and Philanthropists: The Cowper-Temples and High Politics in Victorian Britain* (London and New York: Tauris Academic Studies, 2010), pp. 158, 172, 178, 191–2, 248. Article on Lady Mount-Temple by Virginia Surtees in the *Oxford Dictionary of National Biography*.

80 'Band of Mercy treat', *The Band of Mercy Advocate*, 2:24 (December 1880), 90.

81 G. Stringer Rowe, *T.B. Smithies (Editor of 'The British Workman'): A Memoir* (London: T. Woolmer, 1884), pp. 62–4. George John Stevenson, *Methodist Worthies: Characteristic Sketches of Methodist Preachers of the Several Denominations*, vol. 4 (London: Thomas C. Jack, 1885), 'Thomas Bywater Smithies', pp. 588–91. Article on Smithies by Frank Murray in the *Oxford Dictionary of National Biography*.

82 'C.S.' [Catherine Smithies], *A Mother's Lessons on Kindness to Animals* (London: S.W. Partridge, undated [c.1862]). 'The late Mrs Smithies', *Band of Mercy Advocate*, 1:1 (January 1879), 6.

83 'Sixty-sixth anniversary of the R.S.P.C.A. first meeting', with report on the Band of Mercy, *Animal World*, 21:251 (1 August 1890), 119. Roswell C. McCrea, *The Humane Movement: A Descriptive Survey* (New York: Columbia University Press, 1910), pp. 94–6.

84 Rowe, *T.B. Smithies*, pp. 15–16, 27–8, 49–55. Stevenson, *Methodist Worthies*, pp. 590–1.

85 *Band of Mercy Advocate*, 1:9 (September 1879), 69–70.

86 'The village school', *Band of Mercy Advocate*, 1:6 (June 1879).

87 Letter from George Eliot to Caroline Bray, 3 February 1876, in Gordon S. Haight (ed.), *The George Eliot Letters* (London: Oxford University Press and New Haven: Yale University Press, 1956), vol. 6, p. 220.

88 'Sylvia and the blackbird', *Band of Mercy Advocate*, 1:9 and 1:10 (September–October 1879), 70–1, 78–9; 'The merciless boy', 2:19 (July 1880), 51. Monica Flegel, '"How does your collar suit me?": the human animal in the RSPCA's *Animal World* and *Band of Mercy*', *Victorian Literature and Culture*, 40:1 (March 2012), 247–62.

89 'Robert the stone-thrower' and 'The pleasure van', *Band of Mercy Advocate*, 2:18 (June 1880), 45–6.

90 '"Prince" and the kitten: a story for little boys', *Band of Mercy Advocate*, 2:13 (January 1880), 3.

91 George T. Angell, *The New Order of Chivalry: Band of Mercy Information* (Boston: Band of Mercy and the Massachusetts Society for the Prevention of Cruelty to Animals, 1883). Diane L. Beers, *For the Prevention of Cruelty: The History and Legacy of Animal Rights Activism in the United States* (Athens, OH: Swallow Press/Ohio University Press, 2006), pp. 88–9. Materials relating to the American Band of Mercy can be accessed via the National Museum of Animals and Society at Los Angeles.

92 Marshall Saunders [pen name of Margaret Saunders], *Beautiful Joe: An Autobiography*, facsimile edn (Bedford, MA: Applewood Books, undated), pp. 143–63, 176.

93 Angell, *New Order of Chivalry* (unpaginated), 'Appeal to the teachers and Sunday school teachers of Massachusetts'.

94 Milton, 'Taking the pledge', p. 107.

95 Florence Horatia Nelson Suckling, *The Humane Educator and Reciter* (London: Simpkin, Marshall, Hamilton, Kent, 1891), pp. 78, 304–8, 423–35.

96 Florence Horatia Nelson Suckling, *The Humane Play-Book: Being a Collection of Dialogues, Action Pieces, and Plays, Suitable for Entertainments* (London: George Bell & Sons, 1900), pp. 2, 30.

97 Milton, 'Taking the pledge', pp. 291–5.

98 Flora Thompson, *Lark Rise to Candleford* (1939), chapter 9, 'Country playtime'.

99 Miss Levvy, 'Hunt or no hunt (written for five boys)', in Suckling's *Humane Educator*, pp. 420–2.

100 Brightwen, *Life and Thoughts*, p. 112.

101 Cheshire Archives, D5749, minute book of the Knutsford Band of Mercy. The five honorary vice-presidents were all clergymen. At a meeting of 4 December 1900, Payne, an antiquarian and literary scholar as well as a minister, asked to hand over the secretary's role to 'someone who had more time and greater interest'.

102 Minute book, meetings of 28 October 1898, 6 March 1899, 8 May 1900.

103 Cheshire Archives, DET 3229/60/2, game diaries etc. of Maurice Egerton. MacKenzie, 'Chivalry, social Darwinism', p. 55. Mangan and McKenzie, *Militarism, Hunting, Imperialism*, pp. 127–8, 143, 152–5, 180–2. 'Bachelor Baron's death', *Knutsford Guardian* (6 February 1958), p. 7.

104 Revd Alfred Charles Smith, 'On the persecution of birds and animals, unhappily so general in this country', *Zoologist*, 11:128 (June 1853), 3901–5. Archibald Stodart Walker (ed.), revised Peter Jeffrey Mackie, *The Keeper's Book: A Guide to the Duties of a Gamekeeper* (London and Edinburgh: T.N. Foulis, 7th edn. 1910), pp. viii, 103f. F.D.

Smith and Barbara Wilcox, *Sold for Two Farthings: Being the Views of Country Folk on Cruelty to Animals* (London: James Barrie, 1950), pp. 47, 65–8, 72–4, 100f., 197.

105 Frances Power Cobbe, 'Humanity', *The Times* (18 October 1886), p. 4.

106 Susan Chitty, *The Woman Who Wrote 'Black Beauty': A Life of Anna Sewell* (London: Hodder & Stoughton, 1971). Adrienne E. Gavin, *Dark Horse: A Life of Anna Sewell* (Stroud: Sutton Publishing, 2004). There are innumerable editions of the book, including *The Annotated Black Beauty*, ed. Ellen B. Wells and Anne Grimshaw (London: J.A. Allen, 1989), with many illustrations.

107 RSPCA *Report* for 1899–1900, p. 117. Anna Sewell, *Black Beauty*, edited and introduced by Adrienne Gavin (Oxford: Oxford University Press, 2012), pp. xiii–xiv. Subsequent page references are to this edition. Coral Lansbury, *The Old Brown Dog: Women, Workers, and Vivisection in Edwardian England* (Madison: University of Wisconsin Press, 1985), pp. 5, 40, 63f., 97f.

108 George T. Angell, *Autobiographical Sketches and Personal Reflections* (Boston: American Humane Education Society, undated [c.1897–1898]), pp. 94–9. Beers, *For the Prevention of Cruelty*, pp. 26, 31.

109 McCrea, *Humane Movement*, pp. 112, 115–16.

110 Tess Cosslett, *Talking Animals in British Children's Fiction, 1786–1914* (Aldershot: Ashgate, 2006). Teresa Mangum, 'Narrative dominion or the animals write back? Animal genres in literature and the arts', in Kathleen Kete (ed.), *A Cultural History of Animals*, vol. 5, *In the Age of Empire* (Oxford and New York: Berg, 2007).

111 Anon., *Memoirs of Dick, the Little Poney, Supposed to be Written by Himself; and Published for the Instruction and Amusement of Good Boys and Girls* (London: J. Walker, 1800). 'M. Pelham' [Dorothy Kilner], *The Rational Brutes; Or, Talking Animals*, 1st edn 1799 (London: J. Harris; Darton and Harvey, 1803). Ellis, 'Our pets', 16.

112 Anon. [Mrs E. Burrows], *Tuppy; Or, The Autobiography of a Donkey* (London: Griffiths and Farran, 1860). Anon., *The Adventures of a Donkey, Written by Himself* (London: Ward, Lock and Tyler, undated [c.1870]).

113 Donald, *Picturing Animals*, pp. 216–32.

114 Ralph Fletcher, *A Few Notes on Cruelty to Animals* (London: Longman, 1846), p. 3. Kathryn Miele, 'Horse-sense: understanding the working horse in Victorian London', *Victorian Literature and Culture*, 37:1 (March 2009), 129–40.

115 Sewell, *Black Beauty … With Recollections … by Margaret Sewell* (London: George G. Harrap, 1935), p. 3. Chitty, *Woman Who Wrote 'Black Beauty'*, pp. 102–3. Gavin, *Dark Horse*, p. 88. Donald, *Picturing Animals*, p. 201. These pictures, still in a private collection, do not seem to have been engraved.

116 The shortness of the chapters may reflect Sewell's experience of teaching working men and boys in evening classes, but also the sporadic nature of her work on the book due to illness.

117 Sewell, *Black Beauty*, p. 16.

118 Mary Bayly, *The Life and Letters of Mrs Sewell* (London: James Nisbet, 3rd edn, 1889), p. 272.

119 Sewell, *Black Beauty*, pp. 46–8, 66–8.

120 Peter Hollindale, in 'Plain speaking: *Black Beauty* as a Quaker text', *Children's Literature*, 28:1 (2000), 95–111, is at pains to emphasise the book's purely literary qualities, as somehow distinct from its 'well-intentioned functionalism' or 'propaganda'.

121 Ruth Padel, 'Saddled with Ginger: women, men and horses', *Encounter* (November

1980), 47–54. Moira Ferguson, 'Breaking in Englishness: *Black Beauty* and the politics of gender, race and class', *Women: A Cultural Review*, 5:1 (1994), 34–52, and Ferguson, *Animal Advocacy and Englishwomen, 1780–1900* (Ann Arbor: University of Michigan Press, 1998), pp. 75f. Robert Dingley, 'A horse of a different color: *Black Beauty* and the pressures of indebtedness', *Victorian Literature and Culture*, 25:2 (Fall 1997), 241–51. Adrienne Gavin, 'The Autobiography of a Horse? Reading Anna Sewell's *Black Beauty* as autobiography', in Martin Hewitt (ed.), *Representing Victorian Lives* (Leeds: Leeds Centre for Victorian Studies, 1999). Gina M. Dorré, 'Horses and corsets: *Black Beauty*, dress reform, and the fashioning of the Victorian woman' in her *Victorian Fiction and the Cult of the Horse* (Aldershot: Ashgate, 2006). Deborah Denenholz Morse, '"The mark of the beast": animals as sites of imperial encounter from *Wuthering Heights* to *Green Mansions*', in Deborah Denenholz Morse and Martin A. Danahay (eds), *Victorian Animal Dreams: Representations of Animals in Victorian Literature and Culture* (Aldershot: Ashgate, 2007). Essays by Monica Flegel and Kathryn Yeniyurt in Laurence W. Mazzeno and Ronald D. Morrison (eds), *Animals in Victorian Literature and Culture: Contexts for Criticism* (London: Palgrave Macmillan, 2017) refocus attention on Sewell's evocation of horses' experience of suffering.

122 Burrows, *Tuppy*, p. 98.

123 Anon., *Adventures of a Donkey*, pp. 119–20, 133, 184.

124 *The Adventures of a Donkey. By Arabella Argus*, 1st edn c.1815 (London: William Tegg, 1864), p. 171.

125 Cosslett, *Talking Animals*, pp. 63f., especially pp. 69–70.

126 *Black Beauty ... With Recollections ... by Margaret Sewell*, pp. 3–4.

127 Several members of the Sewell family, including Anna, were converted to a more evangelical form of belief, and left the Society of Friends, but retained much of its culture. Gavin, *Dark Horse*, pp. 40–4, 57–9. Elizabeth Isichei, *Victorian Quakers* (London: Oxford University Press, 1970), pp. 2–23, 44–53.

128 Bayly, *Life and Letters*, pp. 56–7, 106–20. Mary Sewell's *Poems and Ballads ... With Memoir by Miss E.B. Bayly*, 2 vols (London: Jarrold & Sons, undated [1886]), includes many verses exhorting boys to be kind to animals.

129 Thomas Clarkson, *A Portraiture of Quakerism*, 3 vols (London: Longman, Hurst, Rees, and Orme, 2nd edn, 1807), vol. 1, pp. 54, 132–51; vol. 3, pp. 179–81.

130 Sewell, *Black Beauty*, pp. 127, 151–3. *Black Beauty ... With Recollections ... by Margaret Sewell*, p. 3.

131 Bayly, *Life and Letters*, pp. 274–5.

132 Gavin, *Dark Horse*, p. 189.

133 Anne Wright, *What Is a Bird?* (London: Jarrold and Sons, 1857), pp. 20–6. Another aunt, Maria Wright, wrote the equally fundamentalist *The Bow of Faith: Or, Old Testament Lessons for Children* (London: Routledge, Warnes, and Routledge, 1859).

134 Bayly, *Life and Letters*, pp. 70, 264, 280–1, 306, 315.

135 Sewell, *Poems and Ballads*, p. vii.

136 Bayly, *Life and Letters*, pp. 157, 245–7.

137 Horace Bushnell, 'Of the animal infestations', in *Moral Uses of Dark Things* (New York: Charles Scribner, 1868), pp. 277, 282, 286.

138 Bayly, *Life and Letters*, pp. 250–2. I am grateful to Conrad Cherry for confirming that 'Of the animal infestations' must be the sermon Bayly remembered. As she dates her conversation with Anna Sewell to 1863, she presumably read it as a separate work before the publication of *Moral Uses*.

139 Sewell, *Black Beauty*, pp. 15, 23.

140 Ibid., pp. 29, 131–2, 154.

141 Margaret Gatty, *Parables from Nature. Fourth Series* (London: Bell and Daldy, 1864), pp. 100–1. Cosslett, *Talking Animals*, pp. 98–9.

142 Sewell, *Black Beauty*, pp. 11–13, 109–12.

143 Ibid., pp. 72, 74–5, 113–14, 134, 145–6.

144 Hilda Kean, *Animal Rights: Political and Social Change in Britain since 1800* (London: Reaktion Books, 1998), pp. 57–8, 77–8.

145 *The Cabman's Chronicle: An Advocate of Sabbath Rest*, 1:1 (October 1859), 1–2.

146 Sewell, *Black Beauty*, pp. 118–22.

147 See, for example, 'The power of kindness', *The Cabman*, 1:5 (January 1875), 40, and 'The horse: his use and abuse', 1:8 (April 1875), 83–5. David Hayes, 'Mission and suspicion at King's Cross: The London Cabmen's Mission, 1871–c.1910', *Camden History Review*, 21 (1997), 25–9.

148 *Cabman's Chronicle*, 1:1, 3–4.

149 Sewell, *Black Beauty*, pp. 128–30. Alice Quinn, 'Blame, Black Beauty, class and cruelty: scapegoats and horses in the 19th century', uploaded to www.academia.edu, accessed May 2019. Huge numbers of horses were kept by railway and tram companies, hotels and livery stables etc.

150 Sewell, *Black Beauty*, pp. 29–30, 73–6, 151–3.

151 *Animal World* (March 1890), 41. Suckling, *Humane Educator*, p. 482. Charles H. Allen, 'Bearing reins', *The Times* (19 October 1893), p. 14.

152 Bracy Clark, *A Treatise on the Bits of Horses* (no imprint, 1835), pp. 4–5, 8.

153 Gavin, *Dark Horse*, pp. 193–4.

154 Edward Fordham Flower, 'Cruelty to horses', *The Times* (12 August 1874), p. 6. Edward Fordham Flower, *Bits and Bearing-Reins; With Observations on Horses and Harness* (London: Cassell, 7th edn, 1885), published posthumously by Flower's sons, pp. 19–20, 25–6, 30, 37–8. Sir Arthur Helps had also repeatedly condemned bearing reins in *Some Talks About Animals* (1873), discussed in our chapter 3.

155 RSPCA *Report* (1876), p. 38. Court report and correspondence in the *Times* (23 June 1875), p. 14; (24 June 1875), p. 11; (25 June 1875), p. 7; (26 June 1875), p. 10.

156 Nimrod [Charles James Apperley], 'On the abolition of the bearing-rein', *Sporting Review* (March 1839), 197–202.

157 Among many examples: Anon., *Observations on the Effects of the Fixed Bridle or Bearing Rein* (London: RSPCA, 1860), p. 9; 'J.M.', 'The evil effects of the bearing rein, etc.', *Animal World*, 1:2 (1 November 1869), 42–3.

158 Sewell, *Black Beauty*, pp. 72–5. Miele, 'Horse-sense', p. 137.

159 See also, for example, Caroline (Cara) Bray, *Elements of Morality, in Easy Lessons, For Home and School Teaching* (London: Longmans, Green, 3rd edn, 1897), p. 96.

160 Examples are the works by Padel, Ferguson and Dorré, as cited in note 121.

161 Sewell, *Black Beauty*, p. 154.

162 Anon., *Some Remarks on Cruelty to Animals, and the Principles in Human Nature from Which That Vice Proceeds* (London: S. Lowe, Son, & Marston and Birmingham: Josiah Allen, junior, 1865), pp. 3–8.

163 Anna Kingsford, 'The uselessness of vivisection', *Nineteenth Century*, 11:60 (February 1882), 171–83.

5

Anti-vivisection:
a feminist cause?

During the last quarter of the nineteenth century and the first decade of the twentieth, one kind of cruelty to animals aroused the public to a degree that was quite unprecedented: scientific experiments on live animals, or (as such experiments were collectively and popularly described) vivisection.[1] The resulting controversy was remarkable not simply in the depth of the passions that were stirred, but in the fact that – as one expert observer remarked – it 'interested the people of England from the Sovereign on the throne to the humblest of her subjects'.[2] Labouring-class men and women as well as aristocrats, parliamentarians, middle-class leaders of opinion, literary celebrities, church leaders and religious thinkers and of course doctors and scientists actively participated in the increasingly bitter and polarised battles between the defenders and the opponents of vivisection. There were endless petitions, parliamentary bills, deputations to the Home Office, and two Royal Commissions (in 1875 and 1906) that produced lengthy published reports. Several anti-vivisection societies were established, using prosecutions, pamphlets, dedicated journals and poster campaigns to convey their views to the public. Latterly there were even shops displaying propagandist literature and visual imagery of vivisection, mass meetings and processions with provocative banners (figure 20), which sparked physical violence between the anti-vivisectionists' working-class stewards and hostile medical students.[3] The serious journals of the day carried many polemical articles on vivisection, with the arguments of one side being immediately controverted by those of the other, and newspapers, too, admitted long series of correspondence arising from particular episodes in the struggle. More remarkably, there was a whole genre of novels reviling vivisection, while Tennyson and Browning among others wrote poems full of pathos on the subject.[4]

Accounts of painful vivisection experiments aroused deep and furiously

20 Photograph of 'The Brown Dog's Day in Trafalgar Square', a demonstration organised by the Animal Defence and Anti-Vivisection Society in 1910 to protest against the destruction of a monument to the dog, which had been a victim of repeated vivisection. *The Anti-Vivisection Review*, vol. 1 (1909–10).

indignant feelings of sympathy with suffering animals. At the same time, it is clear that the polemic over this issue developed into something more far-reaching: a debate about the fundamental moral values of the nation, in an age when technological and commercial developments seemed to be only doubtfully matched by progress in 'civilisation', and when the old religious certainties were crumbling under the impact of evolutionary science. As the leader of the anti-vivisection movement, Frances Power Cobbe, reflected in a *Fortnightly Review* article of 1882, 'It is not surprising that strong feeling should be exhibited on both sides of this controversy', as its 'narrow strait of the "waters wide of agony"' is filled by 'eddying currents from the opposite poles of the moral compass':

> and here will probably be decided questions embracing a larger scope than that of scientific cruelty; perhaps the whole problem of the rights of man over the lower animals; perhaps in a measure the yet wider contest between the principles of which the Christian Beatitudes are the symbol, and those which may be

embodied in the newer gospel of the Survival of the Fittest, 'Blessed are the strong, the self-asserting, and they that hunger and thirst after Science. Blessed are the merciless, – for they shall obtain – useful knowledge'.[5]

Cobbe's friends indeed credited her with opening up, through her countless publications on vivisection, 'the dark continent of our relations to our dumb fellow creatures'.[6] The metaphor is suggestive of the obscurity and barbarism that would then have been associated with Africa, but it also hints at the multiplicity of the cruelties that for the first time, through debate on the issues surrounding vivisection, impinged on the consciousness of the public. It was a consciousness that soon appeared to be sharply divided on gendered lines. Given the record of female involvement in animal protection throughout the nineteenth century, a high level of participation by women in anti-vivisection campaigns was predictable. However, it can be argued that the issue brought to the surface wider discontents: militant opposition to vivisection was gradually aligned with overtly feminist causes, and ultimately became one form of expression among many of a growing attack on patriarchy.[7] In this chapter and the next, I shall trace the process through which leading female anti-vivisectionists shaped their oppositional discourse: a discourse that countered the arguments of 'men of science' on the basis of distinctively feminine psychological responses to suffering, but at the same time drew attention to the power structures of late Victorian society and their malign effects on subordinated groups – groups that included both women and animals.

The events of the 1870s: emergent female leadership of opposition to vivisection

Experimentation on living animals was an ancient practice that had always incurred the execration of animal lovers.[8] It was not until the 1860s, however, that the gradual institutionalisation of vivisection in scientific research and teaching led to widespread public alarm. At that time Britain lagged behind continental Europe in experimental physiology, but from the 1870s onwards it became a required part of medical education. Chairs in physiology and well-funded laboratories were successively created in the leading universities, and medical schools attached to hospitals also fostered vivisection.[9] An impression that the widely publicised cruelties of French and German physiologists might be imported into Britain along with their operating techniques seemed to receive unwelcome confirmation when a *Handbook for the Physiological*

Laboratory compiled by John Burdon-Sanderson and others was published in 1873.[10] Intended as a textbook for the use of students, it inadvertently reached a wider lay readership, and many were appalled by the air of routine conferred on obviously painful experiments, with no mention of the use of anaesthetics. In 1874, the RSPCA prosecuted the perpetrators of an experiment on dogs performed in the semi-public forum of a British Medical Association meeting at Norwich, but acquittal of the accused men only proved the insufficiency of the existing anti-cruelty laws to encompass the collective activities of scientists, and the extreme difficulty that would be encountered in amending those laws acceptably.[11]

The recent passing of two Acts to protect wild birds may have suggested to animal advocates the feasibility of extending legal protection into other areas. Shortly after the Norwich trial, in January 1875, a 'memorial' drafted by Frances Power Cobbe, requesting action against untrammelled vivisection, was presented to the executive committee of the RSPCA by a large deputation that included Cobbe herself and two other women. Many members of the Society's ladies' committee, led by Angela Burdett-Coutts, were also present at the meeting – an exceptional concession by this conservative institution – and Burdett-Coutts, probably with more enthusiasm than her male colleagues, thanked the visiting party for coming.[12] The wording of the memorial pulled no punches: vivisection of animals had 'become the every-day exercise' of British physiologists, and – more worryingly – of their impressionable students. Moreover, the 'indefinite multiplication' of such experiments was confidently predicted, especially in research on the nervous system, for which use of anaesthetics was impossible. The RSPCA, with its substantial funds and prestigious record, was implored to solicit the banning of such practices. The Society's work would 'remain altogether one-sided and incomplete, if, while brutal carters and ignorant costermongers are brought to punishment for maltreating the animals under their charge, learned and refined gentlemen should be left unquestioned to inflict far more exquisite pain upon still more sensitive creatures; as if the mere allegation of a scientific purpose removed them above all legal or moral responsibility'. Cobbe's proposals for the control of vivisection went beyond anything then contemplated by the RSPCA, a society which included many doctors and scientists among its members.[13] Yet, according to the RSPCA's own *Animal World*, the memorial had nearly a thousand signatories mustered by Cobbe and her helpers, and it reads like a roll call of the great and good of Victorian society, from archbishops and aristocrats to military leaders, members of parliament and writers, including Leslie Stephen, Ruskin,

Lecky, Tennyson, Browning and Carlyle. While anti-vivisection was a cause with which women readily identified, it was not, or not yet, a specifically feminist movement, but one that embraced a large segment of the upper classes and the intelligentsia in Britain.

In her autobiography, written in the 1890s, Cobbe – anxious to justify her own role as leader of the anti-vivisection campaign – stressed the lukewarm and ineffectual nature of the RSPCA's response to the memorial.[14] However, it is fascinating to find in the minutes of the RSPCA executive committee of May 1875, that a special private meeting was convened to discuss parliamentary action. It was attended by Burdon-Sanderson (for the physiologists) and by medical experts known to be hostile to vivisection, including two of the first women doctors in Britain – both of them active supporters of female suffrage – Elizabeth Blackwell and Frances Hoggan.[15] For a society that still excluded members of its own ladies' committee from representation on the executive body, this attempt to secure an understanding between the two sides in the vivisection dispute marks also a recognition of the special importance it had for women. In the various dedicated anti-vivisection groups that sprung up during 1875 after perceived RSPCA backsliding, women assumed important leadership and committee roles, as well as providing a majority of the foot soldiers. The creation of committees in which the sexes were represented equally, or with a slight female majority, is much more significant for the future of the movement, and for female activism in general, than establishment of traditional ladies' subcommittees would have been. In the leading group, the Society for the Protection of Animals Prone to Vivisection (known for short as the Victoria Street Society (VSS)), Lord Shaftesbury was president, but Cobbe, as one of the two honorary secretaries, was always the leading spirit in the early years. Female membership of the VSS executive rose from an initial 40 per cent to reach, in the 1880s, about 60 per cent of the total.[16] Rank and file membership of the VSS has been estimated as about 70 per cent female, while features and correspondence in the Society's journal, the *Zoophilist*, reveal that women made up a large percentage of contributors and readers.[17]

The Royal Commission on Vivisection, 1875: a first airing of the ethical issues

Such pressure groups could, however, accomplish little unless they could influence the legislature. In Spring 1875, two rival bills were introduced into parliament to provide for the humane regulation, but not the prohibition, of vivisection: one, presented to the House of Lords by Lord Henniker, was framed in consultation with Cobbe, while the other, supported by many scientists, and notably by Charles Darwin, was brought to the Commons by Lyon Playfair.[18] In this impasse, the government, impelled by the pressure of public opinion, set up a Royal Commission to interview expert witnesses from both sides (none of them were women), and its report, published early in 1876, was a huge and impressive document. It showed that the activities lumped together as 'vivisection' actually ranged from forensic toxicology to the fast-developing fields of bacteriology and pharmacology; but physiological research involving mutilation of animals was by far the most emotive topic. Some examples discussed at length by the commissioners were constantly cited in subsequent polemic between the two sides, and took on an element of the monstrous in the minds of vivisection's opponents. David Ferrier's work on localisation of mental functions involved the application of electrodes to the exposed brains of great numbers of mammals, especially monkeys, and the excision of selected lobes; the animals being left alive afterwards in a defective state for further study.[19] William Rutherford's analysis of organic secretions, especially bile, was achieved by opening the bodies of dogs, starved for eighteen hours beforehand. His experiments lasted many hours and had to be performed without anaesthetics. The animals were immobilised and silenced by the use of curare, a substance which inactivated the muscles (necessitating artificial respiration through an apparatus with a tube piercing the windpipe), but did not prevent pain. 'It is wonderful', Rutherford remarked, 'what one may do to a sheep-dog without the animal making any commotion'.[20] The work of Emanuel Klein, who infected animals with the pathogens of diseases such as septicaemia, tuberculosis and diphtheria (the bacterium of the latter was injected into cats' eyes), owed its special notoriety to the unguarded candour with which he gave his evidence to the Commission. He 'never used anaesthetics' except to keep a troublesome animal quiet, and paid 'no regard at all' to the signs of suffering.[21]

In these exchanges with scientists and with critics of vivisection, the commissioners elicited opinions as well as facts. They had to confront a central paradox: the practice of vivisection was scientifically validated by the close physical similarities between animals and humans; yet physiologists assumed that animals, unlike humans, might legitimately be made to suffer. In this situation, the unprecedented task of arriving at an *ethical* judgement on vivisection required the establishment of criteria for judging the permissibility of causing such distress and pain to animals. Professor Burdon-Sanderson explained his 'principle ... that the question of right and wrong depends upon the relation between the purpose of the experiment and the pain inflicted'. If the purpose is good, 'the whole thing is a right action'. However, Sir Henry Acland, Professor of Medicine at Oxford, pointed out that fixing the ratio between pain and gain in any instance involved a 'graduated difficulty'. It was necessary to appraise the scientific value of a given experiment, but also to predict the degree of pain that would be caused, weighing up the balance between them before inflicting any 'necessary torture'. On this analysis, the end did still in some sense justify the means – a return to the old assumption that an action was cruel only when it involved merely 'wanton' or gratuitous infliction of pain.[22] Supporters of vivisection argued that the animals' agonies were conscientiously minimised by medical scientists, who were allegedly as humane as they were expert in their vocation; but they were always conscious of a greater moral obligation than kindness to animals – that of relieving *human* suffering through research into the causes of disease. In these debates, it was never denied that the 'higher' mammals – those with which, in the light of Darwin's evolutionary theory, man had the greatest physiological and psychological affinities – could suffer agony akin to that of humans in the same situation; and domestic animals, whose sensibilities were believed to be rendered more acute through human tutelage, seemed especially susceptible to pain. On these grounds, Richard Hutton, editor of the *Spectator*, who represented the anti-vivisection case on the Commission, unsuccessfully tried to gain exemption from experimentation for dogs and cats; and it was the potential fate of these beloved companions of man that would ever after dominate the thoughts of the anti-vivisectionists.[23]

Yet whatever the claims made on behalf of animals, it was never seriously questioned by witnesses to the Commission that man had an absolute right of disposal, conferred by his supremacy in nature. A view inherited from Christian theology now received a different kind of legitimation from another aspect of Darwinism – consciousness of a principle of survival of the fittest in the natural world, and therefore of the rightness and inevitability of human power over other species. As George Humphry, Professor of Anatomy at Cambridge, put it: 'a large part of the animal kingdom lives and maintains its perfection by the death of other animals ... necessarily attended with more or less pain', so 'it is quite a justifiable thing for man to inflict death and a certain amount of pain on other animals when there is a reasonable prospect of his condition being benefited by it'.[24] In these circumstances concern for the animals was a voluntary gesture arising from human self-respect, not a moral requirement laid on scientists. Man owed it to *himself*, as the superior being, to exercise 'mercy', while at the same time the benign motives for his actions provided an unchallengeable justification for them.[25] This thought proved especially useful in gaining public acceptance of vivisection, through endless comparisons with other pursuits that inflicted pain on animals but could claim no such ethical basis – a revival of the *tu quoque* gambit that had been used so effectively by William Windham over seventy years earlier. Thomas Huxley, one of the commissioners and a strong supporter of the physiologists, remarked in a letter to Darwin that a parliament full of fox hunters and shooting enthusiasts could hardly pass draconian laws restricting vivisection, without incurring charges of gross hypocrisy or establishing a principle that might bring cruel field sports themselves under judicial scrutiny.[26]

Meanwhile the commissioners' report, weighing up the evidence they had heard, favoured the introduction of a law that would regulate vivisection without impeding its useful operation. They affirmed, what was afterwards often denied by the scientific lobby, that some restrictions were necessary. 'It is manifest that the practice is from its very nature liable to great abuse', and 'It is not to be doubted that inhumanity may be found in persons of very high position as physiologists'.[27] A bill that was introduced by Lord Carnarvon in 1876 to institute controls of the kind envisaged by the Commission was, however, gradually weakened and whittled down through the interventions of physiologists and doctors, who on one occasion invaded the Home Office in their massed ranks.[28] As finally passed in the Commons in August 1876, the 'Cruelty to Animals Act' decreed that vivisectionists were to be licensed, their laboratory premises registered, and systems of official inspection and reporting of experiments were instituted. Anaesthetics were to be used whenever possible, and animals must normally be killed before they recovered consciousness. *Painful* experiments – those that did not employ anaesthetics and those that kept the animal alive afterwards for further study – were subject to special restrictions: they could not be performed in lectures to medical students, or in public. However, such painful procedures were still allowable for bona fide research purposes, subject to special certification. If cats, dogs or horses were involved, the applicant must additionally show that there was a scientific need to use an animal of the particular species indicated. Finally, any prosecution of a license holder needed the permission of the Home Secretary.[29]

In the view of opponents of vivisection like Frances Power Cobbe, these impressive-sounding provisions actually protected scientists from prosecution, *not* animals from suffering.[30] Certification allowed painful vivisection to continue without hindrance, in contravention of the letter and spirit of the existing 1835 law against cruelty to animals. Moreover, the secretiveness and privilege of a system where inspectors and operators were bonded by *esprit de corps*, and private prosecutions needed the say-so of the government, offered little reassurance to the public. In 1882, the founding of the Association for the Advancement of Medicine by Research provided a means by which scientists, working with the Home Office, were able to assume responsibility for the regulation of their own practices. Thenceforth, outside interventions stood less and less chance of success, and several speculative bills for total abolition of vivisection in the decades that followed were easily defeated.[31] No wonder that Cobbe, looking back, saw the 1876 Act as the commencement rather than the resolution of the struggle over vivisection – a struggle that preoccupied her for the rest of her life. 'The world has never seemed to me quite the same since that dreadful time', she wrote:

> My hopes had been raised so high to be dashed so low as even to make me fear that I had done harm instead of good, and brought fresh danger to the hapless brutes for whose sake, as I realised more and more their agonies, I would have gladly died. I was baffled in an aim nearer to my heart than any other had ever been, and for which I had strained every nerve for many months ... Justice and Mercy seemed to have gone from the earth.[32]

The mission of Frances Power Cobbe: direct action against vivisection

Modern biographers of Cobbe (figure 21) – a brilliant, witty journalist, a leading writer on cultural, theological and social matters, a champion of the poor in workhouses and an effective campaigner on behalf of women's causes, including the suffrage movement – often marvel that she should have devoted her life from the mid-1870s onwards to an obsessive, harrowing and (as it proved) utterly fruitless effort to end vivisection.[33] After all, her other projects were at this time beginning to prosper. In 1878, the Matrimonial Causes Amendment Act, which Cobbe had actively promoted, offered a measure of security to battered women; the University of London at length agreed to admit women, including medical students, to its examinations – a measure for which she had pressed since 1862; and her articles in support of a woman condemned to hang for killing her husband secured a reprieve.[34] Yet now specifically feminist causes were secondary to her campaigning on behalf of animals.[35] Organising

21 Photograph of Frances Power Cobbe, from the frontispiece of *Life of Frances Power Cobbe by Herself*, volume 1, 1894.

the VSS, writing endless pamphlets against vivisection, arguing her case in the press, lecturing and canvassing support – it had all involved, her friend Blanche Atkinson explained, 'immense sacrifices'. She now had little time for more congenial and remunerative literary work, but worse was the loss of 'many friends, and much social influence and esteem'.[36] Only by interpreting Cobbe's opposition to vivisection as part of a much larger protest against the malign tendencies of the age – as a development rather than a narrowing of her moral passions – can it be fully understood. As we shall see, it was deeply rooted in her religious convictions and in her understanding of the state of contemporary society, involving considerations that went much beyond the 'pain versus gain' pragmatism of the scientists.

The mortification of being outflanked by the powerful scientific lobby and the evident impossibility of monitoring what went on in closed laboratories led Cobbe to rethink her position on vivisection. As the RSPCA's writers also noted, the regulatory apparatus introduced by the 1876 law was both feeble and easily flouted, especially with respect to the certification of painful experiments.[37] It became clear to Cobbe that the soothing reassurances which physiologists conveyed to the public in journals for a general readership were belied by the brutal realities glimpsed in scientific reports: only a total end to vivisection would prevent these subterfuges.[38] By 1878 abolition, rather than restriction, of experiments on animals had become the official policy of the VSS, causing the first of many internal rifts in the anti-vivisection movement.[39] Since legislative pressure had so far proved unavailing, Cobbe contemplated more drastic measures, even including publication of the names and addresses of vivisectors.[40] This was not carried through, but the VSS did adopt the high-risk tactic of a dramatic appeal to public opinion across all social classes, for which Cobbe was prepared by her long experience as a leader writer on the *Echo*. The recent partial enfranchisement of working men and Forster's education act were beginning to engender more articulate views on public issues among the lower classes – views that were now capable of exerting some pressure on parliament. There was in fact widespread popular repugnance against vivisection, which was seen as a parallel to, and even a possible cause of, medical experimentation on pauper patients in charity hospitals: repugnance which would later surface in working-class support for anti-vivisection campaigners during the 'old brown dog' affair.[41]

In 1877, an idea that seems to have originated with Anna Kingsford – of whom more anon – was taken up by Cobbe and the VSS.[42] They commissioned handbills and posters or 'placards' with horrifying and pathetic images of vivisection experiments, such as Cobbe also used in her lectures and pamphlets (figure 22).[43] The posters were apparently printed in colour, and displayed at railway stations and on street hoardings in London and across the country. There was also a leaflet, *The Vivisection Pictures: What Do They Mean?*, making the connection between vivisection and the treatment of hospital patients explicit.[44] The poster designs were handed on in some form to a notoriously sensational popular paper, the *Illustrated Police News*, and published across

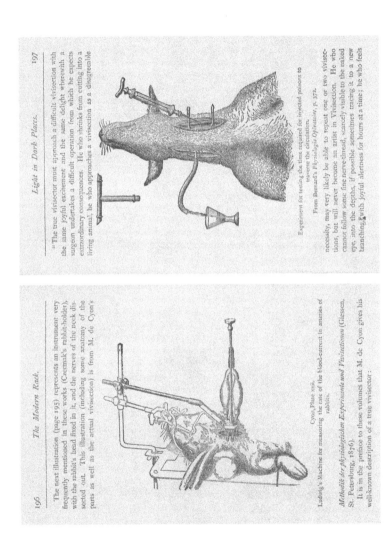

22 Frances Power Cobbe, *The Modern Rack: Papers on Vivisection*, 1889; 'Light in Dark Places', with diagrams reproduced by photo-zincography from those in Elie de Cyon's *Methodik der physiologischen Experimente und Vivisectionen* and Claude Bernard's *Physiologie Opératoire*. Alongside these horrific images of experiments on live animals, Cobbe bitterly quotes de Cyon's description of the 'joyful excitement' and 'delight' of the 'true viviector'.

23 'More vivisection horrors', wood engravings in the *Illustrated Police News* (21 April, 1877), based on the design of posters commissioned by Frances Power Cobbe.

its pages in the form of crude wood engravings. Seen there in close proximity to the images of violent robbery and murder which were the paper's usual fare, they took on additional powers of suggestion, with brutish vivisectors ignoring 'A pet dog begging for mercy' or 'The mute appeal of the poor monkey' (figure 23).[45] Other posters issued by Cobbe's society showed animals strapped down and mutilated; they were taken directly from the diagrams in Elie de Cyon's *Physiologische Methodik* (figure 22), and these copies were often reprinted in anti-vivisection journals. It is little wonder that the physiologists, already hostile to Cobbe on account of the charges made against them in her memorial to the RSPCA and in her pamphlets, were enraged by the 1877 posters. The 'hysterical sentimentality' of women had its public dangers; according to Richard Owen, the 'mendacious daubs' were plastered across the most poverty-stricken and 'excitable' districts of the East End of London, where he claimed to have seen crowds of ignorant people viewing them eagerly.[46] Even some observers sympathetic to the anti-vivisection cause feared that the posters might rouse the rabble, provoke a propaganda war in the streets (medical students scrawled on them), or titillate sadists.[47] For whatever reason, one hears nothing of any further campaigns exploiting the power of visual imagery in public places until the end of the century.

Instead, Cobbe imposed on herself the 'heavy and heart-sickening work' of reading all the descriptions of experiments in scientific journals, together with Home Office records of licensees and their experiments, in order to monitor the implementation of the 1876 Act.[48] In 1881, a large International Medical Congress was held in London, which resoundingly endorsed vivisection, and was followed by a series of strident polemical articles in *Nineteenth Century* and other journals for a general readership, both for and against the practice. At this juncture, the VSS decided to prosecute David Ferrier, whose controversial work on localisation of brain functions has already been mentioned.[49] Reports in the *Lancet* and the *British Medical Journal* indicated that Ferrier had presented his theories, techniques and results at the medical congress, and displayed monkeys in their maimed post-operative state to interested parties; but Cobbe ascertained that he was not licensed as a vivisector, and apparently had no certification for keeping the animals alive after the experiments. Ferrier was nevertheless acquitted, after representatives of the medical journals vouched for the inaccuracy of their own earlier reports, and it was claimed implausibly that the experiments had actually been done by Ferrier's colleague Yeo on his behalf. What is striking in this affair is not so much the apparent perjury of the journal editors and the easy acceptance of the defence's evidence by the magistrate – Cobbe had always expected a rigged outcome – but rather the strongly gendered element in the courtroom and its proceedings. According to the *Times* report, 'Several ladies, among whom were Miss Frances Cobbe, interested in anti-vivisection, were accommodated with seats upon the bench', while a large crowd of boisterous male medical students was 'howling and cheering' outside.[50] Besides this intimidation, one has to consider that the presiding magistrate, the defending counsel, the strongly supportive professional colleagues and the scientific journalists backing Ferrier were all men, and all invested with authority in the public sphere; Cobbe and her companions sat mute, their discomfiture apparently causing laughter in court. In pressing a cause that was especially important to women, anti-vivisection, like the suffrage movement, was always handicapped by male monopolisation of the levers of power. Yet the *Times*, quoting the *British Medical Journal*, frothed with indignation over the 'persecution' of Ferrier and Yeo: 'they have been interrupted, and dragged to the police-court as criminals, at the moment that science and humanity are hailing their work as of the most beneficent character and the largest promise'. Even Darwin eagerly subscribed to Ferrier's legal expenses, arising from what he believed to be an 'absurd and wicked prosecution'.[51]

There was indeed a dawning recognition of the salience of gendered distinctions in attitudes to vivisection, which journal articles and newspaper correspondence were making ever more marked. Elie de Cyon, mortified by the abuse of his treatise and its diagrams, blamed the poster campaign on ugly and frustrated 'old maids', whose 'tenderness, despised by man, has flung itself in despair at the feet of cats and parrots'. 'Let my adversaries contradict me, if they can show among the leaders of the agitation … one young wife who has found in her home the full satisfaction of her affections!'[52] A letter in the *Times* in 1885, during yet another long dispute about the value of Ferrier's experiments, classed Cobbe among the 'sickly sentimentalists, who can shed tears over a dead donkey but are deaf to the loud and importunate cries of human suffering'.[53] For Richard Owen too, Cobbe was the prime example of 'bestiarianism' – a view of the world that put the wellbeing of animals before that of the human race. This was an absurd but nevertheless a very hurtful charge. As Ernest Bell later pointed out in an obituary of Cobbe, she was in truth the 'champion' of *all* 'the weak and the downtrodden', whether animal or human, anticipating the holistic social vision of the Humanitarian League in the 1890s.[54] However, as a device to discredit the anti-vivisectionists' cause, and to deter women from committing themselves to it, such ancient stereotypes of sexually frustrated, animal-obsessed spinsters and their skewed values, which I traced in chapter 1 (compare figure 1), still did useful work. On important public issues, such women could have no opinion worth heeding. As early as June 1876 the *Times* warned 'the ladies who seem disposed to inflame the agitation' on vivisection, 'that it is one which must always be very much out of their sphere'.[55] Evidently women's alleged maudlin sentimentalism was, in the eyes of their accusers, entirely compatible with 'shrieking' militancy. Even the interventions of the highly respected and influential philanthropist Baroness Burdett-Coutts were treated with ignominy: when the British Medical Association met in Edinburgh in 1875, the news that she had written many earnest letters about vivisection to the Lord Provost of the city was greeted with derisive mirth.[56] Women's lack of scientific and medical knowledge, indeed their assumed incapacity for such knowledge, was frequently cited. This, it was thought, made them especially prone to deny the guiding principle of the Royal Commission's hearings, that the end (man's medical benefit) justified the means. Thus the surgeon Jonathan Hutchinson, in an article of 1876, summarily dismissed the opposition of Burdett-Coutts and Cobbe to every 'infliction of vicarious suffering' on animals. 'It is hopeless for any lady, however eminent in philanthropy, however famed in literature – or, indeed, for any class of women or men, excepting trained physiologists, to form an opinion of the slightest value on this point.'[57] In 1882 a writer in *Nature* went further: the writings of Cobbe and Anna Kingsford on vivisection 'are so extravagant and ill-advised that even an ignorant reader must feel their judgment upon this head to be valueless'.[58]

Theoretical works by Frances Power Cobbe and Vernon Lee, opposing vivisection

One would not guess from such comments that the leading female writers actually wrestled with the ethical and philosophical problems of vivisection in ways that transcended the stock self-justifications of the scientists. Time and experience would prove to Cobbe 'the sorrowful limitation of literary influence', especially in the face of misogynistic prejudice.[59] Yet almost until her death in 1904 she maintained a vast output of publications at every level of discourse, which returned repeatedly to the same religious and moral themes.[60] No one in her circle doubted that her resistance to vivisection arose initially from agonised identification with the animals, not from a consciousness of having theoretical axes to grind, or collateral wars to fight through this issue. In her *Life*, she noted that the animals' pain alone entitled them to 'measureless compassion', regardless of their status as presumed creatures of God or kindred of man.[61] Nevertheless, it was the 'large principles' of ethics explored even in her first publications that she now applied 'solely to protect the science-tortured brutes from cruel wrong'.[62] Her thoughts, so far from reflecting a monomaniac, over-emotional or misanthropic attitude to the subject, as alleged by her enemies, had deep implications for the whole tenor of Victorian society.

Born in 1822 into the conservative Anglo-Irish gentry, Cobbe was brought up as an evangelical Anglican, but experienced a 'spiritual landslip' of doubt and confusion in her adolescent years before rejecting traditional Christianity and emerging as a Theist, close to the Unitarians.[63] Belief in original sin, Christ's vicarious atonement, the everlasting damnation of the sinful, and supernatural interventions such as miracles, all seemed to her to be relics of an earlier phase of human mental and moral development. Christ must be deprived of his supposititious godhead, but still revered as the supreme moral teacher, whose message of mercy and love was, she believed, applicable to the treatment of all living things. Guided by Kant, she believed in universal principles of absolute good and evil cognisable to the human mind and soul. God was the loving father and mother of all creatures, and He promised a path to perfection beyond the grave. However, He could not be known by revelation, nor (in the light of the modern Darwinian view of nature) by the 'argument from design' embedded in the old natural theology. His existence must be apprehended by the vital human faculty of 'intuition', a term which figures constantly in Cobbe's writings.[64]

The stress on this word 'intuition' is highly interesting, in fact daringly tendentious. It could be used in a purely philosophical sense; for example, Professor Henry Sidgwick, in *The Methods of Ethics* (1874), defined 'Intuitionism' as an ethical approach opposed to utilitarianism. It 'recognises rightness as a quality inherent in actions', irrespective of their effects, 'rightness or virtuousness being intuitively ascertained'. However, outside philosophical parlance, and especially in many eighteenth- and nineteenth-century works on the differing characteristics of the sexes, 'intuition' had gendered associations. The male capacity for reasoning was contrasted with female 'intuition' as routes to understanding; but these alternatives were by no means equal in status. Darwin, in the *Descent of Man* (1871), reiterated the traditional view that women evinced 'greater tenderness' towards their fellow-creatures than men did, and more marked 'powers of intuition, of rapid perception'; but he added that 'some, at least, of these faculties are characteristic of the lower races, and therefore of a past and lower state of civilisation', allied to the instinctual behaviour of savages and animals.[65]

Cobbe, too, was in some ways an essentialist in her view of male and female characteristics, albeit differing sharply from Darwin in her valuation of them.[66] Thus in her writings of the 1860s she reversed his negative judgements on 'intuition', without discarding its sexual connotations. In *Dawning Lights* of 1868, she foresaw that 'rapid, intuitive minds, perchance of a somewhat feminine cast' would overcome masculine reliance on the old, grim doctrinal 'authority' to usher in a more enlightened and a kinder religion.[67] Cobbe's *Essays on the Pursuits of Women* (1863) claimed that women's 'vividness of intuitive faith' and 'moral intuitions' were productive of open-minded, even experimental ways of thinking about God and human destiny – a remarkable reversal of the conventional view that women's ideas were more tradition-bound, less original than those of men.[68] In *Broken Lights* (1865), intuition was linked with mankind's 'everlasting, unresting progress' towards spiritual insight; and to love God in this way was to love his creatures, 'even the poorest and meanest – even the brutes … Before His eyes we all admit there must be equality'.[69] Thus the concept of intuition as a religious faculty in women by no means detracted from its old association with women's greater capacity for sympathy with the powerless and oppressed, especially animals. Like Sarah Stickney Ellis, whose ideas I discussed in the last chapter, Cobbe believed that women had a special vocation to care for animals and to protect them from male cruelty. As late as 1895, in 'The ethics of zoophily', she *welcomed* a sneering characterisation of her anti-vivisection arguments as a 'philosophy of sentiment' that was quintessentially female in its lack of recourse to hard logic: 'I claim, as a woman … to have the better right to be heard in such a cause than a man … If my sex has a "mission" of any kind, it is surely to soften this hard old world', according to the 'higher law of love'.[70]

As a friend of William Lecky, Cobbe was particularly conscious of his historiographical schema (discussed in our chapter 2): a gradual progress in humane values through the nineteenth century, with women playing a key role in transforming attitudes to animals.[71] She was indeed preoccupied with the nature and degree of this moral progress, as were many thinking Victorians.[72] Darwin's theory of evolution by natural selection offered little scope for the consideration of a First Cause guiding events, but it was possible for religious believers like Cobbe to extend the biological data into a more general theory of directed or providential development of human societies towards enlightenment: God, she discerned in *Broken Lights*, 'is the Author of the Tale'.[73] As part of the process of human elevation, continued in the hereafter, attitudes to suffering would gradually be transformed, both in individuals and societies. A quality she called 'heteropathy' and identified with the German term *Schadenfreude* – for her the worst of sins – signified the primitive emotion of pleasure in causing or observing the suffering of others, especially of weaker beings like women and animals, and this was an emotion which could linger even in outwardly cultured men.[74] In an appropriately medical metaphor, Cobbe suggested that heteropathy could be described as 'infectious or epidemic quite as justly as idiopathic or endemic'.[75] The Royal Commission of 1875 had heard from Professor George Rolleston that the 'unworked-out beast which exists in man' was especially prone to surface when scientists and their students were gathered in a crowd to watch the victimisation of an animal in a physiological experiment.[76] However, civilised peoples could, Cobbe believed, rise above heteropathy, passing through mere aversion or indifference to the misfortunes of others, to reach the positive state of universal sympathy with the suffering. In *The Hopes of the Human Race* (1874), Cobbe explained that the pinnacle of civilisation would be a development of the 'Social Sentiment', such that people would feel 'the joys and sorrows of all sentient beings', bringing 'the notion of duties towards the animal world' within 'the range of ethics'.[77]

Darwin, too, reflected – often in conversation with Cobbe – on the proto-human sensitivities and moral impulses of animals themselves, especially of dogs.[78] The continuity of life forms revealed in *Origin of Species* and *The Descent of Man* included a psychological kinship between humans and other species, bringing with it a sense of animals' entitlement to humane consideration. Darwin thought that a physiologist, lovingly licked by the dog he was vivisecting, 'unless he had a heart of stone, must have felt remorse to the last hour of his life'. However, in the second edition of *Descent*, published at the height of the furore over vivisection, a further caveat was inserted in this passage: 'unless the operation was fully justified by an increase of our knowledge'.[79] Cobbe lamented Darwin's enlistment as figurehead of the lobby supporting the experimental physiologists.[80] However, this tragedy was linked to a far greater one – the new theory of the origins of the human conscience proposed in *Descent*, which was, she felt, utterly destructive of her teleological view of evolution. Darwin came to believe that notions of right and wrong conduct had evolved by natural selection, along with man's other faculties, as functional adaptive traits conducive to social bonding and the survival of the species. Their pure moral relativity was such that if 'men were reared under precisely the same conditions as hive-bees, there can hardly be a doubt that our unmarried females would, like the worker-bees, think it a sacred duty to kill their brothers', and 'no one would think of interfering'.[81]

Cobbe had once hopefully lent Darwin a copy of Kant's *Groundwork of the Metaphysic of Morals*, which he returned to her after only a cursory reading.[82] His extrinsic approach to the study of human mentality, developed through analogies with animal behaviour, differed wholly from Cobbe's belief in 'independent or intuitive morality' – the existence of absolute, unalterable goodness and evil revealed to the mind by God.[83] From her point of view, the utilitarianism implied by Darwin's theory of conscience threatened 'descent into a moral abyss', and a reversal of the steady progress in humanitarianism for which she had fondly hoped.[84] It was a 'Philosophy of Selfishness', in which the teachings of Plato and Kant, Christ and St Paul, had been replaced by those of 'humble vivisectors' such as polecats and wasps.[85] Of that tendency, indeed, real vivisection presented the most striking example. The physiologists' easy assumption that the end (human physical benefits) justified the means (infliction of pain on animals) destroyed the ideal of selfless altruism which for her constituted the true human *differentia*; and the reduction of helpless animals to mere objects for disassembly spoke of a materialism and expediency that was capable of indefinite extension. Far from profiting society, it threatened *all* subalterns – not just animals but also weaker humans – with cruel exploitation for the advantage of the survival of the fittest. In a dystopian fantasy, *The Age of Science: A Newspaper of the Twentieth Century* (1877), Cobbe imagined the world a century hence as a hell where 'Science reigns supreme'. Physical health is a fetish, euthanasia is the norm, religion and the humanities have been destroyed, men and women are vivisected at will, and watching animal experiments (now so numerous that dogs are a threatened species) is a moral duty for all citizens.[86]

Cobbe's grounds for condemning vivisection make an interesting comparison with those of another opponent of the practice, the novelist and polymath author Vernon Lee, whose real name was Violet Paget. The two women knew each other well, and discussed moral questions from differing philosophical viewpoints, but with respect for each other's positions. Both understood fully the ethical problems created by Darwin's dismissal of the notions of absolute moral truths, or of supernatural authority for particular courses of action, that arose from the acceptance of human animality.[87] In 1882 Vernon Lee published an article in the *Contemporary Review* entitled 'Vivisection: an evolutionist to evolutionists', which was afterwards largely assimilated into a fictional work, *Baldwin: Being Dialogues on Views and Aspirations* (1886). In her article, Lee had deplored the polarisation of opinions on vivisection in the press, with a tendency to pious 'sentimental twaddle' on one side, and unscrupulous dissimulation on the other. This dichotomy inhibited the development of individuals' more nuanced thoughts on the subject: a subject which presented an 'almost unique psychological anomaly ... most singular in the history of moral dilemmas'. Lee pondered it for the rest of her life without reaching a categorical conclusion.[88]

Baldwin, as a series of imagined conversations between friends, allowed Vernon Lee to explore conflicted views of the legitimacy of vivisection, as of other philosophical problems, and to give her own ambivalent feelings full expression. The central male protagonist Baldwin represents Lee herself: he is 'Negative, self-contradictory, abstract ... I agree in all his ideas; yet I can place myself at the point of view of some of his opponents'.[89] One of those opponents is a woman called Agatha (the name, significantly, comes from the Greek word for 'good'), whose beliefs correspond to Cobbe's.[90] Agatha chides Baldwin – as Cobbe chided Lee – for his atheism; she explains that she has herself discarded the biblical doctrines of Christianity, but continues to believe 'that there is a God, and that He is Love', directing the world and the human mind aright, and promising a recompense for suffering in this world – the suffering of both humans and animals – by a blissful life in the hereafter. Baldwin cannot believe such things: it is just wishful thinking, an unconscious reflection of Agatha's own virtues, rather than a revelation of those of a benign God. The natural world is amoral, the First Cause is unknowable, and all scientific research now suggests the identity of mind and brain, precluding belief in the existence of an immortal soul. What assurances can there be 'that there is for any of these creatures ... the dog tied down for hours while disembowelled by the physiologist ... the stag rushing along with the teeth of the hounds already upon him, and for the woman hounded by society from one stage of infamy and misery to another ... what assurance have you that when death releases them from their miseries, death does not also put an end to all possibilities of compensation and justice?' The 'horrible purposelessness of suffering', the lack of a spiritual afterlife to give meaning to present wickedness and affliction: this was indeed the nightmare that haunted Cobbe and many others in the wake of the Darwinian revolution in thought. The brutal materialism of vivisection might, it seemed, represent the future of the human race, rather than being a temporary and corrigible mistake in the course of predestined moral progress.

Vernon Lee was as troubled as Cobbe was by the implications of agnosticism or atheism for the moral order. In the case of vivisection, she was far from treating it *only* as an intellectual conundrum, in which one had to weigh up the opposed claims and entitlements of humans and animals. Physiologists rightly adopted the experimental methods that were used in the other natural sciences; yet the necessity to cause suffering to live animals entailed a great evil. In *Baldwin*, a young man called Michael enters the debate.[91] He once 'talked evolution by the hour', but has now turned furiously against science after learning the facts of vivisection. Opposition to it was not, as he had previously assumed, just a ridiculous female fad, typified by his aunt's pamphlets:

> Of course they were rather rubbishy as literature, and had a deal of sentimentality and piety, and the 'Faithful Dog' and 'Merciful Creator' sort of thing. But they contained facts … and they induced me to open the various physiological treatises … And the result has been that I feel … as if all science were dishonoured … the strapped-down monkey, the poison-paralyzed dog … opening the living stomach, removing fragments of the living brain, injecting the living veins with drugs and purulent matter … sending streams of electricity through the living nerves … how impressions are received, and writhings and yells are ordered by the uncovered living brain mass.[92]

The repetitions of *living* symbolise the distance between abstract ethical discourse and this terrible reality. The school of Utilitarian thought to which Vernon Lee belonged might suggest, as indeed the scientists did constantly suggest, that the suffering of individual dogs, cats and monkeys was to be countenanced for the sake of the greater good of the majority – the human patients whose chances of successful diagnosis and surgery were enhanced by the findings from animal experimentation. But this argument was in truth, Baldwin and Michael agree, merely an expression of the notion that might is right, self-preservation a duty, according to the 'evolutionary morality' derived from Darwinism. It ignored the more refined insights of nineteenth-century thought – the civilised humanitarianism that now seemed to rise above an amoral natural order. Vernon Lee as a rationalist could not take refuge in a 'philosophical creed in the unintelligible'. Instead she invoked the ideas, not of pity or mercy, but of honour and justice, as more vital to the progress of society than scientific discovery. Animals themselves gained nothing from vivisection. Their sufferings were vicarious, involuntary and unreciprocated: they could not be accommodated within the more enlightened versions of Utilitarian philosophy, and it was shabby and dishonourable to pretend that they could. The idea of 'honour' had ancient, chivalric connotations which might have seemed inapplicable in the modern context, but Baldwin tries to square the circle by *identifying* honour with Darwin's inherited conscience or 'natural morality'. Just as the Creation was now understood as 'the mere inevitable adjustment and development of physical things', so honour is 'now comprehensible as the instinct, the ingrained habit due to ages of deliberate choice, of preferring certain sets of motives to certain other ones'.[93] Justice was more conducive to the survival of the race than expediency, for 'we have evolved beyond the law of the jungle'. Frances Power Cobbe deplored Vernon Lee's attempts to reconcile altruism with Darwin's theory of inherited and contingent morality, and Lee's own fictional Michael in *Baldwin* too is unimpressed.[94] He cannot foresee an end to vivisection; indeed, in his present mood, he feels that 'modern civilization has a sort of mark of the beast – something hideous and Moloch-like … The angel of progress makes a sound with his wings, and has a sulphurousness in his breath which is oddly suggestive of hell'.[95]

Women, scientists and doctors: anti-vivisection as one aspect of a protest against endemic misogyny

Cobbe's single-minded and increasingly intransigent opposition to vivisection, and her incrimination of Darwinian science in the cruelties of the physiologists, had personal repercussions. Until the early 1870s, she had viewed scientists as allies in the assault on Judaeo-Christian mythology.[96] She was a friend of Darwin and his extended family, awed by his scientific achievements, 'enchanted' by his character, including his gentle fondness for animals, and no doubt flattered by his respect for her intellect.[97] Darwin sent her an advance copy of *Descent of Man* for review before any other potential reviewers received one – and this in full expectation that her interpretation of his theories about the human conscience would be damning.[98] It was not in fact her criticism of *Descent* but rather her anti-vivisection memorial to the RSPCA in early 1875 that led to a breach between them, culminating in a particularly bitter exchange of letters in the *Times* in 1881. Through such clashes, Cobbe lost not only Darwin's friendship, but also that of Huxley, Herbert Spencer and William Carpenter – champions of scientific progress who felt embattled against the perceived forces of reaction; 'there came', Cobbe later sadly told a friend, 'the absolute cut'.[99]

Yet even within Darwin's family circle, views on vivisection were divided on gendered lines. He had to warn the militant pro-vivisectionist George Romanes not to raise the subject when in the company of the ladies at Down House, especially as Romanes and his allies were prone to a kind of macho jocularity about vivisection which even Darwin found offensive.[100] In a letter of January 1875, Darwin had explained to Cobbe some of his own reasons for declining to endorse her memorial. 'I believe that Physiology will ultimately lead to incalculable benefits', and 'Any stringent law' against animal experiments 'would stop all progress in this country which I should deeply regret'. Certainly vivisectionists were guilty of 'atrocious' cruelty when they operated without use of anaesthetics, in cases where an experiment did not require the animal to be conscious; but people who described them as '"demons let loose from hell"', ignored the greater cruelties of 'those who shoot birds for mere pleasure', 'besides the indirect suffering of traps' set by their gamekeepers. However, Emma Darwin wrote by the same post, explaining more fully Darwin's difficulties with anti-vivisection, in an attempt to mitigate Cobbe's disappointment – and her own. 'I do trust and believe that some good will be done' by the memorial, and she would be happy to collect some more signatures for it, if Cobbe would like her to.[101] Following the parental pattern of contrarieties on this topic, Darwin's son Francis joined the Physiological Society, but his daughter Henrietta opposed vivisection so passionately that Darwin felt it necessary to write her a long letter setting out his position, though fearing that 'my conclusions ... will appear very unsatisfactory to you'.[102] The Wedgwoods – Emma's brother Hensleigh, his wife Fanny and daughter Julia 'Snow' Wedgwood – were all active in the VSS, and Julia in particular became a friend of Cobbe.[103] In *Why Am I an Anti-Vivisectionist?* (1910), Julia noted that she had needed to reject 'arguments in favour of unfettered medical research' which 'have been in my mind for thirty-seven years, weighted with the influence of some whose influence has gone for much with me, and touched by the shadow of tender memories' – perhaps an allusion to the moral as well as the scientific authority of Darwin, and to the unbreakable affections of the family circle.[104] It was a different matter in the family of the French physiologist Claude Bernard, who, unlike Darwin, was an active, indeed a notoriously ruthless vivisector. Michael Foster, Professor of Physiology at Cambridge, in a biography of Bernard, noted that 'dissensions with his wife' over his treatment of animals led to their 'early separation'. Bernard's two daughters were also estranged from him, and one of them, Foster noted scornfully, 'was so far removed from sympathy with her father's labours' that she spent her inheritance on 'founding hospitals for dogs and cats, with the view of atoning for what she considered the crimes of vivisection which her parent had committed'.[105] Elsewhere Foster, in an article on vivisection of 1874, deplored the 'mawkish sentimentalism which is stealing over the present generation, and by a lessening of manliness is curtailing the good effects of increased enlightenment'.[106]

Of course, individuals of both sexes could be found in the ranks of both supporters and opponents of vivisection, and, as the benefits of bacteriological research became clear later in the century, with the production of vaccines on an industrial scale, women were won over to vivisection in increasing numbers. Nevertheless, anti-vivisection continued to be seen as pre-eminently a women's cause, embracing a host of concerns that went beyond cruelty to animals, but were perceived as being associated with it. There was, first of all, the obnoxious degree of professional power wielded by the 'men of science', a power from which women were excluded. Like the records of big game hunting which I discussed in the last chapter, the language used by vivisection's male apologists exudes a strange blend of physical pleasure in mastery over an animal's body with rationalistic analysis and measurement of that body's vital processes. Thus Foster, whose disapproving view of Bernard's daughters and other 'sentimentalists' has just been quoted, wrote enthusiastically of how any expert physiologist, operating on an anaesthetised animal, 'brings to bear on this breathing, pulsating, but otherwise quiescent frame, the instruments which are the tools of his research':

> He takes deft tracings of the ebb and flow of blood … measures the time and the force of each throb of the heart, while by light galvanic touches he stirs this part or quiets that … divides this nerve … brings subtle poisons to bear … and having done what he wished to do … obtained … answers to the questions he wished to put, he finishes a painless death by the removal of all the blood from the body, or by any other means that best suits him at the time.[107]

To many women, it seemed that their bodies provided the same kind of passive, depersonalised objects on which doctors could exercise their skills, as though they were, in Cobbe's words, 'a mere animal link in the chain of life', devoid of individual mind or will.[108] In cases of 'hysteria', supposedly a disease of women leading to moral degeneracy, the symptoms of mental distress were pathologised. Patients might be isolated under a doctor's control, exposed to male students as medical exhibits, or operated on for removal of female organs, including clitoridectomy (genital mutilation).[109] The treatments practised in gynaecological hospitals also threw up periodic scandals of lubricious use of the speculum or unwarranted and dangerous recourse to ovariotomy and hysterectomy, while poor women in charity hospitals were exposed to humiliating examination and testing by medical students.[110] However, one gynaecologist allegedly affirmed that one could learn more from animal vivisection even than from 'experimenting on women'.[111] Not only did there seem to be a parallel between the vivisection of animals and the medical abuse of women: it was widely suggested by anti-vivisectionists that the one led on to the other, as ruthless objectification of weaker beings became a habit.[112]

Elsewhere, family doctors were accused of inducing hypochondria and invalidism in their female patients. Cobbe's articles on 'The little health of ladies' and 'The medical profession and its morality' especially criticised doctors' unfeeling arrogance, both in the sphere of general practice, and in the Medical Council's 'meddling and despotic' interventions in the field of public health – a trait which she linked directly to their propagandising of vivisection.[113] There had actually been a move among female readers of the anti-vivisectionist *Home Chronicler* to reject the services of family doctors who supported the practice.[114] However, if respectable, moneyed women allegedly fell prey to doctors' cynicism and avarice, their 'fallen' sisters endured a much worse fate. The Contagious Diseases Acts (1864–1869), which were largely supported by the medical profession, aimed to check the spread of venereal diseases to men in the armed forces; under the Acts' provisions, suspected prostitutes were arrested, forcibly examined and incarcerated in lock hospitals if found to be infected.[115] For Cobbe (a late convert to the oppositionist cause) as for Josephine Butler, Elizabeth Blackwell and fellow-campaigners against the Acts, this was 'an abominable oppression', reflecting the 'gross materialism' of the doctors involved, as well as their hypocrisy.[116] Yet Butler, like Cobbe and like many other women who campaigned for moral reforms, complained that she was accused of 'mere sentiment, and of carrying away my hearers by feeling rather than by facts and logic'.[117] In an essay titled 'In the long run', Cobbe noted that such accusers, 'mainly the same who uphold the vivisection of animals', had ultimately been defeated by the 'Conscience of England' when the Contagious Diseases Acts were repealed in 1886, giving hope to those who, as anti-vivisectionists, still did battle with the autocratic men of science.[118]

From a feminist viewpoint, the sins of medical men went beyond such physical and psychological oppression of helpless beings. As out-and-out materialists who maintained that all states of mind were purely physical phenomena, scientists were able to frustrate women's intellectual and political aspirations by an appeal to 'nature'. In the ongoing process of mental evolution, women were believed to lag behind men, a phenomenon which Darwin in *Descent of Man* had linked to sex-specific transmission of characteristics through the generations.[119] This discrepancy was supposedly widening as civilisation advanced: women represented a less developed phase of human progress, as was evident even in the form of their skulls – linked by their more prognathous form to those of apes and 'primitive' human races, and condemned by their smaller cranial capacity to a shortfall in intelligence.[120] Physiological data were cited to reinforce such spurious claims based on anatomy. According to the theory of conservation of energy, human vigour was finite, and the functions of female bodies, especially menstruation and childbearing, exhausted the energy that might otherwise have been given to study and concentrated thought. Therefore opening higher education or professional training to women could cause their physical and mental breakdown; it could, moreover, have a disastrous effect on their all-important role as mothers, risking a collapse of population and a diminution of the nation's power.[121]

Arguments such as these, based on preconception rather than on the kind of scrupulous interrogation of evidence advocated by Victorian scientists themselves, were refuted by many women writers. The suffragist Lydia Becker forcefully presented a case that there was no sex in mind – women were as competent as men to undertake scientific research.[122] Dr Elizabeth Garrett Anderson similarly dismissed biological determinism on the grounds that it conflicted with actual experience.[123] It is unsurprising that, when confronted with the baselessness of assumptions made by sexual theorists, many women (but not Garrett Anderson) should also have disbelieved the physiologists' claims for the validity and fruitfulness of vivisection as a scientific methodology. Admittedly, a number of pro-vivisection scientists, notably Darwin, Burdon-Sanderson and the *British Medical Journal*'s editor Ernest Hart, supported higher education for women, including their qualification as doctors.[124] However, some key figures who advocated vivisection as part of an ultra-materialist approach to natural science were particularly prone to misogynistic theorising about women's incapacities on the basis of somatic data. The psychiatrist Henry Maudsley who, in *Body and Mind*, defined emotion as 'the special sensibility of the vesicular neurine to ideas', also cited the reflex movements of decapitated frogs and pigeons as proof that the operations of the mind originate in the body and the nervous system, not in a spiritual sphere beyond the reach of 'physical research'. In 'Sex in mind and education', Maudsley went on to affirm that women 'cannot rebel successfully against the tyranny of their organization' by intellectual competition with men: like vivisected animals, women had an exclusively physical value – in their case, to bear children.[125] Darwin's acolyte George Romanes, who has already been mentioned as a champion of vivisection in press debates, was also the author of an article on 'Mental differences between men and women', which reached conclusions only slightly less dogmatic than Maudsley's.[126] As a crowning example of this tendency, the influential evolutionist Carl Vogt, who explained in *Lectures on Man* (1864) that 'whenever we perceive an approach to the animal type, the female is nearer to it than the male', was, according to Cobbe, known for making vivisection his 'daily bread'.[127]

To many feminists, including Cobbe, it seemed that only the entry of women to the medical profession would counterbalance such attitudes by a more sympathetic and holistic approach to the workings of the human body, especially to women's disorders. Female doctors would, it was hoped, give greater attention to the mental state of patients, to sanitary reform and to the environmental causes of communicable disease; less attention to germ theory and physiological research. Renouncing the cruelties of live experiments, whether on animals or on hospital patients, was a crucial aspect of this mission: and British women, who necessarily travelled to continental European countries to get a medical education, had often been unwilling witnesses of both these horrors. Thus when the London School of Medicine for Women opened in 1874, Burdon-Sanderson, a council member, recommended the French scientist Eugène Dupuy as lecturer in physiology, but the Royal Commission on vivisection was informed in 1875 that Dupuy had resigned the post within a month, 'because the young women would not attend at vivisectional experiments'.[128] Some members of the school's council were blamed for this debacle, and must have been at loggerheads with Burdon-Sanderson on the issue. Among them was Elizabeth Blackwell, who was the first woman to qualify as a doctor and to open a women's infirmary and medical college in the United States.[129] She now devoted her time to the promotion of distinctive roles for women as doctors, and to the reform of public attitudes to sexual morals; but, in her mind, the suppression of vivisection seemed critically important to these feminist enterprises.

In *Pioneer Work in Opening the Medical Profession to Women* (1895), Blackwell expressed a religious conviction as strong as Cobbe's that there was 'a great providential ordering of our race's progress' – a plan for the moral 'redemption of mankind', to which women would make a vital contribution. 'I have long since realised that conscience and humanity must guide intellectual activity.'[130] In *Essays in Medical Sociology* (1902), she insisted that there could in fact be no conflict or division between religion and science. God could not will evil that good might come, and therefore vivisection must be not only wicked but fallacious as a method of medical research. It was a kind of 'narrow and superficial materialism' that ignored the link between mind and body. The medical student 'becomes familiar with the use of gags, straps, screws, and all the paraphernalia ... invented for overpowering the resistance of the living creature', but never learns to reverence the principle of *vitality* – 'the spiritual essence' of his victim.[131] 'We are linked to living creatures ... by all those varying relations involved in the mystery of life' – a truth which women, 'whose distinctive work is joyful creation' as mothers, were peculiarly able to comprehend. Blackwell went further:

> Our relation to the lower animals has never yet been brought fully into the clear light of reason and conscience. Yet in the order of Providential development it must so come forward. As advancing humanity has gradually recognised natural rights as existing in the various races of mankind ... so the time has come when the natural rights of inferior living creatures must be seriously studied.[132]

This study still lay in the future. Meanwhile, in the last decades of the nineteenth century, the triumphs of Pasteur's bacteriology and the development of effective vaccines tended to discredit thinkers such as Cobbe, Blackwell and Anna Kingsford, who had all dismissed Pasteur's experiments as both scientifically unsound and morally reprehensible.[133] Moreover, as women themselves qualified as doctors in increasing numbers, their majority acceptance of the ethos and practices of the profession was inevitable. Blackwell grieved when the women's medical college that she had founded in New York decided in 1891 to equip a laboratory for vivisection.[134] Similarly, when science students at the recently founded Oxford and Cambridge women's colleges began to observe experiments on animals as part of their grounding in physiology, Frances Power Cobbe was appalled, and started bitter quarrels over the issue with fellow-feminists – her erstwhile friends, now heads of such colleges and active in academe.[135] No woman was registered as a vivisectionist under the 1876 act until 1898, and even then it was still unusual for experiments to take place actually within women's medical schools; but the notion of a distinctive spiritual mission for women doctors, in which abolition of vivisection played a key part, seemed to most of them to be a thing of the past.[136] The change was signalled by Elizabeth Garrett Anderson's measured article on 'The ethics of vivisection', which appeared in the *Edinburgh Review* in 1899. She weighed up pros and cons, but concluded, as most of her male colleagues would have done, that the medical benefits and therefore the morality of vivisection legitimated a degree of animal suffering.[137] She sympathised with physiologists 'who are continually smarting under unjust and most damaging imputations' from their opponents; but, alas, she ignored the fact that two of the most prominent and bitter of those accusers were Elizabeth Blackwell, Garrett Anderson's first inspirational mentor, and Frances Power Cobbe, whose efforts to get London

University to admit women to its examinations had been undertaken principally in order to facilitate Garrett Anderson's qualification as a doctor.[138] Feminism and anti-vivisection were, it seemed, not necessarily coextensive; but one anti-vivisection campaigner in the 1870s and 1880s – also a qualified doctor – brought them together in new and startling ways.

The vision of Anna Kingsford

Anna Kingsford struck the people who encountered her as a kind of phenomenon: a woman of extraordinary beauty, inspiration, passion and eloquence to whom the rules of Victorian society seemingly did not apply (figure 24).[139] Married to an Anglican clergyman, she defied convention by living, intermittently but publicly, with the writer and mystic Edward Maitland, who described himself as her 'colleague' or 'companion escort'.[140] He might have added that he was also, paradoxically, the nurse, custodian and spiritual interpreter of this fiercely independent woman – or tried to be. After her death in 1888 at the age of forty-one, he became her literary executor and biographer too; and his destruction of all her papers, after the massive two-volume *Life* was completed, has entailed an undue dependence on this tendentious portrayal of her character and views.[141] Severally or together, Kingsford and Maitland produced many books and were active in a variety of groups dedicated to anti-vivisection, vegetarianism and religious enquiry – causes which Kingsford also promoted through a series of lecture tours in Britain and other European countries. Her achievement was to unite these causes with an idiosyncratic kind of feminism: a synthesis which in many ways anticipated the mindset of the 'new women' of the 1890s and early 1900s.

Not even Maitland professed to understand Anna Kingsford. When they first met, 'Never had I seen anyone so completely and intensely alive, or comprising so many diverse and incompatible personalities'. Her protean nature could only be explained by the supposition that she had existed as many other people in previous lives. Maitland also fell back on the traditional gendered notion that Kingsford's mentality was a compound of male intellect and female intuition – a categorisation which she resisted.[142] However, it remains true that her writings encompass an extraordinary variety of modes, from scientific analysis based on her medical knowledge to the expression of deep emotion, and from polemic to imaginative fiction. Like Cobbe, she could cater to many readerships, producing everything from romantic tales or beauty tips for popular magazines to abstruse metaphysics. Yet the causes she wrote and spoke for were *one* in her own mind, heralding the more comprehensive view of human

24 Photograph of Anna Kingsford, based on an undated 'carte de visite' published by Elliott and Fry.

interactions with animals that characterised the *fin de siècle*. Only through an insight into Kingsford's religious beliefs can one understand her attitude to vivisection. She was nominally a convert to Roman Catholicism, and certainly enamoured of the cult of the Virgin Mary – indeed, the spiritual name that Maitland conferred on Kingsford was Mary.[143] She claimed to be a prophetess with psychic powers; with Maitland, she developed a form of hermeticism, fusing Christian imagery, the Kabbala and ancient mythologies in an attempt to recover the root of all religions, and embracing belief in metempsychosis as the key to continuity and inheritance of spiritual ideas through the ages. This tendency to syncretism made it possible to identify actual people or things with counterparts in the spirit world, and hence to deal with concrete issues like vivisection or the oppression of women within a visionary schema.

What was new in the mystical writings of Kingsford and Maitland was an emphasis on the supremacy of woman or of the female principle in the divine hierarchy. In *The Perfect Way; Or, The Finding of Christ*, published in 1882, they affirmed that 'the Soul' is 'the feminine element in man'. 'The heavenly Maria ... As Soul or Intuition' (that word again), 'is the "woman" by whom man attains his true manhood'. So far from 'being an inferior part of humanity' as traditionally believed, real women, when 'glorified', will enable humanity to 'attain to Christhood'.[144] *'Clothed with the Sun': Being the Book of the Illuminations of Anna (Bonus) Kingsford*, published in 1889 after Kingsford's death but purporting to record her revelations, gave these ideas a more ecstatic and controversial expression. 'Maria, the God-woman, or feminine presentation of the supreme power and goodness, delivers mankind and destroys evildoers.' These godless 'evildoers' were readily identified. In *The Perfect Way*, Kingsford and Maitland found 'Little wonder ... that between Mystic and Materialist' a 'gulf so impassable, feud so irreconcilable' should intervene; 'seeing that while the one seeks by the sacrifice of his own lower nature to his higher ... to prove man potential God, the other – turning vivisector – makes him actual fiend'.[145] Kingsford seems to have dramatised her own mission to conquer such devilry, which estranged men from women, and mankind from the divine principle of sympathy.[146] One of her dream-stories concerned 'The Armed Goddess' preparing for battle, and Maitland explained that this divinity represented Kingsford herself on the eve of an anti-vivisection lecture tour of Switzerland; as it turned out, her lectures aroused a 'fierce conflict' with physiologists who despised women, so that her premonitions were 'amply fulfilled'.[147] If Maitland is to be believed, Kingsford once contemplated offering *herself* as a subject for vivisection, 'making it the condition that the practice should thereafter be forever abandoned' – an impulse that he attributed to her psychological need to make a heroic 'sacrifice of herself ... at once an expiation and a redemption'. Indeed, she typically claimed that a self-imposed visit to Pasteur's laboratory in driving rain had brought on pneumonia, accelerating the tuberculosis that would cause her early death. In her brother's words, 'she died a martyr to the scrupulous conscientiousness with which she followed M. Pasteur's experiments ... the fallacies of which ... she was desirous to make patent to all'.[148]

Like Cobbe, Kingsford considered herself to be at war with the materialism of the age, as being the root cause of the cruelty to animals involved in vivisection. However, unlike Cobbe, she seems to have dismissed almost entirely the implications of modern evolutionary science. When arguing that man was a natural vegetarian, Kingsford was happy enough to point out humans' physiological and anatomical resemblances to anthropoid apes.[149] Yet at another level of thought she envisaged a spirit world that formed a moral hierarchy: through metempsychosis the souls of men and animals were constantly being rein-carnated in higher or lower life forms according to the degree of merit they had attained, or the evil ways into which they had fallen, during an earthly life – passing and repassing each other in a kind of snakes and ladders, as they endeavoured to ascend towards perfection and enlightenment. Thus the need to treat animals kindly did not rest on a notion of their 'rights' such as Elizabeth Blackwell began to spell out, but on a respect for the fulfilment of their spiritual destiny, which would be disastrously interrupted by cruel victimisation and a violent death. In *Dreams and Dream Stories*, Kingsford's most fascinating book, 'The laboratory underground' is a nightmare in which she sees scientists operating on the living bodies of half-dissected and mutilated animals.

> But, as I looked at the creatures ... they no longer appeared to be mere rabbits, or hounds, for in each I saw a human shape ... hidden within the outward form. And when they led into the place an old worn-out horse, crippled with age and long toil in the service of man, and bound him down, and lacerated his flesh with their knives, I saw the human form within him stir and writhe as though it were an unborn babe moving in its mother's womb. And I cried aloud – 'Wretches! You are tormenting an unborn man!'[150]

Such a tormented soul was predestined to a spirit of cruelty and revenge in its next earthly existence as a human being. In 'The perfect way with animals' (a deliberate allusion to *The Perfect Way; Or, The Finding of Christ*), the spirit of a deceased cart horse explains to her that 'Kindness to animals of the gentler orders is the very foundation of civilisation':

> Brutal usage creates brutes; and the ranks of mankind are constantly recruited from spirits [of animals] already hardened and depraved by a long course of ill-treatment ... For the spirit learns by experience and imitation ... Humanity will never become perfected until this doctrine is understood.[151]

Men must abjure the notion of survival of the fittest or 'the rule of the strong' in favour of a higher and purer code of conduct. It followed that a vegetarian diet was the *sine qua non* of human progress, and all herbivorous creatures were more advanced on the upward path of virtue than carnivores; indeed, noxious reptiles and the most ferocious mammal species became the receptacles of fallen and irredeemable human souls, and could be exterminated without guilt. Kingsford's chosen pets were symbolically appropriate guinea pigs, not dogs or cats (the two species normally of most concern to anti-vivisectionists), which had periods of penance and cleansing to undergo before they could rise in the spiritual scale. Her influential book on *The Perfect Way in Diet* (1881), rests its argument for vegetarianism on considerations of human health and the economic use of land, as well as on the prevention of cruelties to livestock, and the corruption of human character by meat-eating; but here too the philosophical substructure of her ideas is always in evidence.[152] While later generations of anti-vivisectionists might deplore the more outré aspects of Kingsford's mystical and vitalist beliefs, her convictions undeniably predisposed her to view the relations between human and animals in a more inclusive way. *All* cruelties to animals exude a 'spirit' which is 'inherently antagonistic to the needs, intuition, and progress of civilised humanity' – its ultimate 'perfectionment'.[153] Thus when vivisectors resorted to their favourite *tu quoque* argument – that women were inconsistent in their attitudes to the exploitation of animals, Kingsford defied them. In a letter on 'Vivisection' published in *Nature* in 1882, she explained that she never bought 'furs, feathers, ivory, kid gloves, stuffed birds or other creatures' and was trying to find a vegetable substitute for shoe leather.

> I detest all 'sport' which necessitates the pain and suffering of living creatures, and have written many articles and letters … against seal-hunting, pigeon-shooting, coursing, battues, and rabbit-gins. Of late years I have added 'vivisection' to the list. My husband's horses wear no bearing-reins; and I never see cruelty without interfering at the risk – as I know but too well – of personal insult. Finally, it is twelve years since I tasted flesh or fowl of any kind.[154]

The adoption of a personal code of conduct was one thing: effective public action against vivisection was quite another. According to Maitland, Kingsford's decision in c.1873 to train as a doctor had little to do with relief of *human* suffering. Rather, she wished to 'qualify for accomplishing the abolition of that which she regarded with a passionate horror as the foulest of practices'. The knowledge and status which came with medical qualification would enable her to elevate at one and the same time 'purity of diet, compassion for the animals, the exaltation of womanhood, and mental and moral unfoldment through the purification of the organism'.[155] Kingsford studied briefly at the London School of Medicine for Women, where she certainly would have supported the students' boycott of Eugène Dupuy's demonstration experiments. However, most of her medical education took place in Paris, where physiologists like Claude Bernard, Paul Bert and many others practised vivisection with none of the sensitivity to public opinion which was necessary in Britain, and often with no pretence of direct medical purposes. Kingsford steadfastly refused to watch vivisections in the course of her studies.[156] At the same time, the medical knowledge that she acquired in Paris (qualifying as a doctor in 1880) enabled her to prove that she was not anti-science. She could argue for the proven merits, indeed the greater reliability, of diagnostic alternatives to vivisection, such as clinical observation, pathology and post mortem dissections; and her graduation thesis on the health benefits of a vegetarian diet became an influential book. In the letter to *Nature* quoted above, she explained that vivisection was a method of research 'which I wholly dissociate from "science" properly so called. And it is a charge not lightly made, but based on sound experience and thoughtful observation, unbiased by "emotion" of any kind'.

The strange combination of dissimilar traits in Kingsford's own mind did indeed make it possible for her to alternate between the driest analyses of scientific data and the most passionate and visionary anathemas on vivisection. Her polemical article on 'The uselessness of vivisection' in *Nineteenth Century* (1882) pointed out the differences between human and animal physiology, the variability of individual animal subjects and the unnaturalness of operative conditions: all these discrepant factors invalidated scientific findings from experiments, and hence destroyed the plea that potential benefits to humans justified animal suffering.[157] Similarly, when someone signing himself 'F.R.S.' (perhaps to be read as 'Fellow of the Royal Society') claimed in a letter to the *Times* that knowledge gained from Ferrier's experiments on animals' brains was now guiding surgery on human patients suffering from tumours, she was able to reply as 'a graduate of the Paris Faculty of Medicine', denying both the primacy and the medical applicability of Ferrier's data; but 'F.R.S.' soon reappeared as the imaginary vivisector 'Professor Effaress' in Kingsford's *Dreams and Dream Stories* – a soulless 'ogre' who can see nothing in living nature but material for experiments.[158] In *Unscientific Science* of 1883 she railed, as Cobbe had done, against Darwin's dismissal of a guiding providence in evolution and human history, and especially against the moral relativism proposed in the *Descent of Man*. The Darwinian materialist treats sympathetic impulses as 'idiosyncrasies': 'he laughs at appeals to sentiment, and boasts of being inaccessible to the "hysterical attacks" of "sensitive and weak-minded fanatics" ... the words "pity" and "justice" have no sense for him', because he fails to understand the 'philosophic unity' of intellect and conscience in human development. In actual fact, such 'physiologists of the modern school' are themselves weak-minded, in not recognising the contradiction inherent in their ideas: they are 'only anxious to prove our common origin with the animals ... the ties of brotherhood ... in order the more tranquilly to claim the right to torture and misuse them'.[159] Kingsford's article on '"Violationism" or sorcery in science' (1882), originally a

lecture to an audience of spiritualists, went so far as to describe modern experimental physiology as a credulous 'resuscitation of the old and hideous cultus of
the black Art', in its Faustian rites of secret animal sacrifice, taking the place of
the 'reverent and loving study of nature' that produces true cures of disease.[160]

In such protests one senses a feeling of doom, which surfaced in vivisection
nightmares like 'The city of blood' in *Dreams and Dream Stories*, but which was
never far from the surface even in Kingsford's most scientifically dispassionate
writings.[161] In an essay of 1886 in *The Heretic*, she noted that Pasteur's commercial development of vaccines necessitated 'a perpetual sacrifice of multitudes of
creatures – rabbits, dogs, monkeys, guinea-pigs, with circumstances of peculiar
horror and protracted torment'. They died of rabies after 'long drawn-out agonies of madness artificially induced'. Yet 'the practices of Pasteurism', if proved
successful, 'will afford a solid basis, a *raison d'être*, for the entire art and science
of vivisection … the principle that it is lawful to do evil for good's sake will be
definitively affirmed', and the great principle of harmony of the 'One Mind' at
the core of the universe will be denied by a false opposition between knowledge
and virtue. In contrast to that tendency, the 'increasing consideration shown
by advancing nations towards women and towards animals has the same basis
… recognition of the principle of abstract justice' towards groups that cannot
defend themselves from abuse by more powerful beings. For Kingsford, this
sense of identification with suffering animals was not intellectual but visceral,
as her memories of medical study in Paris made clear. One morning, while
studying alone in the museum of natural history, she heard 'a frightful burst of
screams … more distressing than words can convey' which the porter told her
was 'only the dogs being vivisected in M. Béclard's laboratory … *"Que voulez-
vous? It is for science"'*:

> Much as I had heard, and said, and even written before that day about vivisection,
> I found myself then for the first time in its actual presence, and there swept over
> me a wave of such extreme mental anguish, that my heart stood still under it. It
> was not sorrow, nor was it indignation merely that I felt, it was nearer despair
> than these; it seemed as if suddenly all the laboratories of torture throughout
> Christendom stood open before me … and the awful future an atheistic science
> was everywhere making for the world rose up and stared me in the face. And then
> and there, burying my face in my hands, with tears of agony I prayed for strength
> and courage to labour effectually for the abolition of so vile a wrong.[162]

According to Maitland, these labours included uttering maledictions against
vivisectors, the potency of which seemed to be proved by the sudden death
of Claude Bernard; but such claims about Kingsford's actions, impossible to

verify, epitomise the eccentricities that prevented the couple from working successfully within existing anti-vivisection societies.[163] Maitland accused Cobbe of having cold-shouldered and maligned Kingsford, through jealousy or a wish to domineer – an imputation that has been uncritically accepted by many later writers. Cobbe was certainly antipathetic to vegetarianism, socially conservative, as averse to moral aberrations like adultery as she was to mysticism, and concerned that the anti-vivisection movement should not be embarrassed by association with crankiness.[164] She could not but be riled by the assertion in Maitland's *The Soul, and How It Found Me* (1877) that Kingsford's 'championship of the animals' initiated 'the present vigorous opposition to the barbarous practice of vivisection' – an assertion he credited to the spirit of a dog, writing messages from the beyond.[165] More importantly, Cobbe knew that Kingsford and Maitland were prone to divide or fall out with every group they joined, notably the London Theosophical Society. Their spiritual pronouncements, published without authorisation under the aegis of the International Society for the Total Suppression of Vivisection, were disowned by its committee.[166] As a result, Kingsford and Maitland resigned, and the International Society soon quietly amalgamated with Cobbe's VSS.[167]

Anna Kingsford was emphatically not a team player, but rather an original spirit who dramatically projected herself as prophetess and martyr into all her undertakings. Her emphasis on 'sentiment' or passionate feeling as the mainspring of moral action on behalf of animals certainly influenced feminist writers of the following decades. However, in the last analysis, what she *was*, her striking presence when lecturing or conversing, had more effect on contemporaries than anything she wrote. 'Who that ever met her' asked the journalist and editor William T. Stead rhetorically, 'can forget that marvellous embodiment of a burning flame in the form of a woman, divinely tall and not less divinely fair! ... her sentences flowed in one unending flood. She talked literature'.[168] Roden Noel remembered her 'luminous exposition, beautiful expression' and 'vivid poetic imagination'.[169] Apparently actors attended her Hermetic Society lectures, just to learn from her perfect elocution, and on lecture tours, dramatically costumed, she evidently fascinated her audiences.[170] However, such ephemeral gifts could not ensure her legacy as an important thinker on man's relations with animals. By 1896, the *Times* could refer to her as 'a lady doctor well known in her day', and even Henry Salt of the Humanitarian League wrote of her as 'in her time a distinguished and memorable figure'. He wished that her important work as 'a humanitarian and food-reformer' could be detached from the 'mystic doctrines and revelations' and the reputation for haughty misanthropy which clouded her posthumous reputation. She saw herself as the *redeemer* of animals as humble lower beings, but had not 'grasped the vital idea which the more advanced humanitarian thinkers are now beginning to grasp – that the emancipation of animals can only be brought about through … the emancipation of men – that in *democracy* … is to be found the only solution of the humanitarian problem'. The 'reconciliation of man and Nature' depended on 'gradual enlightenment from within, the growing sense of perfect equality and brotherhood'.[171] Such new 'vital ideas' form the subject of our last chapter.

Notes

1   Richard D. French, *Antivivisection and Medical Science in Victorian Society* (Princeton and London: Princeton University Press, 1975). Hilda Kean, *Animal Rights: Political and Social Change in Britain since 1800* (London: Reaktion Books, 1998), pp. 96–112. Chien-hui Li, *Mobilizing Traditions in the First Wave of the British Animal Defence Movement* (Palgrave Macmillan, forthcoming).

2   Speech of Lord Cardwell, chair of the 1875 Royal Commission on vivisection, as reported in 'Parliamentary intelligence, House of Lords, Monday May 22', *The Times* (23 May 1876), p. 6.

3   Coral Lansbury, *The Old Brown Dog: Women, Workers, and Vivisection in Edwardian England* (Madison: University of Wisconsin Press, 1985).

4   Browning, 'Tray', from *Dramatic Idyls* [*sic*], 1st series (London: Smith, Elder, 1879); Tennyson, 'In the Children's Hospital: Emmie', from *Ballads and Other Poems* (London: C. Kegan Paul, 1880).

5   Frances Power Cobbe, 'Vivisection: four replies', *Fortnightly Review*, new series 31 (January–June 1882), 88–104. Cobbe slightly misquotes Shelley's 'In the waters of wide agony' from 'Lines written among the Euganean Hills'.

6   Blanche Atkinson's introduction to *Life of Frances Power Cobbe as Told by Herself* (London: Swan Sonnenschein, 1904), p. xvi, quoting the 'congratulatory address' to Cobbe on her eightieth birthday in 1902.

7   Mary Ann Elston, 'Women and anti-vivisection in Victorian England, 1870–1900', in Nicolaas A. Rupke (ed.), *Vivisection in Historical Perspective* (London and New York: Routledge, 1987). Hilda Kean, 'The "smooth cool men of science": the feminist and socialist response to vivisection', *History Workshop Journal*, 40:1 (1995), 16–38. Susan Hamilton (ed.), *Animal Welfare & Anti-Vivisection 1870–1910: Nineteenth-Century Woman's Mission*, 3 vols (London and New York: Routledge, 2004), Introduction. Robert G.W. Kirk, 'The experimental animal: in search of a moral ecology of science?', in Hilda Kean and Philip Howell (eds), *The Routledge Companion to Animal-Human History* (London and New York: Routledge, 2019), especially pp. 124–5.

8   James Turner, *Reckoning with the Beast: Animals, Pain, and Humanity in the Victorian Mind* (Baltimore and London: Johns Hopkins University Press, 1980), pp. 83f. Andreas-Holger Maehle and Ulrich Tröhler, 'Animal experimentation from antiquity to the end of the eighteenth century: attitudes and arguments', in Rupke (ed.), *Vivisection in Historical Perspective*; Anita Guerrini, *Experimenting with Humans and Animals: From Galen to Animal Rights* (Baltimore and London: Johns Hopkins University Press, 2003).

9   French, *Antivivisection*, pp. 36–60.

10 John Burdon-Sanderson (ed.), *Handbook for the Physiological Laboratory*, with contributions from Emanuel Klein, Michael Foster and Thomas Lauder Brunton (London: J. and A. Churchill, 1873).

11 'Prosecution at Norwich', *British Medical Journal* (12 December 1874), pp. 751–4. French, *Antivivisection*, pp. 55–60.

12 RSPCA executive committee minutes, book 13, pp. 100–2, meeting of 25 January 1875. 'Vivisection', *The Times* (26 January 1875), p. 7 and (28 January 1875), p. 9. 'Memorial against vivisection', *Animal World*, 6:66 (1 March 1875), 38. *Life of Cobbe*, pp. 628f.

13 French, *Antivivisection*, pp. 82–3.

14 *Life of Cobbe*, p. 636.

15 RSPCA executive committee minutes, book 13, pp. 132–4, meeting of 5 May 1875.

16 *Life of Cobbe*, pp. 678–9. Details of office holders and committee membership for the Victoria Street Society and the other groups are regularly given in anti-vivisectionist journals like the *Home Chronicler* and the *Zoophilist*. An advertisement for the International Society for the Total Suppression of Vivisection in the *Times* (6 April 1877), p. 8, reveals that, while all the main functionaries were men, subscribers comprised over twice as many women as men.

17 Elston, 'Women and anti-vivisection', p. 267. Frank K. Prochaska, *Women and Philanthropy in Nineteenth-Century England* (Oxford: Clarendon Press, 1980), pp. 31, 243.

18 Leonard Huxley, *Life and Letters of Thomas Henry Huxley*, 2 vols (London: Macmillan, 1900), vol. 1, pp. 436f. *Life of Cobbe*, pp. 639–42. French, *Antivivisection*, pp. 69–79.

19 *Report of the Royal Commission on the Practice of Subjecting Live Animals to Experiments for Scientific Purposes; with Minutes of Evidence and Appendix* (London: HM Stationery Office, 1876), pp. viii–ix, 82–3, 167–77, 212, 243. 'Monkeys' brains once more: Schaefer v. Ferrier', *Zoophilist* (2 April 1888), 198–200. Michael A. Finn and James F. Stark, 'Medical science and the Cruelty to Animals Act 1876: a re-examination of anti-vivisectionism in provincial Britain', *Studies in History and Philosophy of Biological and Biomedical Sciences*, 49 (2015), 12–23.

20 'The British Medical Association', *The Times* (9 August 1875), p. 10. *Report of the Royal Commission*, pp. 148–56. Arthur de Noé Walker, *Reflections on Professor Rutherford's Experiments on the Biliary Secretion of the Dog* (London: M. Walbrook, 1881).

21 *Report of the Royal Commission*, pp. vii, 182–8. Huxley was furious with Klein, whose admissions damaged the pro-vivisection cause: *Life and Letters of Huxley*, vol. 1, pp. 472–3.

22 *Report of the Royal Commission*, pp. 41, 145, and cf. p. 94.

23 Ibid., pp. xxii–xxiii.

24 Ibid., p. 30.

25 Cf. for example Sir William Gull's 'The ethics of vivisection', *Nineteenth Century*, 11 (March 1882), 456–67 (462). A.W.H. Bates in *Anti-Vivisection and the Profession of Medicine in Britain: A Social History* (London: Palgrave Macmillan, 2017) analyses the ethical debate between medical scientists and their opponents.

26 *Life and Letters of Huxley*, vol. 1, p. 437. Evelleen Richards, 'Redrawing the boundaries: Darwinian science and Victorian women intellectuals', in Bernard Lightman (ed.), *Victorian Science in Context* (Chicago and London: University of Chicago Press, 1997), p. 130.

27 *Report of the Royal Commission*, p. xvii.

28 French, *Antivivisection*, pp. 112–58. A deputation from the Victoria Street Society to the Home Office urged the government to introduce the strongest possible restrictions on vivisection: *The Times* report (21 March 1876), p. 8. However, its influence was greatly outweighed by that of 'a very large deputation of the medical profession': 'The government and the vivisection bill', *The Times* (16 June 1876), p. 5.

29 'Cruelty to Animals' law (39 & 40 Vict. Ch. 77), passed in August 1876.

30 Frances Power Cobbe, 'The vivisection bill', *Home Chronicler*, 9 (19 August 1876), 40.

31 French, *Antivivisection*, pp. 204f. Cobbe, 'Comments on the debate in the House of Commons (April 4, 1883), on Mr Reid's Bill for the Total Prohibition of Vivisection', in her book *The Modern Rack: Papers on Vivisection* (London: Swan Sonnenschein, 1889), p. 88. Lori Williamson, *Power and Protest: Frances Power Cobbe and Victorian Society* (London, New York and Sydney: Rivers Oram Press, 2005), p. 149.

32 *Life of Cobbe*, p. 654.

33 Williamson, *Power and Protest*, pp. 96, 173–6, 213. Sally Mitchell, *Frances Power Cobbe: Victorian Feminist, Journalist, Reformer* (Charlottesville and London: University of Virginia Press, 2004), pp. 229, 245, 262, 277–8.

34 Williamson, *Power and Protest*, pp. 82–3. Mitchell, *Cobbe*, pp. 127, 256–63, 265.

35 *Life of Cobbe*, pp. 437, 647. Barbara T. Gates, *Kindred Nature: Victorian and Edwardian Women Embrace the Living World* (Chicago and London: University of Chicago Press, 1998), pp. 124–9.

36 Atkinson, introduction to *Life of Cobbe*, p. ix. Cf. Revd John Stuart Verschoyle, 'Frances Power Cobbe', *Contemporary Review*, 85 (June 1904), 829–40 (835).

37 A number of articles in *Animal World* reported shortcomings and infringements of the law: 'The vivisection act', 7:84 (1 September 1876), 130–4; 'Defects of the vivisection act', 7:86 (1 November 1876), 162–3; 'Vivisection act, article 3', 8:89 (1 February 1877), 18–19.

38 'Comments on the debate in the House of Commons', 'The Janus of science', 'The fallacy of restriction applied to vivisection' and 'Four reasons for total prohibition of vivisection', all in *Modern Rack*. 'Vivisection and its two-faced advocates', *Contemporary Review*, 41 (April 1882), 610–26.

39 Cobbe, 'The policy of the future' and 'The Society for the Protection of Animals Liable to Vivisection', *Home Chronicler*, 13 (16 September 1876), 200–1, and 24 (2 December 1876), 378–9. *Life of Cobbe*, pp. 657, 662f.

40 Mitchell, *Cobbe*, pp. 246, 253, 299.

41 Lansbury, *The Old Brown Dog*. French, *Antivivisection*, pp. 272–3.

42 'Placards' and 'The placard fund', *Home Chronicler* (10 February 1877), 536; (17 February 1877), 552; (24 February 1877), 570; (3 March 1877), 588. Edward Maitland, *The Soul and How It Found Me. Being a Narrative of Phenomena Connected with the Production of 'England and Islam'* (London: the author, 1877), pp. 188–9, 203. Edward Maitland, *Anna Kingsford: Her Life, Letters, Diary and Work*, 2 vols, ed. Samuel Hopgood Hart (London: John M. Watkins, 3rd edn, 1913), vol. 1, pp. 149–50, 154.

43 *Life of Cobbe*, p. 657. See the illustrations in 'Light in dark places', in *Modern Rack*, and a publication that Cobbe produced with Albert Leffingwell, *Illustrations of Vivisection; Or, Experiments on Living Animals* (Philadelphia: American Society for the Restriction of Vivisection, 1887).

44 'The placards' and 'The picture placards', *Home Chronicler* (10 March 1877), 602; (21 April 1877), 696, 700; (12 May 1877), 746–7. French, *Antivivisection*, pp. 255–6.

45 'The horrors of vivisection', *Illustrated Police News*, 684 (24 March 1877), cover and

p. 2, quoting a recent lecture by Cobbe; 'More vivisection horrors', 688 (21 April 1877), cover and p. 2; 'The horrors of vivisection' (7 July 1877), p. 2 and whole back page. The connection between these designs and the VSS posters is confirmed by a reference in George Jesse's *Correspondence with T. Spencer Wells ... On Ovariotomy*, 3rd edn (London: Pickering, 1882), p. 5, and by Barrett's letter, cited in note 47 below. The *IPN*'s attacks on vivisection reflected the views of its editor, George Purkess.

46 Richard Owen, *Experimental Physiology. Its Benefits to Mankind* (London: Longmans, Green, 1882), pp. 2–4, 107–8. Samuel Wilks, 'Vivisection: its pains and its uses, 3', *Nineteenth Century*, 10:58 (December 1881), 937, 944. Williamson, *Power and Protest*, pp. 133–4.

47 'The picture placards', *Home Chronicler* (21 April 1877), 696; 'The placards', letter from the Revd Richard Barrett, *Home Chronicler* (26 May 1877), 779.

48 Cobbe, *Modern Rack*, p. 174.

49 *Life of Cobbe*, pp. 672f.

50 'Police', *The Times* (4 November 1881), p. 12. 'The charge against Professor Ferrier', *The Times* (18 November 1881), p. 10.

51 'Dr. Ferrier's researches', *The Times* (19 November 1881), p. 12. Francis Darwin and A.C. Steward (eds), *More Letters of Charles Darwin: A Record of His Work in a Series of Hitherto Unpublished Letters*, 2 vols (London: John Murray, 1903), vol. 2, pp. 437–9. Contrast 'Vivisection correspondence' and editorials in *Zoophilist*, 1:8 (1 December 1881), 139–42, and 1:9 (2 January 1882), 159–61. Cobbe, in 'Vivisection: four replies', 97–8, cites the clear evidence on which the prosecution was based. Queen Victoria wrote to the Home Secretary to express her horror at the animal suffering revealed: Rod Preece (ed.), *Awe for the Tiger, Love for the Lamb: A Chronicle of Sensibility to Animals* (New York and London: Routledge, 2002), pp. 326–7.

52 Elie de Cyon, 'The anti-vivisectionist agitation', *Contemporary Review*, 43 (April 1883), 498–510 (499, 502, 506, 509).

53 'F.R.S.', 'Surgery and vivisection', *The Times* (9 January 1885), p. 3.

54 Owen, *Experimental Physiology*, pp. 34, 36, 52, 55–6, 133, 164, 197. Ernest Bell, 'Miss Frances Power Cobbe', *The Animals' Friend*, 10:8 (May 1904), p. 121. Owen revived another old misogynistic label, when describing Cobbe's polemic as 'the railing of a scold' (p. 200).

55 *The Times* leading article (21 June 1876), p. 11.

56 'The British Medical Association', *The Times* (9 August 1875), p. 10.

57 Jonathan Hutchinson, 'On cruelty to animals', *Fortnightly Review*, new series, 20 (July–December 1876), 307–20 (308–9).

58 'Vivisection', editorial in *Nature*, 25:645 (9 March 1882), p. 430.

59 *Life of Cobbe*, p. 438.

60 Barbara Caine, *Victorian Feminists* (Oxford: Oxford University Press, 1992), 'Frances Power Cobbe', and Susan Hamilton, *Frances Power Cobbe and Victorian Feminism* (Basingstoke: Palgrave Macmillan, 2006) relate her ideas on vivisection to the range of her writing.

61 *Life of Cobbe*, p. 546.

62 Cobbe, *Modern Rack*, preface, p. vi.

63 *Life of Cobbe*, p. 91. Sandra J. Peacock, *The Theological and Ethical Writings of Frances Power Cobbe, 1822–1904* (Lewiston, Queenston and Lampeter: Edwin Mellen Press, 2002).

64 Cobbe's first book was *An Essay on Intuitive Morals, being an Attempt to Popularise*

Ethical Science. Part 1: Theory of Morals (London: Longman, Brown, Green and Longmans, 1855).

65 Henry Sedgwick, *The Methods of Ethics* (London: Macmillan, 1874), p. 80. Charles Darwin, *The Descent of Man, and Selection in Relation to Sex* (1871), 2nd edn (1879), part 3, chapter 19, section on 'Difference in the mental powers of the two sexes'; ed. James Moore and Adrian Desmond (London: Penguin, 2004), p. 629.

66 In *The Duties of Women: A Course of Lectures* (Boston: George H. Ellis and London: Williams and Norgate, 1881), Cobbe trusted that the enfranchisement of women would not result in a loss of the distinctive feminine virtues of moral purity, unselfishness etc. Richards, 'Redrawing the boundaries', pp. 128f., relates Cobbe's take on Darwin's sexual theories to the vivisection issue.

67 Frances Power Cobbe, *Dawning Lights: An Inquiry concerning the Secular Results of the New Reformation* (London: Edward T. Whitfield, 1868), p. 25.

68 Frances Power Cobbe, *Essays on the Pursuits of Women* (London: Emily Faithfull, 1863), pp. 30, 32, 90. In contrast, Carl Vogt in *Lectures on Man: His Place in Creation, and in the History of the Earth*, ed. James Hunt (London: Anthropological Society, 1864), p. 82, represents woman as the often foolish 'conservator of old customs and usages'. Ludmilla Jordanova, 'Natural facts: a historical perspective on science and sexuality', in Carol P. MacCormack and Marilyn Strathern (eds), *Nature, Culture and Gender* (Cambridge: Cambridge University Press, 1980), especially pp. 53, 62.

69 Frances Power Cobbe, *Broken Lights: An Inquiry into the Present Condition and Future Prospects of Religious Faith* (London: Trübner, 2nd edn, 1865), pp. 131, 186–7.

70 Frances Power Cobbe, 'The ethics of zoophily: a reply', *Contemporary Review*, 68 (October 1895), 497–508. This was a riposte to an article by the Jesuit George Tyrrell in the Catholic journal *The Month*, 85 (September 1895), which had attacked Cobbe's *The Divine Law of Love, in its Application to the Relations of Man to the Lower Animals* (1895).

71 See Cobbe on Lecky in 'The right of tormenting', *Modern Rack*, pp. 49f., and in 'The evolution of the social sentiment; or, heteropathy, aversion and sympathy', in *The Hopes of the Human Race, Hereafter and Here* (London: Williams & Norgate, 1874), p. 196.

72 See e.g. Cobbe's *Broken Lights*, pp. 128–35, and her essay 'What is progress, and are we progressing?', *Fortnightly Review*, 7 (March 1867), 357–70.

73 Cobbe, *Broken Lights*, p. 139.

74 Cobbe, 'The evolution of the social sentiment', pp. 151f. 'Those who are appointed to die', *Modern Rack*, pp. 253f. 'Schadenfreude', *Contemporary Review*, 81 (May 1902), 655–66. Peacock, *Theological and Ethical Writings of Cobbe*, pp. 181, 222f.

75 Cobbe, 'The evolution of the social sentiment', p. 151.

76 Frances Power Cobbe, 'The education of the emotions', *Fortnightly Review*, new series 43 (January–June 1888), 223–36 (230). *Report of the Royal Commission*, p. 64.

77 Cobbe, *Hopes of the Human Race*, pp. xx, 207–8.

78 On 28 November 1872, Darwin wrote to tell Cobbe that her article on 'The consciousness of dogs', in *Quarterly Review*, 133:266 (October 1872), was 'the best analysis of the mind of an animal' he had ever read (Darwin Correspondence Project, letter 8652). *Life of Cobbe*, pp. 489–90. Darwin's *The Expression of the Emotions in Man and Animals* was published in 1872.

79 Darwin, *Descent of Man*, 'Comparison of the mental powers of man and the lower animals', 1st edn (1871), vol. 1, chapter 2; 2nd edn (1879), part 1, chapter 3.

80 *Life of Cobbe*, pp. 490–1. F. Burkhardt et al. (eds), 'Darwin and vivisection', in *The*

Correspondence of Charles Darwin, vol. 23 for 1875, appendix 6, pp. 579–84: on line at the Darwin Correspondence Project.

81 Darwin, *Descent of Man* (edition cited in note 65), part 1, chapter 4, p. 122.

82 *Life of Cobbe*, pp. 487–8. Cobbe's letter to Darwin, recommending Kant (Darwin Correspondence Project, letter 7149). Janet Browne, *Charles Darwin: The Power of Place* (London: Jonathan Cape, 2002), pp. 297–8.

83 Frances Power Cobbe, *Darwinism in Morals, and Other Essays* (London and Edinburgh: Williams and Norgate, 1872). Frances Power Cobbe, 'The scientific spirit of the age', *Contemporary Review*, 54 (1888), 126–39. 'The new morality', in *Modern Rack*, pp. 65f.

84 Cobbe, 'Darwin and vivisection' (1881), in *Modern Rack*, pp. 105–6.

85 Frances Power Cobbe, *The Significance of Vivisection* (London: Victoria Street Society, c.1891), pp. 2–3.

86 'Merlin Nostradamus' [Cobbe], *The Age of Science: A Newspaper of the Twentieth Century* (London: Ward, Lock, and Tyler, undated [1877]).

87 Mitchell, *Cobbe*, pp. 266, 274, 281–2, 296, 312.

88 Vernon Lee, 'Vivisection: an evolutionist to evolutionists', *Contemporary Review*, 41 (May 1882), 788–811 (788–9, 797). Peter Gunn, *Vernon Lee: Violet Paget, 1856–1935* (London: Oxford University Press, 1964), pp. 82, 149, 188–9.

89 Vernon Lee, *Baldwin: Being Dialogues on Views and Aspirations* (London: T. Fisher Unwin, 1886), p. 13.

90 Lee, *Baldwin*, 'The consolations of belief', pp. 76f.

91 Lee, *Baldwin*, 'Of honour and evolution', pp. 129f.

92 Ibid., pp. 130, 133–4.

93 Ibid., p. 165.

94 Peacock, *Theological and Ethical Writings of Cobbe*, pp. 249–51.

95 Lee, *Baldwin*, p. 180.

96 Cobbe, *Dawning Lights*, pp. 5–13, 73–4. Peacock, *Theological and Ethical Writings of Cobbe*, p. 96.

97 *Life of Cobbe*, pp. 485–7.

98 Ibid., p. 489. The publisher of *Descent*, John Murray, begged Darwin not to let Cobbe publish her review before others had received copies of the book: Darwin Correspondence Project, letter 7486, 18 February 1871.

99 *Life of Cobbe*, pp. 483–5. Francis Darwin (ed.), *The Life and Letters of Charles Darwin*, 3 vols (London: John Murray, 1887), vol. 3, pp. 205–8. Mabel Collins, 'Pioneers of anti-vivisection. No. 1: Frances Power Cobbe', *The Anti-Vivisection Review* (October 1909), 188, 191–2.

100 Darwin's letter to Romanes, Darwin Correspondence Project, letter 9916, 7 April [1875]. Romanes's letters defending 'Surgery and vivisection': *The Times* (20 January 1885), p. 4; (27 January 1885), p. 7. *Life and Letters of Darwin*, vol. 3, p. 210.

101 Hull History Centre, UDBV/25/1, typescript copies of letters to Cobbe. Darwin Correspondence Project, letters 9814F and G, 14 January [1875]. Mitchell, *Cobbe*, p. 228.

102 Edward Sharpey-Schafer, 'History of the Physiological Society, 1876–1926', *Journal of Physiology*, 64:3, supplement (1927), p. 8. *Life and Letters of Darwin*, vol. 3, pp. 202–3. Henrietta Litchfield (ed.), *Emma Darwin: A Century of Family Letters, 1792–1896*, 2 vols (New York: D. Appleton, 1915), vol. 2, pp. 219–20, letter from Darwin to Henrietta, 4 January 1875.

103 *Life of Cobbe*, p. 646.

104 Julia Wedgwood, *Why Am I an Anti-Vivisectionist?* (London: The Animal Defence and Anti-Vivisection Society [1910]), p. 1.

105 Michael Foster, *Claude Bernard* (New York: Longmans, Green, 1899), p. 204.

106 Michael Foster, 'Vivisection', *Macmillan's Magazine*, 29:172 (February 1874), 367–76 (368).

107 Ibid., 371.

108 Frances Power Cobbe, 'The final cause of woman', in Josephine Butler (ed.), *Woman's Work and Woman's Culture* (London: Macmillan, 1869), p. 9.

109 Isaac Baker Brown, *On the Curability of Certain Forms of Insanity, Epilepsy, Catalepsy, and Hysteria in Females* (London: Robert Hardwicke, 1866), pp. v–vii, 12, 17–19. Ornella Moscucci, *The Science of Woman: Gynaecology and Gender in England, 1800–1929* (Cambridge: Cambridge University Press, 1990), pp. 102, 104–5, 129. Sander L. Gilman et al., *Hysteria Beyond Freud* (Berkeley and London: University of California Press, 1993), especially Elaine Showalter's 'Hysteria, feminism, gender'.

110 Mary Poovey, '"Scenes of an indelicate character": the medical "treatment" of Victorian women', in Catherine Gallagher and Thomas Laqueur (eds), *The Making of the Modern Body: Sexuality and Society in the Nineteenth Century* (Berkeley and London: University of California Press, 1987). Moscucci, *Science of Woman*, pp. 98, 110–11, 119, 122–3, 125, 134, 158, 160–4.

111 Jesse, *Correspondence with T. Spencer Wells*, p. 6.

112 *Life of Cobbe*, p. 602. Williamson, *Power and Protest*, pp. 162f. Lynda Birke, 'Life as we have known it; feminism and the biology of gender', in Marina Benjamin (ed.), *Science and Sensibility: Gender and Scientific Enquiry, 1780–1945* (Oxford: Blackwell, 1991), p. 250. Lansbury, *Old Brown Dog*, pp. x, 58–9, 83–95. Moscucci, *Science of Woman*, pp. 98, 111, 124. Showalter in Gilman et al., *Hysteria Beyond Freud*, p. 311. Jordanova in 'Natural facts', pp. 57–8, notes the affinity between images of dissections of women's bodies and images of animal vivisections.

113 Frances Power Cobbe, 'The little health of ladies', *Contemporary Review*, 31 (January 1878), 276–96; 'The medical profession and its morality', published anonymously in *Modern Review*, 2 (April 1881), 296–328.

114 Gertrude Douglas, 'Our new anti-vivisection society', *Home Chronicler*, 8 (12 August 1876), 140. French, *Antivivisection*, pp. 279–81.

115 Josephine Butler, *Personal Reminiscences of a Great Crusade*, new edn (London: Horace Marshall, 1910). Judith R. Walkowitz, *Prostitution and Victorian Society: Women, Class, and the State* (Cambridge: Cambridge University Press, 1980).

116 Cobbe, 'The medical profession', 321. Butler reciprocally condemned vivisection and other cruelties to animals in *An Autobiographical Memoir*, ed. George and Lucy Johnson (Bristol: J.W. Arrowsmith and London: Simpkin, Marshall, Hamilton, Kent, 1909), pp. 261–2.

117 Jane Jordan, *Josephine Butler* (London: Hambledon Continuum, 2007), p. 174.

118 Cobbe, 'In the long run', in *Modern Rack*, pp. 270–1. Nevertheless, Cobbe had initially been ambivalent about the campaign against the Contagious Diseases Acts, as were some other feminists and suffragists. Mitchell, *Cobbe*, p. 194. Lise Shapiro Sanders, '"Equal laws based upon an equal standard": the Garrett sisters, the Contagious Diseases Acts, and the sexual politics of Victorian and Edwardian feminism revisited', *Women's History Review*, 24:3 (15 January 2015), 389–409.

119 Darwin, *Descent of Man*, 'Difference in the mental powers of the two sexes'.

120 Brian Easlea, *Science and Sexual Oppression: Patriarchy's Confrontation with Women and Nature* (London: Weidenfeld & Nicolson, 1981), pp. 143f. Cynthia Eagle Russett, *Sexual Science: The Victorian Construction of Womanhood* (Cambridge, MA: Harvard

University Press, 1989). Barbara T. Gates (ed.), *In Nature's Name: An Anthology of Women's Writing and Illustration, 1780–1930* (Chicago and London: University of Chicago Press, 2002), pp. 9–79.

121 Edward H. Clarke in *Sex in Education; Or, a Fair Chance for Girls* (Boston: J.R. Osgood, 1874). Russett, *Sexual Science*, pp. 104f., 'The machinery of the body'.

122 Russett, *Sexual Science*, p. 189. Report on Lydia Becker's paper on women's education at a BAAS meeting, *The Times* (26 August 1868), p. 4. Lydia Becker, 'On the study of science by women', *Contemporary Review*, 10:3 (March 1869), 386–404. Gates, *In Nature's Name*, pp. 11–12, 14–32.

123 Elizabeth Garrett Anderson, 'Sex in mind and education: a reply', *Fortnightly Review*, n.s., 15:89 (May 1874), 582–94, a riposte to Henry Maudsley's 'Sex in mind and education', *Fortnightly Review*, n.s., 15:88 (April 1874), 466–83. Gates, *Kindred Nature*, pp. 15–16.

124 Darwin was a 'friend and patron' of the London School of Medicine for Women: *The Times* (15 June 1882), p. 8.

125 Henry Maudsley, *Body and Mind: An Inquiry into Their Connection and Mutual Influence* (London: Macmillan, 1873), pp. 7–10, 13, 18. Maudsley, 'Sex in mind and education'.

126 George Romanes, 'Mental differences between men and women', *Nineteenth Century*, 21 (May 1887), 654–72.

127 Carl Vogt, *Lectures on Man: His Place in Creation, and in the History of the Earth*, ed. James Hunt (London: Longman, Green, Longman and Roberts, for the Anthropological Society, 1864), p. 180. *Life of Cobbe*, p. 663.

128 *Report of the Royal Commission*, p. 147. Letter in *Home Chronicler*, 12 (9 September 1876), 188–9. Neil McIntyre, *How British Women Became Doctors: The Story of the Royal Free Hospital and Its Medical School* (London: Wenrowave Press, 2014), pp. 51–2.

129 *Oxford Dictionary of National Biography* (British Academy and Oxford: Oxford University Press, 2004) article on Elizabeth Blackwell by Mary Ann Elston.

130 Elizabeth Blackwell, *Pioneer Work in Opening the Medical Profession to Women: Autobiographical Sketches* (London and New York: Longmans, Green, 1895), pp. 35, 93, 146.

131 Elizabeth Blackwell, *Essays in Medical Sociology*, 2 vols (London: Ernest Bell, 1902), vol. 2, pp. 19, 41, 112.

132 Ibid., vol. 2, pp. 26, 89–90, 99.

133 Mitchell, *Cobbe*, p. 318.

134 Blackwell, *Essays*, vol. 2, pp. 35–45, '"Erroneous method in medical education", addressed originally [in 1891] to the Alumnae Association of the Woman's Medical College of the New York Infirmary'.

135 Frances Power Cobbe and G.M. Rhodes, *The Nine Circles of the Hell of the Innocent* (London: Swan Sonnenschein, 1892), pp. 91–2. *Life of Cobbe*, p. 388, re: her attempt to block the election of Mrs Burdon-Sanderson, wife of the physiologist, to the council of Somerville College. Mitchell, *Cobbe*, pp. 321, 333–4. Williamson, *Power and Protest*, pp. 153–6. Anne De Witt, *Moral Authority, Men of Science, and the Victorian Novel* (Cambridge: Cambridge University Press, 2013), p. 137.

136 McIntyre, *How British Women Became Doctors*, p. 52.

137 Elizabeth Garrett Anderson, 'The ethics of vivisection', *Edinburgh Review*, 190:389 (July 1899), 147–69.

138 Ibid., p. 159. *Life of Cobbe*, p. 467. Mitchell, *Cobbe*, pp. 127–8, 252. Williamson, *Power and Protest*, pp. 70–1. Blackwell, *Pioneer Work*, pp. 218–19, 228–32, 248. Jo Manton, *Elizabeth Garrett Anderson* (London: Methuen, 1965), pp. 50–2, 69–70, 75, 95.

139 Maitland, *Kingsford*, vol. 2, p. 62. Gates, *Kindred Nature*, pp. 147–52. Alan Pert, *Red Cactus: The Life of Anna Kingsford* (Watsons Bay: Books and Writers Network, 2006), pp. 113, 168.

140 Maitland, *Kingsford*, vol. 1, pp. 56, 92.

141 Florence Fenwick Miller, Kingsford's close friend, considered Maitland's biography a travesty of her real character, exaggerating her belief in occultism, which he had himself fostered. See Miller's autobiographical sketch, 'An uncommon girlhood', an undated and unpaginated typescript (Wellcome Library, GC/228). Pert, *Red Cactus*, pp. 2–3, 187f.

142 Maitland, *Kingsford*, vol. 1, pp. 31–2, 59, 392; vol. 2, pp. 285, 288. Pert, *Red Cactus*, p. 51.

143 Maitland, *Kingsford*, vol. 1, pp. 14–16; vol. 2, pp. 98–9.

144 Anna Kingsford and Edward Maitland, *The Perfect Way; Or, The Finding of Christ* (London: Field and Tuer, and New York: Scribner and Welford, 1882), pp. xvii, 282.

145 Edward Maitland (ed.), *'Clothed with the Sun': Being the Book of the Illuminations of Anna (Bonus) Kingsford* (London: George Redway, 1889), p. 29. Kingsford and Maitland, *Perfect Way*, p. 277.

146 Maitland, *Kingsford*, vol. 1, p. 83.

147 Anna Kingsford, *Dreams and Dream Stories*, ed. Edward Maitland (London: George Redway, 1888), 'The armed goddess'. Cf. Maitland, *Kingsford*, vol. 2, pp. 78, 83, 116–18. The audience for her lectures at Geneva included the arch vivisectors Moritz Schiff and Carl Vogt; the latter's contemptuous view of women has already been cited.

148 Maitland, *Kingsford*, vol. 1, p. 249; vol. 2, pp. 298, 373–4. Charles Walter Forward, *Fifty Years of Food Reform: A History of the Vegetarian Movement in England* (London: Ideal Publishing Union, 1898), p. 123. Pert, *Red Cactus*, pp. 156, 172.

149 Anna Kingsford, *The Perfect Way in Diet: A Treatise Advocating a Return to the Natural and Ancient Food of Our Race* (London: Kegan Paul, Trench, Trübner, 5th edn, 1892), pp. 1–4.

150 Kingsford, *Dreams and Dream Stories*, 'The laboratory underground'.

151 Ibid., 'The perfect way with animals'.

152 Maitland, *Kingsford*, vol. 1, pp. 29–30, 46, 143, 152, 317, 422–3; vol. 2, pp. 8, 182, 250–1, 295, 311–12, 328–30, 336–7. Maitland, *The Soul, and How It Found Me*, pp. 207–11, 219. Maitland (ed.), *'Clothed with the Sun'*, p. 93. Charles W. Forward, *Fifty Years of Food Reform: A History of the Vegetarian Movement in England* (London: Ideal Publishing Union, and Manchester: Vegetarian Society, 1898), pp. 122–3, 183. Sarah Richardson, 'Transforming the body politic: food reform and feminism in nineteenth-century Britain', in Francesca Scott, Kate Scarth and Ji Won Chung (eds), *Picturing Women's Health* (London: Pickering & Chatto, 2014).

153 Kingsford, *Perfect Way in Diet*, pp. 117–18.

154 Anna Kingsford, 'Vivisection', *Nature*, 25:647 (23 March 1882), 482. However, according to Florence Fenwick Miller, Kingsford did wear ostrich feathers – presumably from 'farmed' birds.

155 Maitland, *Kingsford*, vol. 1, p. 20. Florence Fenwick Miller confirmed that Kingsford's prime motive for studying medicine was to 'help the animals'.

156 Maitland, *Kingsford*, vol. 1, pp. 60, 72–3, 75–6.

157 Anna Kingsford, 'The uselessness of vivisection', *Nineteenth Century*, 11:60 (February 1882), 171–83.

158 'F.R.S.', 'Brain surgery', *The Times* (16 December 1884), p. 5. Anna Kingsford, 'Surgery and vivisection', *The Times* (25 December 1884), p. 10. Kingsford, *Dreams and Dream Stories*, 'Beyond the sunset: a fairy tale for the times'.

159 Anna Kingsford, *Unscientific Science: A Lecture: Under the Auspices of the Scottish Society for the Total Suppression of Vivisection* (Edinburgh: Andrew Elliot, 1883); anthologised from an intermediate source in Gates, *In Nature's Name*, pp. 135–45.

160 Anna Kingsford, '"Violationism" or sorcery in science', lecture to the British National Association of Spiritualists, January 1882 (Whitefish: Kessinger Publishing, reprint 2010). Maitland, *Kingsford*, vol. 2, pp. 38–9, 47–8. Pert, *Red Cactus*, p. 92.

161 Kingsford's 'The city of blood' in *Dreams and Dream Stories* evoked a deserted street, where vivisected animals could be heard moaning, and blood oozed out from the doorways of shuttered houses.

162 Anna Kingsford, 'The root idea of the anti-vivisection movement', *The Heretic*, 4 (May 1886), 257–62.

163 Maitland, *Kingsford*, vol. 1, pp. 250–2; vol. 2, pp. 269, 290–3. The idea that Kingsford had tried to kill vivisectionists by witchcraft was deplored or doubted by many readers of Maitland's book.

164 Maitland, *Kingsford*, vol. 1, p. 425; vol. 2, pp. 27, 44–6, 57, 232, 418.

165 Maitland, *The Soul, and How It Found Me*, pp. 180–1.

166 The offending work was Maitland's *'The Woman' and the Age: A Letter Addressed to the Rt. Hon. W.E. Gladstone, M.P., by Sundry Members … of the International Association for the Total Suppression of Vivisection* (London: E.W. Allen, 1881). Maitland, *Kingsford*, vol. 2, pp. 7–9. Pert, *Red Cactus*, pp. 82–3.

167 *Life of Cobbe*, p. 661.

168 William T. Stead in *Review of Reviews* (15 January 1896), quoted in Maitland, *Kingsford*, vol. 2, p. 378.

169 Quoted in Maitland, *Kingsford*, vol. 2, p. 368.

170 Maitland, *Kingsford*, vol. 2, pp. 116, 128–9, 258, 366, 371.

171 Review of Maitland's *Kingsford* in 'Books of the week', *The Times* (23 January 1896), p. 8. Henry Salt, 'Anna Kingsford', *Vegetarian Review* (February 1896).

6

Sentiment and 'the spirit of life':
new insights at the fin de siècle

This book opened with Baroness Burdett-Coutts's impressive account, penned in 1893, of 'Woman's work for animals' during the century that was drawing to a close.[1] Yet it is doubtful whether she and her colleagues, looking back, felt that their efforts had been rewarded by a comprehensive change in people's behaviour, in line with the much-vaunted progress of western 'civilisation'. As she noted at the RSPCA's annual meeting in 1897, advances in technology, ease of transport and other amenities often brought new evils in their train, involving 'more or less of animal suffering', such as the 'heart-rending' pain of old horses shipped to the continent in dreadful conditions for slaughter, or the wholesale trapping of wild birds. 'I cannot but believe with many others, that cruelty is inherent in some natures.'[2] True, the street offences of cabbies and costermongers had been quelled by the busy prosecuting policies of the RSPCA. However, by the 1890s it had become clear that the psychology of cruelty was an infinitely more complex affair than had been appreciated in earlier times, and was correspondingly resistant to reform. Abuse of animals was not restricted to an ignorant and vicious underclass, as the pioneers of the 1820s had tended to assume. On the contrary, it was endemic to the whole of 'respectable' British society, shielded from prosecution, even from opprobrium, by its habitual and systemic nature and by the wealth and social privilege of those responsible. The thwarting of anti-vivisection activists was thus compounded by the jibes and reproaches of the scientists they attacked. For example, the *Times*, taking up the cudgels for the insulted physiologists in 1876, noted that 'Hundreds of thousands' of cattle, suffering 'agonies of terror', were cruelly castrated, transported and slaughtered every day without hindrance. Yet a 'sentimental' sector of the public turned 'for the relief of their feelings', not upon the heartless livestock dealer, nor upon the 'reckless trapper or the cruel excitement of the sportsman' but upon 'tender-hearted' vivisectionists. 'Some of the ladies who promote this agitation will probably be wearing, with the greatest complacency, furs and feathers ... procured for them by the cruel torture and death of more innocent animals' than would be 'sacrificed in a lifetime' by all the medical gentlemen together.[3]

It was predictable that women, leaders of the anti-vivisection movement, would be singled out for special criticism by their antagonists. Foolish inconsistency, shallow sentimentalism – these were the perennial charges against them, often making their public participation in animal protection as much a liability as an aid. Burdett-Coutts and many other women did, in point of fact, direct their attention to the *Times*'s full gamut of ingrained societal cruelties, which turned out to be almost as irremediable as vivisection. Frustration and defeat led inevitably to schism among anti-cruelty campaigners. In 1898 Stephen Coleridge, who had succeeded Frances Power Cobbe as Honorary Secretary of the VSS (now renamed the National Anti-Vivisection Society (NAVS)), won a vote to change its policy from outright abolitionism to mere pressure on government for incremental improvements in the treatment of laboratory animals. Such judicious gradualism would, Coleridge thought, be more likely to produce results than 'the barren policy of the last twenty years'. However, for Cobbe the new approach represented a betrayal of all that the VSS had fought for. She angrily seceded from NAVS, taking Lady Mount-Temple and other early members of the VSS with her, and founded the British Union for the Abolition of Vivisection (BUAV), a loose federation of regional groups faithful to the former policy. She closed her last personal letter to Coleridge with 'the assurance that, though you have well nigh ruined the work of my life ... I am still yr. old *friend*'. Actually the two groups remained bitterly hostile for many years, weakening still further their resistance to the ever-expanding practice of vivisection in the form of lymph collection for the industrial manufacture of antitoxins. The death of Cobbe herself in 1904 deprived the movement of its most impressive leader. As the BUAV's journal *The Abolitionist* recorded sadly, 'the spirit of her fervent faith in the unseen Power behind our cause' had produced 'a great reservoir of moral energy and enlightenment, from which lesser souls obtained their power of incandescence'. There was the sense that an age had passed, without attaining the noble victories which such gifts deserved.[4]

The mood of discouragement that characterised animal protectionism in the 1890s was of a piece with the pervasive pessimism and melancholy of the period. As Henry Salt noted, the failure to secure better legal protection for animals contributed to the sense that 'We are in the hollow of a deep depression, where all the progressive movement with which the humanitarian movement is indissolubly bound up, is thwarted and delayed'.[5] Western powers' build-up of armaments and aggressive militarism, their oppression of colonial peoples, the perceived gulf between the social classes, the problems of extreme poverty, and the rise of socialism and anarchism were all causes of acute anxiety. Yet in animal protection, as in other fields, a strain of utopian thinking suggested new, comprehensive approaches to society's problems. A respect for the *rights* of both oppressed humans and animals would stem from an ethical and rational approach to the problem of cruelty, superseding the piecemeal philanthropy of earlier eras. This trend was epitomised in the philosophy of the Humanitarian League, founded in 1891 by Salt and Alice Drakoules.[6] Both had become vegetarians on conscientious grounds – at a time when the vegetarian movement was acquiring a much stronger ideological impetus.[7] In an essay on 'Cruel sports' published in 1892, Salt explained that sporadic and selective 'kindness' to animals was not enough:

> The older humanitarianism was, and is, a somewhat conservative, orthodox, and pietistic form of benevolence, which regarded the objects of its compassion, whether 'the lower orders' or 'the lower animals', with a merciful and charitable eye, but from a rather superior standpoint ... It condemned the ill-usage of animals, and in particular vivisection, as cruel and inhuman, but it did not even consider the vast ethical vistas opened out by the new phase into which the animal question, no less than the human social question, has been carried by the new democratic ideal and the discoveries of evolutionary science. It still believes that poverty is a heaven-ordained evil ... and that there is a great gulf fixed between the dominant human race and the so-called 'brutes', which were created for the use, 'but not the abuse' (it is careful to add) of man.[8]

Salt represented a generation that had made its peace with Darwin's ideas. Rather than dwelling on the battles for survival inherent in nature, with all their capitalist and imperial echoes, many progressive thinkers now emphasised living beings' capacity for co-operation, and the strong evolutionary relationship between humans and other species which Darwin had demonstrated. As Edward Evans explained in his remarkable *Evolutionary Ethics and Animal Psychology* (1897), 'general acceptance of the theory of evolution' had unexpectedly fused with influences coming from the 'more mystical and metaphysical mind of the east', especially belief in metempsychosis. 'It is through the portal of spiritual kinship, erected by modern evolutionary science, that beasts and birds ... enter into the temple of justice and enjoy the privilege of sanctuary against the wanton or unwitting cruelty hitherto authorized by the assumptions and usurpations of man.'[9] Salt too, in his book on *Animals' Rights, Considered in Relation to Social Progress* of 1892, affirmed that, as animals' minds and emotions were proved to be closely similar to those of humans, they had the same entitlement to freedom, happiness and individual self-realisation; yet they were habitually treated by humans as mere slaves, food, or objects of sporting amusement. The practice of vivisection, in particular, exposed this cruel reification, ignoring the 'vital essence' of living animals while tearing apart their material bodies.[10] The 'vital essence' common to all life forms was indeed a key theme of late nineteenth-century writers. At the beginning of *Animals' Rights*, Salt quoted a passage from his friend Edward Carpenter's *Towards Democracy*, published in parts between 1883 and 1902. In that strange visionary compound of socialist aspiration, passionate egalitarianism and quasi-mystical identification with the natural world, Carpenter had exhorted the reader to 'Behold the animals. There is not one but the human soul lurks within it, fulfilling its destiny as surely as within you'.

> I saw where it was born deep down under feathers and fur, or condemned for awhile to roam fourfooted among the brambles. I caught the clinging mute glance of the prisoner, and swore that I would be faithful … Come nigh little bird with your half-stretched quivering wings – within you I behold choirs of angels, and the Lord himself in vista.[11]

A causal connection between the advance of socialism and an acceptance of animals' equality with humans was, however, far from obvious, and Salt did not spell it out. Indeed, he acknowledged that the human 'instinct of compassion and justice to the lower animals' counted for more than abstract philosophy. In fact, even the theory of *human* rights rested not on reasoning but on an apprehension 'by the moral faculty, however difficult it may be to establish it on an unassailable logical basis'.[12] In practice, therefore, an assertion of animals' rights depended on feeling, analogy and association rather than on rational proof. It was part of a nexus of inspirational ideas typical of the turn of the century, embracing also progressive politics, theosophy, vegetarianism and feminism, and implying a critique of patriarchy.[13] John Howard Moore, one of Salt's favourite writers, argued in *The Universal Kinship* (1906) that the message of eastern religions, as of Darwinism, was to 'be true … to the spirit of Universal Compassion – whether we walk with … the feathered forms of the fields and forests … the simple savage', or 'the political blanks whom men call wives'. The sense of fraternity that brought about the abolition of slavery is 'to-day melting the white woman's chains', and 'will to-morrow emancipate the working man and the ox'.[14]

The importance of political and religious ideals in shaping women's attitudes to animals

According to some writers of the time, women were not simply the beneficiaries of this development in thought, but actually its most effective agents. Charlotte Despard – socialist, pacifist, vegetarian and anti-vivisection campaigner – explained in *Theosophy and the Woman's Movement* (1913) that the 'spiritual evolution' represented by theosophy, an ideal of peace and equity embracing all humans and animals, was being led by emancipated women. The sufferings of the suffragettes when subjected to the superior 'physical force' of all-powerful men found a parallel in the sufferings of animals under that same tyranny.[15] Constance Bulwer-Lytton, a willing martyr to the cause of the Women's Social and Political Union, in fact remembered that the sight of a sheep on its way to slaughter being bullied by a crowd of onlookers, first brought home to her 'how often women are held in contempt ... excluded or confined', due to 'the mistakes of a civilisation in the shaping of which they have had no free share'.[16] However, Despard believed that in 'the intuitive heart of woman' the future 'City Beautiful' was already taking shape. 'The awakened instinct which feels the call of the sub-human' expressed itself in vegetarianism and 'in strong protest against the cruel methods of experimental research'; for 'life itself is one'.[17]

The 'spiritual evolution' of the then president of the Theosophical Society, Annie Besant, provided a striking example of the transformative power of these notions.[18] In *Vivisection*, which she published in 1882 with fellow-freethinker Charles Bradlaugh, Besant had accused opponents of vivisection of trying to thwart scientific progress through misplaced concern for animals, ignoring the great benefits to humanity that would accrue from physiological experiments. 'Religion is said to be against vivisection, and we hear a great deal of talk about "the great Father of all"'; but the God of the Theists created a natural world which, to the objective observer, seemed to be full of violence and disease.[19] In *A World Without God* (1885) Besant was even more scornful of the way in which Frances Power Cobbe, one of the anti-vivisection 'weak sentimentalists', clung to belief in divine providence in the direction of history.[20] Yet only nine years later, having become a theosophist in the interim, Besant proposed a very different view of the human–animal relationship. Her lecture on *Vegetarianism in the Light of Theosophy* explained her belief that every earthly life was 'a link in a mighty chain' of existences, originating in 'the divine life itself'; 'divine thought' was expressed or reflected in all of nature. Certainly human beings had a higher spiritual destiny than other species, but through the gift of free will they were also uniquely liable to engender 'disharmony'. Cruelty to animals was one effect of that fall from grace. Man *should* be 'the friend of all, the helper of all, the lover of all'. 'He is not to go amongst the happy creatures of the woods, and bring there the misery ... of terror' through his sports. The 'slaughter of living things' for food, too, creates shock waves in 'the astral world', shocks which reverberate in the human mind. Besant believed that the stockyards of Chicago induced, even at a distance, 'a profound sense of depression ... a sense of shrinking, as it were, from pollution, a sense of horror', as a 'terrible protest comes from the escaped lives of the slaughtered beasts'. Such animal misery is like mire that 'clings round your feet when you would ascend' to 'higher forms of life'.[21] Addressing a congress in Manchester in 1897 that marked the fiftieth anniversary of the founding of the Vegetarian Society there, she appealed particularly to women, whose superior standard of 'refinement, compassion and purity' would best advance the vegetarian cause; and in a speech at the International Anti-vivisection and Animal Protection Congress of 1909, she completed her volte-face by identifying herself with the supposedly 'hysterical' women who attacked vivisection, describing the practice now as 'that apotheosis of cruelty'. In truth, 'The human heart, the human conscience, cannot tolerate such things'.[22]

In many cases it was progressive politics that primarily shaped women's eager support for animal protection, in ways that Henry Salt had optimistically predicted. Certainly not all of the early socialist groups felt that crusading for animals was a necessary corollary of political idealism. Henry Hyndman, leader of the Social Democratic Federation, allegedly believed that 'scientific socialists' should not be 'sentimentalists'; he did not want the labour movement to become 'a depository of odd cranks: humanitarians, vegetarians, anti-vivisectionists and anti-vaccinationists, arty-crafties and all the rest of them'.[23] However, the Independent Labour Party (ILP) founded by Keir Hardie (himself a noted animal lover) embraced a wide range of cultural and moral causes. One of the first women to be elected to its national council, Katharine Glasier, became, in the words of an obituarist, 'an eloquent crusader of the new political evangel'.[24] She travelled the country tirelessly, addressing large audiences in streets and public halls, and conjuring up the socialist society of the future. It was a utopian vision, short on practical strategy but full of a sense, often inspired by the writings of Edward Carpenter, of the *oneness* of all created beings – a sense that made her both a pacifist and a supporter of animal causes. Celebrating the birth of the ILP in 1893, she expressed her conviction that 'The Labour party is in league with life ... every living thing is sacred ... Stray cats and dogs, hungry, forlorn and cold – do you laugh, comrades? I have found too many in your lanes not to know them included in our creed, and the poor, over-driven, worn-out cab-horse, the joke of modern society, disappears with the gold hunger that created him'.[25] In one of her poems, jotted in a notebook, she pleaded that there should be 'One law for all, and that the law of love', extended to all the works of nature.[26] In pursuance of this vision, Glasier signed the Humanitarian League's 1896 petition for the abolition of vivisection.[27] In 1900 she shared a platform with George Bernard Shaw at a 'largely attended and enthusiastic meeting' of the National Anti-Vivisection Society. There she argued that 'at present the lower orders were sacrificed for the benefit of the higher' – a reference to the fact that pauper hospital patients as well as animals were subjected to medical experimentation, making anti-vivisection a working-class cause. The ILP's paper, *Labour Leader*, reported that she also 'got a good point home, which some of the feather-and-fur ornamented ladies in the audience must have felt, when she asked that those who condemned cruelty to animals by means of vivisection should not encourage it by wearing ospreys [egret feathers] and furs. By taking away the legal sanction from cruelty they thereby upheld the conscience of the nation, and to that extent helped to purify modern life'.[28]

Animal protection had by the 1890s become so closely identified with feminist causes that women's associations linked to wider national movements often adopted policies on animals that differed from those of their male colleagues. The Women's Liberal Federation, for example, not only supported the aims of the SPB, but was reported as aiding anti-vivisection bodies by distributing literature and 'diffusing anti-vivisection sentiments'.[29] 'A member of a Women's Liberal Association' who wrote to the *Manchester Guardian* in 1896 passionately believed that, by 'refusing to ignore this subject', the Associations 'have shown not only courage but ... have put themselves into line with what is most honourable and inspiring in advanced democracy'.[30] Membership of Women's Liberal Associations evidently both drew on and inspired local anti-vivisection activism, and gave women the confidence to present their case on public platforms. For example, Nessie Egerton Stewart-Brown of Liverpool, who was elected a member of the Women's Liberal Federation National Executive Committee in 1892, was also a keen suffragist and a very strong-minded leader of the ladies' committee of the Liverpool branch of the RSPCA.[31] A journalist who interviewed her for *The Woman at Home* in 1895 reported that she was 'a lady for whom the word "advanced" has no terrors'; and just as the suffrage cause often brought members of the Women's Liberal Foundation into conflict with their male colleagues in the Liberal party hierarchy, so Stewart-Brown found that the conscientious views of the RSPCA ladies' committee in Liverpool could similarly be ignored by the men who managed the affairs of the branch.[32] In 1896 she led a revolt by the RSPCA ladies against the governing male committee's de facto acceptance of the practice of vivisection in the School of Medicine at Liverpool University College. A deputation of the women led by Stewart-Brown actually invaded the men's committee to expostulate, a proceeding that would have been unthinkable in earlier decades.[33] Members of the two committees were substantially drawn from the same wealthy merchant and industrialist families in the Liverpool region; bold support for anti-vivisection by the women alone therefore had strongly gendered overtones.

It could be argued that, given the unlikelihood of any significant concessions by the scientific lobby to the concerns of women like Nessie Stewart-Brown, anti-vivisection had become a mere badge of feminist militancy, rather than a functioning enterprise. However, it would probably be truer to say that concern for animal suffering, a traditional female trait, had deepened and become more vocal as an effect of women's painful struggle against patriarchy. In 1899 an International Congress of Women in London included a session on 'Our duties to wild animals', with Margaretta Lemon, Honorary Secretary of the SPB, and two of the Society's vice presidents (both MPs), Sir Herbert Maxwell and Sir Edward Grey, as invited speakers.[34] Maxwell had qualms about addressing this well-informed and articulate female audience, 'feeling that men and women view certain subjects in different planes'. In any debate on the 'rights' of wild animals, it was certain that the 'sentiment' of female 'ultra-humanitarians' would obscure 'the serene light of reason' or 'common sense' which he and Grey claimed for themselves. Nevertheless, Maxwell had hardly expected the continual 'hisses' and angry ripostes provoked by his rejection of vegetarianism, his qualified support for vivisection, and especially his defence of shooting and other field sports. The women dismissed as 'casuistry and quibbling' Maxwell's argument that, in a world of ferocious 'survival of the fittest', animals had no *rights* – that their fate depended solely on the degree of 'mercy', often tinged by self-interest, which humans chose to exercise.[35] He even spelled out provocatively the wider implications of this view: any Women's Congress should consider 'whether the cause of what are usually termed Women's Rights' would be better described as 'Women's Claims'. A 'right' could be established only by being written into law, and such a law was unlikely to be passed by a male parliament.[36] The parallels between animals and women in their state of subjection to the rule of 'might is right' could not have been made clearer.

Polemical and imaginative literature as vehicles of feminist opposition to cruelties

While women's practical campaigning for animals' rights was constantly thwarted, their writings might still succeed in reforming public opinion. In 1903 the anti-vivisection movement produced a literary masterpiece, in the form of a book written by two young Swedish women, Louise Lind-af-Hageby and Liesa Schartau.[37] As students at the London School of Medicine for Women from 1902, they attended physiology demonstrations involving vivisection at University College London and King's College, and apparently made notes on what they observed. They approached Stephen Coleridge of NAVS, who decided to cite their damning eyewitness accounts in a public lecture, as a result of which he was prosecuted for libel by one of the physiologists concerned, Dr William Bayliss of University College.[38] Before the case came to court, a version of the women's script was published by Ernest Bell as *Eye-Witnesses*; but when Coleridge was convicted and fined, this work was withdrawn, and few copies of it remain.[39] Lind-af-Hageby and Schartau, undeterred, produced several revised and suitably expurgated editions of their book, retitled *The Shambles of Science*, which were published by Lind-af-Hageby's Animal Defence and Anti-Vivisection Society.[40] It was widely reviewed, and formed the background to all her contentious public utterances in the period leading up to the First World War.

Shambles in its definitive form retained the episodic nature of a diary, but with its elegant citations of a cloud of witnesses (famous men of history who had opposed vivisection), its philosophical framework and the subtle wit of the text, it was anything but improvisatory. Vivisection demonstrations at University College London were open to a general audience, and it is their performative aspect which fascinated these authors. The jocular panache of the lecturers with their battery of ingenious machines, and the varied affective responses of the students, including appreciative mirth, seemed like additional insults to the mutilated animals that lay bound and gagged, apparently still semi-conscious and in helpless agony on the table. However, the authors' anger was veiled in irony, and all the more powerful for that. The chapters have *faux naïf* titles such as 'The dog that escaped', 'The quiet cat' or 'Where do the animals come from?' which are redolent of the nursery, and even the page format of the later editions of *Shambles* resembles that of an attractive story-book rather than a tract. Kipling's *Just So Stories* had been published in 1902, with stories variously entitled 'The cat that walked by himself', 'The butterfly that stamped' and so on. In echoing this idiom, and referring to the animals as though they, rather than the humans in attendance, were the *subjects* of the various episodes – empowered agents rather than denatured victims – the authors of *Shambles* pointed the contrast between the Victorians' fond anthropomorphic whimsy in animal stories and their callous objectification of the once-domestic animals that ended up in the laboratory.[41] It transpires that the dog 'escaped' by dying, while the cat was 'quiet' because, according to Lind-af-Hageby and Schartau, it had been treated with curare, which produced immobility without deadening pain:

> he is very firmly fixed to the operation-board with paws in leg-holders and head in a fork … the jaws are squeezed together by a string … He may have tried to scratch the noble specimen of the superior human race who tied him to the board – you cannot expect better behaviour from a cat.

At the end of the (largely abortive) experiment, the cat was left in its disembowelled but still live state, while the students 'descended the stairs chatting and laughing … It is nice to have taken part in some important scientific work, and to feel how one's knowledge and intellectual worth are growing'.[42]

The bitter sarcasms of Lind-af-Hageby and Schartau were founded in the belief that vivisection was not just cruel but also scientifically 'bankrupt', due partly to the abnormal physiological state of the animals under scrutiny. Under the heading, 'The death of vitalism' they affirmed that any attempt to penetrate and explain 'the depths of the phenomena of life' through disassembly of the physical organs was doomed to failure, for it ignored the mysterious 'spirit of life' that united all created beings. Moreover, 'In emancipating themselves from the old vitalistic and reverent views, the adherents of this school have also expunged the unscientific and misty attributes of mercy and kindness towards inferior creatures which are coveted by less advanced men'.[43] *Shambles* constantly sets up an opposition between the sophisticated electrical machines used by the physiologists to maintain organic function, or to measure and analyse physical data, and the tender and fragile inner life of the animals involved. Ambitious medical students were 'deeply impressed with the magnificence of the elaborate apparatus of clever men, dumb animals, and costly instruments', and here 'men' must be understood in the sexual sense.[44] Lind-af-Hageby, like fellow-vegetarians and vitalists Charlotte Despard and Annie Besant, viewed the contemporary ideal of the masculine mind – materialistic, coolly rational, exact and exacting, as the antithesis of the imaginative capacity for fellow-feeling with other species which represented the true evolutionary future of mankind. In these historical circumstances, militant feminism involved a *celebration* of the female capacity for strong emotion or sentiment, not women's traditional, shamefaced denial of it. In the course of an epic court case in 1913, when Lind-af-Hageby unsuccessfully sued her detractors for libel, she 'admitted she was guided by sentiment … All great movements had sentiment behind them, and men did not follow the dictates of mere reason, even in their politics'.[45] The defiance conveyed by this declaration becomes clear when one reads the *Observer*'s comments on the court case, which were typical of mainstream press opinion: the jury's verdict against Lind-af-Hageby proved 'that we have not yet reached an autocracy of hysterics in this country … The sentimentalist is the most deadly traitor to a half-educated democracy'.[46] Nothing daunted, the many women supporting Lind-af-Hageby in the courtroom wept, cheered and applauded her speech, 'with a heartiness which seemed more appropriate to a public meeting than a court of justice'.[47] In another London courtroom at the same historical moment, the conviction of Mrs Pankhurst on a charge of incitement to violence similarly caused a 'scene of uproar … A number of women repeatedly shouted "Shame"'.[48] It is not surprising that the general public, including the medical students who reportedly disrupted both pro-suffrage and anti-vivisection meetings or demonstrations, often acted as though the two movements had effectively converged.[49]

Another leading figure in the 'New Woman' movement, Mona Caird (figure 25), did, in fact, treat the connection between the oppression of women and cruelty to animals at many levels. Indeed, in her overt attacks on patriarchy, she anticipates the ways in which the gendered element in animal advocacy is framed by feminist writers at the present day.[50] Caird passionately supported the women's suffrage movement, as vital to 'the future history of the human race'.[51] However, she chose to promote radical feminism principally through literature, moving easily and continuously between polemical essays and fiction. Her article on 'Marriage' in the *Westminster Review* in 1888 created a sensation; as promulgated at a more popular level in the *Daily Telegraph*, it is said to have prompted some 27,000 responses, a selection of which was published under the title *Is Marriage a Failure?*[52] In her essay collection *The Morality of Marriage* (1897), Caird inveighed against the millennia-old system of patriarchy, which gave men virtual ownership of women. The power conferred by mere brute force was masked by the myths of ideal domesticity, 'separate spheres' and female self-sacrifice, thus thwarting all women's aspirations to an independent intellectual life and to relationships of equality with men. Analogies with the treatment of animals were not far to seek. Women

25 Photograph of Mona Caird by Hayman Seleg Mendelssohn, reproduced as an electrotyped wood engraving by the Nops firm. This striking image illustrated an article on 'The novel of the modern woman' in *Review of Reviews*, edited by W.T. Stead, 10 (July–December 1894).

were chained up like watchdogs, and in both cases the 'overwrought instincts' engendered by frustration were perversely used as a justification for chaining. 'Just as a pointer acquires its peculiar powers through hereditary adaptation to its master's convenience, so, in very fact, women have acquired certain ... standards of conduct, through hereditary training in *their* master's service', notably the code of 'honour' and chastity in marriage. By the same token it was assumed that boys and men needed 'something to destroy', and masculine mastery over weaker beings, human or animal, was therefore fostered and naturalised.[53]

Caird's novels pictured the effects of such societal values on individual women's lives, and once again the treatment of animals was an emblem of the larger aspects of patriarchal oppression. In *The Wing of Azrael* (1889), the character of Philip Dendraith – outwardly respectable, but in fact a heartless tyrant and lecher – is first manifested in his cruel teasing of a dog, laming of a cat and violent beating of a horse, forming a prelude to the sexual torture of his wife.[54] There is here a parallel to Sarah Grand's *The Beth Book* (1897) – one example of a prolific genre of anti-vivisection novels – in which Beth's despicable and possessive husband, a doctor, turns out to be a secret vivisector.[55] Conversely, in Caird's *The Daughters of Danaus* (1894), the nobly altruistic Professor Fortescue deplores the whole idea of 'dominion', whether of men over women or of humans over animals, and he devotes his life to the unglamorous task of finding a painless method of slaughtering cattle. Fortescue rejects the argument that violence in nature justifies human brutality, on the principle of survival of the fittest. Instead, ' "the supreme business of man, was to evolve a scheme of life on a higher plane" ', to follow the ' "dictates of pity and generosity in his own soul" ', renouncing anthropocentrism and the egoism of the overlord. Fortescue explains that, as he pursued his humanitarian project for the benefit of animals, ' "a curious decentralizing process took place. I ceased to be the point round which the world revolved ... The world span, and I, in my capacity of atomic part, span with it" '.[56]

Caird's attitude to nature was strangely ambivalent: it was at once a theatre of cruelty to be transcended by the evolving faculty of human kindness, *and* a sphere of freedom and beauty, an expression of universal life for which the human soul longed as an escape from societal oppression. For Hadria, the heroine of *Daughters of Danaus*, the 'rich and ecstatic song' of a robin seemed like an attempt to cheer her, but its vitality was transient: ' "it will die alone, in the horrible great universe; one thinks little of a robin, but it agonizes all the same when its time comes" '. The thought filled her with 'a flood of terrible, unbearable pity for all the sorrow of the world'.[57] In *The Sanctuary of Mercy* Caird suggested that only the poetic mind (perhaps a mind like Edward Carpenter's or John Howard Moore's) recognises 'the great, beautiful truth of universal kinship, the unity of all life and its profound mystery ... a love that stops at no poor barriers of genus and species'.[58] *Beyond the Pale: An Appeal on Behalf of the*

Victims of Vivisection of 1896, explained her sensation of being 'weighed down by a sense of the tragic importance of the subject, not for the victims alone, but also for the oppressors. I am conscious of the extreme difficulty of making clear the deeply momentous character of our relations with the animal world ... perplexed by the problem of how to ... urge the rights of creatures who have been treated almost as if they had no claims and no rights'.[59]

Caird, like Henry Salt, found that this self-imposed task of establishing animals' rights on an indisputable basis was full of difficulties. Her fictional creation Professor Fortescue expressed her own fears: if the social and political ramifications of the theory of 'survival of the fittest' were once accepted as the key to racial progress, and embodied in statist eugenic policies, as Caird presciently feared they might be, then recognition of the equal rights of the weak became impossible. Unvalued individuals might be condemned, on impeccably rational grounds, to undergo hardship, suffering or death for the collective 'greater good', as happened already to vivisected animals and patients in charity hospitals.[60] Yet the human race could never benefit from the suppression of solicitude and respect for individual rights – such suppression led only to a slide into savagery. Caird believed, with Lind-af-Hageby, that 'Sentiment', though sneered at and shamed, 'is at the bottom of most things that we do, and that we refrain from doing', widening 'the boundaries of human sympathy and mercy'. This emotion, *not* utilitarian calculation, was the true guide to the advance of civilisation, and disparagement of it was a malign function of patriarchy.[61]

Thus Caird's first major study of the causation of cruelty was provocatively titled *A Sentimental View of Vivisection* (1895). In it she argued that the standards of humane conduct to which society conformed at any particular historical period conditioned attitudes to the powerless; but these standards shifted over time and were selective in their objects. The bloody spectacles of the ancient Roman arena would strike horror in a nineteenth-century spectator; yet sometimes the cruelty hidden in the human mind seemed ineradicable. In Caird's novel *The Pathway of the Gods* (1898), a young man dozing among the ruins of ancient Rome has a nightmare vision of the mass slaughter of animals and gladiators in the amphitheatre, and, when he wakes, 'could not shake off a sense of something like heart-break ... There was a horrible likeness to modern men and women in those eager Romans, as they watched the massacre ... The same instincts and passions were there, the same strange, deep-seated cruelty, combined ironically with all the respectable virtues'.[62] Human behaviour could appear wildly inconsistent, because 'moral standards are always high in relation to the dominant and influential', but may dwindle down to nothing in treatment of 'the utterly defenceless'. One could imagine a line that marked the always wavering and indefinite division between those included in, or excluded from, the operations of a society's moral code; for the categories of powerless beings 'differ enormously, as to class and kind, in different epochs'. Animals and slaves nearly always find themselves below the line, as do the black races of humanity. 'For centuries, women were below the line', and 'it is yet possible … to treat women as a class apart, to whom obligations and rights may be arbitrarily apportioned or withheld by the governing sex'. Therefore 'It is in regard to women and to animals that we see the clearest and grossest survivals from pure savagery'.[63]

Ouida on the destruction of nature

Mona Caird was not the only *fin de siècle* writer to fear that, in the brave new world of materialistic science, the interests of individuals would be sacrificed for the supposed benefit of a nation. The popular novelist Ouida (Marie Louise de la Ramée) (figure 26) was hostile to 'new woman' circles, yet in her defiantly independent character, her fear of increasing state and institutional powers, her sympathy for the woes of the downtrodden, and, above all, her passionate concern for animals as abused and disregarded beings, she seems to belong in the same company.[64] In fact, many of her essays about society's cruelties, emphasising the value of powerful 'sentiment' when pitted against the callousness of officialdom, anticipated and probably influenced similar affirmations in the writings of Caird and Lind-af-Hageby. In an article on 'The future of vivisection' published in 1882, Ouida remarked that 'Sentiment is the contumelious charge with which all opposition to these brutal experiments is met by those who practise them: it is an easy form of abuse'.

> Every noble movement of the world has been saddled with this name, from patriotism to the abolition of slavery; and every impersonal impulse of the human race is necessarily one of sentiment – *i.e.* of spiritual and generous, as opposed to gross and merely egotistic, inspirations.[65]

To be 'impersonal' in this sense was to care for the rights of all living beings, irrespective of one's own interest. Ouida believed that the typical physiologist, in contrast, felt entitled to sacrifice the lives of animals at will, and was correspondingly callous to helpless humans, who were likely to become the next victims.[66] She could be described as a romantic libertarian, for whom personal autonomy was a right to be fiercely defended; and the higher animals, as beings with their own idiosyncrasies, loves, friendships, thoughts and impulses, and

26 Photograph of Ouida (Marie Louise de la Ramée), by Adolphe Paul Auguste Beau; reproduced as a line and stipple engraving by Auguste Weger and published by Bernhard Tauchnitz, Leipzig, c.1872.

with the same capacity (she believed) for grief and suffering as humans, should be accorded that same right to self-fulfilment. 'Yet such feelings as these' were never 'considered for an instant'; animals were 'sold from owner to owner, and hustled from place to place', as if they were mere chairs and tables. 'What they suffer from strange voices … unfamiliar treatment … no one cares', for the owner's convenience and profit were the only considerations.[67]

According to Ouida, this state of unrequited servitude was not the only evil endured by animals. Human avarice, caprice and desire for mastery entailed more gratuitous forms of cruel exploitation, whether in sport or so-called 'taming', involving the imprisonment of wild species. 'Dancing dogs, dancing bears, performing wolves, enslaved elephants, would one and all, from the lion tortured on a bicycle in a circus, to the little guinea-pig playing a drum in the streets, be so sickeningly painful to a truly civilised public, that the stolid human brutes who live by their sufferings would not dare to train and exhibit them.'[68] Ouida greatly admired Pierre Loti's *Le livre de la pitié et de la mort*, and some of the best passages in her own essays and stories evoke, in a comparable way, the free, vital spirit in animals, '"the soul within speaking and calling"' to human intimates.[69] Yet that 'soul' was often violently extinguished through human agency. In Ouida's novel about life in post-Risorgimento Italy, *A Village Commune* (1882), the fate of dogs killed by heartless local officials due to the supposed danger of rabies, symbolises the snuffing out of the villagers' former liberties. When one loved dog was shot, 'Blood was pouring from its mouth, but it moved its little curly tail feebly in welcome and farewell. Then the little bright eyes glazed and seemed to sink into its head, its heart beat convulsively through a few seconds more, it stretched its limbs out feebly, and then was still forever'.[70] Such intent, moment-by-moment observation of the parting of body and soul expresses the frailty and preciousness of life and the kinship of all living beings. It is striking that Lady Florence Dixie, trying to explain her dramatic conversion from globe-trotting sportswoman to animal defender, similarly recalled watching the slow deaths of stricken animals. 'I have seen the beautiful eye of deer … glaze and grow dim, as the bright Life, [that] my shot had arrested in its happy course, sped onward into the unknown … The memory of those scenes … haunts me with a huge reproach.'[71]

'Life' with a capital 'L' was the bond between all of nature's creations, but it was also, for Ouida, the antithesis of the dead hand of the industrialised state, which seemed to be inexorably destroying the natural world.[72] Her short stories obsessively pictured this malign force at work, and very few have a happy ending. As Henry Salt, who knew Ouida well as a contributor to the work of the Humanitarian League, perspicaciously remarked, 'through all that she wrote there ran that pessimistic tone which marked her whole attitude to modern life'.[73] She lived and wrote in Italy, where the regime of Francesco Crispi seemed to have betrayed the ideals of the Risorgimento, through savage military suppression of political revolts, 'suffocation of all public expression of feeling', and the empowerment of big business to ride roughshod over citizens' interests.[74] However, this situation merely represented in an extreme form trends which were, she believed, common to the whole of Europe. 'Modern life' for her signified untrammelled capitalism, with all its coarsening effects: the philistinism which swept away the beauties of historic architecture and gardens in the name of 'progress'; the worship of money and vulgar ostentation that had corrupted (so she believed) the refined culture of the aristocracy; worst of all, the destruction of the natural world through the growth of heavy industry and military installations, urban sprawl and the introduction of intensive forms of agriculture. The killing of dogs on the pretext of rabies prevention was an epitome and a symbol of the callous treatment of the poor, who found themselves powerless against corrupt 'municipal despotism'.[75] In Ouida's short story 'The stable boy', set in Florence, orphaned Gino lives in a livery stable, once a church, where 'the pavement, with its marbles and mosaics' – symbol of a nobler and more refined past – is now 'slippery with dung and urine'. When Gino's beloved dog Stellina, a bitch suckling her young, is carried off by local guards 'swollen with the accursed official tyranny' to be incarcerated and vivisected, he attempts her rescue. His trek to the dog pound, which abuts the grim municipal slaughter-house, takes him through 'hideous modern streets and vulgar squares, which have sprung up like wens and tumours', passing 'dirty tramway stations ... stinking soap factories, mounds of cinder and peat'. This nightmarish vision of the loss of all cultural sensibility finds its corollary in the utter heartlessness of a system which Gino resists in vain, and the story ends with his suicide, hanged in the stable with Stellina's dead puppies slung round his neck.[76]

Morality and aesthetics were inseparable. Ouida's essay on 'The ugliness of modern life' published in 1901, expressed her feeling that 'The beauty of the earth is dying, dying like a creature with a cancer in its breast'. The reckless destruction of nature arose from the demoralisation of the moneyed classes; 'all true sense of art must be lacking in a generation whose women wear the spoils of tropical birds, slain for them, on their heads and skirts, and whose men find their principal joy ... in the slaughter of tame creatures [artificially reared pheasants], and bespatter with blood the white hellebore of their winter woods'.[77] In an appreciation of Wilfrid Scawen Blunt's *Satan Absolved*, a poem lamenting the wholesale destruction of nature arising from western imperialism, Ouida added some accusations to the charge sheet. 'To blast the harmless, gentle, colossal whale with the coward's tool of dynamite; to strip the fur coat off the living seal ... to penetrate into virgin forests and plunge in untroubled streams to seize the heron on her nest, and poison the lyre-bird in his haunts and snatch his golden plumes from the bird of paradise ... that commerce may flourish and women be adorned – all these things ... are human sins, and human sins alone.'[78] It was not only tropical paradises that were thus despoiled. Ouida's 'The passing of Philomel' suggested that:

In the guano-dressed, phosphate-dosed, chemically-treated fields and gardens of the future, with their vegetables and fruits ripened by electric light, and their colouring and flavouring obtained by the artificial aids of the laboratory, there will be no place for piping linnet, rose-throated robin, gay chaffinch ... and none amidst the frames, the acids, the manures, the machines, the hydraulic engines, for Philomel ... It is very probable that the conditions of human life in the future will be incompatible with the existence of the nightingale at all.

The effects of intensive, monoculture farming, which also involved the grubbing up of hedgerows and draining of marshes, were aggravated by the practice of killing wild birds as a culinary delicacy or as a supposed threat to profitable agriculture, when in truth insectivores were vital to the interests of farmers. 'The sticks, the guns, the nets, the traps, the birdlime of the accursed bird destroyer, are carried by train and tram into the green heart of once tranquil wolds and woods.'[79] The capture of wild birds for caging as pets was for Ouida an equally grievous wrong. In 'Birds and their persecutors' (1896), she described meeting on the road in Tuscany 'a person, well clothed, followed by a boy carrying nets and poles and osier cages, in which were, recently captured, many chaffinches, two goldfinches, some fieldfares, and one of those useful and rare birds the great woodpecker, who sat upright and tragic as a figure of Napoleon on the Rock'. Such a miserable prisoner would die quickly, and its ultimate destination was a glass case in a collection of specimens. Ouida thought that no one who truly loved nature 'could bear to skin and stuff forms late instinct and radiant with life ... the immobility of death is horrible, because it stands in such cruel contrast to the vivacity and vitality which have been destroyed'.[80] She noted that there was 'an excellent association for the protection of birds, but its aims are so little in touch with its generation that it obtains only the most meagre support'.[81] How indeed could a small group of women hope to change the ingrained habits of society, or to combat the malign effects of commercial greed on the natural world?

The founding of the Society for the Protection of Birds

The SPB was the first national body set up in Britain to defend the interests of a class of 'wild' creatures. In gradually embracing the international dimensions of bird protection, it was also one of the first to apprehend that human actions in any zone had implications for the whole of nature. As the *Royal* Society for the Protection of Birds, or RSPB (from 1904), it has become a major force in conservation and research on ornithology, with a high public profile. Yet its beginnings were modest in the extreme. Like the Band of Mercy movement, it evolved as a coalescence of small-scale initiatives started by women to oppose cruelty to animals – in this case, the mass slaughter of birds to provide plumes for hats, bonnets and gowns.[82] In 1889 Mrs Emily Williamson, who lived in Didsbury, near Manchester, began canvassing people in her circle and writing to the press, in an effort to end the destruction.[83] It was obvious that an international agreement to ban the trade was then unattainable; but if enough women were prepared to band together and swear that they would forego the wearing of feathered millinery, the fashion would die. According to a history of the SPB's beginnings written in 1910–1911, 'Letters of hearty approval and sympathy began to reach Mrs Williamson from many parts of England and Wales', and the burgeoning anti-plumage movement soon transferred to London.[84] It had become too big for one person to manage, and Williamson, who as the wife of a prominent Manchester solicitor would have found it difficult to shift her base to the capital, relinquished the leadership. In London a Plumage League with a similar purpose to Williamson's society had already been initiated by the Reverend F.O. Morris, a prominent writer on bird protection, in collaboration with Lady Mount Temple.[85] We have encountered the latter as a member of the RSPCA ladies' committee, which in the 1870s, under the leadership of Angela Burdett-Coutts, already treated the protection of wild birds as a key part of its mission. Burdett-Coutts wrote to the *Times* in 1872 about the trapping of native songbirds, and again in 1875, about the massacre of humming-birds – letters long remembered.[86] Moreover, her successor as chair of the RSPCA ladies' committee, the Duchess of Portland, became the SPB's first president.[87] In 1886, Revd Morris's Plumage League amalgamated with another nascent organisation, the Selborne Society, which was devoted to the study of natural history and nature conservation.[88] The Selborne's leaders lacked the Plumage League's enthusiasm for a campaign against the feather trade, which therefore played little part in the programme of the merged body. Thus there was a widening rift between the Selborne Society and the SPB. Indeed James Britten, the editor of the Selborne's journal, *Nature Notes*, remarked in 1891 that 'To assume such a very ambitious title as "The Society for the Protection of Birds" for a band of ladies who do nothing but abstain from personal iniquity in the matter of bonnets, may give occasion to the unrighteous to scoff'.[89]

Britten certainly underestimated the ambition of the 'band of ladies'. It is true that the infant SPB had very limited funds, because initially no subscriptions were required of the women members.[90] Yet its moral resources had already been augmented by assimilation of yet another London-based group, the 'Fur, Fin and Feather' society led by Eliza Phillips, which held informal meetings at her house in Croydon; and Mrs Phillips thereupon became a SPB vice president and chair of its committee. She was a veteran of RSPCA work in Tunbridge Wells, where she had formerly lived, and as early as 1874 had admonished women in her branch report never to use 'for dress or ornament ... birds, butterflies, or sealskins'.[91] From c.1886 she collaborated with a Mrs Jarvis of Kirkliston near Edinburgh in producing leaflets for children under the aegis of a 'Bird Protection Society' attached to the Tunbridge Wells RSPCA. Some of these texts seem also to have appeared in the *Women's Penny Paper*; they were imaginary 'Letters' from various birds, explaining their tender feelings and the usefulness of their lives under the dispensation of a loving God, which entitled them to the children's care.[92] This was very much in the spirit of the RSPCA's Band of Mercy, and in fact Mrs Suckling, a moving spirit in the Band (see chapter 4), also soon became a member of the SPB's committee.

Mrs Phillips's strong religious convictions were evidently no barrier to the building of wide alliances in the bird protection cause. She supported the Humanitarian League, and Henry Salt, in his autobiographical *Seventy Years Among Savages*, remembered fondly that 'through the hospitality of Mrs. E. Phillips ... an ardent bird-lover and humanitarian, I had the good fortune to be introduced' to the writer W.H. Hudson, who became a close friend and 'inspiration'. Soon, Hudson was to be an inspirational mentor for the SPB too.[93] Several early supporters of the Society had, like Lady Mount-Temple and Mrs Phillips, strong links with other animal-protection causes, especially the anti-vivisection movement. For example, the SPB's first treasurer, Miss C.V. Hall, a close friend of Mrs Phillips, was a member of the executive council of Lind-af-Hageby's Animal Defence and Anti-Vivisection Society, while Frances Power Cobbe was an early and keen 'life associate' of the SPB.[94] Thus the SPB's long-term Honorary Secretary, Margaretta Lemon, reflected many years later that, when the Society started, 'its object was humanitarian, – its war was against cruelty, its cradle was the R.S.P.C.A.; its early teachings were modelled on the writings of Mrs Suckling, author of the "Humane Educator," of Mrs Brightwen, who wrote "Wild Nature won by Kindness," and on Coleridge's imperishable maxim, – "He prayeth best who lovest best all things both great and small"'.[95] Indeed, Lemon herself became a member of the RSPCA governing council in 1906, and relations between the two bodies remained close and cordial.[96]

Such humane sentiments might have sufficed for a women's group concerned only with self-admonition, or with instruction of the young. However, the programme of the SPB soon expanded to take in active protection of birds in general – threatened native species as well as the tropical birds killed for their plumage. A society that aimed to destroy a vast international trade network, to defeat vested interests that threatened bird populations, and to put pressure on the British parliament for the introduction of comprehensive bird-protection laws, needed more than humanity to guide it. Specifically, it needed the publicity provided by distinguished patrons, the scientific knowledge of academic ornithologists, legal expertise, experience of public life and political clout. During the 1890s and early

1900s, therefore, the power of men in the affairs of this once all-women society steadily increased – a trend epitomised in the appointment of Frank Lemon, a lawyer, as Honorary Secretary in place of his wife Margaretta, when the Society gained its royal charter in 1904.[97] The tact and purposiveness of Mrs Phillips and Mrs Lemon, who still did most of the organisational work, evidently prevented an open clash of cultures. The ecumenical spirit of the early days is well conveyed by Eliza Brightwen's account of a SPB meeting, held at the offices of the RSPCA in 1894. There were several distinguished speakers: Professor Alfred Newton, the leading figure in ornithological research with a chair at Cambridge; Sir Edward Grey, a prominent Liberal MP, and Henry Salt. When Brightwen's turn came to speak, she 'showed the lovely pictures of birds published by the Society for Promoting Christian Knowledge, which I urged should be hung up in all our national schools'.[98] Her address was politely received, but one can imagine the disdain of some of the listeners, who were far from being natural sympathisers with women's aspirations to public, crusading roles. Grey, though theoretically a supporter of women's suffrage, was to be noisily barracked by Christabel Pankhurst and Annie Kenny of the WSPU when he declined to answer their questions on the subject at a Liberal party meeting in 1905, while Newton's misogyny extended to the length of banning women from access to his collection of ornithological specimens at Cambridge.[99]

Although Newton acted as an expert adviser and generous donor to the SPB, he declined all invitations to become a vice president or committee member. Margaretta Lemon remembered that 'During the first years of the Society's existence, scientific ornithologists looked askance at its aims and objects on account of its determined efforts to curb the rapacity of unscrupulous egg-collectors, and the lucrative traffic by commercial dealers in rare specimens'.[100] Such 'scientific ornithologists' were indeed more often concerned at that time with the recording of extinct or threatened species preserved in museum collections than they were with promoting the study of *living* birds in the field, which, under the guidance of William Henry Hudson, was foremost among the SPB's 'aims and objects'. As one of Newton's former students, Francis Guillemard explained, observational studies of animal behaviour such as migration would, in the 1880s–1890s, have been 'considered trifling, and altogether beneath the horizon of professional teaching'.[101] Newton wanted above all to establish the intellectual dignity of ornithology as an autonomous scientific field, not to increase the number of bird enthusiasts. He had a morbid dread of anything that smacked of emotive response to the sights of nature, and, according to his biographer Wollaston, he 'mistrusted' what he considered to be the SPB's 'somewhat amateurish methods ... "The worst is that people will gush and be sentimental"'.[102]

'Sentimentality' was, as we have seen, a standard term of male disparagement of women's efforts on behalf of animals, a term which feminists increasingly redefined and turned back on their detractors. However, the women who founded the SPB were intelligent pragmatists with conservative views in religion and politics (Margaretta Lemon opposed women's suffrage) – not 'new woman' combatants of the order of Caird and Lind-af-Hageby. Moreover, their focus on the sins of other women in the matter of feather-wearing did not conduce to feminist militancy. W. Kennedy in his lecture on *Birds and Their Protection*, published for the SPB in 1895, remarked that the Society was 'founded by ladies ... but happily they did not refuse admission to the men who soon came clamouring at the door', proving that 'it is not a society of mere sentimentalists and faddists'.[103] Margaretta Lemon in her carefully argued, moderate paper on 'Dress in relation to animal life' at the International Congress of Women in 1899 apparently heeded the warnings of Sir Herbert Maxwell and Sir Edward Grey on that same occasion, against the dangers of emotional 'ultra-humanitarianism' in animal advocacy.[104] Indeed Maxwell (editor of *The Sportsman's Library*, author of *Sports and Natural History of the Highlands* and several similar titles) praised the SPB for its 'discretion' in adopting a 'strictly neutral' position on field sports. In a SPB leaflet on *Fowls of the Air*, he maintained the 'apparent paradox, that among no class of persons – no! not even among the fair sex – are animals in general more sure of humane treatment than at the hands of a sportsman'.[105] The assertion of both Maxwell and Grey that participants in driven shoots were blameless, while women who wore feathers were monsters of cruelty, struck many female SPB members, including the co-founder Mrs Phillips herself, as a glaring moral contradiction. However, W.H. Hudson put it to Phillips that a campaign against shooting, such as the Humanitarian League had threatened, would be pointless, indeed counterproductive. It stood no chance of legislative success, and would only 'set people's backs up', turning the whole landed interest, including a majority of Lords and MPs, against the SPB.[106]

In such ways, the mentality and worldly experience of public men increasingly shaped the Society's policies, and tempered the enthusiasms of its rank and file. Surviving registers indicate that the branch secretaries (about 120 of them by 1892, and increasing by the year) and ordinary members continued to be overwhelmingly female, thus replicating the pattern of a gendered contrast and possible tension between leadership and grass roots which also occurred in the RSPCA.[107] In fact, RSPCA branch secretaries often acted in the same capacity for the SPB; but they were 'little heard of beyond the localities where they quietly and persistently labour for the repression of cruelty'.[108] At this local level, however, the SPB's female members were ranged (often with socially embarrassing implications) against feather-wearing neighbours and local milliners. In 1903, the *Manchester Guardian* reported opaquely that the SPB's annual meeting in London had 'a great preponderance of women in the audience. It is to women that the Society makes its chief appeal, for they are the greatest offenders against what may properly be called the conscience of the Society'.[109]

The SPB and the moral crisis of the plumage trade

This first major issue which the SPB confronted, the fashion for feathered millinery, highlighted the confused and contradictory notions of feminine characteristics which operated in the field of bird protection. Women were often accused of vacuous sentimentalism in their opposition to cruelty, and, as the SPB's female writers complained, the jibe came conveniently to hand for use by the plumage dealers who needed to discredit them. However, women were now also to be transformed into their antitypes, and pictured as callous harpies (figure 28). Kennedy, in the lecture already quoted, remarked that Englishwomen were the source 'of almost all the refinement and elevation of life ... conspicuous ... for their works of charity and beneficence'; yet they were also 'the chief cause' of 'the wholesale destruction of birds now raging all over the world ... accompanied by such revolting cruelty ... that, beside it, the ravages of sportsmen, collectors and bird-catchers sink into insignificance'.[110]

Accusations of this kind echoed through the last decades of the century, but originated earlier, in a lecture by Alfred Newton at the annual meeting of the British Association for the Advancement of Science (BAAS) in 1868. Professor Newton was among the first ornithologists to recognise the detrimental effect of changes in land use, particularly drainage of fens, on bird populations. However, 'if the progress of civilization unconsciously demanded some few victims, we should abstain from wilfully adding to their number'. Gamekeepers should be restrained from wantonly destroying birds of prey; but there were worse destroyers – the self-styled 'sportsmen' brought by excursion trains from London and other cities to shoot sea birds on the east coast during the breeding season. In Newton's eyes, the shooters themselves were not the guiltiest parties. According to the *Times* reporter, he chiefly blamed 'the enormous demand for the feathers of the white gull by the modern fashion of ladies' hat-plumes, and almost electrified his fair hearers by informing them that every lady wearing one of these feathers bore upon her forehead the brand of the murderer'. This was too much for one 'fair hearer', the pioneering suffragist and biologist Lydia Becker, who sprang to her feet to challenge Newton on 'holding ladies responsible' for the slaughter.

> Much mischief was done in the world through ignorance. No lady would will-ingly wear the feather of a bird ... destroyed in the act of feeding its young. Ladies should be instructed on these and other subjects, and should be allowed to meet with the other sex on equal terms, not as listeners only, in the discussion and acquisition of the various branches of knowledge ... instead of meeting, as they did, with discouragement. If that plan were pursued, naturalists would have no reason to complain of the conduct of ladies. (Applause.)[111]

At this same BAAS conference, Becker drew a large and apparently sympa-thetic audience for her paper 'On the supposed differences in the minds of the two sexes of Man': those *supposed* differences deriving from 'a fancy picture of women ... made up of recollections from the poets, and vague notions of what women ought to be, with an ideal picture of man drawn from similar veracious sources'.[112] Becker was probably conscious that this 'fancy picture of women' could include the kind of sexual objectification that resulted in extreme fash-ions in dress. It gave rise to what Julia Wedgwood described scathingly as a 'pic-turesque antithesis' in the personae of Victorian men and women.[113] However, despite the advance of feminism in the years that followed, Becker's confident prophecy that the fashion for plumage would correspondingly diminish proved to be mistaken. The Sea Birds Act of 1869 introduced some protection for gulls during the nesting season; but the plume hunters then ventured further afield. British songbirds were killed for their coloured feathers, or stuffed and mounted whole for the decoration of headgear, dresses and decorative objects like fans and valentines. Moreover the improved accuracy and availability of guns, the opening up of virgin territories across the Empire, and the growth of fashion promotion by department stores as well as by bespoke milliners, led to an extraordinary level of destruction of tropical species.[114] The egrets of Florida and South America, and later of other regions, were shot for their white 'nuptial plumes' ('ospreys' in the terminology of milliners) when they gathered at nesting sites, and the young birds were left to die of starvation – a tragedy that was often described in harrowing terms.[115] Humming-birds from the Americas were also harvested by hundreds of thousands, and exploration in New Guinea brought birds of paradise within reach – the *Paradisaea apoda* with its wonderful orange-yellow plumes being especially coveted.[116]

It was once again Newton who publicly sounded the alarm, in a letter to the *Times* of 1876. The catalogue of a recent London auction of imported feathers and skins – one of many held through the year – had shown him that 'the amount of destruction to which exotic birds are condemned by fashion' could not fail to 'extirpate some of the fairest members of creation' in the near future. The stated weights of the bundles listed by one dealer suggested that this single consignment represented the deaths of some 9,700 herons or egrets (many from India) and over 15,500 humming-birds, while 'parrots, kingfishers, trogons, tanagers, and various other brightly-coloured birds are there by the thousand … If ladies like to attire themselves like salmon flies, let them do so; but I would respectfully remind them that feathers on the outside of any biped but a bird naturally suggest the association of tar'.[117] Newton's frightening statistics were confirmed again and again over the years by opponents of the slaughter, who, moreover, generally agreed with him that women whose tastes in dress stimulated the traffic were principally to blame.[118] This was the common theme of the first pamphlets issued by the SPB in the early 1890s. Eliza Phillips herself, in *Destruction of Ornamental-Plumaged Birds* (1890), was, like Kennedy, shocked at the contradiction between the civilised gentleness natural to women, and their apparent indifference to wanton cruelty in the massacre of nesting birds. Englishwomen, as mothers 'with nurseries at home, wear these decorations even when engaged in the public worship of the Creator of the beautiful and useful life of which they are inciting the continued destruction. This is beyond doubt a woman's question. It is our vanity that stimulates the greed of commerce'.[119] '*As In a Mirror': An Appeal to the Ladies of England* (1891), by the Revd H. Greene reminded women that what they *wore* revealed to other people what they *were*; personal taste was an expression of moral character.[120] Edith Carrington, a writer for the Humanitarian League, developed these ideas in *The Extermination of Birds* (1894). Man's alienation from nature and reckless destruction of animals was for her, as for Edward Carpenter, Henry Salt and indeed Ouida, the great crisis of the time. Women living 'cramped' domestic lives could not comprehend it; but 'The woman of the age is daily growing in capacity for taking broader views, and there is hope that she will soon cease to play with a skull, as a child might play with a ball, not knowing what she does'.[121]

Yet Carrington's hopes were doomed to disappointment as surely as Becker's had been. The plethora of hortatory pamphlets in the 1890s and early 1900s almost entirely failed to discredit the fashion for feathers, which actually grew over this period, and continued until the introduction of an import ban in

1922. By the late 1890s it was impossible to claim that the persistence of the fashion was due to a lack of information about the tragic declines in tropical bird species. The mounting despair of the reformers was reflected in Linley Sambourne's famous series of cartoons in *Punch*. His depictions of feathered women in the 1870s like 'I would I were a bird' were whimsical flights of fancy, but later morphed into the grim image of 'A bird of prey' (1892), a clawed harpy hovering menacingly over her quarry (figures 27 and 28).[122] The defiant ostentation and assertiveness of the guilty women were now increasingly emphasised by their critics – *Punch*, like Ouida, associated 'the harpy Fashion' with the kind of 'New Women' who read Ibsen, decried marriage and were 'fond of platform-posing' in campaigns for female suffrage.[123] The bad example set by upper-class ladies and its influence on their social inferiors were also deplored. In 1904 one young woman, who was honorary secretary for the Blackburn branch of the SPB, sent to Mrs Lemon copies of her correspondence with the local bishop, whose wife flaunted 'Egret's plumes … in her bonnet, on Sundays', though she must know 'what a bad effect it will have with girls & women who are too apt to think that what she does must be right'. The Bishop of Blackburn himself took refuge in sententiousness. 'I confess that I have become – after considerable experience – *very* shy of joining Societies of the kind you mention. They are liable to get into the hands of "faddists" and extreme persons, who … identify them with foolish and narrow and even calumnious utterances.'[124]

Exchanges of this kind provide some insight into the attitudes of the population at large, for whom conformity to social norms seemed more important than heeding the admonitions of suspected 'faddists' and 'extreme persons'. As Bella Löwy and other women pointed out in letters to the *Times* in 1893 and 1897, the supply of feathered fashions created the demand. Women (unlike, say, elephant hunters or pheasant shooters) had no murderous intentions – they just passively accepted the merchandise on offer, and the sales talk that went with it.[125] Indeed, a glance through the women's magazines and fashion journals of the 1890s indicates the prodigious volume and variety of feathered goods and furs, from as far afield as Russia, India, the Far East and Australia that were then being aggressively marketed – the furs often boldly advertised with illustrations of fierce animals being hunted in the wild.[126] Garments made from sealskin (obtained through appallingly cruel methods of seal hunting in the arctic) or astrakhan (the curly fleece of ripped-out foetal lambs) were equally controversial.[127] Nevertheless, hyperbolical descriptions of the fast-changing seasonal modes and of the outfits worn by famous actresses and noblewomen gave these luxury products an irresistible allure. Promoters presented buyers

A BIRD OF PREY.

[Despite the laudable endeavours of "The Society for the Protection of Birds," the harpy Fashion appears still, and even increasingly, to make endless holocausts of small fowl for the furnishing forth of "feather trimmings" for the fair sex. We are told that to obtain this delicate and beautiful aigret plume called the "Osprey," the old birds "are killed off in scores, while engaged in feeding their young, who are left to die a lingering death in their nests by hundreds. Their dying cries are described as "heart-rending." But they evidently do not rend the hearts of our fashionable and slavdom, or induce them to read their much-baptised garments. Thirty thousand hummingbirds have been killed in certain Indian provinces in a few days' time to supply the European demand for their skins. One dealer in London is said to have received, during three months, 32,000 skins of humming-birds, 80,000 aquatic birds, and 800,000 pairs of wings. We are told that some of the birds have their skins stripped down, the wings are wrenched off during life, and the mangled bird is left to die slowly of wounds, thirst, starvation and exhaustion."]

28 'A bird of prey', wood engraving from a cartoon drawing by Linley Sambourne, *Punch* (14 May 1892).

"I WOULD I WERE A BIRD——"

IMPOSSIBLE, MY DEAR; BUT HERE IS A SUGGESTION.—EVER YOUR DEVOTED *PUNCH*.

27 'I would I were a bird', wood engraving from a cartoon drawing by Linley Sambourne, *Punch* (23 April 1870).

with the impression of a *fait accompli* which it would have been pointless to reject; and the prescriptive 'tyranny' of fashion seemed to exculpate in advance anyone who followed its dictates. Magazines catering to a wealthy clientele were often brazen or flippant: 'What strange and delightful liberties we do take with the beasts of the field to-day!' remarked *The Gentlewoman* in 1894; 'We not alone strip them of their skins, but we tie their tails into bows, and tassel their ends with jet. Yet, I doubt not, be they of any chivalrous instinct, but that they would be only too glad ... of the privilege of decking lovely woman in such an elegant fashion'.[128]

More modest journals promoting feathered goods and furs had to deal with the prickings of the middle-class conscience. The author of a typical article on 'Coming fashions' in the *Observer* in 1890 thought the use of whole birds was 'much to be regretted; for the wholesale slaughter of brightly-feathered fowl has been a misfortune for years past'. However, 'The wearers should hardly be blamed so much for this massacre' as the commercial originators of the fashion, who 'make the demand, and send out the decree of so much death to the innocent warblers'. After this moral disclaimer, the writer returned happily to descriptions of seductively feathered and furred costumes.[129] When the SPB's Mrs Lemon wrote to *The Ladies' Treasury for 1894* to remonstrate against similar fashion reports, the editor was forced to agree that 'heads of animals as adornments to ladies' dresses is a device of uncivilized life. However, it has high style to recommend it, as the Princess Alix and her sister the Grand Duchess Elizabeth of Russia, have each a dinner dress ... trimmed with little heads of the fur sable'.[130] Some hats are trimmed with 'excellent imitations of birds' feathers and ospreys, which are not at all the real thing; and the wearer should be punishable if they were', given the cruelty involved in obtaining the genuine article.[131] Fashion promoters' disingenuous claims that feathers were artificial or had been harmlessly moulted by the birds were quickly exposed and disproved by the SPB's staff and supporters. On one occasion Darwin's daughter Henrietta bought feathers which were supposedly artificial, but then sent them for scientific analysis and indignantly publicised in the press the commercial deception that was proved to have occurred.[132]

It is impossible to believe that the fashion for furs and feathers would have proved so pertinacious, had it failed to appeal to male onlookers. Its hint of female animality certainly chimed with current notions arising from evolutionary theory, such as we encountered in chapter 5, and seemed to confirm scientists' view that European women remained closer than their more 'evolved' male counterparts to the state of feather-bedecked 'savages'. At the same time,

Society for the Protection of Birds. No. 23.

THE TRADE IN BIRDS' FEATHERS.

(REPRINTED FROM THE TIMES.)

"THE SHUDDERING ANGEL."

(From a photograph of a picture being painted by G. F. Watts, R.A., representing
an angel standing over an altar covered with birds' wings.)

LONDON:
PRINTED AND PUBLISHED BY GEORGE EDWARD WRIGHT,
AT THE TIMES OFFICE, PRINTING HOUSE SQUARE.
1898.

29 Society for the Protection of Birds leaflet, *The Trade in Birds' Feathers* (1898), with a half-tone photographic reproduction of George Frederic Watts's painting, then unfinished, of *A Dedication* or *The shuddering angel* (see the cover image).

the fashion pleasingly confirmed the pre-eminence of humans over other species which was central to more muscular interpretations of 'survival of the fittest' – closely associated in British minds with imperial power and acquisition of the profuse riches of the natural world. The Tory MP, rancher and big-game hunter Henry Seton-Karr, who described himself as a 'common-sense' lover of nature, thought that 'a bird, as well as a seal, a fox, a mink, or a sable, can serve no better end than to yield its life and its covering' to adorn a civilised woman. 'While civilized man remains predatory and carnivorous it is impossible to attack the reasonable killing of any animal for his food, his pleasure, or his family's adornment.'[133] From such attitudes a paradox arose. The refinement and domesticity of the Victorian lady supposedly represented the antithesis of rough business in the wilder reaches of the Empire; yet she was enveloped in its spoils. As well as furs, skins and feathers, she wore whalebone stays and decorations made of beetle wings. She played drawing-room music on ivory piano keys, and her toilet objects and card-cases were often made of brutally obtained tortoiseshell.[134] George Frederic Watts's painting of *The Shuddering Angel* (1897), shows a winged woman – kindred spirit of the birds – weeping over an altar piled with brilliant tropical feathers, and the artist gifted the copyright in this image to the SPB, to be reproduced in its publications or sold as a print (figure 29).[135] However, it is important to note that it also appeared as frontispiece to *Satan Absolved* by Watts's friend Wilfrid Scawen Blunt – the work praised by Ouida as an indictment of the destructive forces of the British Empire. Blunt's Satan tells God that He erred in creating men, who in the course of world conquest have committed crimes against nature such as to make the angels weep, especially when 'the birds of all the Earth' are 'unwinged to deck the heads/ Of their unseemly women'.[136] The violence intrinsic to imperialism was not masked by the 'civilised' culture of the home country, but actually writ large in it.

As though marking the extinction of the spirit of wild nature, the glorious colours of tropical birds' plumage were defiled and dimmed when thus reduced to a simulacrum of their live state. Such violent destruction involved blindness to true beauty as well as extreme cruelty to living creatures, and Watts's 'aesthetic' style of painting encapsulates this association. Indeed, when whole stuffed birds, set up to seem alive, or perversely dismembered, were combined with the extreme artifice of late nineteenth-century tailoring and corseting, there was, to many observers, an impression of gross vulgarity; and pointing this out to the guilty women seemed a promising method of deterrence. As early as 1885, the Hon. Eleanor Vere Boyle, an illustrator in the Pre-Raphaelite mode, wrote to the *Times* to express her disgust over the barbarity of fashion. 'Not content with Nature's gold and enamelled jewel work in such master-pieces as the ruby-crested, emerald-breasted humming bird, she is insulted by the vulgar art of the trade', in being 'encrusted with worthless gilt' painted on the feathers.[137] A few years later, the SPB's annual report described a bonnet bearing 'the lovely little head' of an insectivorous bird, which had been 'split in two, and each half stuck aloft on thin skewers ... the wearer of such a decoration as this must have strange notions of beauty and congruity'.[138] Nature was honoured by artistic interpretation, not by physical appropriation. As G.F. Watts explained in a letter to a teacher of needlework, 'intellectual, interested observation of natural beauty in ... graceful combinations of line' might 'go far towards correcting errant taste in dress, and supplying for it some definite principles'.[139] Those principles were ethical as much as artistic; Henry Salt argued in *Humanitarianism* (1891), that 'humaneness bears a close affinity to the love of beauty, there being a natural connection between the horror with which we witness human or animal torture and the disgust excited by the wanton desecration of any beautiful scene'.[140]

The protection of native birds: inculcation of new habits of mind at the century's end

The purposive appropriation of aestheticism to the cause of animal protection is a striking phenomenon of the time. It drew on the fact that natural history in Britain had always been connected with belles-lettres and imaginative literature, especially of the Romantic period; Shelley was a favourite poet of *fin-de-siècle* nature lovers, particularly the socialists and vegetarians among them. In seeking to gain the public's active support for protective measures, therefore, the SPB represented British birds in all their attractive cultural dimensions. Scientific information and endless 'declamation' about the wanton destruction that was taking place would be ineffectual, 'unless an interest in the birds themselves and an appreciation of their beauty can first be created'.[141] Therefore the SPB's 'Educational Series' of booklets on particular bird species initiated in 1897 (expertly edited by the ornithologist Henry Dresser) adopted a holistic approach. They combined fine quality illustration, taxonomy, physical description, 'characteristics' (especially usefulness to man), and information on legal protection with popular lore, poetic allusions and citation of revered naturalists of the past such as Gilbert White of Selborne. The authors especially dwelt on threats to survival: 'The Lark arising from its dewy bed to hymn the morning sun has won the title of *Alauda* – bird of song; *arvensis* it earns by its care of field and fallow. Surely we have for it a word of praise and a little care to save its frail life from destruction' at the hands of bird-trappers.[142] To hold the attention of lay audiences, especially children, the Society depended especially on vivid impressions 'made through the eye'.[143] Already in the later 1890s, it was producing postcards and Christmas cards with tasteful pictures of birds, and had a growing collection of lantern slides, assembled by Margaretta Lemon, which was lent out for use in lectures. The images included reproductions of Japanese wash drawings, academy paintings, Thorburn's and George E. Lodge's illustrations for deluxe ornithological works, as well as photographs of bird life in natural settings by R.B. Lodge and others.[144] By such means, viewers could learn to appreciate the distinctive traits of each species and gain insight into their lives in the wild, no longer wishing to molest, cage or 'collect' them.

The whole emphasis of the SPB from the start was on bird watching as a substitute for bird killing, and in this it was abreast of the most progressive tendencies of the time.[145] In the last decades of the nineteenth century there was a tense divide between scientific ornithologists like Alfred Newton and his allies in the British Ornithologists' Union, who focused on the collection and analysis of specimens, and field ornithologists like Edmund Selous and William Henry Hudson, for whom the intricate, varied patterns of behaviour of birds in their natural habitats were an all-absorbing study.[146] Selous's extraordinary *Bird Watching* (1901) recorded his sustained observations of particular species and suggested interpretations of their actions, which were to inspire biologists of the next generation like Julian Huxley.[147] Selous's work was imbued with Darwinian theory, especially on sexual selection and inherited characteristics, which he tested out in the field; but he also believed that a bird watcher should have 'the soul in the eyes', and seek original means of conveying visual impressions in words.[148] In fact both Selous and Hudson drew on the wider implications of Darwinism, in their sense of the vitality and interdependence of natural phenomena, and of the bond of sympathetic emotion which united the human observer to all living things; and it was this humane vision that Hudson in particular transmitted to the women who shaped the policies of the SPB. He was a conscious follower of Ruskin (especially of *Love's Meinie*) in the lyricism with which he remembered and recorded the fleeting effects of colour, form and movement in wild birds.[149] As he noted in *Birds and Man*, the human lust for possession of such wonders was self-defeating: 'the best work of the taxidermist … produces in the mind only sensations of irritation and disgust'. A kingfisher that has been shot and stuffed 'is no longer the same thing', except in memory;

the iridescent blue which surpassed 'in beauty and brilliancy any blue ... ever seen in sky or water' has departed, along with 'the spirit of life which is within and the atmosphere and miracle-working sunlight which are without'.[150] The 'spirit of life' is a phrase used by many *fin-de-siècle* vitalists – we have found it already in Lind-af-Hageby's *Shambles of Science*; and in both cases there is the sense of fragility and imminent loss, of threats too powerful to be resisted.

Hudson repeatedly drew attention to the plight of British species; they were endangered by the depredations of the bird catchers and collectors who proliferated in the later decades of the nineteenth century, and (in the case of raptors) by the gamekeepers' ruthless extermination of any creatures deemed a threat to pheasants. In attempting to counter these destructive forces, the SPB built on a body of legislation going back to the 1860s.[151] Already in 1869, an Act was passed to ban the shooting of sea birds on coastal cliffs during the breeding season – they were useful to fishermen at sea in pinpointing the location of fish shoals, and in foggy weather their cries warned sailors of the proximity of rocks. In 1871–1872 Alfred Newton, representing the British Association for the Advancement of Science, pressed for a follow-up Act with equally restricted and practical motives: to protect some valuable species of 'wild fowl' such as snipe and plovers, which were endangered by shooters and egg-takers supplying London markets. However, this BAAS-sponsored bill was hijacked in 1872 by Auberon Herbert MP, who expanded its provisions to cover a large proportion of British bird species.[152] For Herbert – an idealistic freethinker and near-anarchist – the protection of *all* birds from massacre or imprisonment was an acknowledgement of their natural rights, irrespective of their rarity or commercial value. The bill in his amended version gained enough public and parliamentary support to pass into law, to the considerable irritation of Professor Newton and his BAAS colleagues. The long schedule of British species that were now to be protected during a close season was full of anomalies, errors and omissions, and, as Newton predicted, the Act proved virtually unenforceable.[153] Nevertheless, as the RSPCA's *Animal World* noted jubilantly, it established a 'principle' of support for protection of wild birds in general which underpinned all subsequent legislation, and which certainly inspired the SPB's initiatives.[154] The latter's mission was consciously encapsulated in Auberon Herbert's words: ' "all who wish that the friendship between man and animals should become a better and a truer thing than it is at present, must make it so by countless individual efforts" '.[155]

Those efforts met with as much difficulty and discouragement as the campaign against feathered millinery. During the 1890s a succession of further laws allowed county and borough councils to vary the provisions of existing legislation – for example, to protect particular species or sites in their localities throughout the year. However, the complication and confusion arising from this legal patchwork only aggravated the problems of defending birds effectively. Moreover, the SPB, anxious not to appear hostile to the 'progress of civilisation' and commercial interests, was seldom vocal on the subject of environmental degradation and loss of habitats, which writers of books on the birds of particular counties had frequently pointed out. It was human turpitude, not the irreversible effects of industrialisation and the spread of cities and railways, which ostensibly preoccupied the SPB's team of authors in these early days. The unscrupulous ruffians who haunted the rural suburbs on Sundays, catching songbirds such as linnets, goldfinches and even nightingales for sale as cage birds in London's East End; the wealthy collectors who paid commercial dealers or village youths to shoot rare visiting species; the poulterers' agents who destroyed skylarks by the thousand as a culinary delicacy for epicures; the gamekeepers whose pole traps left live hawks and owls hanging by their feet in agony for hours on end: all these *men* were as guilty as the *women* who wore feathers, and there was, seemingly, as little hope of ending the abuses in the one case as in the other.[156] Monitoring of key sites was obviously a priority, and in 1902 Margaretta Lemon, with her customary energy, organised a system of voluntary or paid 'watchers' – forerunners of the wardens of present-day nature reserves – to guard threatened species. However, the exiguous resources of the SPB did not yet allow either acquisition of land or round-the-clock surveillance of nest sites. The Society was greatly dependent on co-operation with local authorities, sympathetic landowners, the police and the RSPCA. The latter prosecuted large numbers of offenders on the SPB's behalf, but succeeded in gaining convictions in only about 50 per cent of cases.[157] The elusiveness, wealth or high social status of the men who instigated the crimes often put them beyond the reach of the law.

In this situation, education of the young once again seemed the most promising long-term means of bringing about a change of heart in the public, and the SPB's women wrote many leaflets aimed specifically at children.[158] If boys, in particular, were made aware of the intelligence and varied emotions that wild birds displayed, they might desist from the age-old practices of egg-collecting or killing the birds with missiles. The SPB's salaried secretary Linda Gardiner, who was appointed in 1899 after a spell working for the RSPCA, therefore collaborated with her close friend Hudson in setting up 'Bird and Tree' competitions for elementary schools on a county basis. Each child was to choose a

CROWNING THE MAIDEN.

30 Society for the Protection of Birds leaflet, *Bird and Tree Day Celebration* (1902), illustrating a scene in a children's play by Mrs Florence Suckling. A boy has stolen a tit's nest, which is restored to the tree by a 'merciful maiden'. She is crowned by the birds and the 'army of kindness'.

particular bird and tree, then watch and record their evolving characteristics through the summer season as the basis for a diary, letter or essay – the format was apparently not prescribed. The school whose pupils produced the best work was awarded the SPB's shield for the year at a local ceremony, and the Society hoped that these events might in time become a national holiday, like the 'Bird and Arbor Days' in the United States and Australia.[159] The shield presentations were often accompanied by tree planting or by the performance of children's songs and plays, some devised by Mrs Suckling (figure 30).[160] The links with the RSPCA ladies' committee's essay competitions and Band of Mercy shows were clear enough here. However, the criteria for the SPB's competition entries were unprecedented. Rather than relying on book-learning or the examination of specimens, the children were to make their own first-hand observations of living nature, as Hudson himself did. They had to find imaginative ways of setting down what they saw or (just as important) heard – with 'enthusiasm and reality', and this could include leaf rubbings, photographs or sketches of birds' movements in the manner of Japanese artists. Indeed, for Hudson, the spontaneous visual notations made by amateur artists were often preferable to the products of professional illustrators like Thorburn and Joseph Wolf, who rendered birds' plumage as though it were 'made of zinc'.[161] The open-endedness and sensory emphasis of the competitions are made clear by the fact that the versatile Linda Gardiner herself apparently devised a way of recording birdsong in musical notation; and in judging the entries, she drew on her own wide knowledge of botany and entomology, as well as the ornithological exper-tise she acquired from Hudson.[162] The success of this SPB project is impossible to gauge; what is certain, however, is that the interactive emphasis of the 'bird and tree' brief was fully attuned to the developing interest in ecology that would characterise the twentieth century. While hopefully imbuing entrants with the notion that the countryside and its wildlife were assets for the whole commu-nity, it must also have helped to foster solicitude for garden birds, expressed in winter feeding, the installation of nest boxes and bird tables (both were sold by the SPB from an early date), and even participation in national surveys of bird populations and migration.

Conclusion: the vindication of 'sentiment' in animal protection

A history of the now *Royal* Society for the Protection of Birds, published in 1910–1911, concluded on an optimistic note. 'Given the united efforts of all who value bird-life … the time should not be far distant when knowledge, common-sense, sentiment and humanity combined procure a sound, com-prehensive and comprehensible Act for the protection of birds.'[163] Common sense *and* sentiment: this imagined balance or reconciliation of traits, with all their gendered connotations, epitomised the early history of the Society. Yet Linda Gardiner, reflecting on *The Fight for the Birds* three years later, com-plained bitterly that enemies of the RSPB still wielded an ancient but deadly weapon against herself and the Society's other female leaders, who might be 'kept under by … constant application of the term "sentimentalists"'.[164] The stereotype of the unbalanced, foolishly doting female animal-lover – always set in antithesis to the rational, moderate and well-judging male – was as common at the end of the nineteenth century as at its beginning, and remained a useful means of discrediting the inconvenient efforts of women to gain recognition of animals' entitlements. However, as Mona Caird in particular had discerned, while accusations of female sentimentalism were consistent through the centuries, the actions and causes to which they referred were temporal and shifting. Thus the allegedly 'extreme' responses of some women to particular forms of animal suffering often anticipated or even shaped the mainstream opinions of later years. Among many examples: in 1854, during a House of Lords debate on a bill to ban the use of dogs to pull carts, Earl Granville, speaking against the measure (which nevertheless passed into law), did not doubt that 'the idea of using some dogs for any useful purpose would excite the horror and indignation of all their female relations. But they ought not to yield to these feelings. They ought to consider the abstract justice of the case'.[165] Yet only six years later a leader writer in the *Times* cited the passing of that law in 1854 as an occasion when rational and humane men had rightly stood between 'the brute creation and the infliction of unnecessary suffering'; whereas, in contrast, Mrs Tealby's current project for a dogs' home represented a descent into 'ridiculous sentimentalism'.[166] We have already seen that such scornful perceptions of the dogs' home, in turn, quickly transmuted into public acceptance and approval, while women's opposition to animal experimentation soon presented a new target for attacks on female 'hysteria'.

Routine accusations of this kind shaped the roles that women wanted, or were allowed, to take on in the animal protection movement. I have shown that they far outnumbered men as ordinary subscribers to animal charities, often donating very large sums of money to the cause. Yet the RSPCA's executive committee felt it necessary to assure the public that even so magnanimous and praiseworthy a patron as Baroness Burdett-Coutts had no say at all in the formulation of the Society's policies.[167] More subtly, women's reaction to accusations of emotional excess often involved a measure of denial or self-censorship: Frances Power Cobbe was always urging the VSS's female members to refrain from 'hysterical and tearful' outbursts against vivisection, though 'There is reason enough for our womanly tears, God knows!'. Instead, they should acquire knowledge of the facts and construct sound arguments to defeat their male opponents on the basis of fundamental ethics.[168]

As this last chapter has shown, the 1890s were marked by a significant shift in consciousness. Writers like Mona Caird, Ouida and Louise Lind-af-Hageby – even Cobbe herself in an article on 'The ethics of zoophily' – began to *embrace* the notion of spontaneous sentiment as a female trait, and represented it as the key to kinder treatment of animals.[169] Why did this change occur? Partly it must have arisen from a more sophisticated understanding of human psychology. The reasoning powers and the emotional urges which prompted human actions could no longer be neatly separated; and, furthermore, 'right' and 'wrong' could not, after Darwin's exposition of his theory of inherited conscience, be understood as eternal absolutes. In earlier times, cruelty to animals had been viewed by their protectors as the outgrowth of an individual's innate, godless and perhaps incorrigible wickedness, setting him apart from decent people. However, by the end of the nineteenth century it was recognised that human moral behaviour was (and is) strikingly inconsistent – ruled not by principle, but by impulses that are scarcely apparent to the conscious mind. People were inured to many cruel practices by the power of tradition, social convention, group dynamics or simply considerations of profit. They were partial and discriminatory in the exercise of their sympathies, selfishly protective of human prerogatives, and hence wilfully indifferent to cruelties such as seal hunting, which were not witnessed at first hand in all their physical horror. At the same time, the assimilation of Darwinian views on the struggle for survival in nature, and the concomitant decay of belief in divine providence, narrowed the grounds on which kindness to animals could be enjoined. Everything now depended on spontaneous *feelings* of kindness – the mysterious moral imperatives that apparently represented the only hope of human progress; and in such sympathetic concern for the oppressed and helpless, women had always been recognised as pre-eminent.

The feminists of the 1880s and 1890s, who directly challenged the power of patriarchy, were able to reappraise the importance of qualities of mind that seemed antithetical to notions of masculine authority. For them, the fellow-feeling aroused by sights of suffering far transcended in importance such 'masculine' traits as the exercise of reasoning powers or the Earl of Granville's 'abstract justice'; and these alternative constructs are still partly operative in present-day approaches to animal protection. As Josephine Donovan wrote in 2007, animal rights theory and utilitarianism tend to 'unite in their rationalist rejection of emotion or sympathy as a legitimate base for ethical theory about animal treatment. Many feminists have urged just the opposite, claiming that sympathy, compassion, and caring are the ground upon which theory about human treatment of animals should be constructed'.[170] I hope my study of their Victorian forebears will contribute fruitfully to this ongoing debate.

Notes

1 'Woman's work for animals', in Angela Burdett-Coutts (ed.), *Woman's Mission*, produced for the Royal British Commission, Chicago Exhibition, 1893 (facsimile edn, Warrington: Portrayer Publishers, 2002).

2 RSPCA *Report* for 1897, pp. 163–4. From c.1910 Ada Cole took up the cause of the old horses sent to Belgium for slaughter. Joyce Rushen, *She Heard Their Cry: The Life of Ada Cole* (ACMS Publishing [unlocated, 1992]), pp. 46f.

3 Leading article, *The Times* (12 July 1876), p. 9.

4 Hull History Centre, UDBV/35/2, letter dated 31 January 1898 from Stephen Coleridge to NAVS members, and letter dated 22 June [1898] from Cobbe to Coleridge. DBV/25/3, Cobbe, *Why We Have Founded the British Union for the Abolition of Vivisection*, printed pamphlet dated 1 June 1898. UDBV/3/1, BUAV Half-yearly Report, 1898, pp. 1–2. Review of the new edition of Cobbe's *Life*, in *Abolitionist*, 5:9 (15 December 1904), 81. Emma Hopley, *Campaigning Against Cruelty: The Hundred Year History of the British Union for the Abolition of Vivisection* (London: BUAV, 1998), pp. 6–7.

5 [Henry Salt], 'Thoughts on the Jubilee', *Humanity*, 2:29 (July 1897), 49–51.

6 Hilda Kean, *Animal Rights: Political and Social Change in Britain since 1800* (London: Reaktion Books, 1998), pp. 134f., and her entry for Drakoules in the *Oxford Dictionary of National Biography* (British Academy and Oxford: Oxford University Press, 2004). Chien-hui Li, *Mobilizing Traditions in the First Wave of the British Animal Defence Movement* (London: Palgrave Macmillan, 2019), pp. 113–19.

7 Henry Stephens Salt, *A Plea for Vegetarianism, and Other Essays* (Manchester: Vegetarian Society, 1886). Howard Williams, *The Ethics of Diet: A Catena of Authorities Deprecatory of the Practice of Flesh-Eating* (London and Manchester: F. Pitman, John Heywood, 1883), preface. Julia Twigg, 'The vegetarian movement in England, 1847–1981: a study in the structure of its ideology' (PhD thesis, London School of Economics, 1981), chapter 6. Colin Spencer, *The Heretic's Feast: A History of Vegetarianism* (London: Fourth Estate, 1993), pp. 275f. Kean, *Animal Rights*, pp. 120–8. Leah Leneman, 'The awakened instinct: vegetarianism and the women's suffrage movement in Britain', *Women's History Review*, 6:2 (1997), 271–87. James Gregory, *Of Victorians and Vegetarians: The Vegetarian Movement in Nineteenth-century Britain* (London: Tauris, 2007).

8 Henry Stephens Salt, 'Cruel sports', *Westminster Review*, 140:1 (July 1893), 545–53 (552–3).

9 Edward Payson Evans, *Evolutionary Ethics and Animal Psychology* (New York: D. Appleton, 1898), pp. 18, 162, 166.

10 Henry Stephens Salt, *Animals' Rights, Considered in Relation to Social Progress*, first published 1892 (New York and London: Macmillan, 1894), p. 73. Salt was himself a doting animal lover: Stephen Winsten, *Salt and His Circle* (London: Hutchinson, 1951), pp. 146, 182, 190.

11 Edward Carpenter, *Towards Democracy*, complete edition (London: Allen & Unwin, 1918), pp. 174–5.

12 Salt, *Animals' Rights*, pp. 1, 87. Cf. Henry Stephens Salt, *Humanitarianism: Its General Principles and Progress*, 1891, new edn (London: Humanitarian League, 1906), p. 3, stressing 'compassion, love, gentleness, and universal benevolence' rather than abstract principles.

13 Hilda Kean, 'The "smooth cool men of science": the feminist and socialist response to vivisection', *History Workshop Journal*, 40:1 (1995), 16–38. Rod Preece, 'Animal sensibilities in the Shavian era', in *Animal Sensibility and Inclusive Justice in the Age of Bernard Shaw* (Vancouver and Toronto: University of British Columbia Press, 2011).

14 John Howard Moore, *The Universal Kinship* (Chicago: Charles H. Kerr, 1906), pp. 327, 329.

15 Charlotte Despard, *Theosophy and the Woman's Movement* (London: Theosophical Publishing, 1913), pp. 1–2, 15.

16 Constance Lytton and Jane Warton, Spinster, *Prison & Prisoners: Some Personal Experiences* (London: William Heinemann, 1914), pp. 12–13. 'Jane Warton' was the name that Lytton assumed when disguising herself as a working-class woman.

17 Despard, *Theosophy*, pp. 21, 23, 44.

18 Li, *Mobilizing Traditions*, pp. 95–6, 245.

19 Annie Wood Besant, *Vivisection* (London: A. Besant and C. Bradlaugh, 1882), p. 3.

20 Annie Wood Besant, *A World Without God: A Reply to Miss Frances Power Cobbe* (London: Freethought Publishing, 1885), p. 19.

21 Annie Wood Besant, *Vegetarianism in the Light of Theosophy*, 1894 (Adyar: Theosophical Publishing House, 3rd edn, 1932), pp. 4, 7–8, 14–19.

22 'The jubilee of vegetarianism: meetings in Manchester', *Manchester Guardian* (19 October 1897), p. 5. 'Speech by Mrs. Annie Besant, at the … Meeting of the Congress on July 8th', *Anti-Vivisection Review* (September 1909), pp. 85–7.

23 Winsten, *Salt and His Circle*, pp. 64–5. Kean, *Animal Rights*, p. 133.

24 'Obituary, Mrs. Katharine Bruce Glasier', *Manchester Guardian* (15 June 1950), p. 5. See also article in the *Oxford Dictionary of National Biography* by Chris Wrigley.

25 Laurence Thompson, *The Enthusiasts: A Biography of John and Katharine Bruce Glasier* (London: Gollancz, 1971), p. 75. I have not been able to trace the source of Thompson's quotation.

26 'Fragments', in Glasier's undated notebook: Liverpool University Library, Glasier archive, GP/3/3/2.

27 Kean, *Animal Rights*, p. 135.

28 'Anti-vivisection', report on Katharine Glasier's speech in *Labour Leader* (9 June 1900), p. 181.

29 Society for the Protection of Birds, annual report, 1899, p. 10.

30 'Vivisection and the Women's Liberal Associations', letter from 'a member' of the WLA, *Manchester Guardian* (20 May 1896), p. 7.

31 Krista Cowman, *Mrs Brown is a Man and a Brother: Women in Merseyside's Political Organisations, 1890–1920* (Liverpool: Liverpool University Press, 2004), pp. 45f., 51–2, 125. Article on Nessie Stewart-Brown by Cowman in the *Oxford Dictionary of National Biography*.

32 Sarah A. Tooley, 'Ladies of Liverpool: Mrs Egerton Stewart-Brown', *The Woman at Home*, 4:21 (June 1895), pp. 173–4.

33 Liverpool Record Office, 179 ANI 6/3 (1891–7), RSPCA ladies' committee, minutes of meetings held on 11 February, 31 March, 9 May, 5 September 1896, and 5 April 1897.

34 'International Congress of Women', *The Times* (4 July 1899), p. 4.

35 Sir Herbert Maxwell, 'Our obligations to wild animals', *Blackwood's Edinburgh Magazine*, 166:1006 (August 1899), 224–37.

36 Ibid., 225.

37 Lisa Gålmark, 'Women antivivisectionists: the story of Lizzy Lind af Hageby and Leisa Schartau', *Animal Issues*, 4:2 (2000), 1–31. Nina Boyd, *Animal Rights and Public Wrongs: A Biography of Lizzy Lind af Hageby* (published by the author, 2014). Article on Lind-af-Hageby by Mary Ann Elston in the *Oxford Dictionary of National Biography*.

38 'High Court of Justice, King's Bench Division', *The Times* (12 November 1903), p. 13; (14 November 1903), p. 6; (18 November 1903), p. 3; (19 November 1903), p. 3.

39 A chapter titled 'Fun' that appeared in the 1903 text and was afterwards suppressed is

reprinted by Barbara Gates in *In Nature's Name: An Anthology of Women's Writing and Illustration, 1780–1930* (Chicago and London: University of Chicago Press, 2002), pp. 155–7.

40 L. Lind-af-Hageby and L.K. Schartau, *The Shambles of Science: Extracts from the Diary of Two Students of Physiology* (London: Animal Defence and Anti-Vivisection Society, 5th edn, 1913).

41 Henry Salt in 'Edith Carrington's writings', *Vegetarian Review* (November 1896) criticised Kipling's anthropomorphism in *The Jungle Book*.

42 *Shambles of Science*, 1913 edn, pp. 27–8, 31, 55–60. Lind-af-Hageby's and Schartau's allegations about the fate of an 'old brown dog' that had allegedly been vivisected several times in contravention of the 1876 law, led to the dog's public commemoration in a statue erected in Battersea; the monument was attacked by medical students, and soon removed. Coral Lansbury in *The Old Brown Dog: Women, Workers, and Vivisection in Edwardian England* (Madison: University of Wisconsin Press, 1985) analyses the whole episode and its context.

43 *Shambles of Science*, 1913 edn, pp. x, 3–8.

44 Ibid., p. 190.

45 'Anti-vivisectionist's claim: Lind-af-Hageby versus Astor and Others', *The Times* (2 April 1913), pp. 3–4. The case was fully reported in the *Times* through April 1913, and brings out many facts about Lind-af-Hageby and her views.

46 'The triumph of mercy', *The Observer* (27 April 1913), p. 12.

47 'End of vivisection case: Miss Lind's forensic powers', *Manchester Guardian* (24 April 1913), p. 9.

48 'Mrs Pankhurst sentenced: three years penal servitude. A disorderly scene in court', *The Times* (4 April 1913), p. 4.

49 Lansbury, *The Old Brown Dog*, pp. 16–17, 21–4, 48.

50 Margaret M. Gullette, afterword to Caird's *The Daughters of Danaus*, facsimile edn (New York: Feminist Press, 1989), pp. 493–534. Lyn Pykett, 'The cause of women and the course of fiction: the case of Mona Caird', in Christopher Parker (ed.), *Gender Roles and Sexuality in Victorian Literature* (Aldershot: Scolar Press, 1995). Ann Heilmann, *New Woman Strategies: Sarah Grand, Olive Schreiner, Mona Caird* (Manchester and New York: Manchester University Press, 2004), pp. 157f. Tracey S. Rosenberg, 'Gender construction and the individual in the work of Mona Caird' (PhD thesis, University of Edinburgh, 2006).

51 Caird, 'The position of women', letter to the *Manchester Guardian* (7 July 1891), p. 12. She joined the Women's Franchise League and then the Women's Emancipation Union in the 1890s, and later subscribed to the WSPU, joining its 1908 Hyde Park demonstration.

52 Elizabeth Cady Stanton, *Eighty Years and More (1815–1897) Reminiscences* (New York: European Publishing, 1898), p. 409. Katharine Tynan, *Twenty-Five Years: Reminiscences* (London: Smith, Elder, 1913), p. 300. Rosenberg, 'Gender construction', pp. 72–81.

53 Mona Caird, *The Morality of Marriage, and Other Essays on the Status and Destiny of Women* (London: George Redway, 1897), pp. 9, 37, 64, 88, 226. Caird explained her views in simpler terms in an interview for the *Women's Penny Paper*, 2:88 (28 June 1890), pp. 421–2. Lucy Bland, 'The married woman, the "new woman" and the feminist: sexual politics of the 1890s', in Jane Rendall (ed.), *Equal or Different: Women's Politics 1800–1914* (Oxford: Basil Blackwell, 1987).

54 Mona Caird, *The Wing of Azrael*, 3 vols (London: Trübner, 1889), vol. 1, pp. 88–90; vol. 2, pp. 18–19, 103.

55 Sarah Grand (Frances Elizabeth Bellenden McFall), *The Beth Book: Being a Study of the Life of Elizabeth Caldwell MacLure, a Woman of Genius* (New York: Appleton, 1897). Anne De Witt, *Moral Authority, Men of Science, and the Victorian Novel* (Cambridge: Cambridge University Press, 2013), pp. 126f., 145–64.

56 Mona Caird, *The Daughters of Danaus*, 3rd edn (London: Bliss, Sands and Foster, 1894), pp. 97–8, 102, 180, 202.

57 Ibid., p. 481.

58 Caird, *The Sanctuary of Mercy* (published by her Independent Anti-vivisection League, c.1892), p. 1; transcript on line at the Victorian Women Writers' Project, Indiana University. Caird was greatly enthused by John Howard Moore's *Universal Kinship*; *Humanitarian* (6 September 1906).

59 Caird, *Beyond the Pale: An Appeal on Behalf of the Victims of Vivisection* (London: William Reeves, [1897]), p. 34.

60 Caird, *Vivisection* (reprinted from *The Clarion* of 10 November 1894, p. 7), undated. Caird, *The Ethics of Vivisection* (London: Society for the Abolition of Vivisection, 1900), pp. 13f., 'Is torture for a good end justifiable?'.

61 Mona Caird, *A Sentimental View of Vivisection* (London: William Reeves [1895]), pp. 19–20.

62 Mona Caird, *The Pathway of the Gods: A Novel* (London: Skeffington, 1898), pp. 26–34.

63 Caird, *Beyond the Pale*, pp. 64–7.

64 George S. Street, 'An appreciation of Ouida', *The Yellow Book*, 6 (July 1895), 167–76. Elizabeth Lee, *Ouida, a Memoir* (London: T. Fisher Unwin, 1914), especially pp. 304f. Pamela Gilbert, 'Ouida and the other new woman', in Nicola Diane Thompson (ed.), *Victorian Women Writers and the Woman Question* (Cambridge: Cambridge University Press, 1999). Mary Sanders Pollock, 'Ouida's rhetoric of empathy: a case study in Victorian anti-vivisection narrative', in Mary Sanders Pollock and Catherine Rainwater (eds), *Figuring Animals: Essays on Animal Images in Art, Literature, Philosophy and Popular Culture* (Basingstoke: Palgrave Macmillan, 2005). Jane Jordan and Andrew King (eds), *Ouida and Victorian Popular Culture* (Farnham: Ashgate, 2013). Ouida's attack on 'The new woman' and 'Female suffrage' appeared in her *Views and Opinions* (London: Methuen, 2nd edn, 1896).

65 Ouida, 'The future of vivisection', *Gentleman's Magazine*, 252:1816 (1882), 415.

66 Ouida, *The New Priesthood* (London: E.W. Allen, 1893). Compare her short story 'Toxin', in *Toxin and Other Papers* (Leipzig: Bernhard Tauchnitz, 1896).

67 Lee, *Ouida, A Memoir*, pp. 311–12. Ouida, 'Death and pity', in *Views and Opinions*, pp. 240–1.

68 Ouida, 'The quality of mercy', in *Critical Studies* (Leipzig: Bernhard Tauchnitz, 1901), pp. 228–9.

69 Ouida, 'Death and pity', p. 226.

70 Ouida, *A Village Commune*, new edn (London: Chatto & Windus, 1882), p. 224, and cf. pp. 99–100. Pamela K. Gilbert, 'Ouida and the canon', in Jordan and King (eds), *Ouida and Victorian Popular Culture*, pp. 44–5.

71 Florence Dixie, *The Horrors of Sport* (London: William Reeves for the Humanitarian League, 1892), pp. 3–4.

72 Ouida, 'Some fallacies of science' in *Views and Opinions*. Lynn Pykett, 'Opinionated Ouida' in Jordan and King (eds), *Ouida and Victorian Popular Culture*.

73 Henry Salt, *Seventy Years Among Savages* (London: George Allen & Unwin, 1921), p. 207.

74 Ouida, 'The Italy of to-day' and 'L'uomo fatale' in *Views and Opinions*.

75 Ouida, 'Cities of Italy' and 'Blind guides', in *Views and Opinions*.

76 Ouida, 'The stable boy', in *Santa Barbara* (New York: John W. Lovell/US Book Company, 1891). 'Toto' in *La Strega, and Other Stories* (London: Sampson Low, Marston, 1899) has a comparable storyline. Pollock, 'Ouida's rhetoric of empathy', pp. 143f.

77 Ouida, 'The ugliness of modern life', in *Critical Studies*, pp. 198, 201.

78 'Wilfrid Scawen Blunt', in *Critical Studies*, p. 161.

79 Ouida, 'The passing of Philomel', in *Views and Opinions*, pp. 138, 142–3.

80 Ouida, 'Birds and their persecutors', in *Toxin and Other Papers*, pp. 168–9, 182.

81 Ouida, 'The quality of mercy', p. 227.

82 The early history and pre-history of the [R]SPB were extensively chronicled in the Society's own journal, *Bird Notes and News*, at various dates. 'Introductory', 1:1 (April 1903). 'The story of bird protection', 4:1 to 4:8 (1910–1911). Margaretta Lemon, 'The story of the R.S.P.B.', 20:5 to 20:8 (1943). Tony Samstag, *For Love of Birds: The Story of the Royal Society for the Protection of Birds, 1889–1988* (Sandy: RSPB, 1988). Tessa Boase, *Mrs Pankhurst's Purple Feather: Fashion, Fury and Feminism – Women's Fight for Change* (London: Aurum Press, 2018). RSPB, 'Our History', at www.rspb.org.uk, accessed May 2019.

83 Editorial article 4, *Manchester Guardian* (30 November 1892), p. 5. 'Introductory', *Bird Notes and News*, 1:1 (April 1903), 1, and 'The story of bird protection', 4:5 (25 March 1911), 49–50. Article on Emily Williamson by Molly Baer Kramer in the *Oxford Dictionary of National Biography*. In a letter to the *Manchester Guardian* (21 October 1893), p. 4, Williamson complained about the mass destruction of larks for gourmet consumption, as well as about the plumage fashion.

84 'The story of bird protection', *Bird Notes and News*, 4:5 (25 March 1911), 49–50.

85 Revd Francis Orpen Morris, 'A Plumage League', *The Times* (18 December 1885), p. 14. Leading article in the *Times* (19 December 1885), p. 11. 'The story of bird protection', *Bird Notes and News*, 4:4 (20 December 1910), 37–8.

86 Angela Burdett-Coutts, 'Protection of Birds', *The Times* (6 June 1872), p. 12, reprinted in *Animal World*, 3:34 (1 July 1872), 147. Burdett-Coutts, 'Humming Birds', *The Times* (2 February 1875), p. 7. See also the minutes of the RSPCA ladies' committee, under the dates of 12 December 1892, 13 March 1893, 12 February 1894, 22 October 1894, 24 February 1896 etc., revealing co-operation with the SPB. Protection of wild birds was part of the RSPCA's established work: Brian Harrison, *Peaceable Kingdom: Stability and Change in Modern Britain* (Oxford: Clarendon Press, 1982), pp. 87–9.

87 The Duchess proved a useful channel of communication with the royal family; for example, in March 1906, she obtained permission to announce publicly that Queen Alexandra rejected the wearing of feathers. RSPB archive, 02.02.00, Margaretta Lemon's papers.

88 Richard Clarke, *Pioneers of Conservation: the Selborne Society and the RSPB* (London: Selborne Society, 2004).

89 'Birds and bonnets', *Nature Notes, the Selborne Society's Magazine*, 2:16 (15 April 1891), 76–7.

90 'Introductory', *Bird Notes and News*, 1:1 (April 1903), 1.

91 The story of bird protection', *Bird Notes and News*, 4:4 (20 December 1910), 37. Article on Eliza Phillips by Jonathan Burt in the *Oxford Dictionary of National Biography*.

92 RSPB archive, 01.03.12. Examples are *A Letter from Little Fathers & Mothers* (1888), and *Letter from a Missel Thrush*. The latter is signed by Phillips, issued by her 'Bird Protection Society', and dated from her (then) home, 'Culverden Castle, Tunbridge Wells April 1st 1890': 'Reprinted from the *Women's Penny Paper*, March 29th, 1890'.

93 Salt, *Seventy Years Among Savages*, pp. 116–18. Henry S. Salt, *Company I Have Kept* (London: George Allen and Unwin, 1930), p. 117. Winsten, *Salt and His Circle*, pp. 12, 86, 182.

94 Boyd, *Animal Rights ... Lizzy Lind af Hageby*, p. 39. *Bird Notes and News*, 1:6 (July 1904), 36–7.

95 Margaretta Lemon, 'Linda Gardiner', obituary, *Bird Notes and News*, 19:5 (Spring 1941), 91. Coleridge's *Ancient Mariner* is slightly misquoted. It was Mrs Suckling who enrolled Linda Gardiner in the New Forest branch of the SPB in 1893; Gardiner's membership card (the SPB's first design) survives in Manchester Central Library, Mike Smith collection of autograph letters, GB127, file 6.

96 In 1906 the RSPCA's executive committee was reconstituted as a council, with branch delegates. Mrs Lemon represented Croydon and various districts of Surrey. RSPCA *Report* for 1906, p. 45.

97 Margaretta Lemon, 'The story of the R.S.P.B', 2, *Bird Notes and News*, 20:6 (Summer 1943), 85.

98 Eliza Brightwen, *The Life and Thoughts of a Naturalist*, ed. Wilfrid Hugh Chesson (London: T. Fisher Unwin, 1909), p. 180.

99 'Miss Pankhurst and the police: assault and obstruction', *Manchester Guardian* (16 October 1905), p. 8. Tim R. Birkhead and Peter T. Gallivan, 'Alfred Newton's contribution to ornithology: a conservative quest for facts rather than grand theories', *Ibis*, 154 (2012), 887–905 (893).

100 Lemon, 'The story of the R.S.P.B.', 3, *Bird Notes and News*, 20:7 (Autumn 1943), 101.

101 A.F.R. Wollaston, *Life of Alfred Newton* (London: John Murray, 1921), p. 266.

102 Ibid., p. 153. Birkhead and Gallivan, 'Alfred Newton's contribution to ornithology', 888, 902–3. Henry M. Cowles, 'A Victorian extinction: Alfred Newton and the evolution of animal protection', *British Journal for the History of Science*, 46:4 (December 2013), 695–714.

103 W. Kennedy, *Birds and Their Protection: A Lecture* (Hertford: Stephen Austin & sons, 1895, for the SPB), p. 5. Kennedy, a member of the SPB committee, intended his lecture to serve as a template for the use of other speakers.

104 Margaretta Lemon, 'Dress in relation to animal life', 'A paper read ... before a Sectional Meeting of the International Congress of Women' on 3 July 1899, reprinted in Gates, *In Nature's Name*, pp. 168–76. Maxwell, 'Our obligations to wild animals', p. 237.

105 SPB, 6th annual report for 1896, p. 9. Sir Herbert Maxwell, *Fowls of the Air*, SPB leaflet no. 23 (1896), pp. 7–9. Boase, *Mrs Pankhurst's Purple Feather*, pp. 91–6.

106 Letter from Hudson to Mrs Phillips, 3 May 1896, in a collection of his letters in Manchester Central Library, Records 34 GB127, E12.

107 The SPB's annual reports listed 'Hon. Local Secretaries' and 'Associates' (members paying annual subscriptions of a shilling or more).

108 SPB, 3rd annual report for 1893, p. 4.

109 'The cruelty of fashion: meeting of the Birds' Protection Society', *Manchester Guardian* (11 February 1903), p. 5.

110 Kennedy, *Birds and Their Protection*, pp. 5–6.

111 'The British Association for the Advancement of Science': 'The Game Laws'; report on Newton's paper on 'The zoological aspect of the game laws' and on Becker's intervention, *The Times* (24 August 1868), p. 7.

112 'The British Association for the Advancement of Science', report on Becker's paper in the Economic Section, *The Times* (26 August 1868), p. 4. Cf. Becker's 'Is there any specific distinction between male and female intellect?', *Englishwoman's Review*, 8 (1868), 483–91, reprinted in Gates, *In Nature's Name*, pp. 14–20; also Becker, 'On the study of science by women', *Contemporary Review*, 10:3 (March 1869), 386–404.

113 Julia Wedgwood, 'Female suffrage, considered chiefly with regard to its indirect results', in Josephine Butler (ed.), *Woman's Work and Woman's Culture: A Series of Essays* (London: Macmillan, 1869), p. 257.

114 Robin W. Doughty, *Feather Fashions and Bird Preservation: A Study in Nature Protection* (Berkeley, Los Angeles and London: University of California Press, 1975). Christopher Breward, 'Femininity and consumption: the problem of the late nineteenth-century fashion journal', *Journal of Design History*, 7:2 (1994), 71–89. Nicholas Daly, 'Fur and feathers: animals and the city in an anthropocene era', in his *The Demographic Imagination and the Nineteenth-Century City* (Cambridge: Cambridge University Press, 2015).

115 William Henry Hudson, *Osprey; Or, Egrets and Aigrettes*, 1891, 2nd edn (London: SPB, 1896). The SPB often republished eyewitness accounts by American writers, for example, *An Egret Hunter's Narrative* (1896).

116 Hudson's letters to the *Times*: 'Feathered women' (17 October 1893), p. 6; 'The trade in birds' feathers' (25 December 1897), p. 5. SPB pamphlets: Margaretta Lemon, *The Bird of Paradise* and Eliza Phillips, *Mixed Plumes* (both 1895). 'The Bird of Paradise', Lemon's letter to the *Manchester Guardian* (27 June 1895), p. 12.

117 'Borrowed plumes', Newton's letter to the *Times* (28 January 1876), p. 10.

118 Doughty, *Feather Fashions*, pp. 26–7, quantifies the imports of feathers into Britain from 1872 to the 1920s.

119 Eliza Phillips, *Destruction of Ornamental-plumaged Birds* (London: SPB, 1890), p. 1.

120 Revd H. Greene, *'As in a Mirror'. An Appeal to the Ladies of England Against the Use of Birds in Millinery*, 1891 (4th edn, London: SPB, 1898).

121 Edith Carrington, *The Extermination of Birds*, Humanitarian League's Publications no. 10 (London: William Reeves, 1894), pp. 7–9.

122 *Punch* (23 April 1870), 167 and (14 May 1892), 231. Cf. Sambourne's 'The "Extinction" of Species', *Punch* (6 September 1899), 110. Jane Munro, '"More like a work of art than of nature": Darwin, beauty and sexual selection', in Diana Donald and Jane Munro (eds), *Endless Forms: Charles Darwin, Natural Science and the Visual Arts* (New Haven and London: Yale University Press, 2009), pp. 280–3.

123 *Punch* (14 May 1892), 230. Ouida, 'The new woman', in *Views and Opinions*, pp. 210–12.

124 Correspondence between Miss Hilda Howard and Revd Samuel Thornton, Bishop of Blackburn, February 1904. RSPB archive, 01.02.11, 'Plumage trade, cuttings and correspondence'.

125 Bella Löwy, 'The wearing of feathers' and two other letters from unnamed women, *The Times* (20 October 1893), p. 5. 'G.E.G.' (also a woman), in the *Times* (21 October 1893), p. 11. 'The trade in birds' feathers', several letters from women, *The Times* (28 December 1897), p. 9.

126 An advertisement for 'The International Fur Store' in Regent Street, London, in *The Queen* (2 October 1897) shows fierce wild animals, bears being hunted etc. The shop's trademark was an elegant lady with a bear begging for her attention. The huge range and

quantity of imported furs is revealed by the business records of Edward Barber and Son, in the London Metropolitan Archives.

127 Frank Buckland, 'A plea for the seals', *The Times* (5 February 1873), p. 7. Joseph Collinson, *The Fate of the Fur Seal* (London: William Reeves and the Humanitarian League, 1902). Daly, *Demographic Imagination*, pp. 165–6, 179f.

128 *The Gentlewoman* (6 October 1894), p. 455.

129 'Coming fashions', *Observer* (28 September 1890), p. 3.

130 'Answers to correspondents', *The Ladies' Treasury for 1894. A Household Magazine*, 764. In 1906, the SPB's publications subcommittee sent a leaflet about Queen Alexandra's disapproval of wearing feathers to 'the leading Court Milliners and Drapery Firms'. The few responses were placatory or noncommittal. RSPB archive, Publications subcommittee minute book, July 1896 – January 1905.

131 *The Ladies' Treasury for 1894*, 52.

132 Sir William Flower, 'Feathers in ladies' hats', *The Times* (25 June 1896), p. 12. Henrietta Litchfield, letter responding to Flower's, *The Times* (27 June 1896), p. 6.

133 Henry Seton-Karr, 'Murderous millinery', *The Times* (17 February 1903), p. 6.

134 Ouida imagined a heartless 'London leader of fashion and politics' wearing such animal products. 'The quality of mercy', *Critical Studies*, pp. 239–40.

135 SPB 7th annual report for 1897, pp. 8–9, and 8th report, 1898, p. 4. Catherine Hilary, *A Picture in Focus: G.F. Watts, A Dedication 1898–9* (Compton: Watts Gallery, 2011). An exhibition reviewer thought the severity of Watts's 'sermon' on feather wearing would startle lady visitors: 'The New Gallery', *The Times* (22 April 1899), p. 4.

136 Wilfrid Scawen Blunt, *Satan Absolved: A Victorian Mystery* (London and New York: John Lane, Bodley Head, 1899), p. 46.

137 Eleanor Vere C. Boyle, 'A Plumage League', *The Times* (25 December 1885), p. 5.

138 SPB 2nd annual report for 1891–1892, p. 6.

139 Mary S. Watts, *George Frederic Watts: Annals of an Artist's Life*, 3 vols (London: Macmillan, 1912), vol. 3, p. 199.

140 Henry S. Salt, *Humanitarianism: Its General Principles and Progress*, 1891, new edn (London: Humanitarian League, 1906), pp. 25–6.

141 SPB 6th annual report for 1896, pp. 5–6.

142 SPB Educational Series No. 22 – *Skylark* by Florence Anna Fulcher, 1897. Hudson told Eliza Phillips, in a letter of 10 March 1901, that Dresser – unlike some of his scientific peers – 'is entirely with us', in support for the SPB's strategies: Manchester Central Library, Records 34 GB127, E13.

143 SPB 6th annual report for 1896, pp. 5–6.

144 SPB 8th annual report for 1898, p. 7; 9th report for 1899, p. 8; 10th report for 1900, p. 9. The subjects of the lantern slides also emerge from Kennedy's lecture, *Birds and their Protection*.

145 David Elliston Allen, *The Naturalist in Britain: A Social History* (Harmondsworth: Penguin, 1976), pp. 200f., 228f. Stephen Moss, *A Bird in the Bush: A Social History of Birdwatching* (London: Aurum Press, 2004), pp. 86f.

146 According to one of Hudson's obituarists, he was 'loathed' by 'scientific or pseudo-scientific bodies': 'his eloquence, and his vision … have banished the credit of their lifeless and life-taking pedagogy to Laputa'. H.J.M., 'Life and Letters: W.H. Hudson', *The Nation and the Athenaeum* (26 August 1922), pp. 708–9.

147 Edmund Selous, *Bird Watching* (London: J.M. Dent, 1901). Julian S. Huxley, 'Bird-watching and biological science: some observations on the study of courtship in birds',

The Auk, 33:2 (April 1916), 142–61. Margaret Morse Nice, 'Edmund Selous: an apprecia-tion', *Bird-Banding*, 6 (July 1935), 90–6.

148 See, for example, Selous's lyrical description of 'the nuptial flight of the wood-pigeon'; *Bird Watching*, pp. 4, 51–2.

149 Hudson, *Birds and Man*, 1901, new edn (London: Duckworth, 1915, reissued 1920), pp. 72, 238.

150 Ibid., pp. 12–13, 269f.

151 J.R.V. Marchant and Watkin Watkins, *Wild Birds Protection Acts, 1880–1896* (London: R.H. Porter, 1897), summarises the complex provisions of the successive Acts. Phyllis Barclay-Smith, 'The British contribution to bird protection', *Ibis*, 101 (1959), 115–22.

152 *Hansard*, Commons debates, vol. 211, columns 1646–1654, 12 June 1872.

153 Marchant and Watkins, *Wild Birds Protection Acts*, p. 27. Wollaston, *Life of Newton*, pp. 140f.

154 *Animal World* (July–August 1872), 147–8, 152.

155 SPB 2nd annual report for 1891–1892, pp. 3–4.

156 Among the many pamphlets on these subjects, see especially Hudson's *Lost British Birds* and *Bird Catching* (both SPB, 1894), and *The Barn Owl* (SPB, 1895). The latter was twice reviewed in *Manchester Guardian*: (23 July 1895), p. 7, and (3 August 1895), p. 5, referring to the cruelty of pole traps.

157 SPB 9th annual report for 1899, pp. 6–7. *Bird Notes and News*, 1:3 (October 1903), 11, 16.

158 For example, Eliza Phillips, *An Appeal to Boys and Girls* (London: SPB, 1894); Linda Gardiner, *Birds and Boys* (London: SPB, 1900).

159 'County Challenge Shield Competition', *Bird Notes and News*, 1:4 (December 1903), 21–2. Margaretta Lemon, 'Linda Gardiner' obituary, *Bird Notes and News*, 19:5 (Spring 1941), 91–3. Lemon, 'The story of the R.S.P.B.', *Bird Notes and News*, 20:6 (Summer 1943), 85–6. One of the attractively decorated shields survives in the RSPB archive.

160 SPB School Series of leaflets, no. 3, *Bird and Tree Day Celebration: An Exercise of Songs and Recitation*, arranged by F.H. Suckling, 1902.

161 *Bird Notes and News*, 1:3 (October 1903), 12; 1:7 (October 1904), 43. *The Royal Society for the Protection of Birds*, leaflet no. 58, undated [1910], p. 4. Hudson's letter to Mrs Hubbard, 17 March 1899: Manchester Central Library, Records 34 GB127, D32.

162 Lemon, 'Linda Gardiner' obituary.

163 'The story of bird protection', *Bird Notes and News*, 4:8 (21 December 1911), 87.

164 Linda Gardiner, *The Fight for the Birds* (London and Bungay: Richard Clay and sons, 1914), p. 9.

165 Hansard, vol. 134, columns 1429–1436, House of Lords debate on 10 July 1854.

166 Leading article, *The Times* (18 October 1860), p. 8.

167 'The luxury of doing good things', *Animal World*, 6:74 (1 November 1875), 162–3.

168 'A charity and a controversy: address by Frances Power Cobbe, at the annual meeting of the Victoria Street Society, June 20th, 1889' in Susan Hamilton (ed.), *Animal Welfare and Anti-Vivisection 1870–1910: Nineteenth-Century Woman's Mission*, 3 vols (London and New York: Routledge, 2004), vol. 1. On the continuing depreciation of female 'sentiment' or 'sentimentality' at this period: Jennifer McDonell, 'Representing ani-mals in the literature of Victorian Britain', in Hilda Kean and Philip Howell (eds), *The Routledge Companion to Animal-Human History* (London and New York: Routledge, 2019), pp. 237–9.

169 Frances Power Cobbe, 'The ethics of zoophily: a reply', in Hamilton (ed.), *Animal Welfare*.

170 Josephine Donovan, 'Attention to suffering: sympathy as a basis for ethical treatment of animals', in Josephine Donovan and Carol J. Adams (eds), *The Feminist Care
Tradition in Animal Ethics: A Reader* (New York: Columbia University Press, 2007),
p. 174. Brian Luke, 'Taming ourselves or going feral? Toward a nonpatriarchal metaethic of animal liberation', in Carol J. Adams and Josephine Donovan (eds), *Animals and
Women: Feminist Theoretical Explorations* (Durham, NC and London: Duke University
Press, 1995).

Index

CPSIA information can be obtained
at www.ICGtesting.com
Printed in the USA
LVHW091902171121
703621LV00007B/254